VOL. 8
Action Edition

Story and Art by
RUMIKO TAKAHASHI

English Adaptation by Gerard Jones

Translation/Mari Morimoto
Touch-Up Art & Lettering/Wayne Truman
Cover Design/Yuki Ameda
Graphics & Design/Yuki Ameda
Editor (1st Edition)/Julie Davis
Editor (Action Edition)/Julie Davis

Managing Editor/Annette Roman
Director of Production/Noboru Watanabe
VP of Publishing/Alvin Lu
Sr. Director of Acquisitions/Rika Inouye
VP of Sales & Marketing/Liza Coppola
Publisher/Hyoe Narita

© 1997 Rumiko TAKAHASHI/Shogakukan Inc. First
published by Shogakukan, Inc. in Japan as "Inuyasha."

Printed in Canada.

Published by VIZ Media, LLC
P.O. Box 77010
San Francisco, CA 94107

1st Edition published 2001

Action Edition
10 9 8 7 6 5 4 3
First printing, December 2003
Second printing, October 2004
Third printing, July 2005

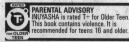

PARENTAL ADVISORY
INUYASHA is rated T+ for Older Teen.
This book contains violence. It is
recommended for teens 16 and older.

store.viz.com

www.viz.com

INUYASHA

VOL. 8 Action Edition

STORY AND ART BY
RUMIKO TAKAHASHI

CONTENTS

THE STORY THUS FAR

Long ago, in the "Warring States" era of Japan's Muromachi period (Sengoku-jidai, approximately 1467-1568 CE), a legendary doglike half-demon called "Inu-Yasha" attempted to steal the Shikon Jewel, or "Jewel of Four Souls," from a village, but was stopped by the enchanted arrow of the village priestess, Kikyo. Inu-Yasha fell into a deep sleep, pinned to a tree by Kikyo's arrow, while the mortally wounded Kikyo took the Shikon Jewel with her into the fires of her funeral pyre. Years passed.

Fast forward to the present day. Kagome, a Japanese high school girl, is pulled into a well one day by a mysterious centipede monster, and finds herself transported into the past, only to come face to face with the trapped Inu-Yasha. She frees him, and Inu-Yasha easily defeats the centipede monster.

The residents of the village, now fifty years older, readily accept Kagome as the reincarnation of their deceased priestess Kikyo, a claim supported by the fact that the Shikon Jewel emerges from a cut on Kagome's body. Unfortunately, the jewel's rediscovery means that the village is soon under attack by a variety of demons in search of this treasure. Then, the jewel is accidentally shattered into many shards, each of which may have the fearsome power of the entire jewel.

Although Inu-Yasha says he hates Kagome because of her resemblance to Kikyo, the woman who "killed" him, he is forced to team up with her when Kaede, the village leader, binds him to Kagome with a powerful spell. Now the two grudging companions must fight to reclaim and reassemble the shattered shards of the Shikon Jewel before they fall into the wrong hands.

THIS VOLUME The resurrected Kikyo, now without a soul, must find a way to survive in her new life.

CHARACTERS

INU-YASHA
A half-human, half-demon hybrid, Inu-Yasha assists Kagome in her search for the shards of the Jewel. The charmed necklace he wears allows Kagome to restrain him with a single word.

KAGOME
A modern-day Japanese schoolgirl, Kagome is also the reincarnation of Kikyo, the priestess who imprisoned Inu-Yasha for fifty years with her enchanted arrow. Kagome has the power to see the Shikon Jewel shards wherever they may be hidden.

KAEDE
The little sister of the deceased priestess Kikyo, now an old woman and head of their village. It's her spell that binds Inu-Yasha to Kagome by means of a string of prayer beads and Kagome's spoken word—"Sit!"

MIROKU
An easygoing Buddhist priest with questionable morals, Miroku is the carrier of a curse passed down from his grandfather. He is searching for the demon Naraku, who first inflicted the curse.

KIKYO
A powerful priestess who died protecting the Shikon Jewel, and has been resurrected by magic. She and Inu-Yasha once shared a special bond.

MYOGA
A flea demon and Inu-Yasha's servant. His bloodsucking seems to have the ability to weaken certain spells.

NARAKU
This enigmatic demon is responsible for both Miroku's curse and for turning Kikyo and Inu-Yasha against one another.

SHIPPO
An orphaned young fox-demon who enjoys goading Inu-Yasha and playing tricks with his shape-changing abilities.

SCROLL ONE

SENSING PRESENCES

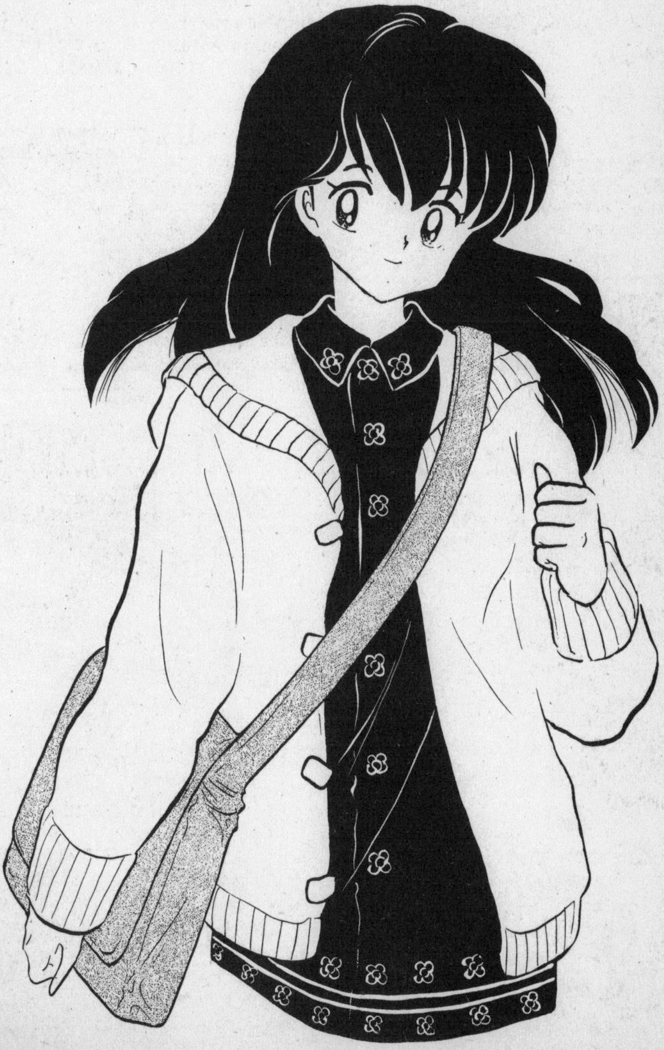

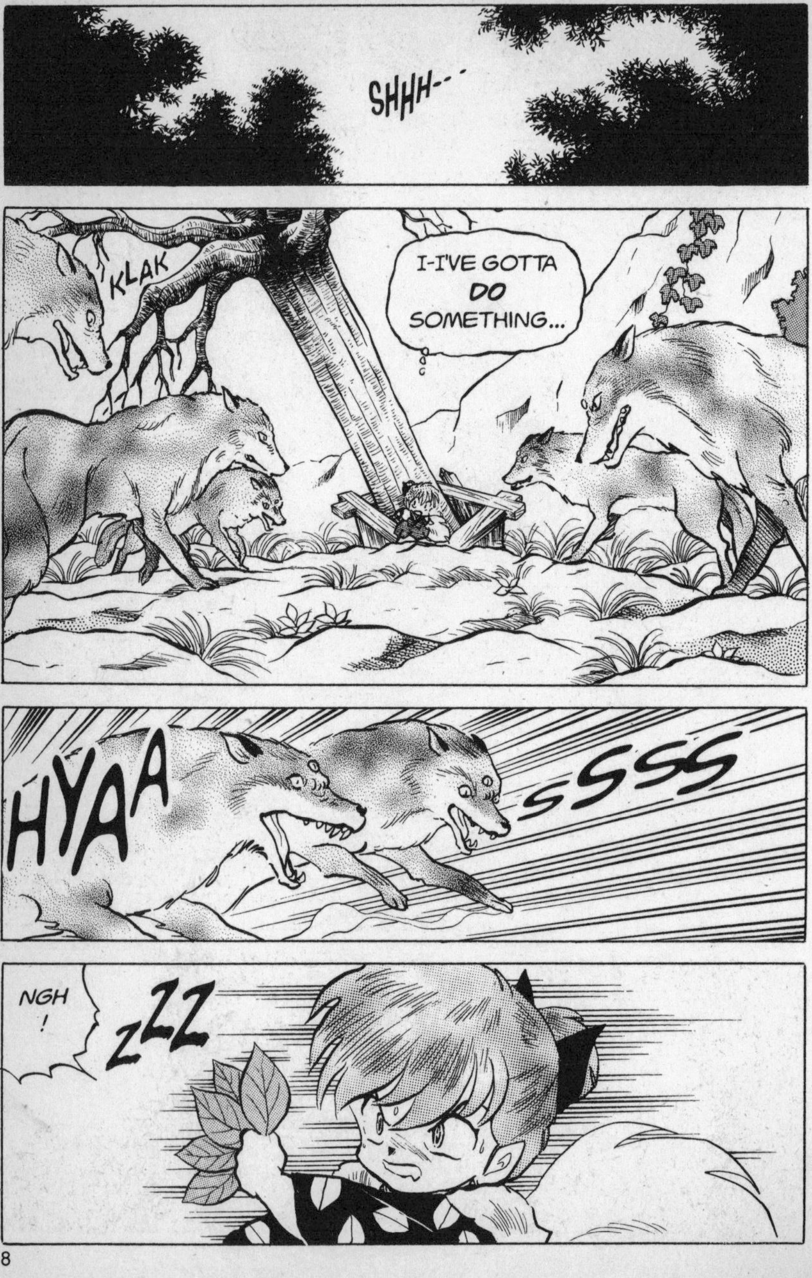
SHHH---
KLAK
I-I'VE GOTTA DO SOMETHING...
HYAA
SSSS
NGH!
ZZZ

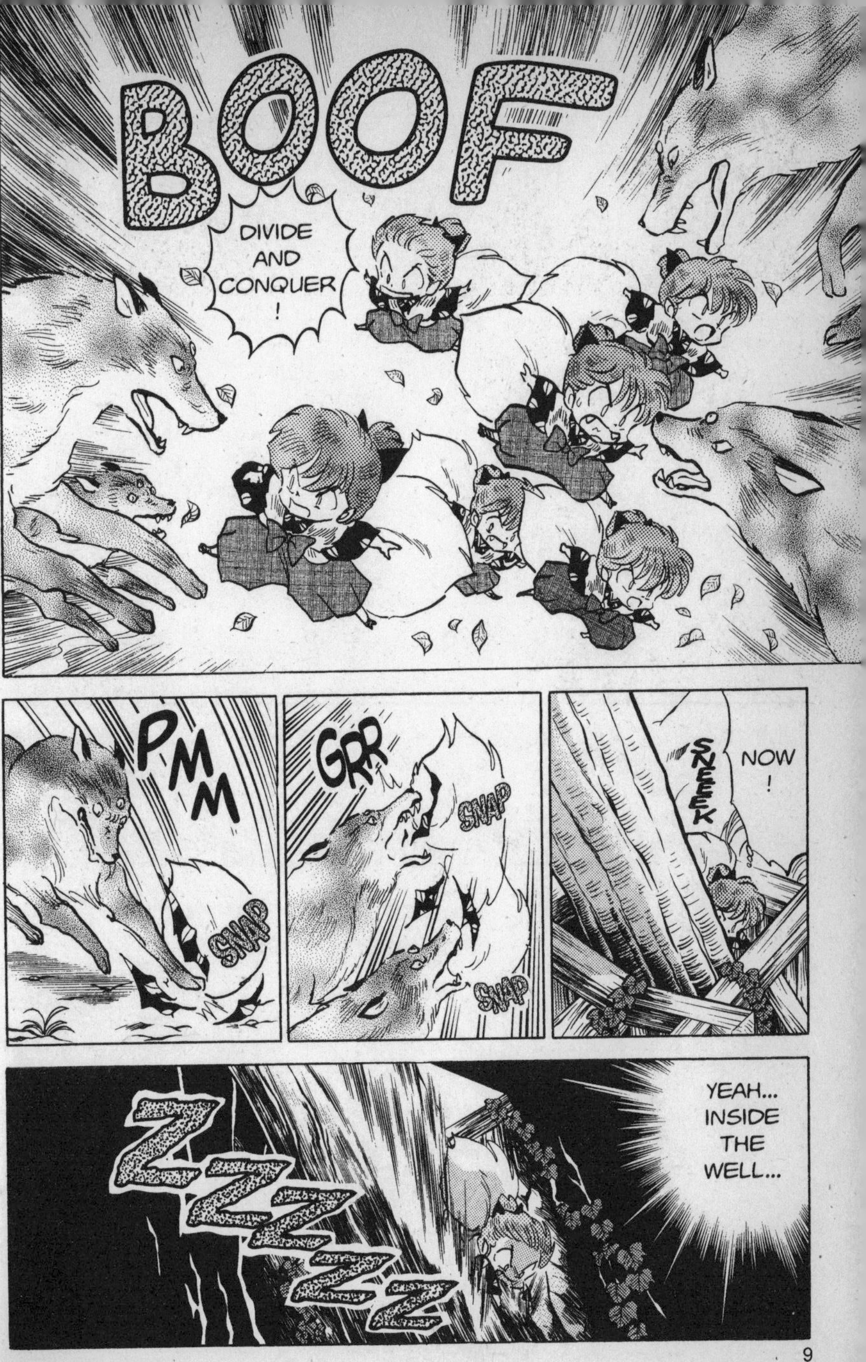
BOOF
DIVIDE AND CONQUER !
PMM
SNAP
GRR
SNAP
SNAP
SNEEEK
NOW !
ZZZZZ
YEAH... INSIDE THE WELL...

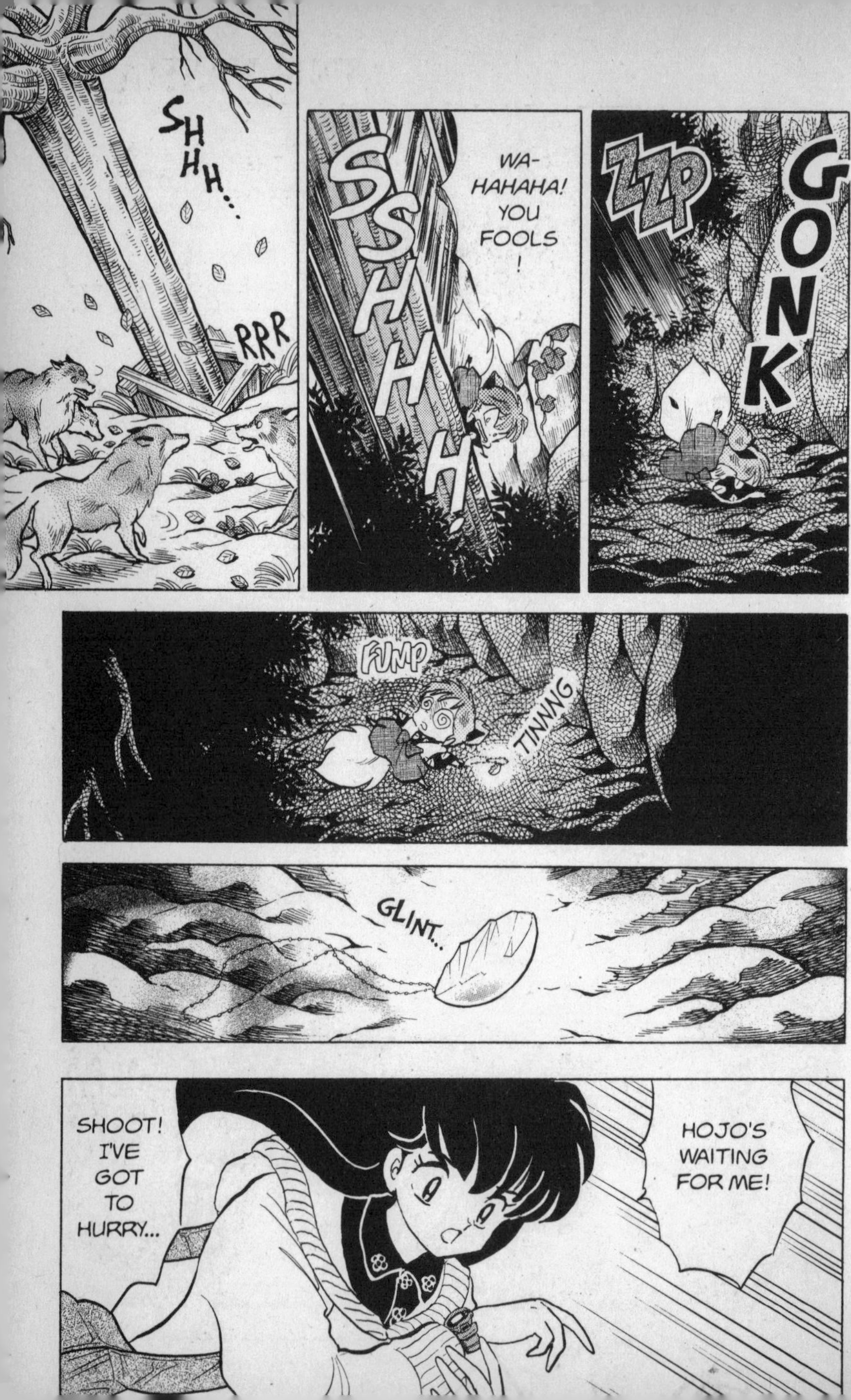
SHHH...
RRR
SSHHH!
WA-HAHAHA! YOU FOOLS!
ZZP
GONK
FUMP
TINNNG
GLINT...
SHOOT! I'VE GOT TO HURRY...
HOJO'S WAITING FOR ME!

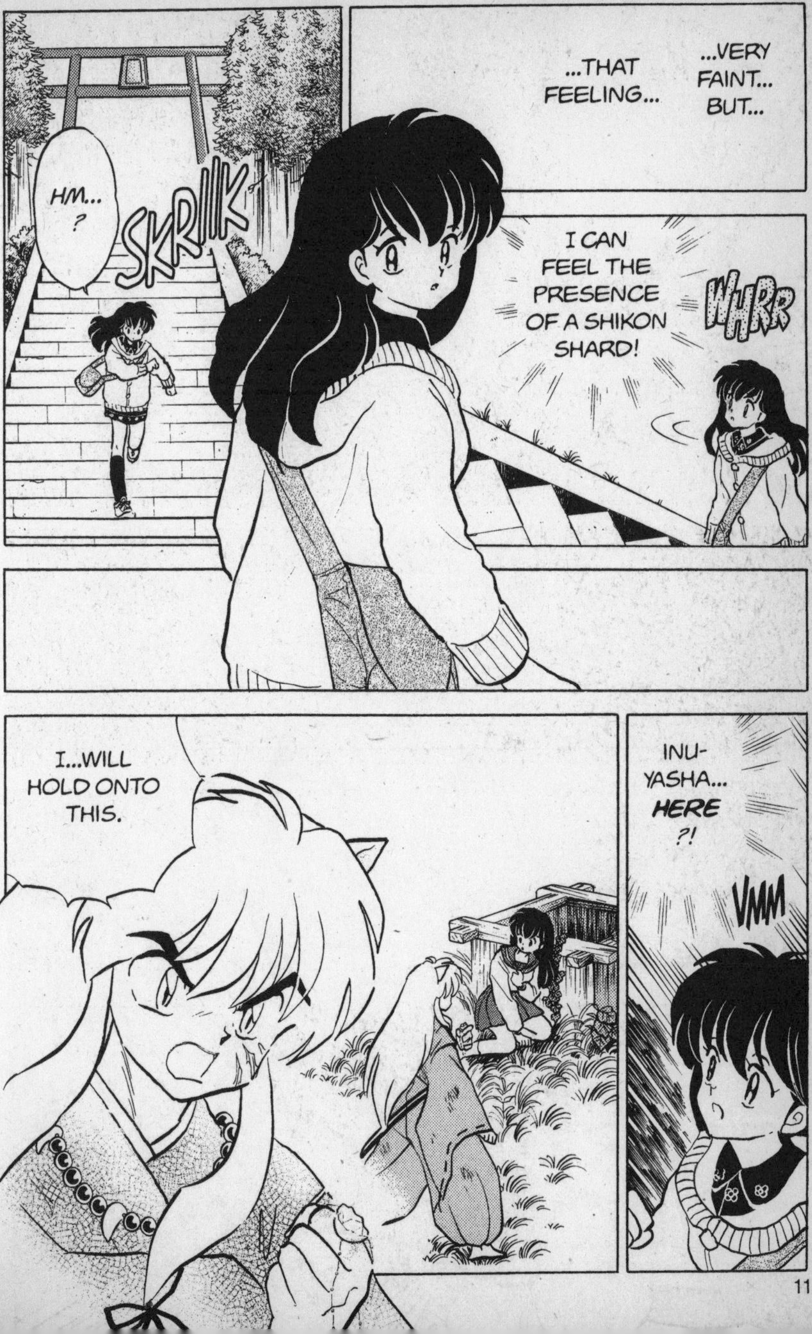
HM...?
SKRIIK
...THAT FEELING...
...VERY FAINT... BUT...
I CAN FEEL THE PRESENCE OF A SHIKON SHARD!
WHRR
I...WILL HOLD ONTO THIS.
INU-YASHA... HERE ?!
VMM

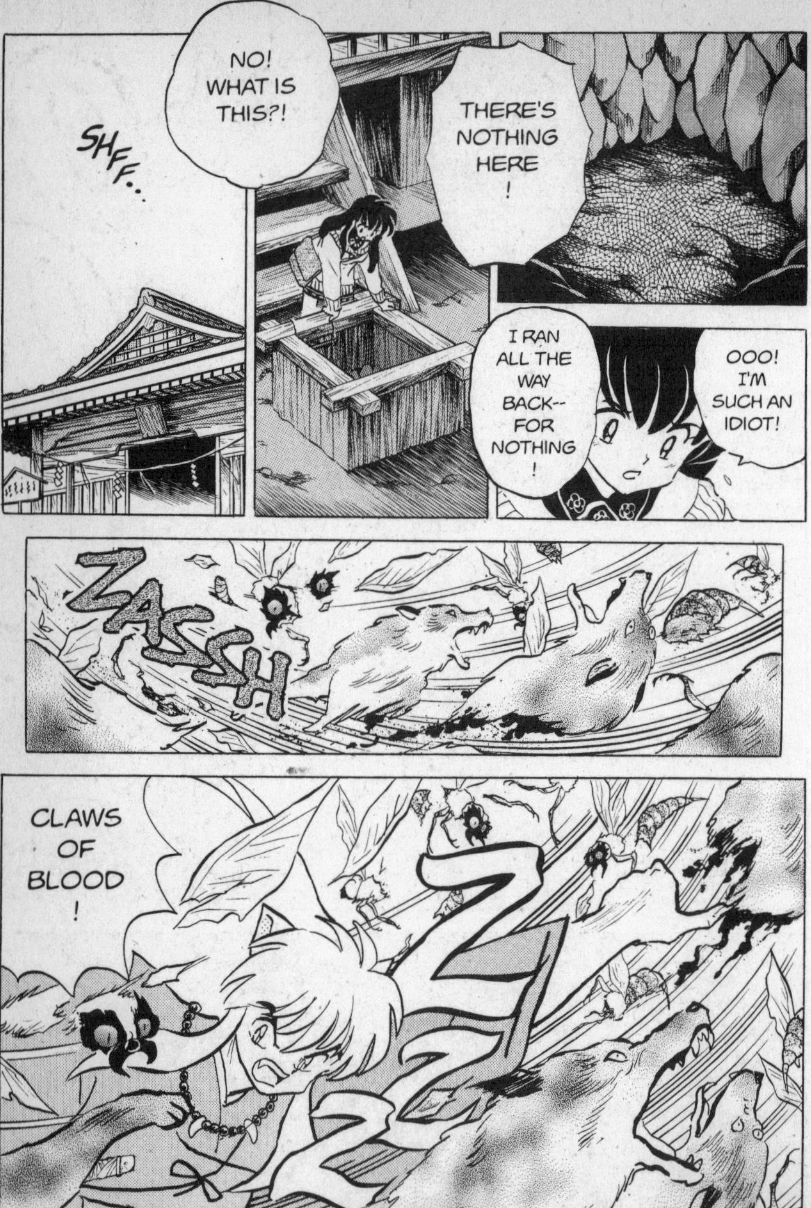
SHFF...
NO! WHAT IS THIS?!
THERE'S NOTHING HERE!
I RAN ALL THE WAY BACK-- FOR NOTHING!
OOO! I'M SUCH AN IDIOT!
ZASSH
CLAWS OF BLOOD!

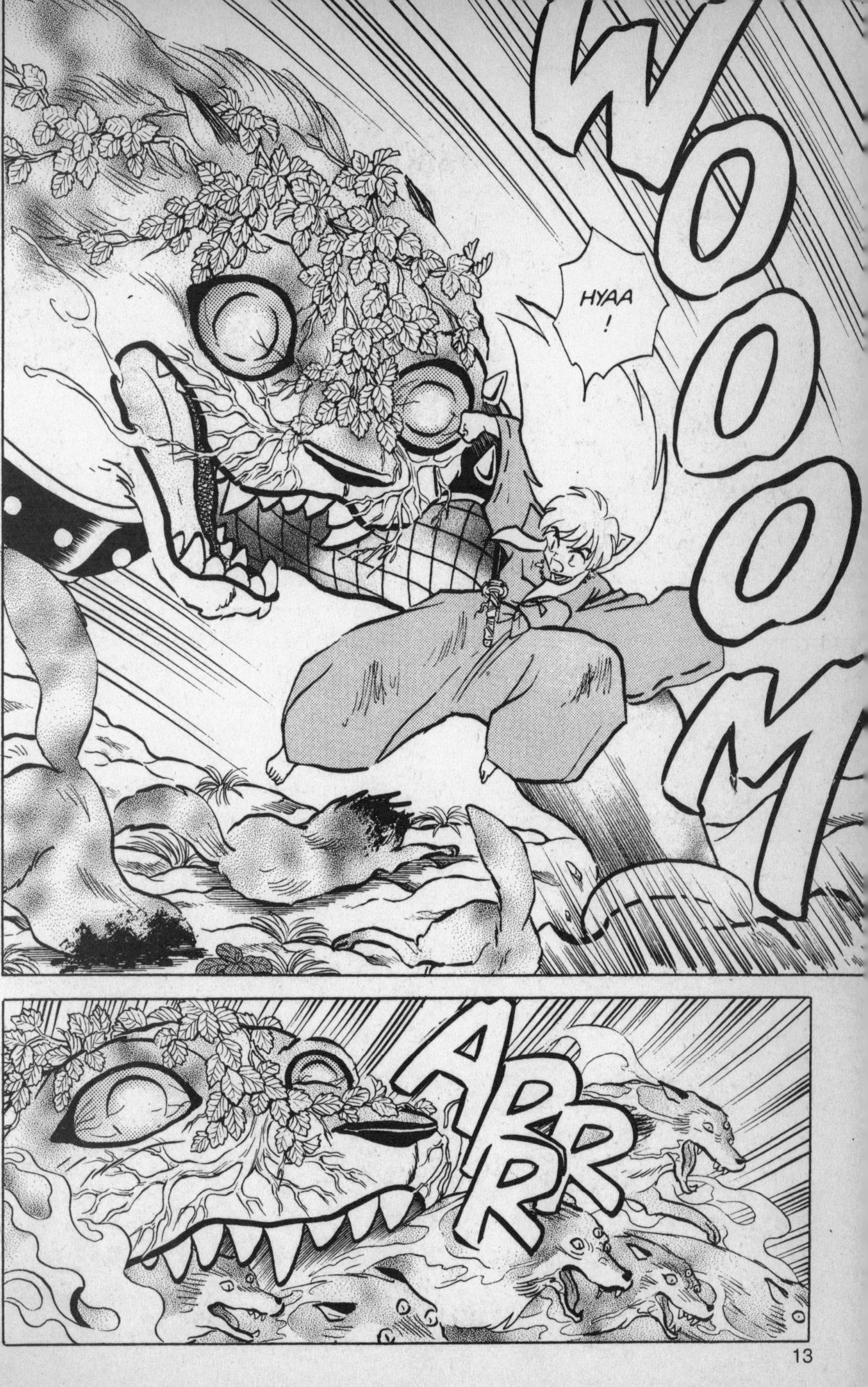
WOOOOM
HYAA!
ARRR

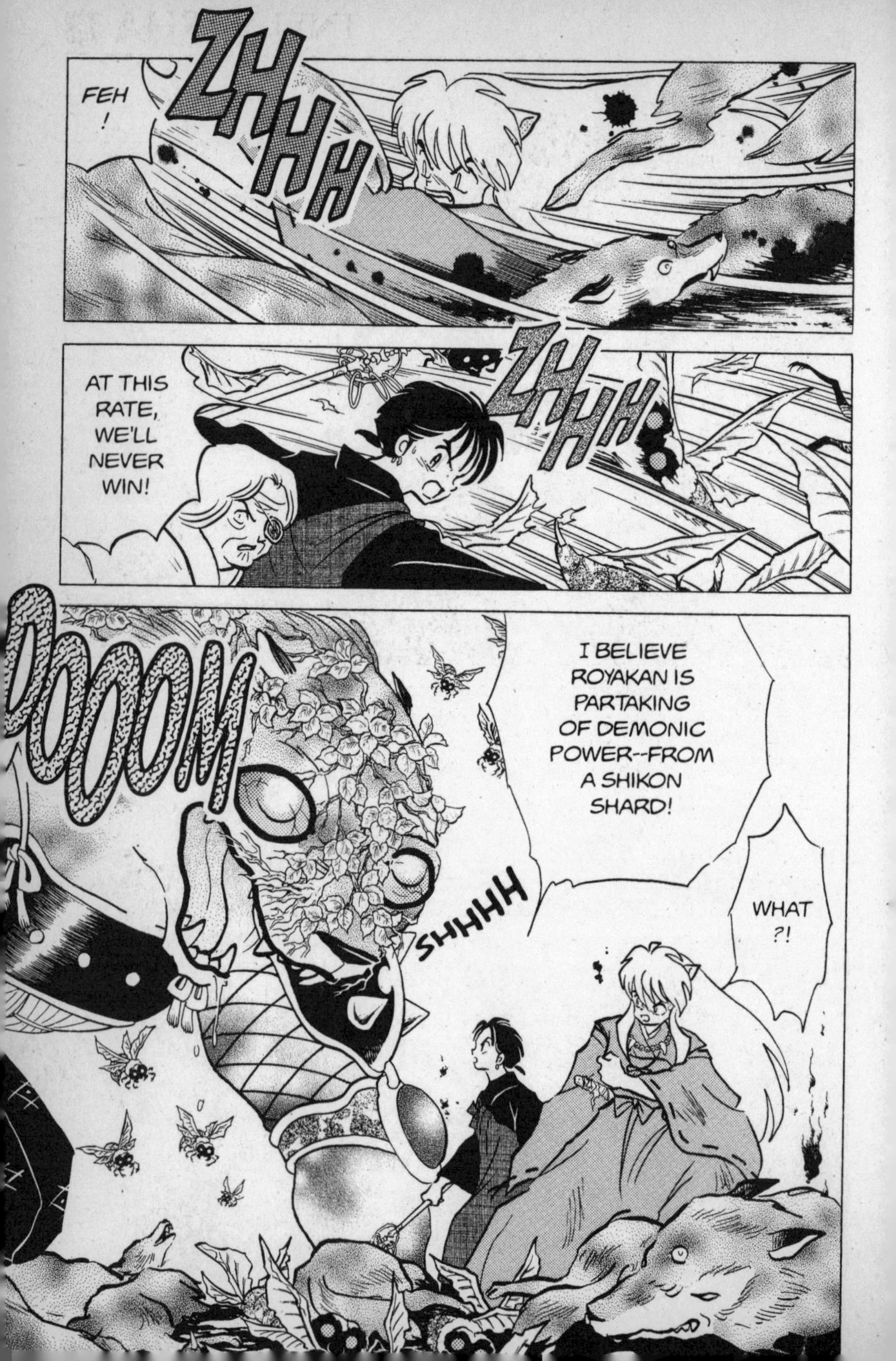
FEH!
ZHHHH
AT THIS RATE, WE'LL NEVER WIN!
ZHHHH
DOOOOM
I BELIEVE ROYAKAN IS PARTAKING OF DEMONIC POWER--FROM A SHIKON SHARD!
SHHHH
WHAT?!

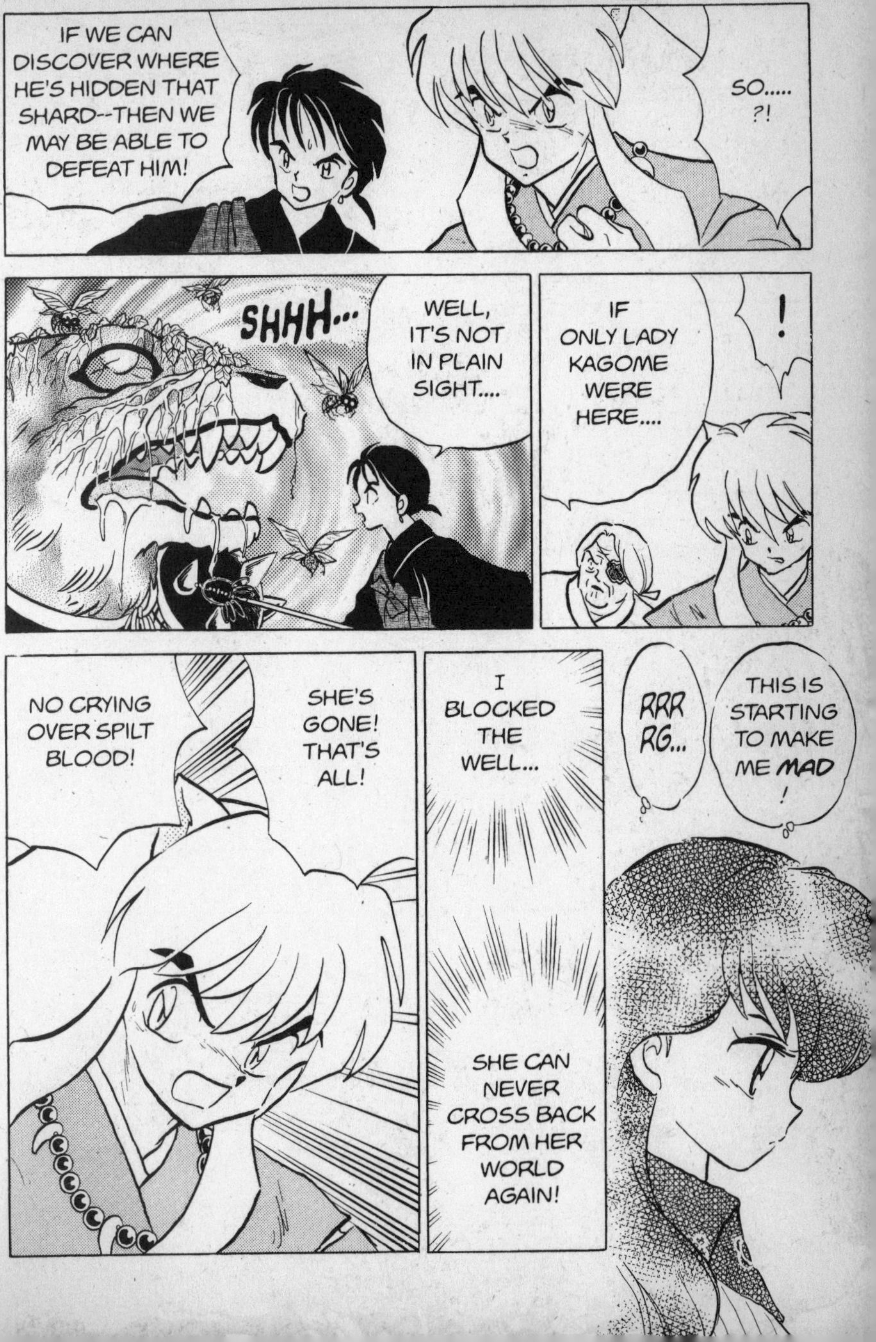
IF WE CAN DISCOVER WHERE HE'S HIDDEN THAT SHARD--THEN WE MAY BE ABLE TO DEFEAT HIM!
SO..... ?!
SHHH...
WELL, IT'S NOT IN PLAIN SIGHT....
IF ONLY LADY KAGOME WERE HERE....
!
NO CRYING OVER SPILT BLOOD!
SHE'S GONE! THAT'S ALL!
I BLOCKED THE WELL...
SHE CAN NEVER CROSS BACK FROM HER WORLD AGAIN!
RRRRG...
THIS IS STARTING TO MAKE ME MAD!

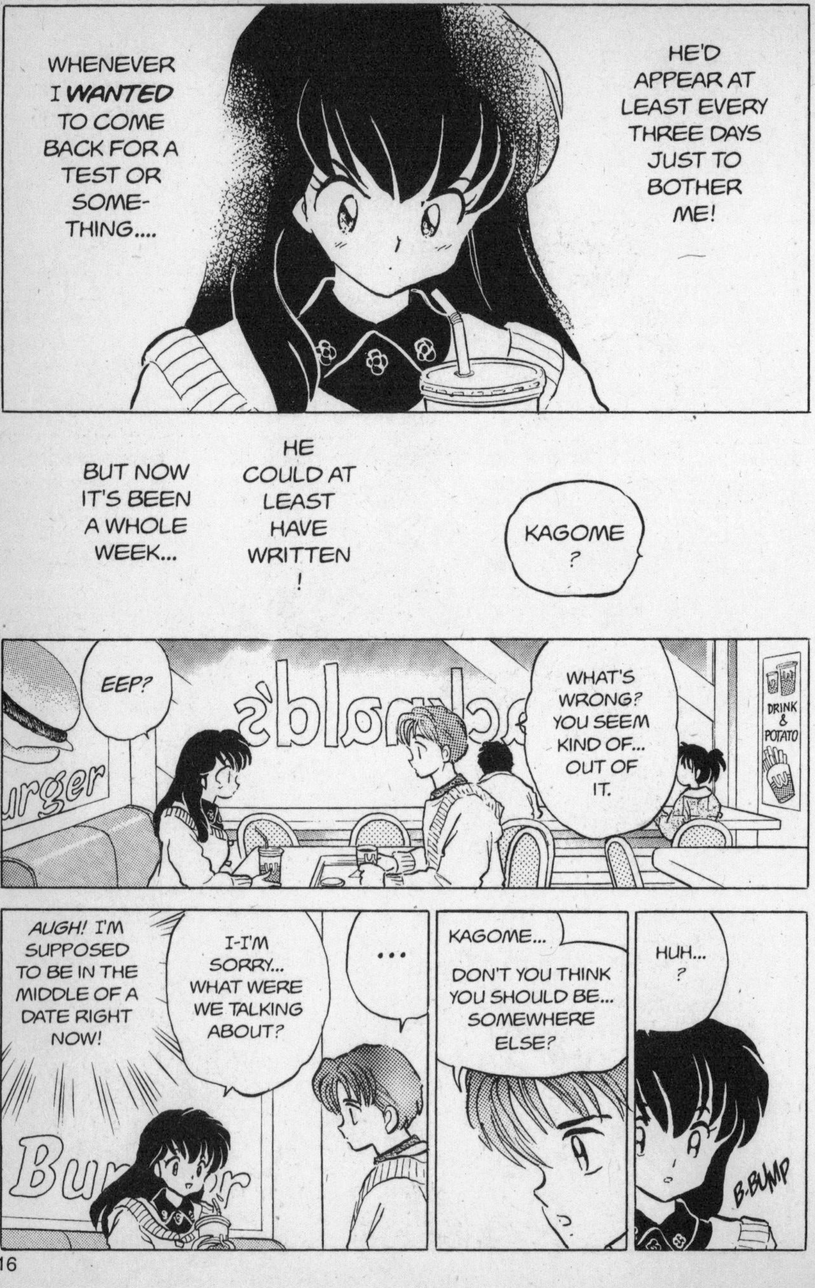
WHENEVER I *WANTED* TO COME BACK FOR A TEST OR SOME-THING....
HE'D APPEAR AT LEAST EVERY THREE DAYS JUST TO BOTHER ME!
BUT NOW IT'S BEEN A WHOLE WEEK...
HE COULD AT LEAST HAVE WRITTEN!
KAGOME?
EEP?
WHAT'S WRONG? YOU SEEM KIND OF... OUT OF IT.
DRINK & POTATO
AUGH! I'M SUPPOSED TO BE IN THE MIDDLE OF A DATE RIGHT NOW!
I-I'M SORRY... WHAT WERE WE TALKING ABOUT?
...
KAGOME...
DON'T YOU THINK YOU SHOULD BE... SOMEWHERE ELSE?
HUH...?
B-BUMP

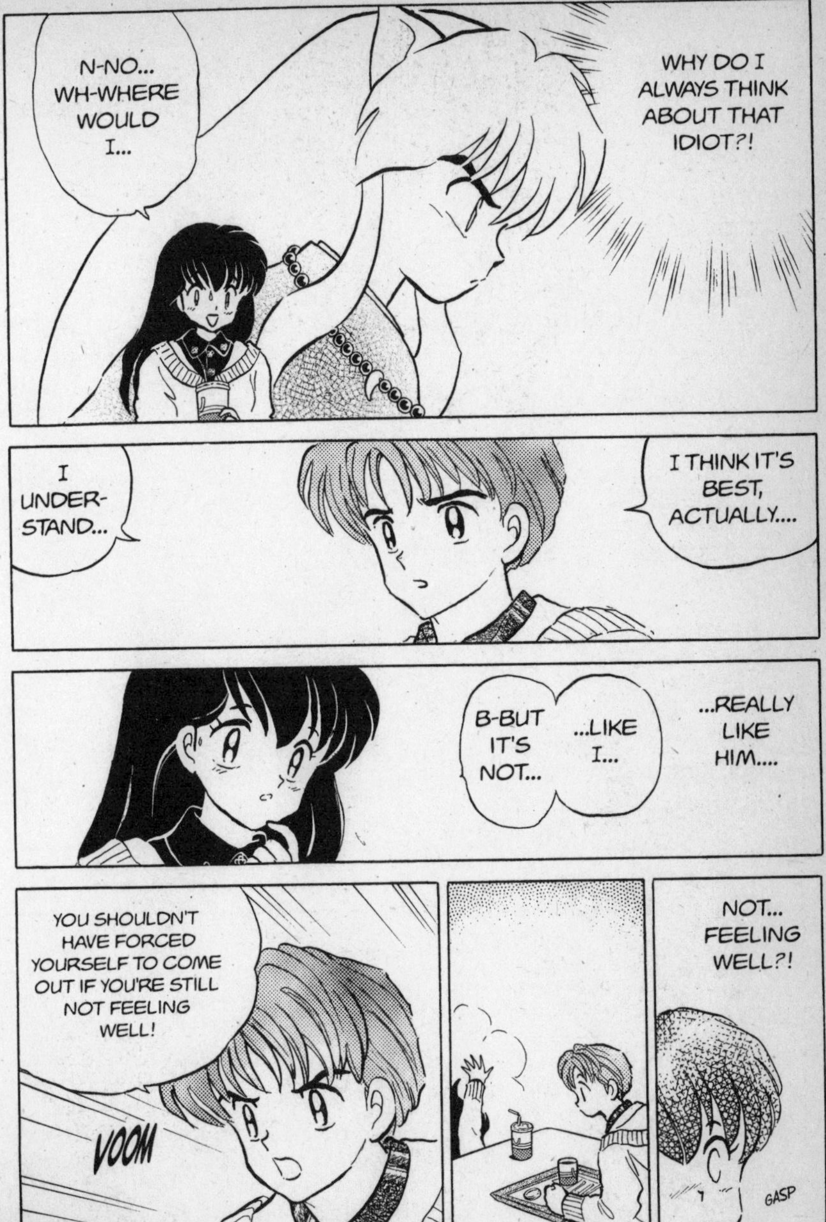
N-NO... WH-WHERE WOULD I...
WHY DO I ALWAYS THINK ABOUT THAT IDIOT?!
I UNDER-STAND...
I THINK IT'S BEST, ACTUALLY....
B-BUT IT'S NOT...
...LIKE I...
...REALLY LIKE HIM....
YOU SHOULDN'T HAVE FORCED YOURSELF TO COME OUT IF YOU'RE STILL NOT FEELING WELL!
VOOM
NOT... FEELING WELL?!
GASP

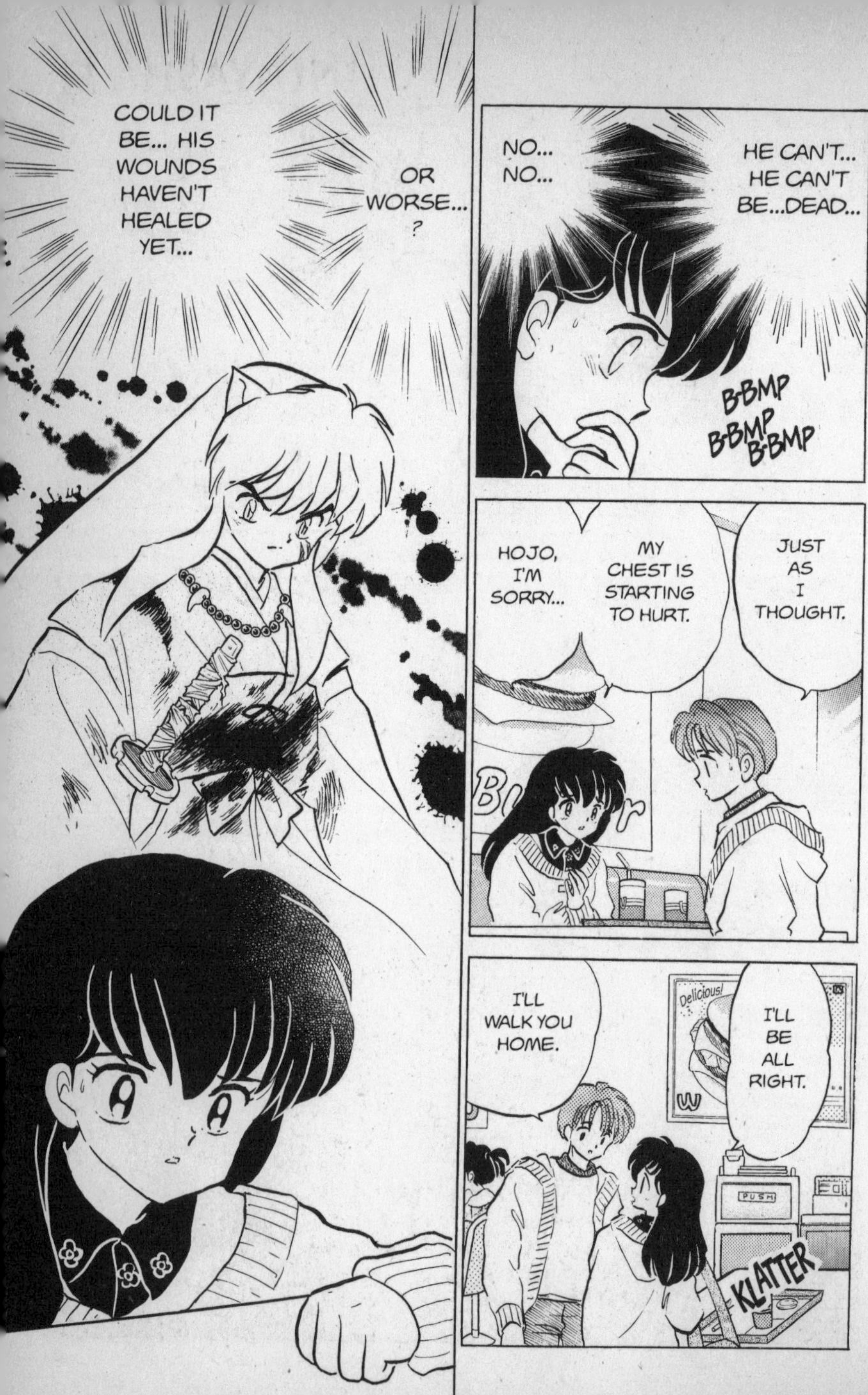
COULD IT BE... HIS WOUNDS HAVEN'T HEALED YET...
OR WORSE...?
NO... NO...
HE CAN'T... HE CAN'T BE...DEAD...
B-BMP B-BMP B-BMP
HOJO, I'M SORRY...
MY CHEST IS STARTING TO HURT.
JUST AS I THOUGHT.
I'LL WALK YOU HOME.
Delicious!
I'LL BE ALL RIGHT.
PUSH
KLATTER

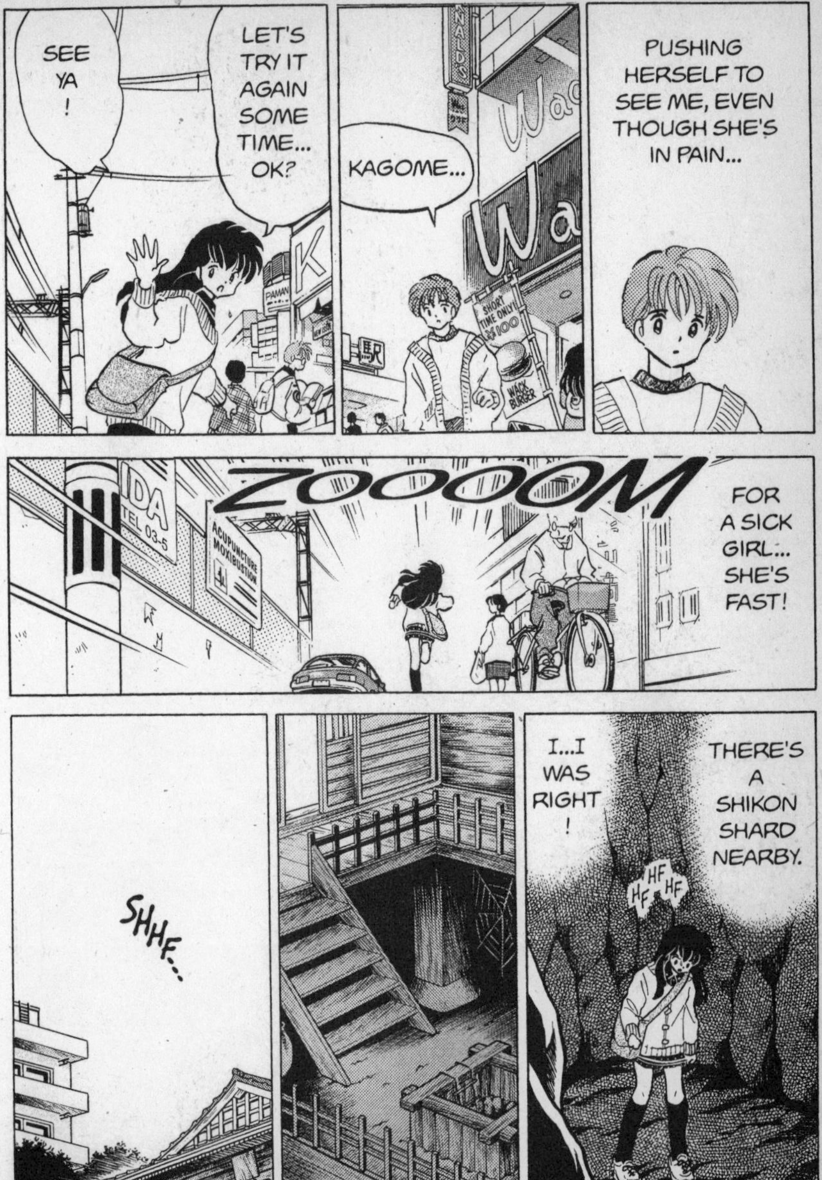
SEE YA!
LET'S TRY IT AGAIN SOME TIME... OK?
KAGOME...
SHORT TIME ONLY ¥100
WACK BURGER
PUSHING HERSELF TO SEE ME, EVEN THOUGH SHE'S IN PAIN...
ZOOOOM
IDA TEL 03-5
ACUPUNCTURE MOXIBUSTION
FOR A SICK GIRL... SHE'S FAST!
SHHF...
I...I WAS RIGHT!
THERE'S A SHIKON SHARD NEARBY.
HF HF HF

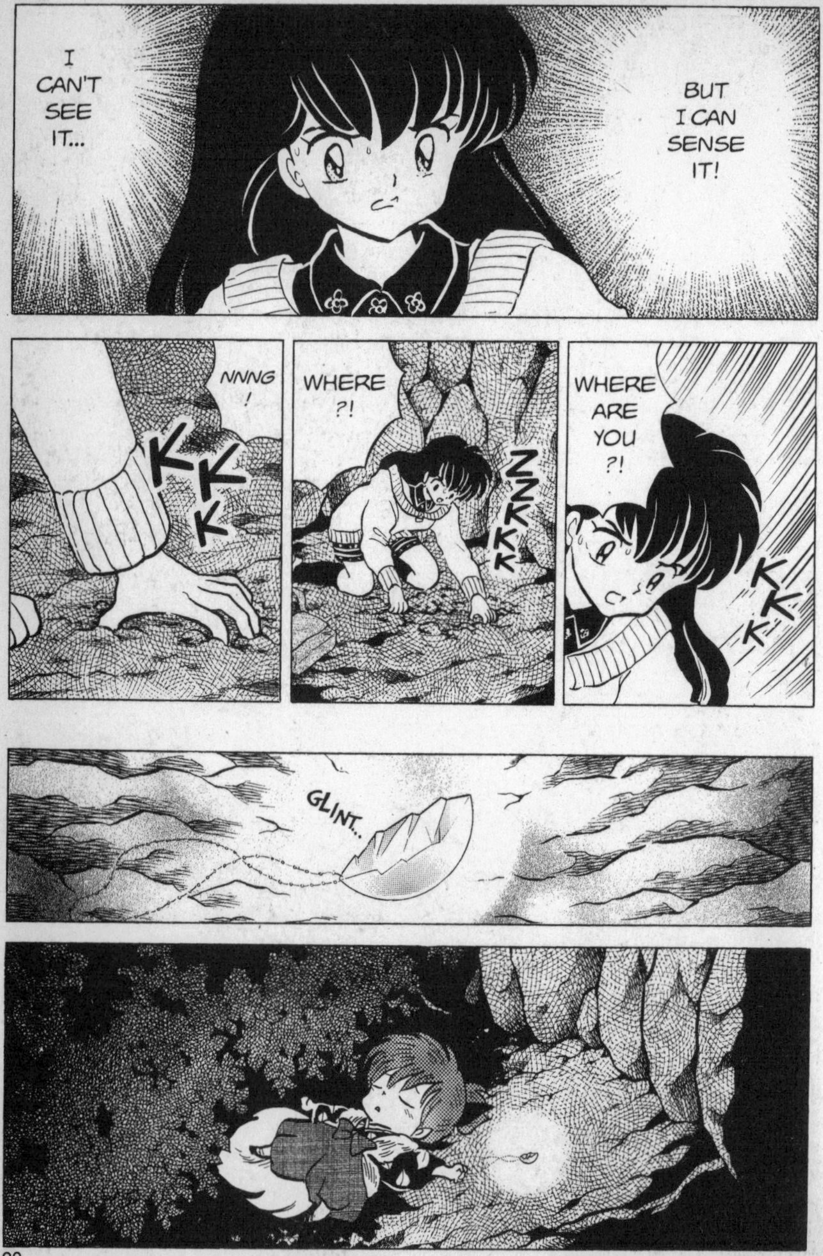
I CAN'T SEE IT...
BUT I CAN SENSE IT!
NNNG!
KKK
WHERE?!
ZZKKK
WHERE ARE YOU?!
KKK
GLINT...

UNNH...

GRRRRrr

RRRR

!

TH-
THEY'VE
FOUND
ME...!

I
HAVE
TO
GET
BACK
!

KKK
K

I HAVE
TO FIND
OUT!

KKK
K

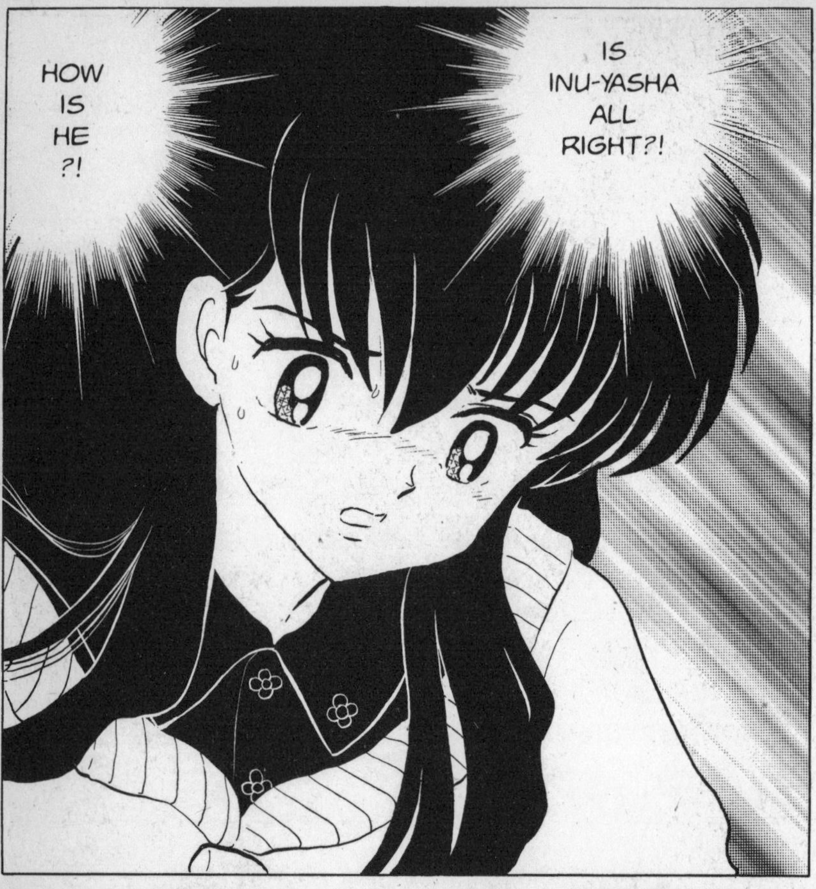
HOW IS HE ?!
IS INU-YASHA ALL RIGHT?!
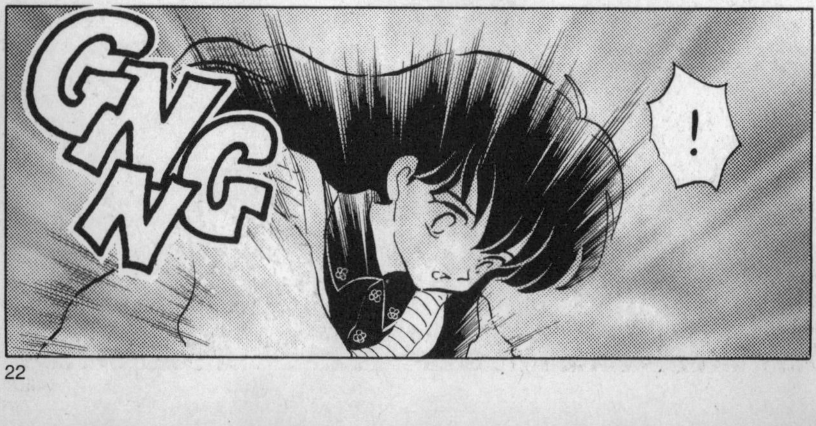
GNG
!

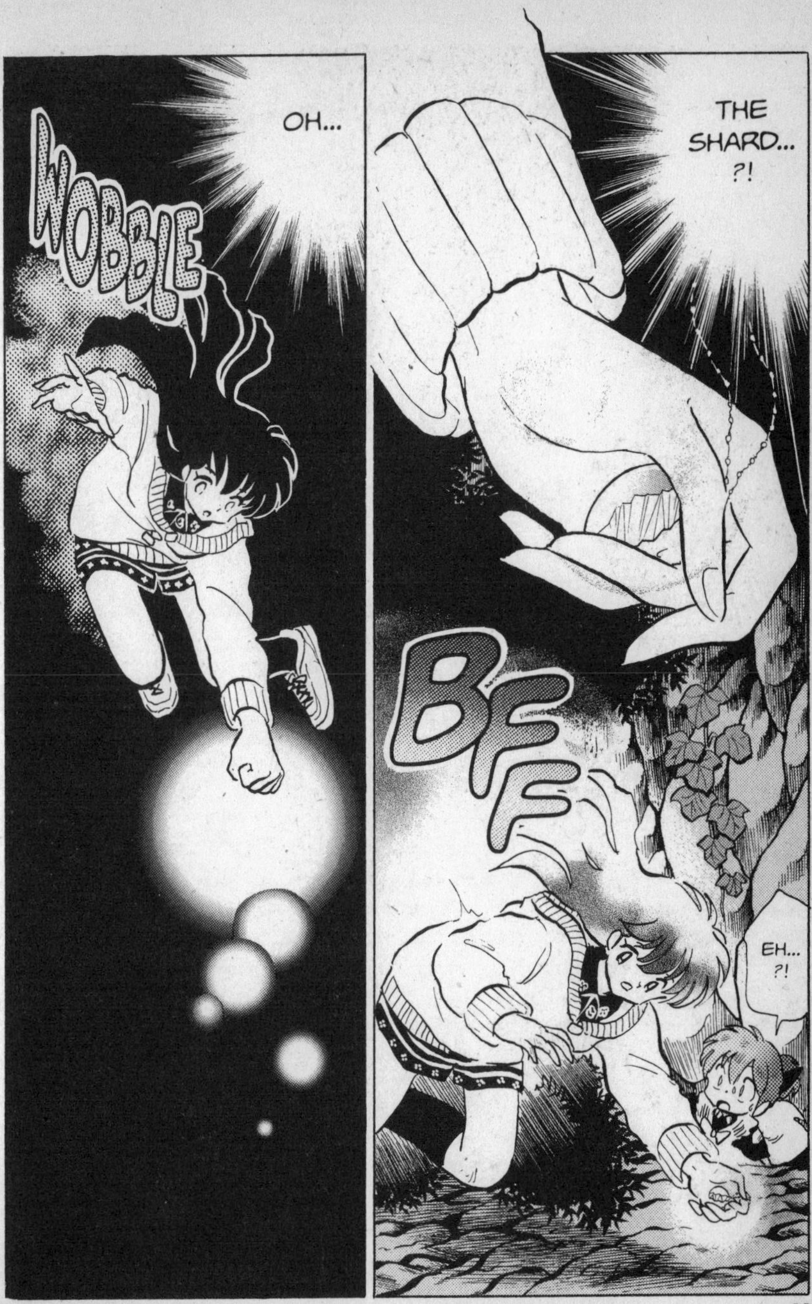
WOBBLE
OH...
THE SHARD... ?!
BFF
EH... ?!

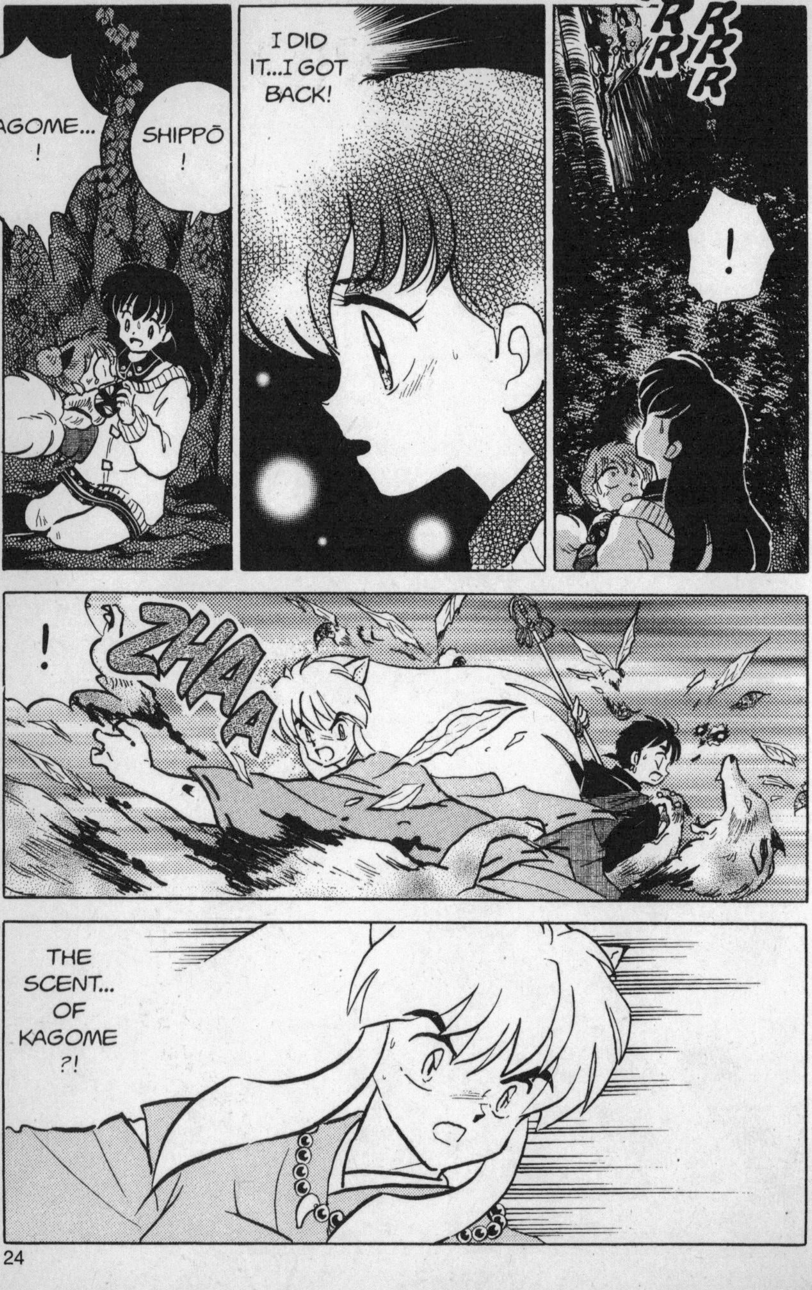

KAGOME... !
SHIPPŌ !
I DID IT...I GOT BACK!
RRRRRR
!
ZHAAA
!
THE SCENT... OF KAGOME ?!

SCROLL TWO

REUNION

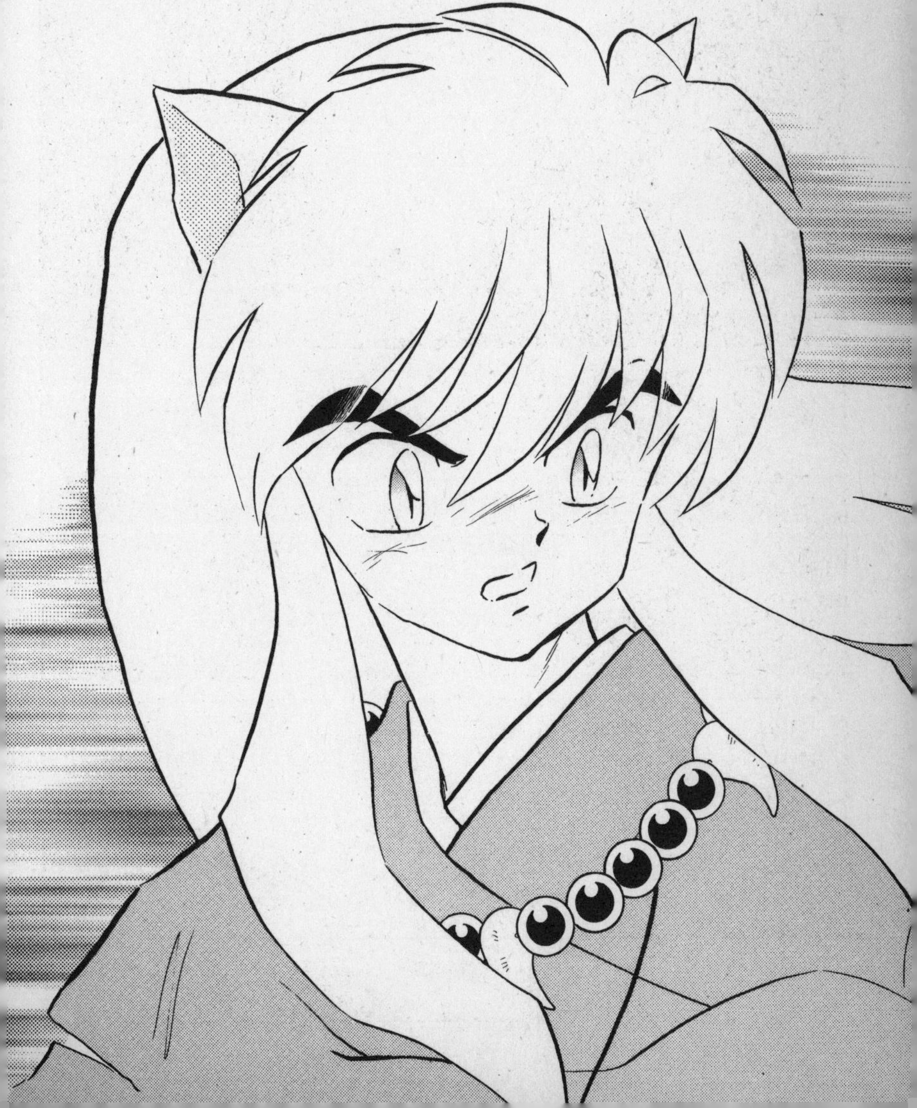

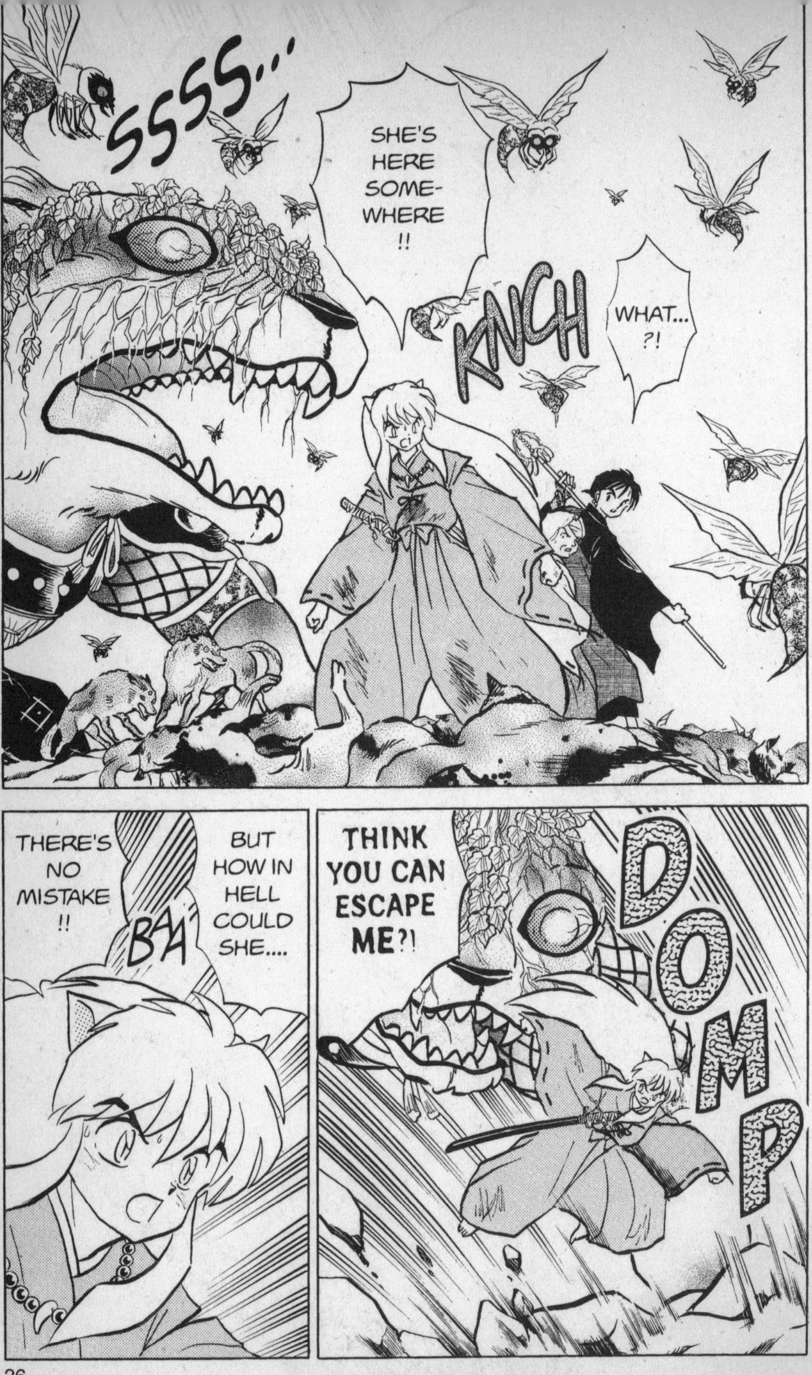
SSSS...
SHE'S HERE SOME-WHERE!!
KNCH
WHAT...?!
THERE'S NO MISTAKE!!
BAA
BUT HOW IN HELL COULD SHE....
THINK YOU CAN ESCAPE ME?!
DOMP

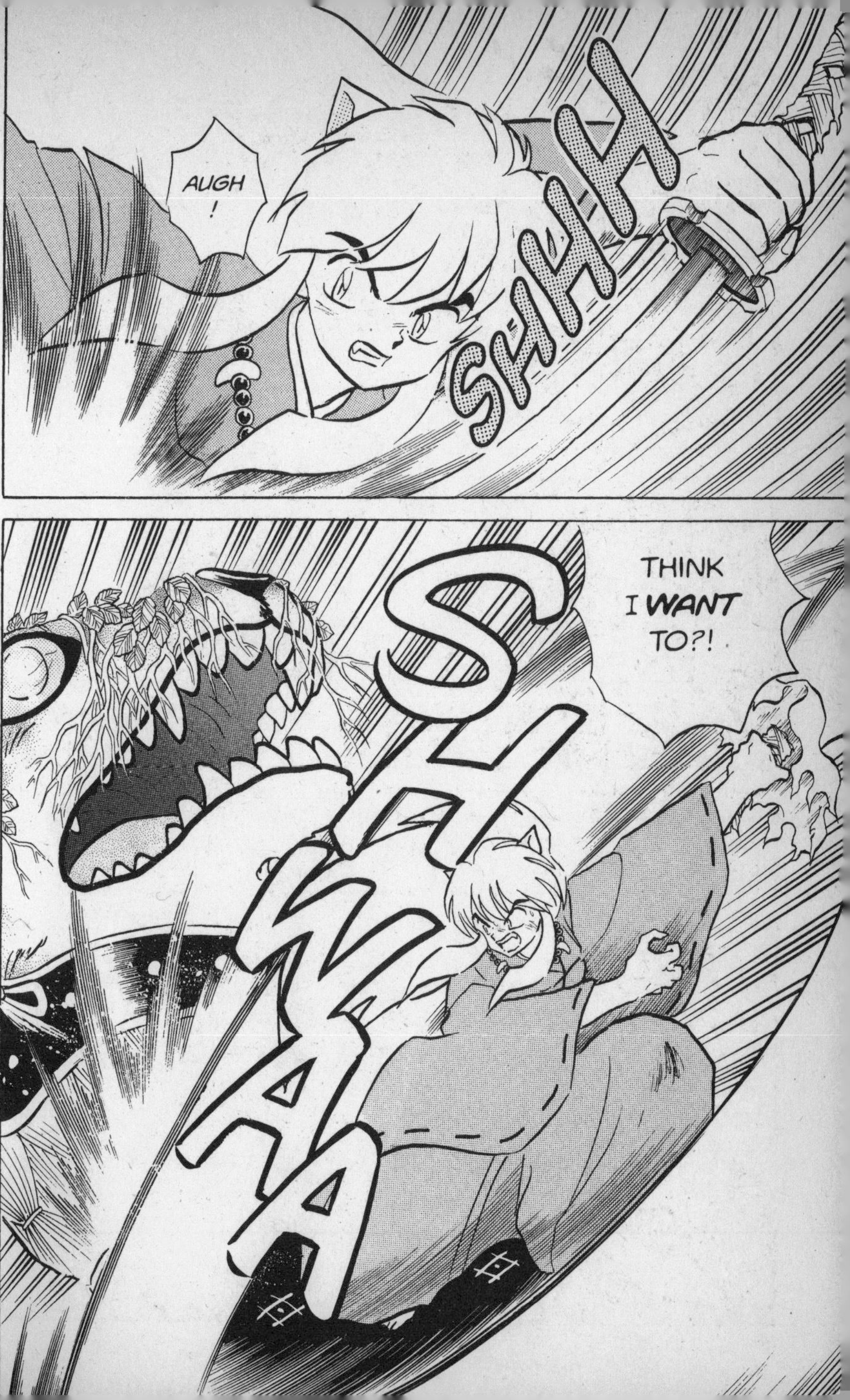
AUGH!
SHHH
THINK I WANT TO?!
SHWAA

KRRRROOM

BY THE GODS!

HAS HE... GAINED STRENGTH....?

ZH ZH...

SHH...

!

WAIT!

ZMMM

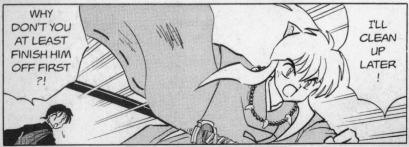

WHY DON'T YOU AT LEAST FINISH HIM OFF FIRST?!

I'LL CLEAN UP LATER!

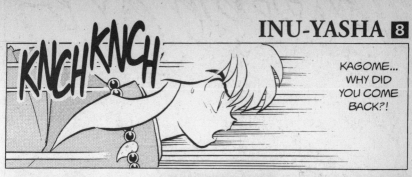

KNCH KNCH

KAGOME... WHY DID YOU COME BACK?!

GRRR GRRR

ZHHH...

WHAT...

IN THE WORLD IS GOING ON?

KAGOME,

INU-YASHA'S WOUNDS HAVEN'T HEALED YET.

OH... !

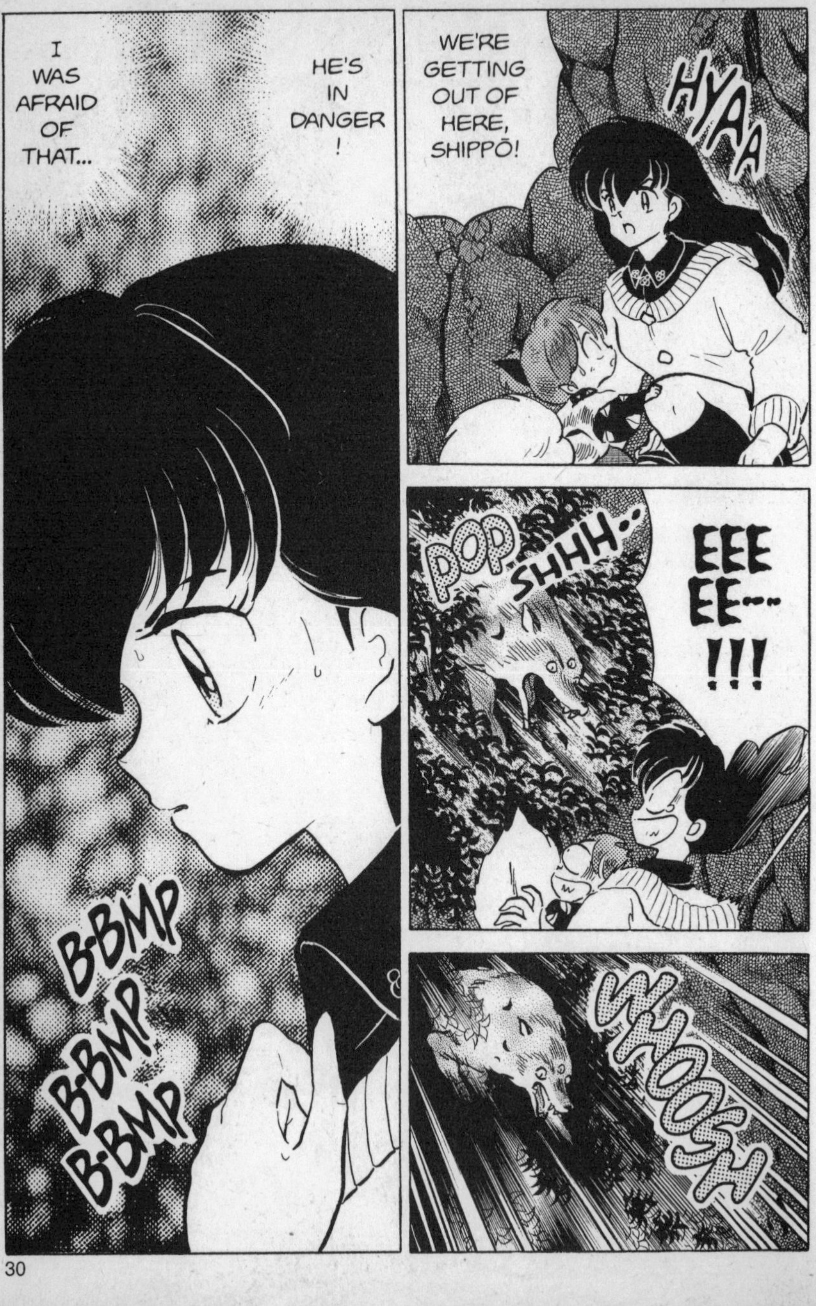

I WAS AFRAID OF THAT...
HE'S IN DANGER !
B-BMP B-BMP B-BMP
WE'RE GETTING OUT OF HERE, SHIPPŌ!
HYAA
POP
SHHH
EEEEE... !!!
WHOOSH

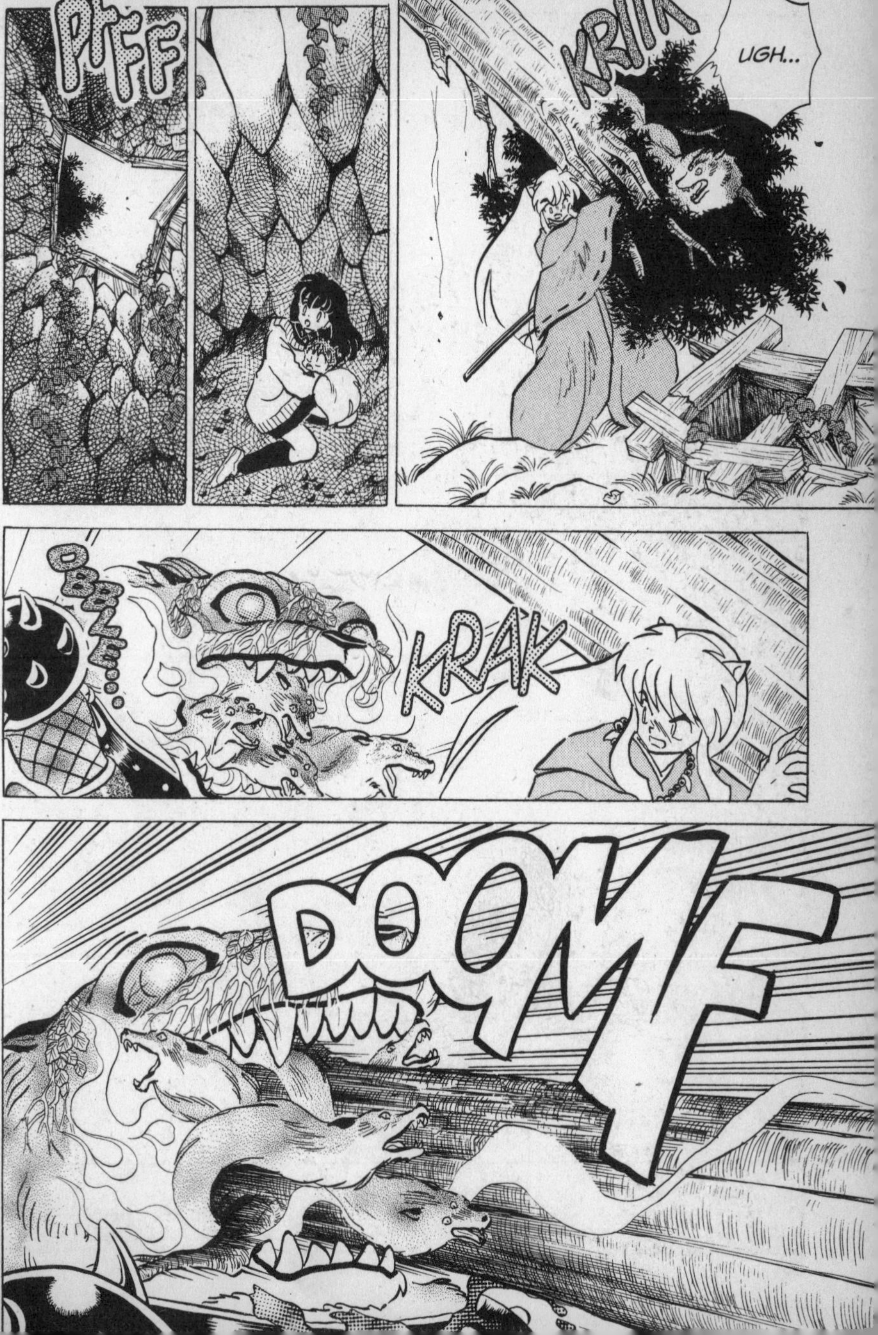
PFFF
KRIIK
UGH...
OBBZE...
KRAK
DOOMF

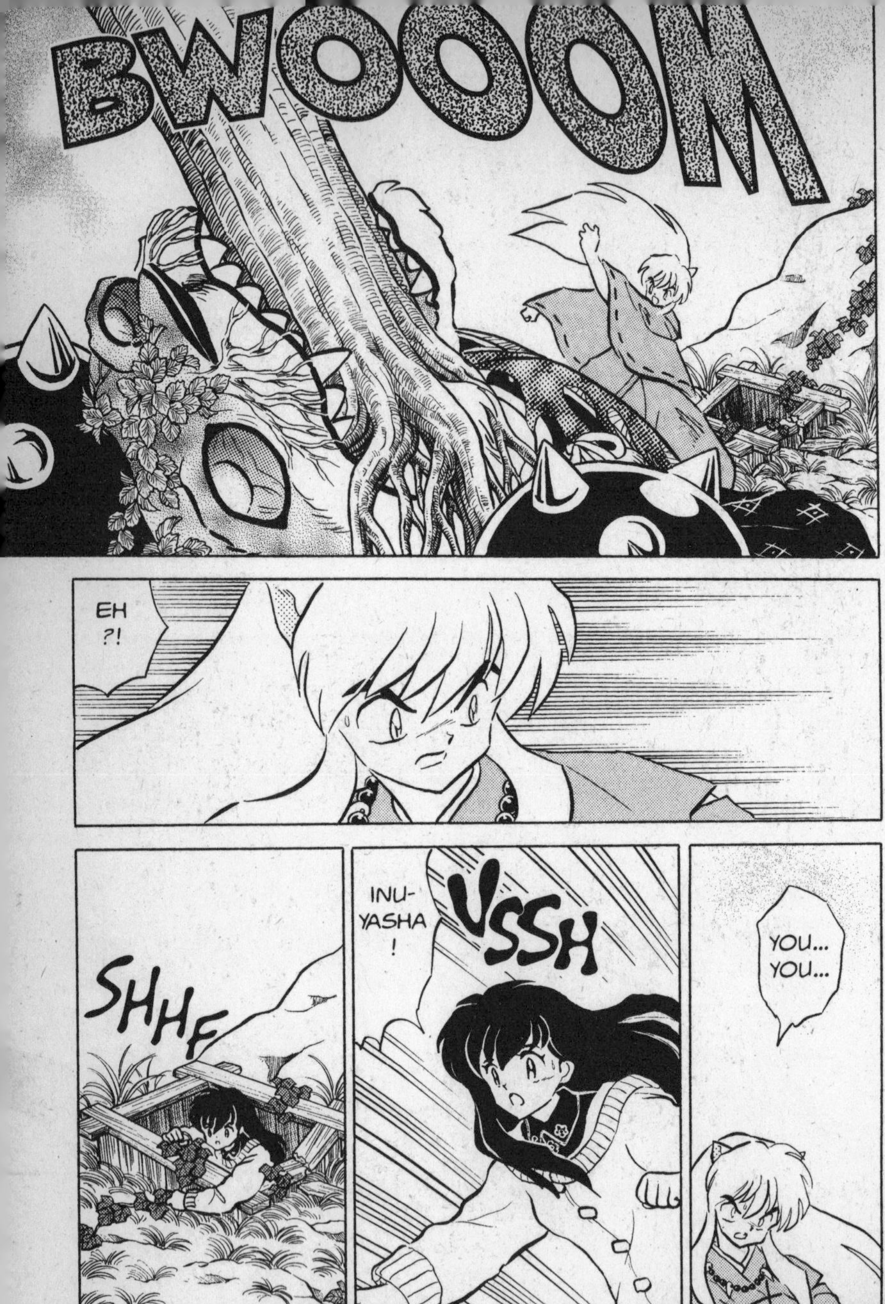
BWOOOM
EH ?!
SHHF
INU-YASHA !
VSSH
YOU... YOU...

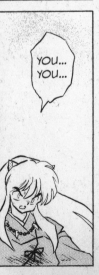

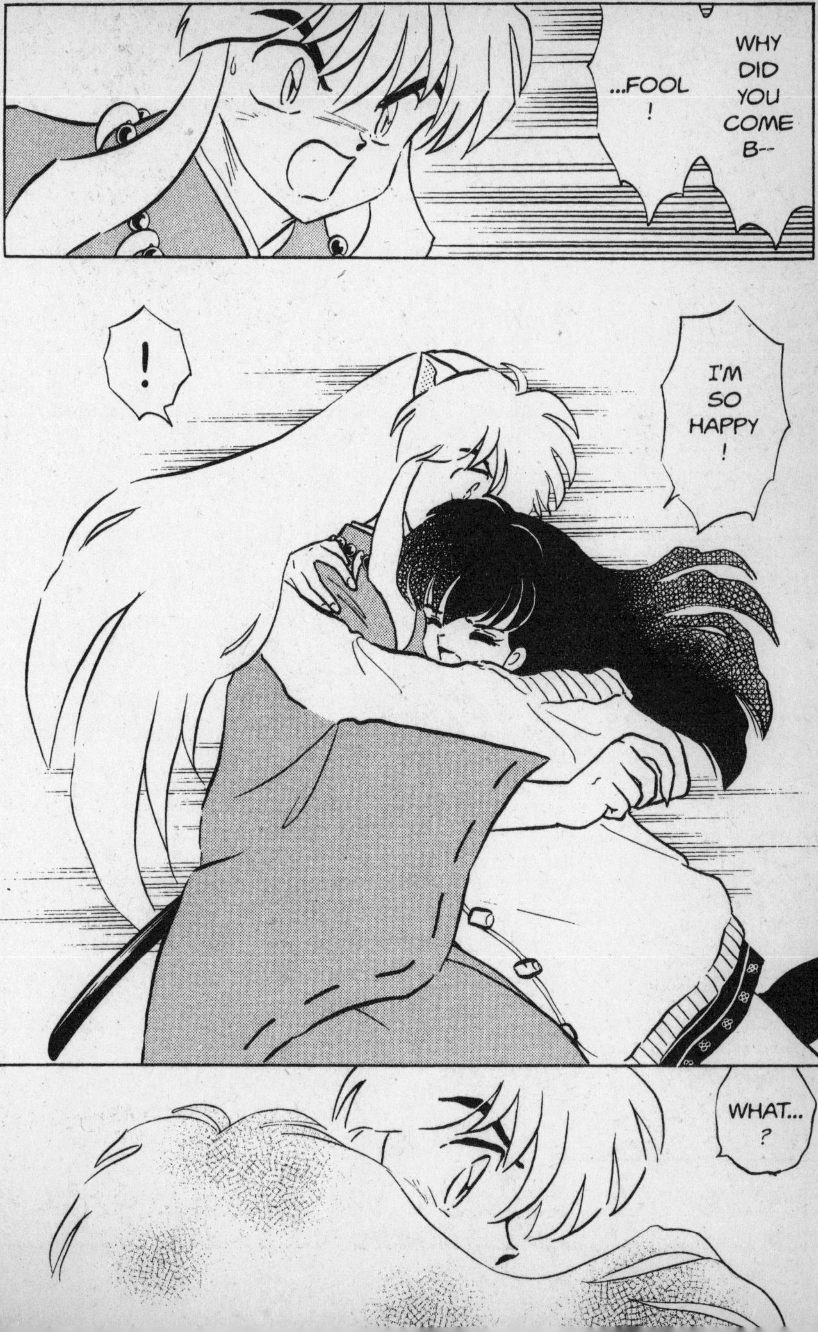
...FOOL !
WHY DID YOU COME B--
!
I'M SO HAPPY !
WHAT... ?

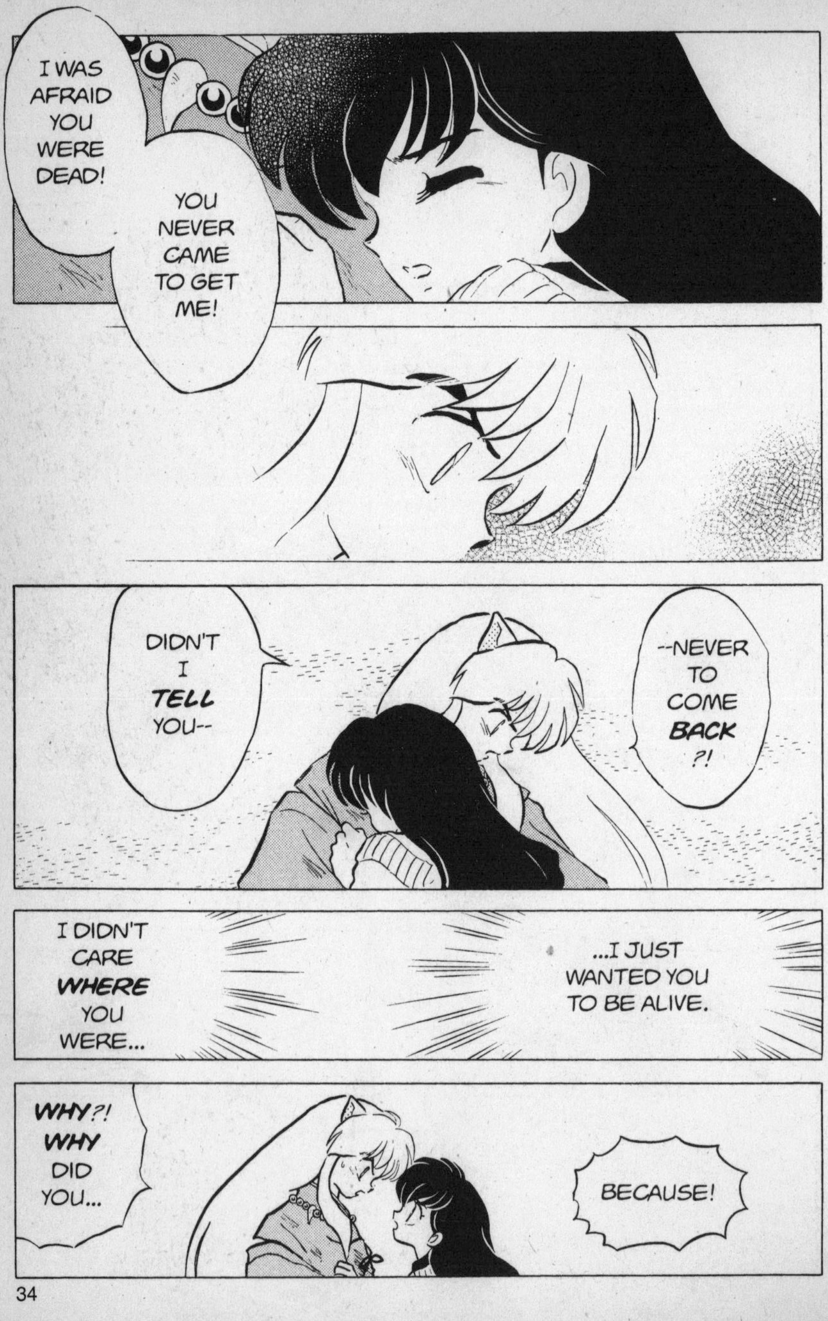
I WAS AFRAID YOU WERE DEAD!
YOU NEVER CAME TO GET ME!
DIDN'T I **TELL** YOU--
--NEVER TO COME **BACK**?!
I DIDN'T CARE **WHERE** YOU WERE...
...I JUST WANTED YOU TO BE ALIVE.
WHY?! **WHY** DID YOU...
BECAUSE!

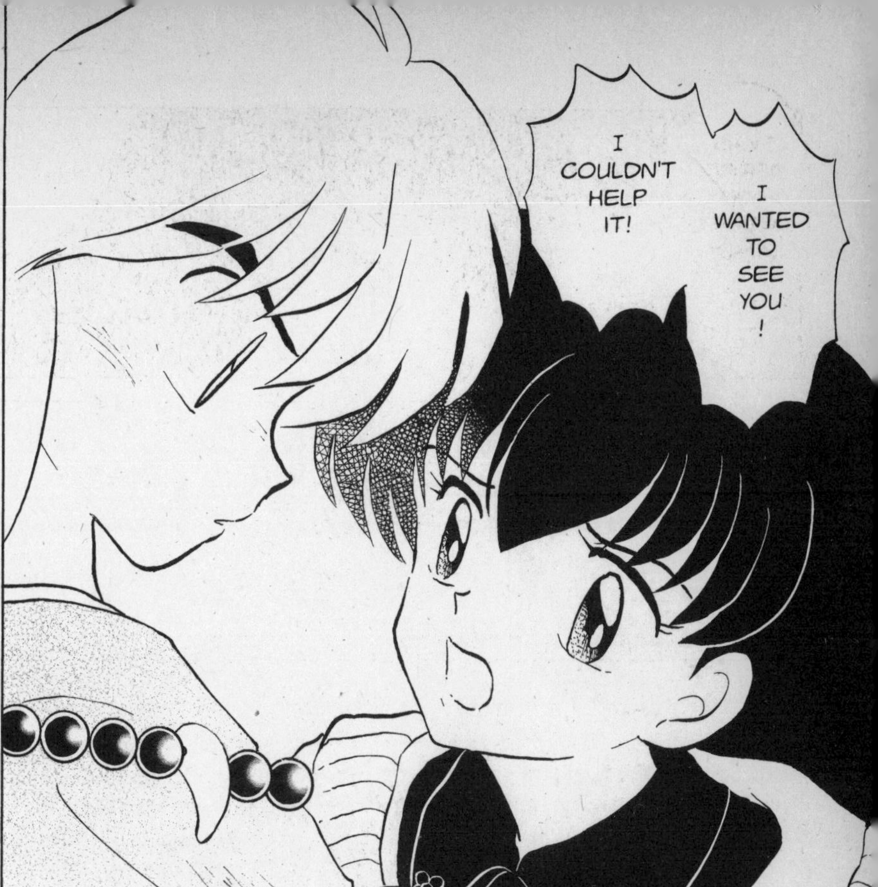
I COULDN'T HELP IT!
I WANTED TO SEE YOU!

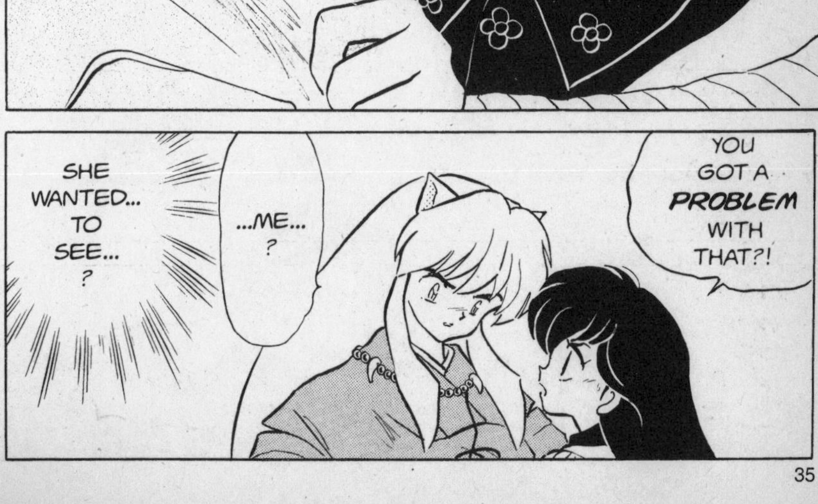
SHE WANTED... TO SEE... ?
...ME... ?
YOU GOT A PROBLEM WITH THAT?!

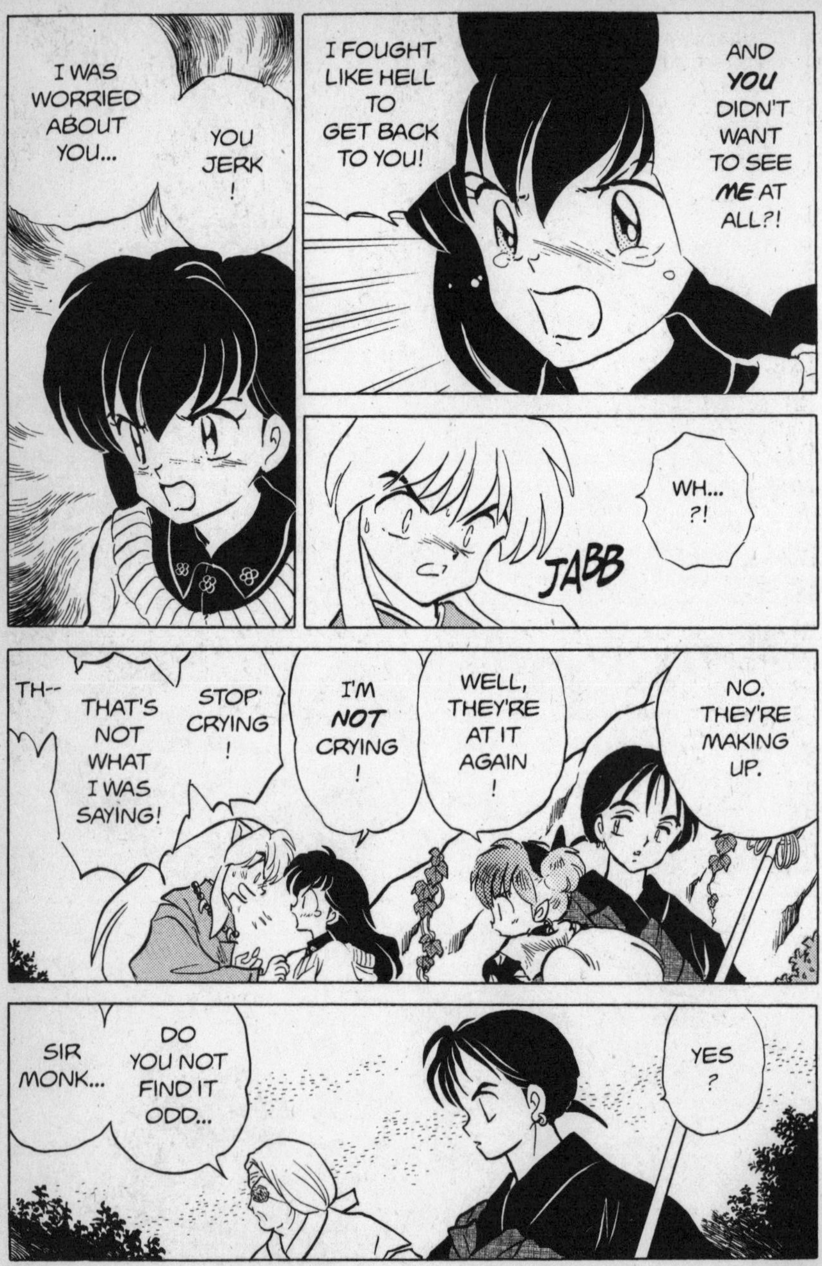
I WAS WORRIED ABOUT YOU...
YOU JERK!
I FOUGHT LIKE HELL TO GET BACK TO YOU!
AND *YOU* DIDN'T WANT TO SEE *ME* AT ALL?!
JABB
WH...?!
TH--
THAT'S NOT WHAT I WAS SAYING!
STOP CRYING!
I'M *NOT* CRYING!
WELL, THEY'RE AT IT AGAIN!
NO. THEY'RE MAKING UP.
SIR MONK...
DO YOU NOT FIND IT ODD...
YES?

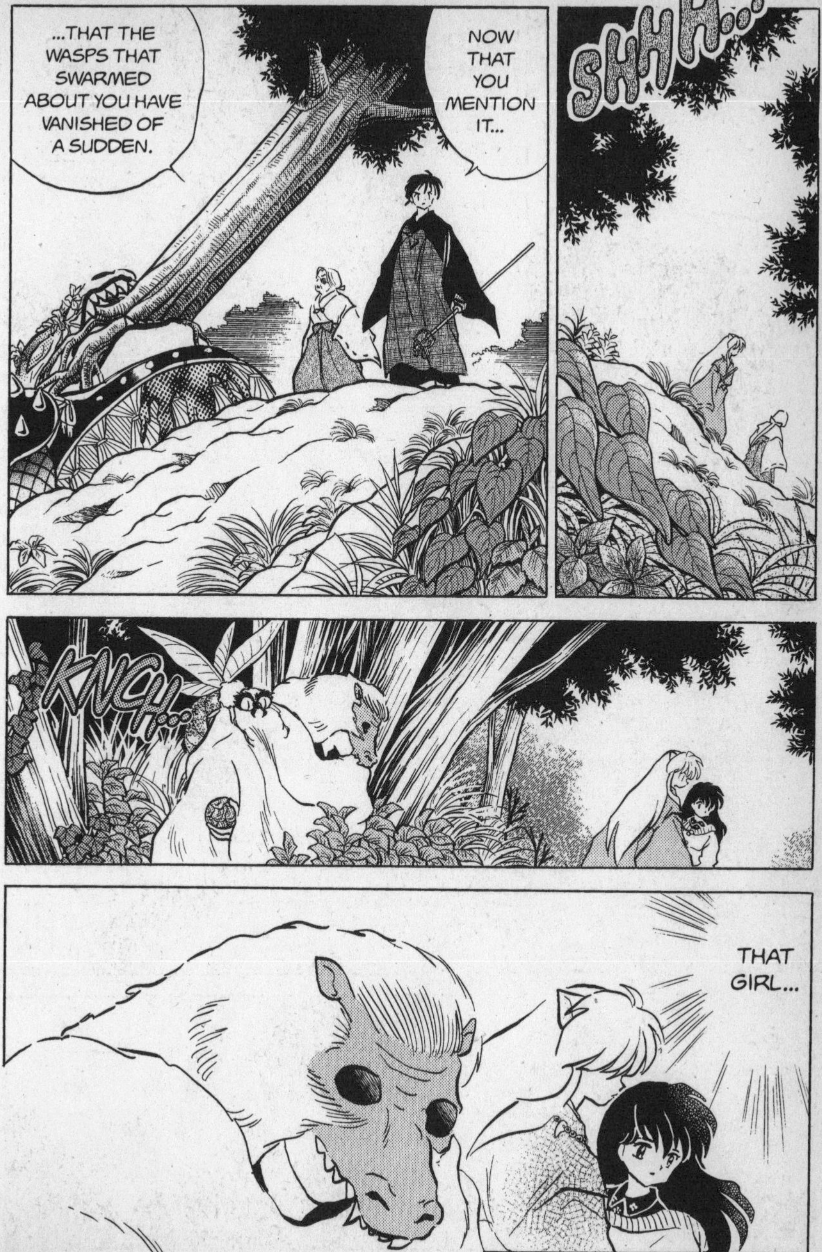
...THAT THE WASPS THAT SWARMED ABOUT YOU HAVE VANISHED OF A SUDDEN.
NOW THAT YOU MENTION IT...
SHHH...
KNCH...
THAT GIRL...

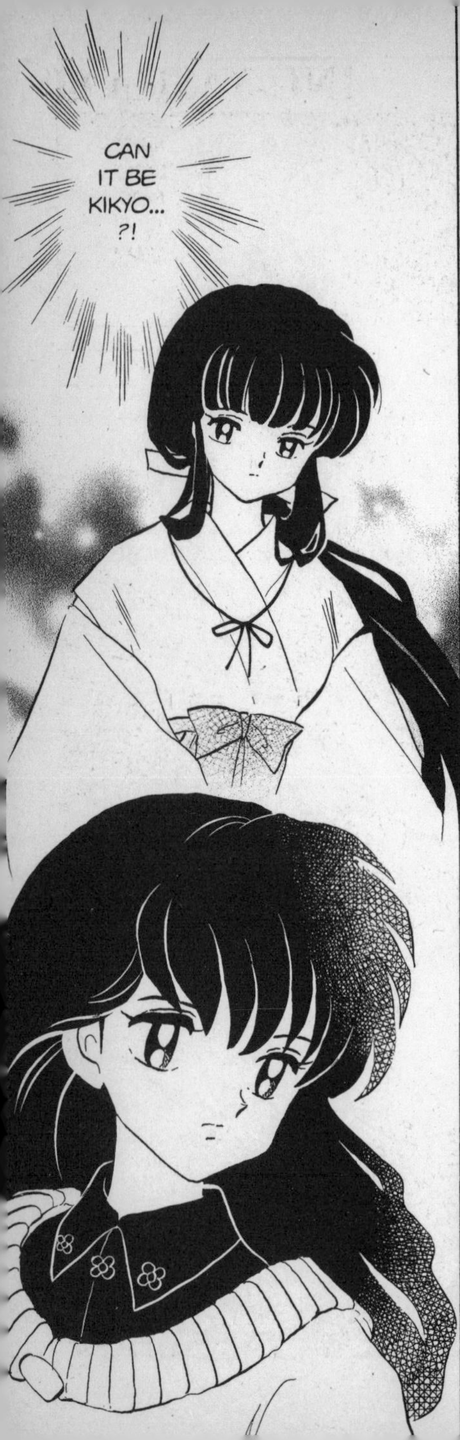
CAN IT BE KIKYO... ?!

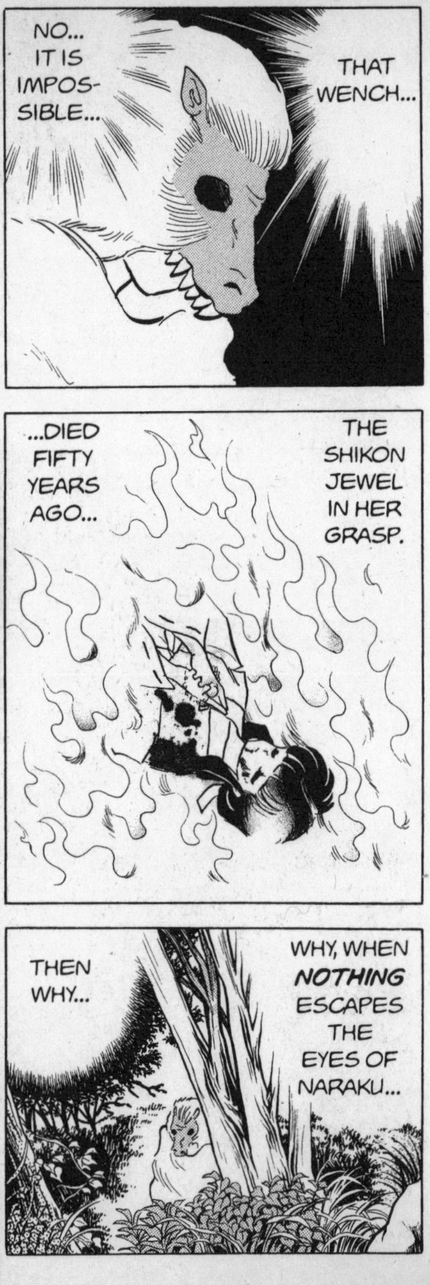
NO... IT IS IMPOS- SIBLE...
THAT WENCH...
...DIED FIFTY YEARS AGO...
THE SHIKON JEWEL IN HER GRASP.
THEN WHY...
WHY, WHEN *NOTHING* ESCAPES THE EYES OF NARAKU...

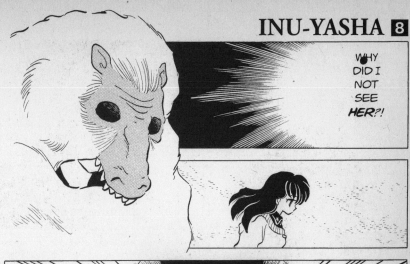

WHY DID I NOT SEE *HER?!*

WHRR

!

THERE'S SOMEONE OVER THERE!

HE'S GOT SHIKON SHARDS!

!

39

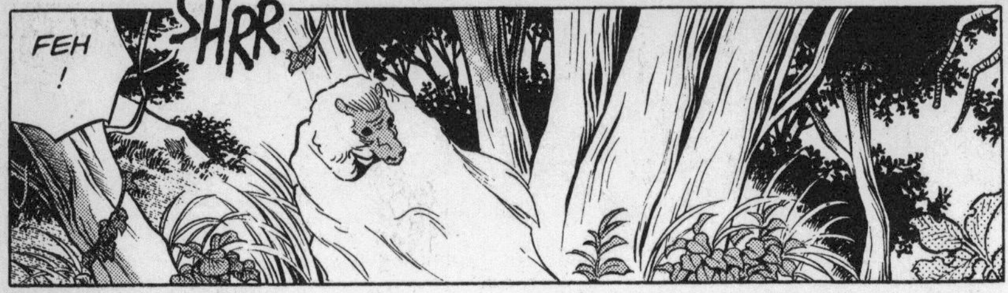
FEH!
SHRR
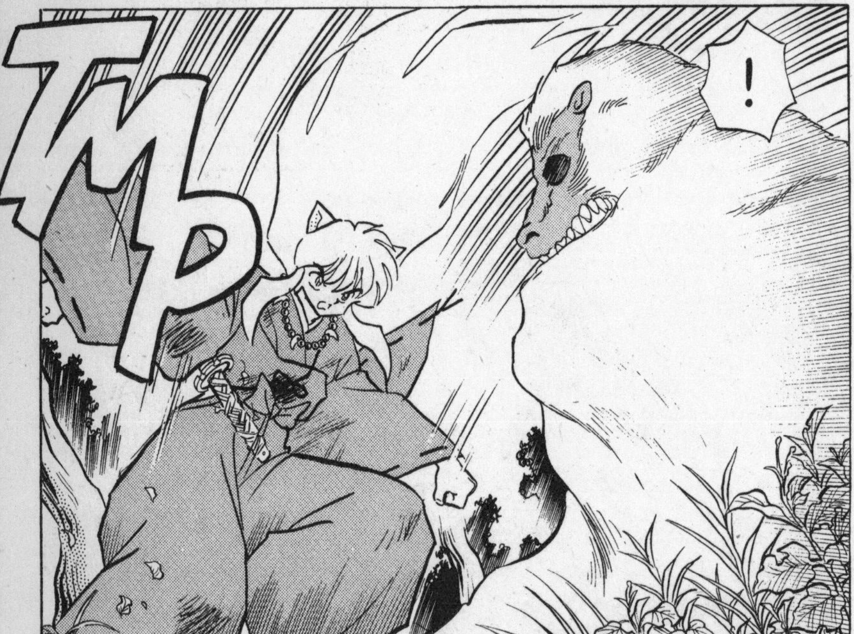
TMP
!
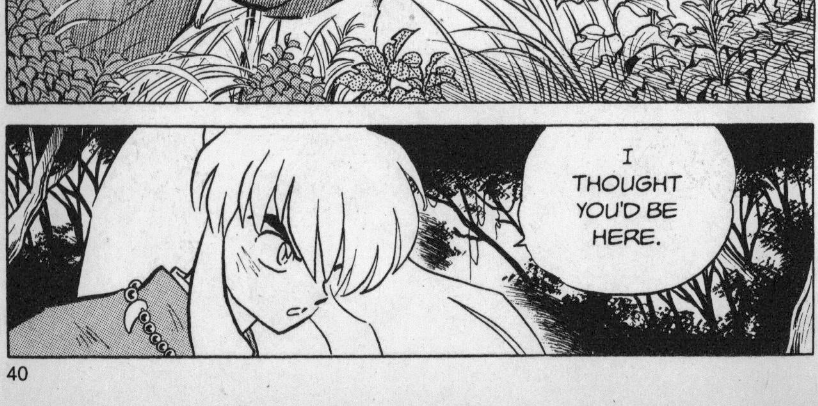
I THOUGHT YOU'D BE HERE.

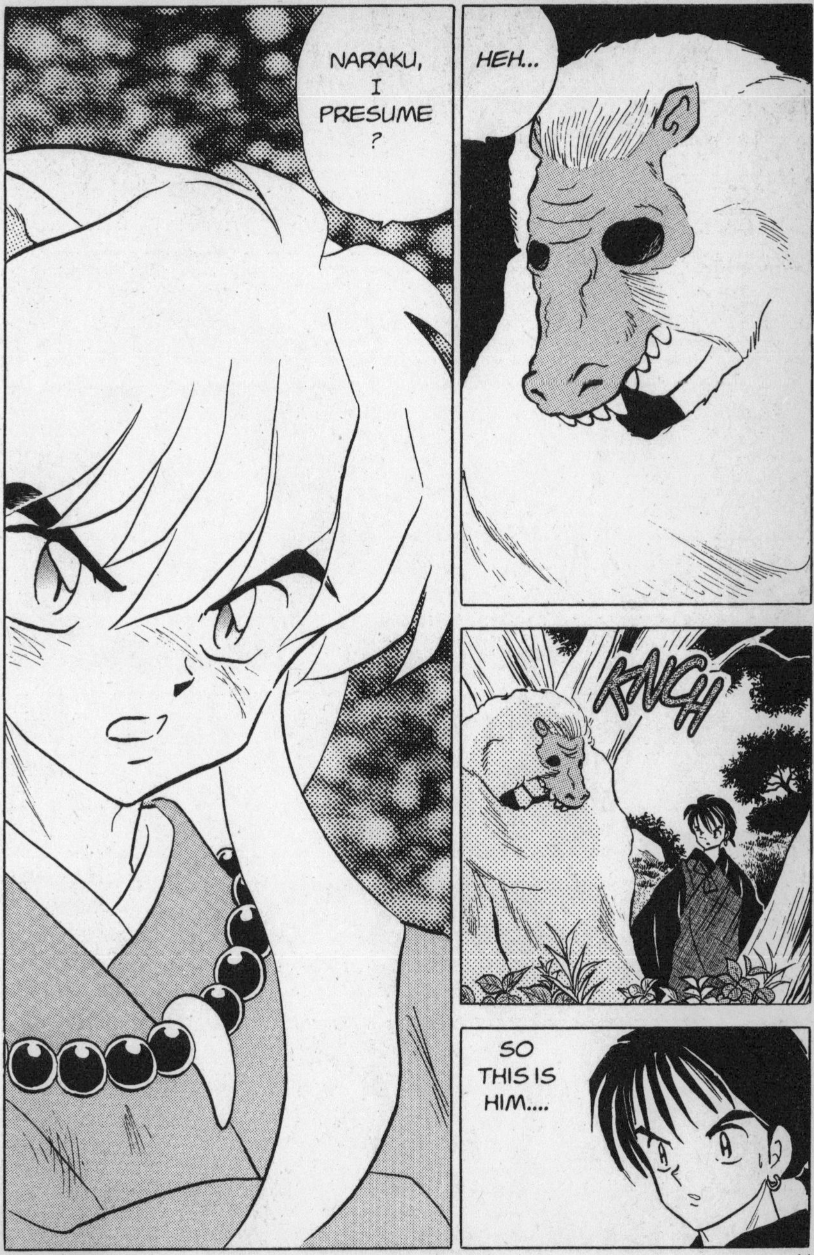
NARAKU, I PRESUME?
HEH...
KNCH
SO THIS IS HIM....

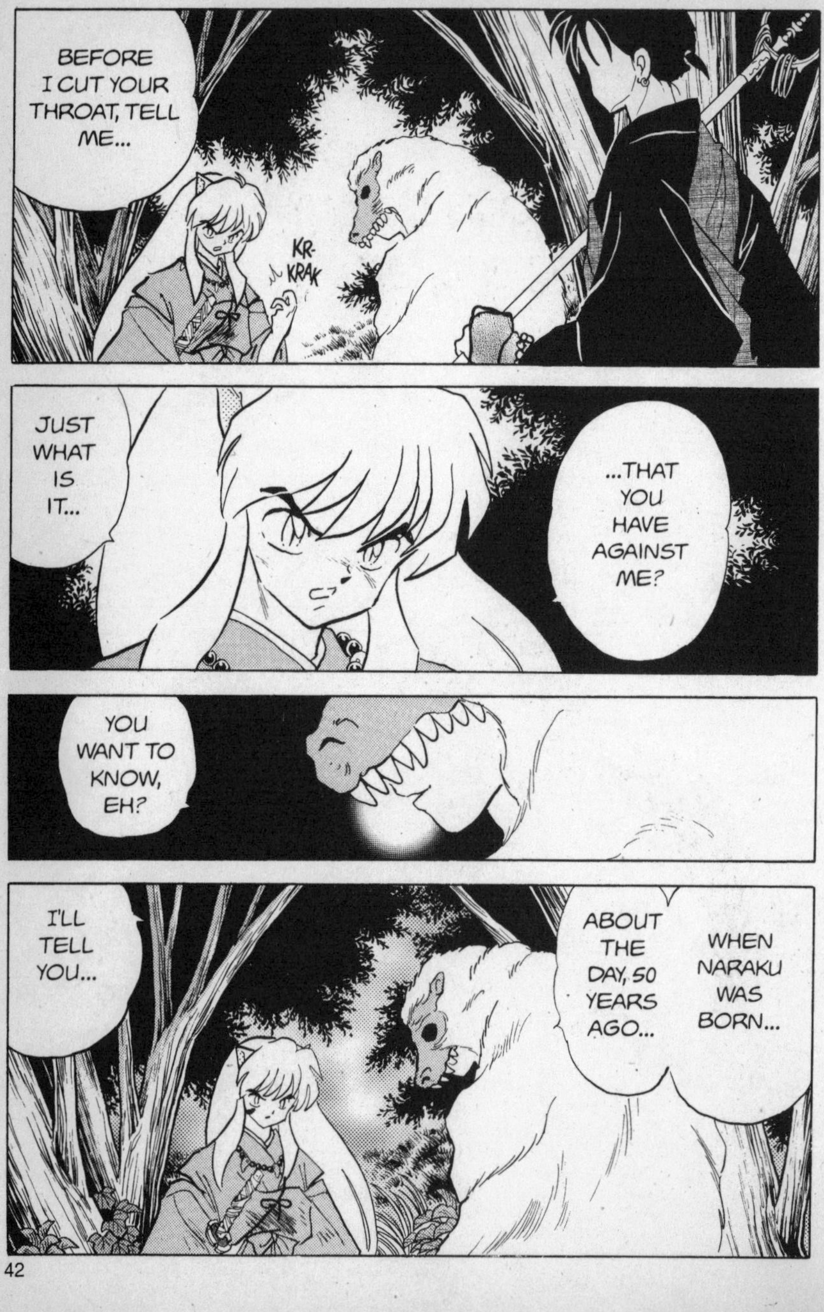
BEFORE I CUT YOUR THROAT, TELL ME...
KR-KRAK
JUST WHAT IS IT...
...THAT YOU HAVE AGAINST ME?
YOU WANT TO KNOW, EH?
I'LL TELL YOU...
ABOUT THE DAY, 50 YEARS AGO...
WHEN NARAKU WAS BORN...

SCROLL THREE
NARAKU

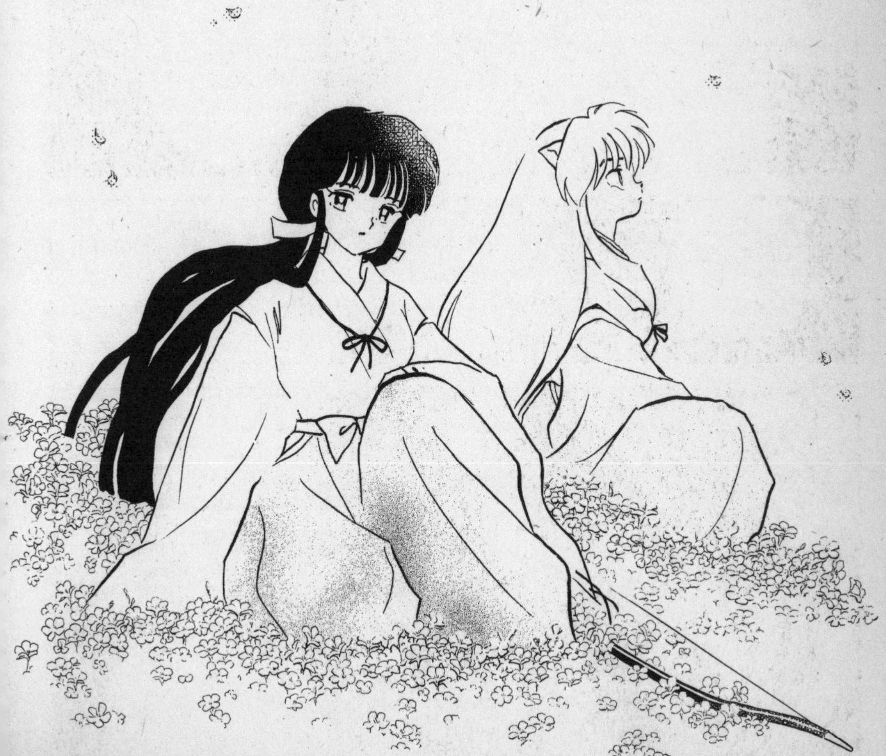

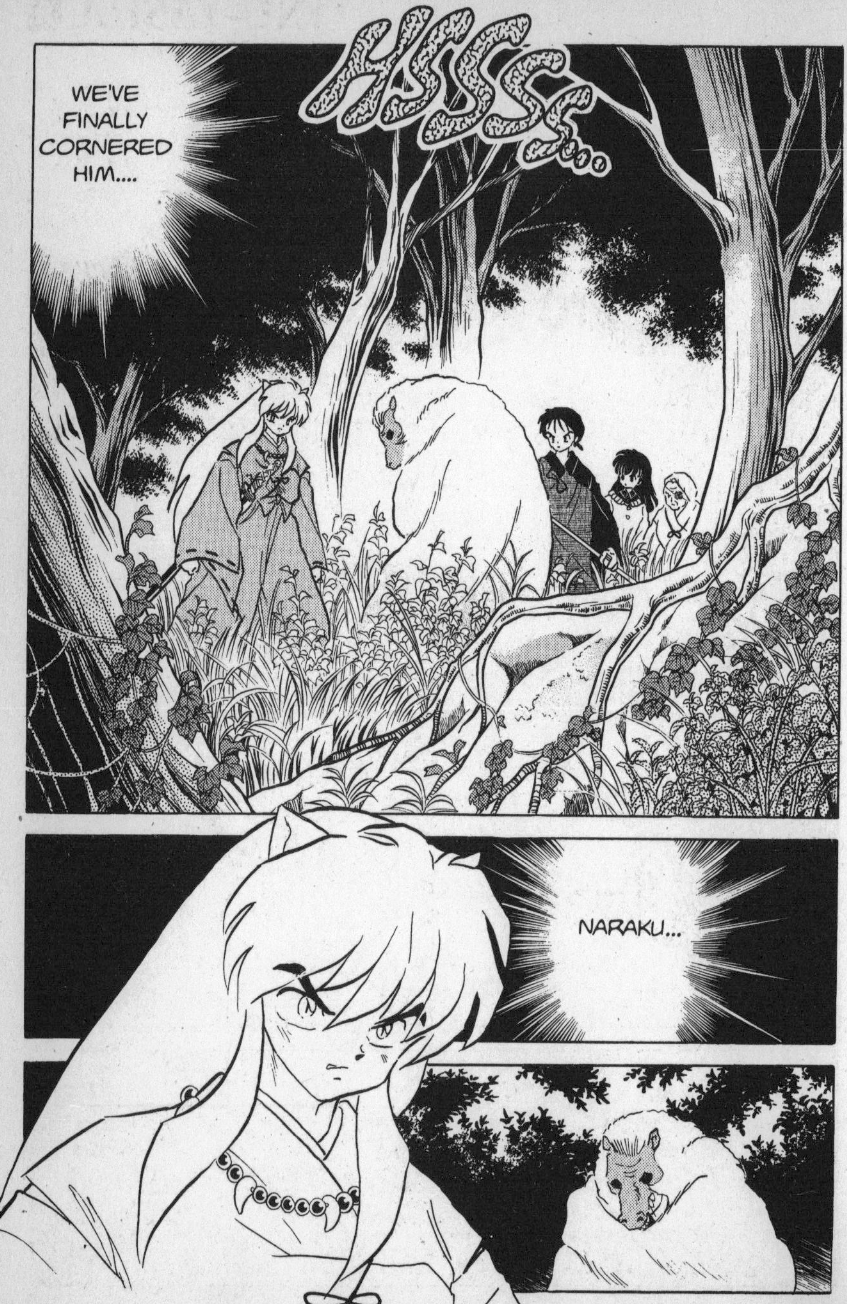
HSSSS...
WE'VE FINALLY CORNERED HIM....
NARAKU...

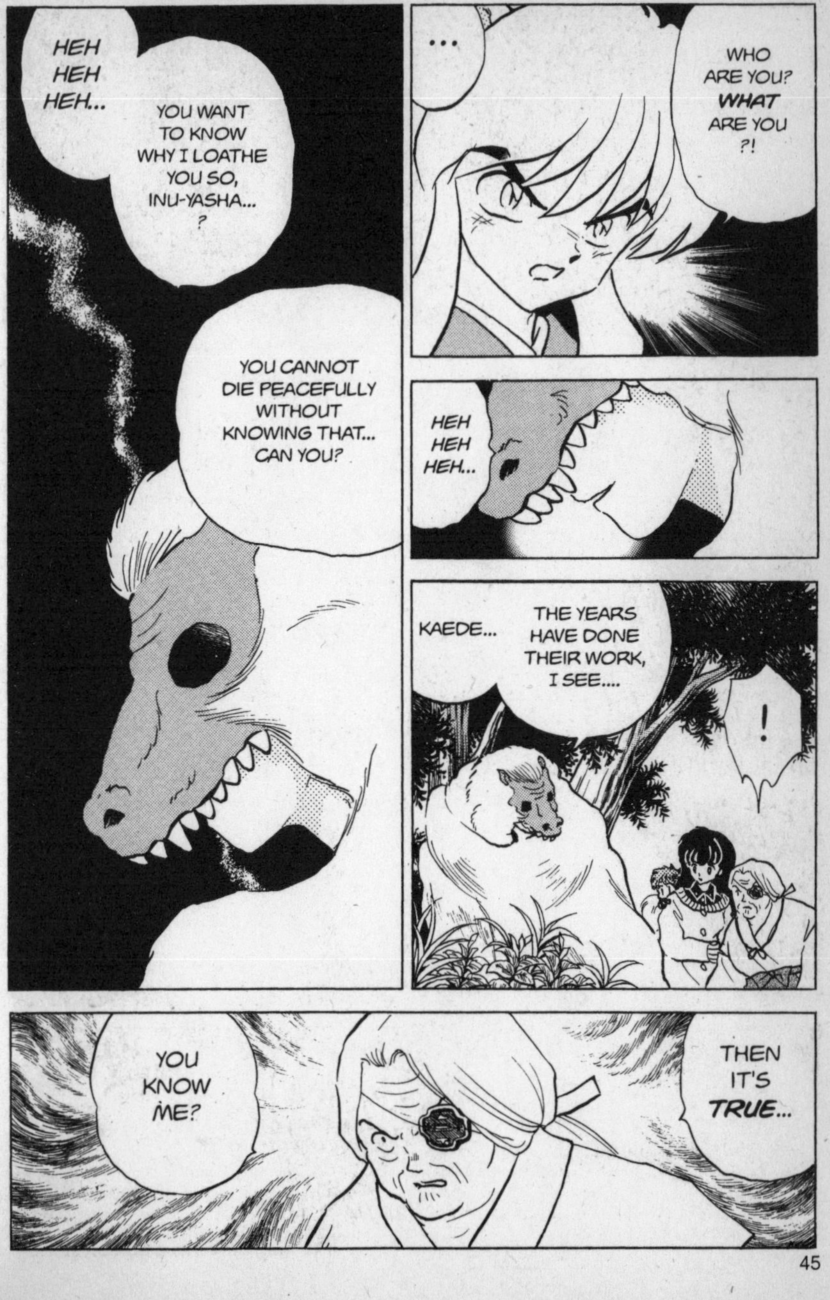
HEH HEH HEH...
YOU WANT TO KNOW WHY I LOATHE YOU SO, INU-YASHA... ?
YOU CANNOT DIE PEACEFULLY WITHOUT KNOWING THAT... CAN YOU?
...
WHO ARE YOU? WHAT ARE YOU ?!
HEH HEH HEH...
KAEDE...
THE YEARS HAVE DONE THEIR WORK, I SEE....
!
YOU KNOW ME?
THEN IT'S TRUE...

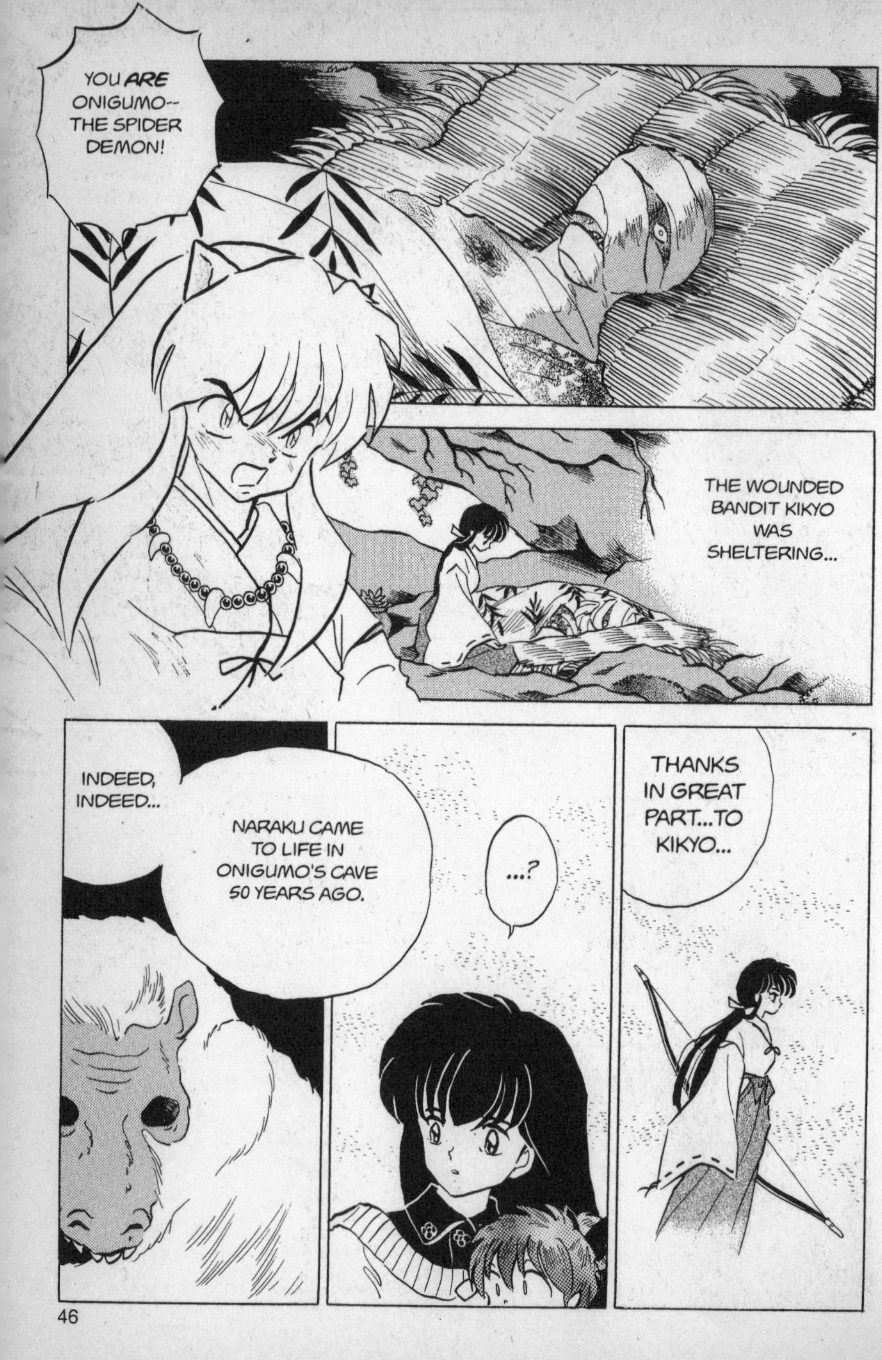
YOU ARE ONIGUMO-- THE SPIDER DEMON!
THE WOUNDED BANDIT KIKYO WAS SHELTERING...
INDEED, INDEED...
NARAKU CAME TO LIFE IN ONIGUMO'S CAVE 50 YEARS AGO.
...?
THANKS IN GREAT PART...TO KIKYO...

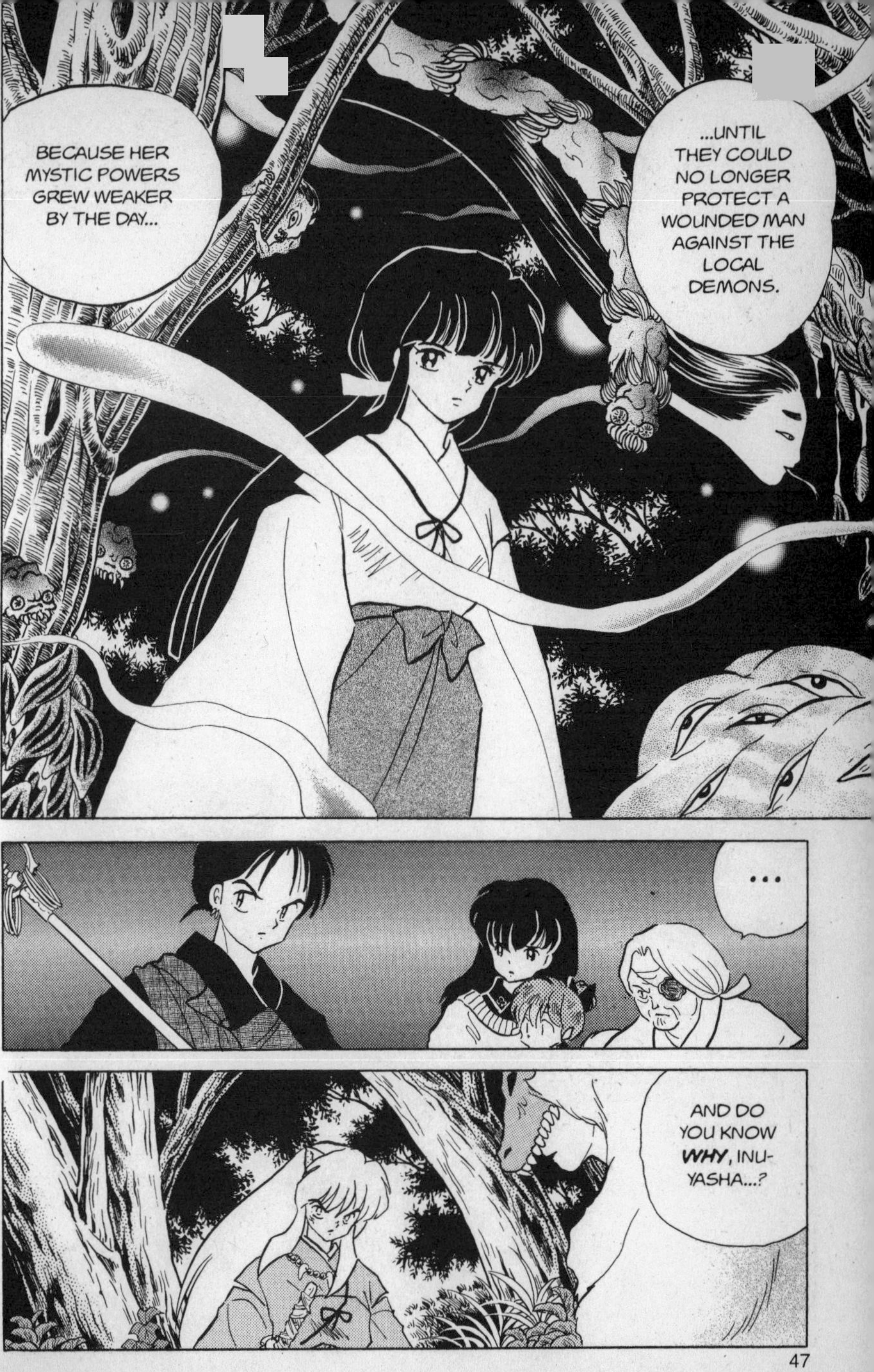
BECAUSE HER MYSTIC POWERS GREW WEAKER BY THE DAY...
...UNTIL THEY COULD NO LONGER PROTECT A WOUNDED MAN AGAINST THE LOCAL DEMONS.
...
AND DO YOU KNOW **WHY**, INU-YASHA...?

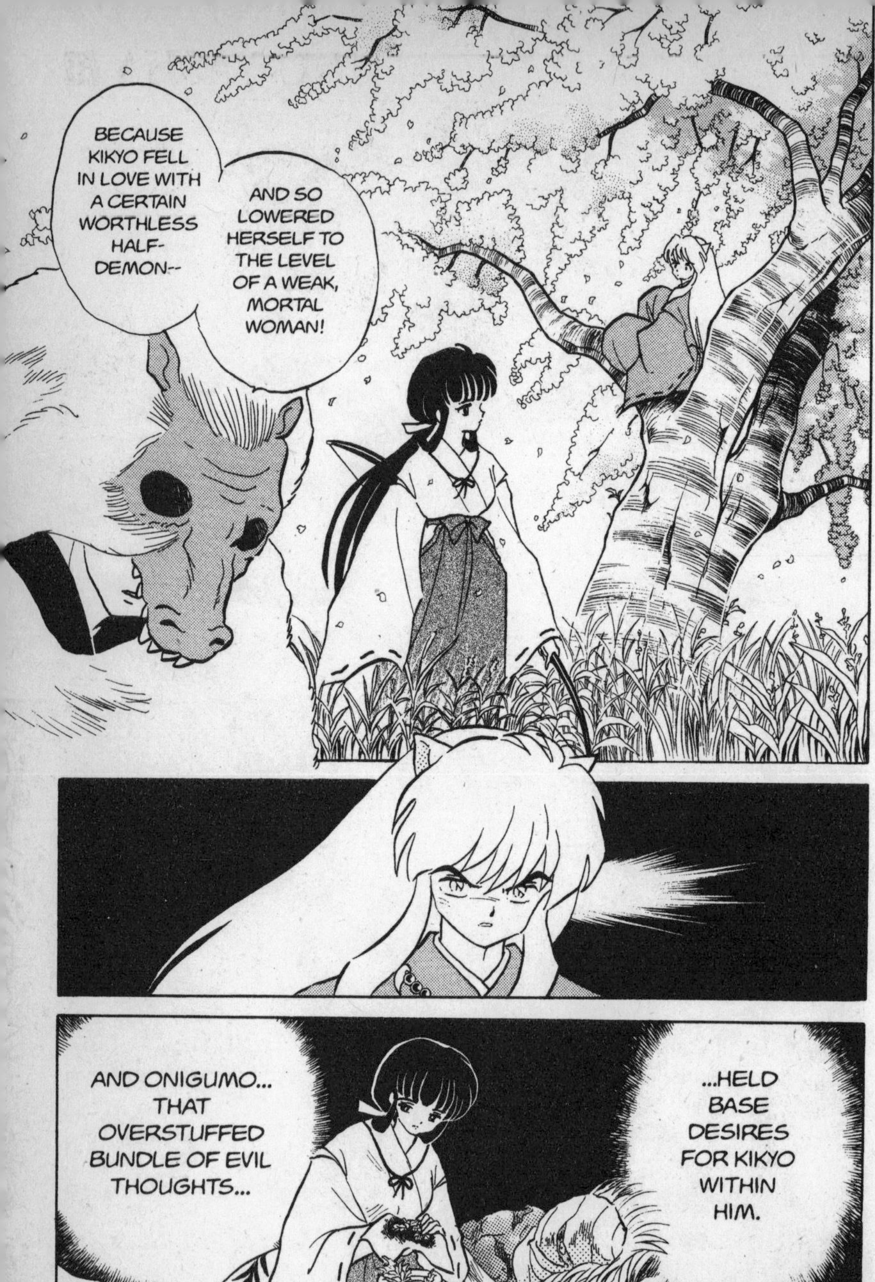
BECAUSE KIKYO FELL IN LOVE WITH A CERTAIN WORTHLESS HALF-DEMON--
AND SO LOWERED HERSELF TO THE LEVEL OF A WEAK, MORTAL WOMAN!
AND ONIGUMO... THAT OVERSTUFFED BUNDLE OF EVIL THOUGHTS...
...HELD BASE DESIRES FOR KIKYO WITHIN HIM.

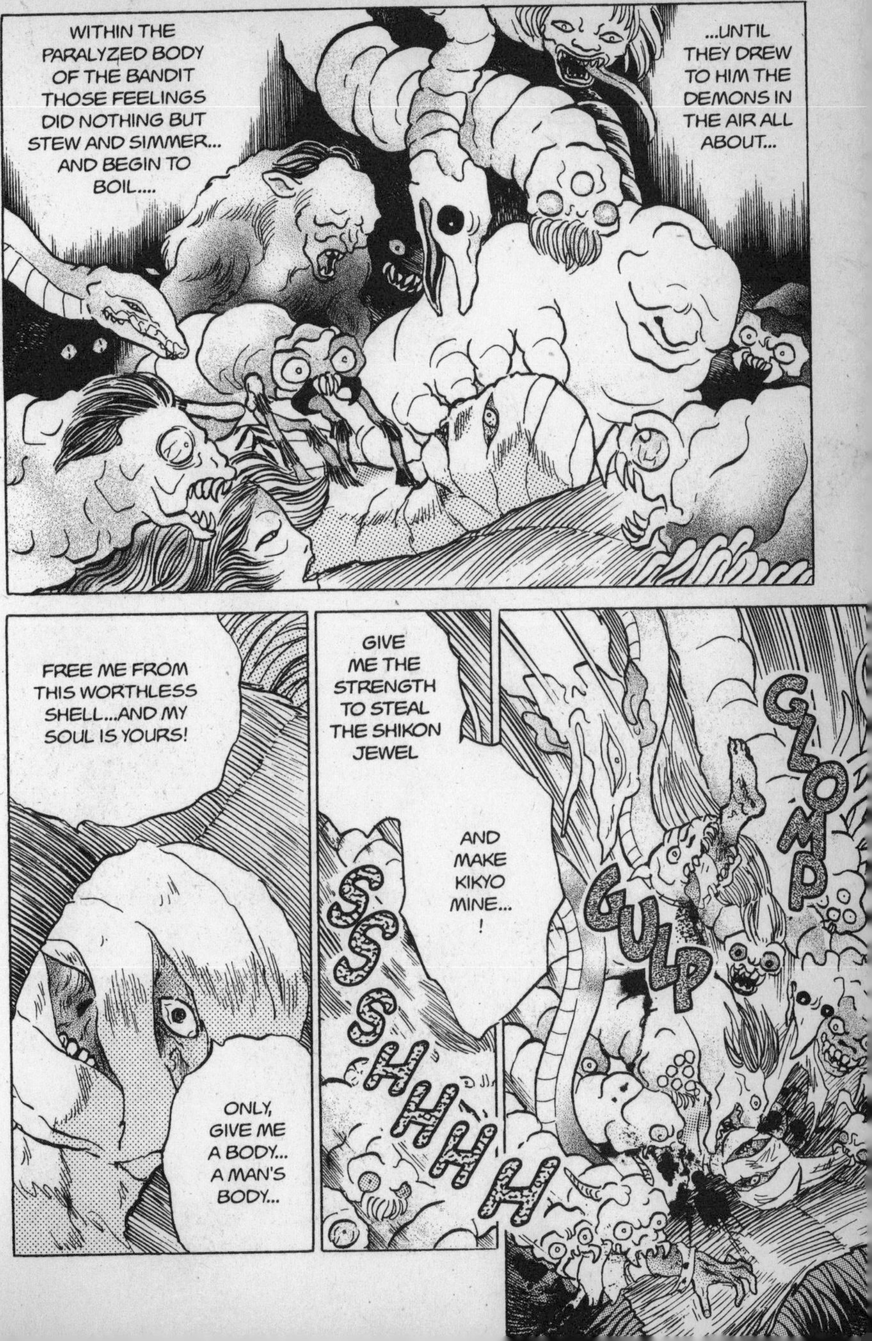
WITHIN THE PARALYZED BODY OF THE BANDIT THOSE FEELINGS DID NOTHING BUT STEW AND SIMMER... AND BEGIN TO BOIL....
...UNTIL THEY DREW TO HIM THE DEMONS IN THE AIR ALL ABOUT...
FREE ME FROM THIS WORTHLESS SHELL...AND MY SOUL IS YOURS!
ONLY, GIVE ME A BODY... A MAN'S BODY...
GIVE ME THE STRENGTH TO STEAL THE SHIKON JEWEL
SSSHHHH
AND MAKE KIKYO MINE... !
GLOMP
GULP

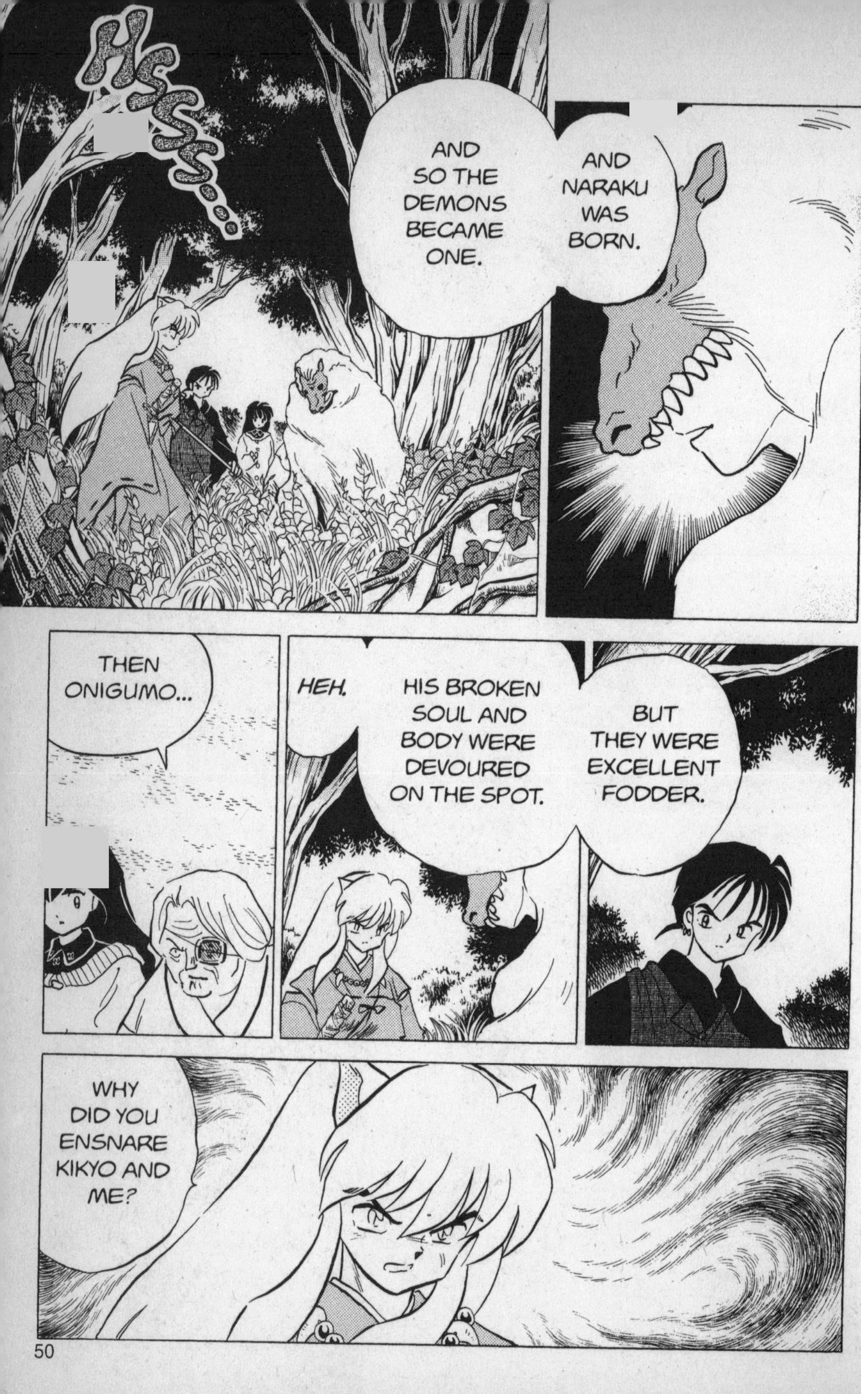
HSSS...
AND SO THE DEMONS BECAME ONE.
AND NARAKU WAS BORN.
THEN ONIGUMO...
HEH.
HIS BROKEN SOUL AND BODY WERE DEVOURED ON THE SPOT.
BUT THEY WERE EXCELLENT FODDER.
WHY DID YOU ENSNARE KIKYO AND ME?

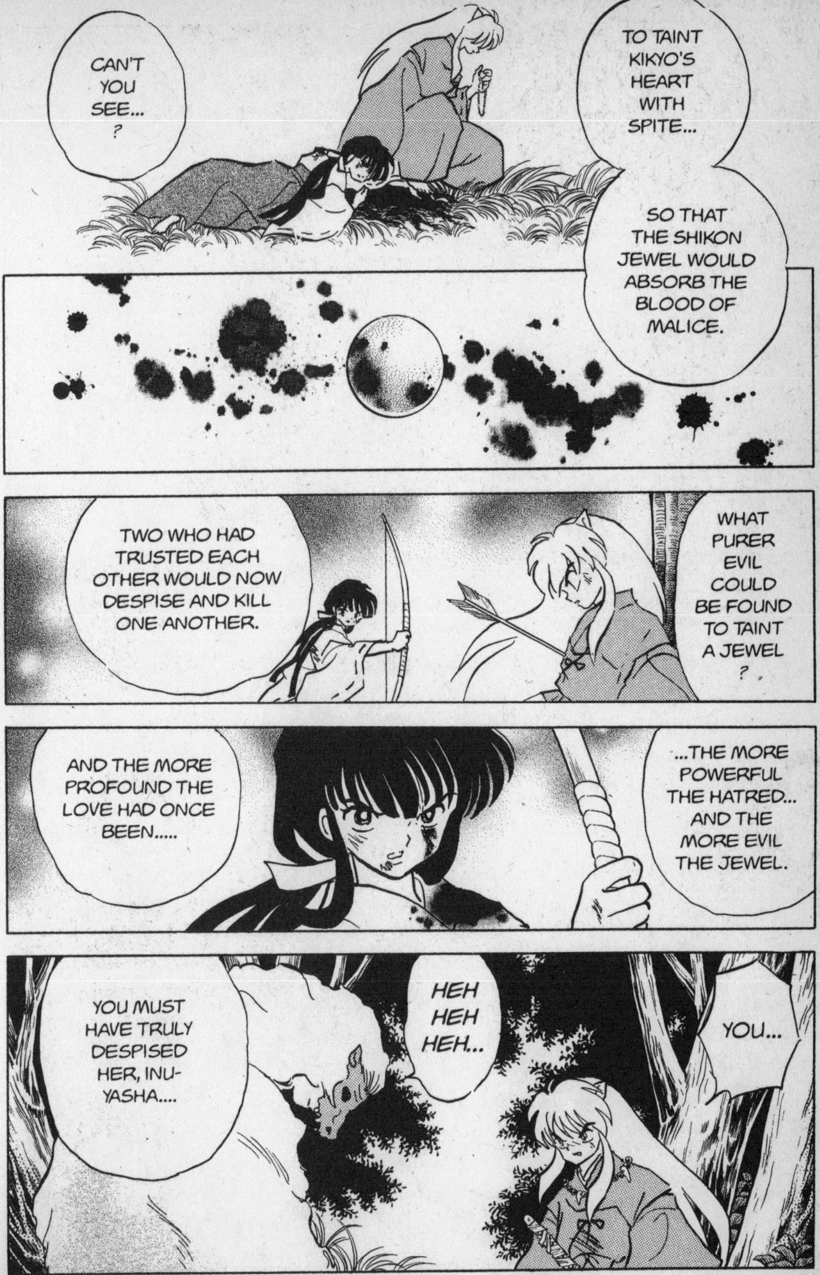
CAN'T YOU SEE... ?
TO TAINT KIKYO'S HEART WITH SPITE...
SO THAT THE SHIKON JEWEL WOULD ABSORB THE BLOOD OF MALICE.
TWO WHO HAD TRUSTED EACH OTHER WOULD NOW DESPISE AND KILL ONE ANOTHER.
WHAT PURER EVIL COULD BE FOUND TO TAINT A JEWEL ?
AND THE MORE PROFOUND THE LOVE HAD ONCE BEEN.....
...THE MORE POWERFUL THE HATRED... AND THE MORE EVIL THE JEWEL.
YOU MUST HAVE TRULY DESPISED HER, INU-YASHA....
HEH HEH HEH...
YOU...

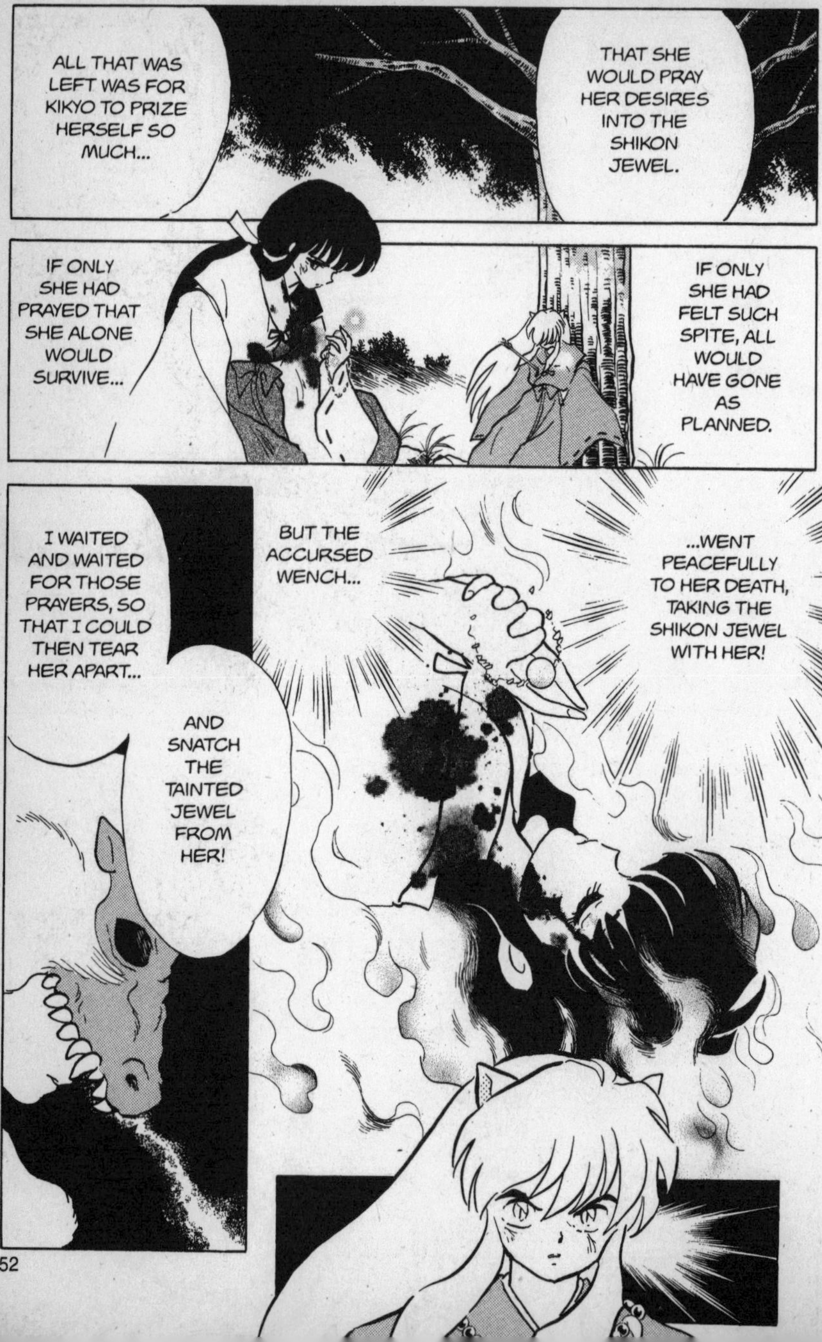
ALL THAT WAS LEFT WAS FOR KIKYO TO PRIZE HERSELF SO MUCH...
THAT SHE WOULD PRAY HER DESIRES INTO THE SHIKON JEWEL.
IF ONLY SHE HAD PRAYED THAT SHE ALONE WOULD SURVIVE...
IF ONLY SHE HAD FELT SUCH SPITE, ALL WOULD HAVE GONE AS PLANNED.
I WAITED AND WAITED FOR THOSE PRAYERS, SO THAT I COULD THEN TEAR HER APART...
AND SNATCH THE TAINTED JEWEL FROM HER!
BUT THE ACCURSED WENCH...
...WENT PEACEFULLY TO HER DEATH, TAKING THE SHIKON JEWEL WITH HER!

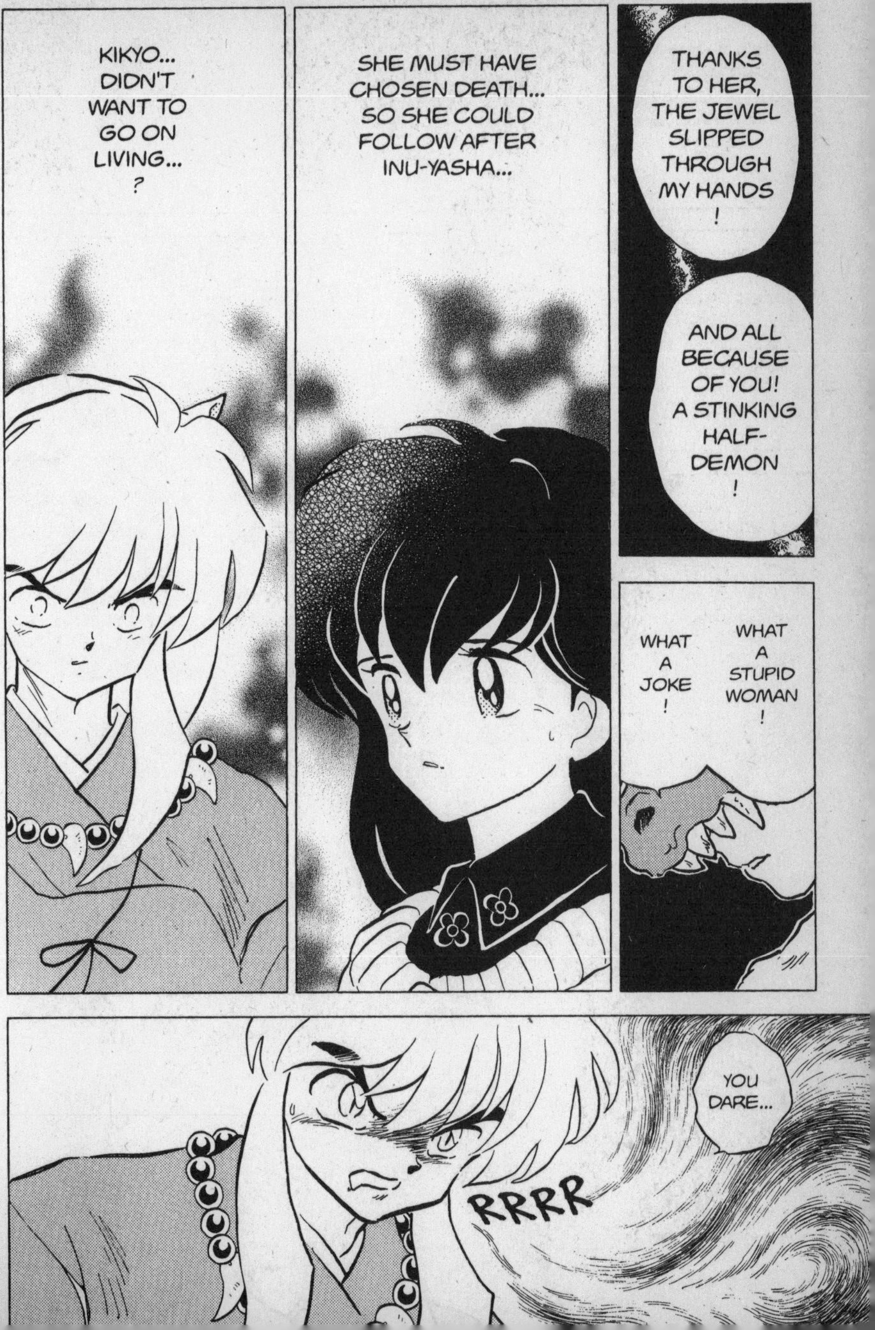
KIKYO... DIDN'T WANT TO GO ON LIVING... ?
SHE MUST HAVE CHOSEN DEATH... SO SHE COULD FOLLOW AFTER INU-YASHA...
THANKS TO HER, THE JEWEL SLIPPED THROUGH MY HANDS !
AND ALL BECAUSE OF YOU! A STINKING HALF-DEMON !
WHAT A JOKE !
WHAT A STUPID WOMAN !
YOU DARE...
RRRR

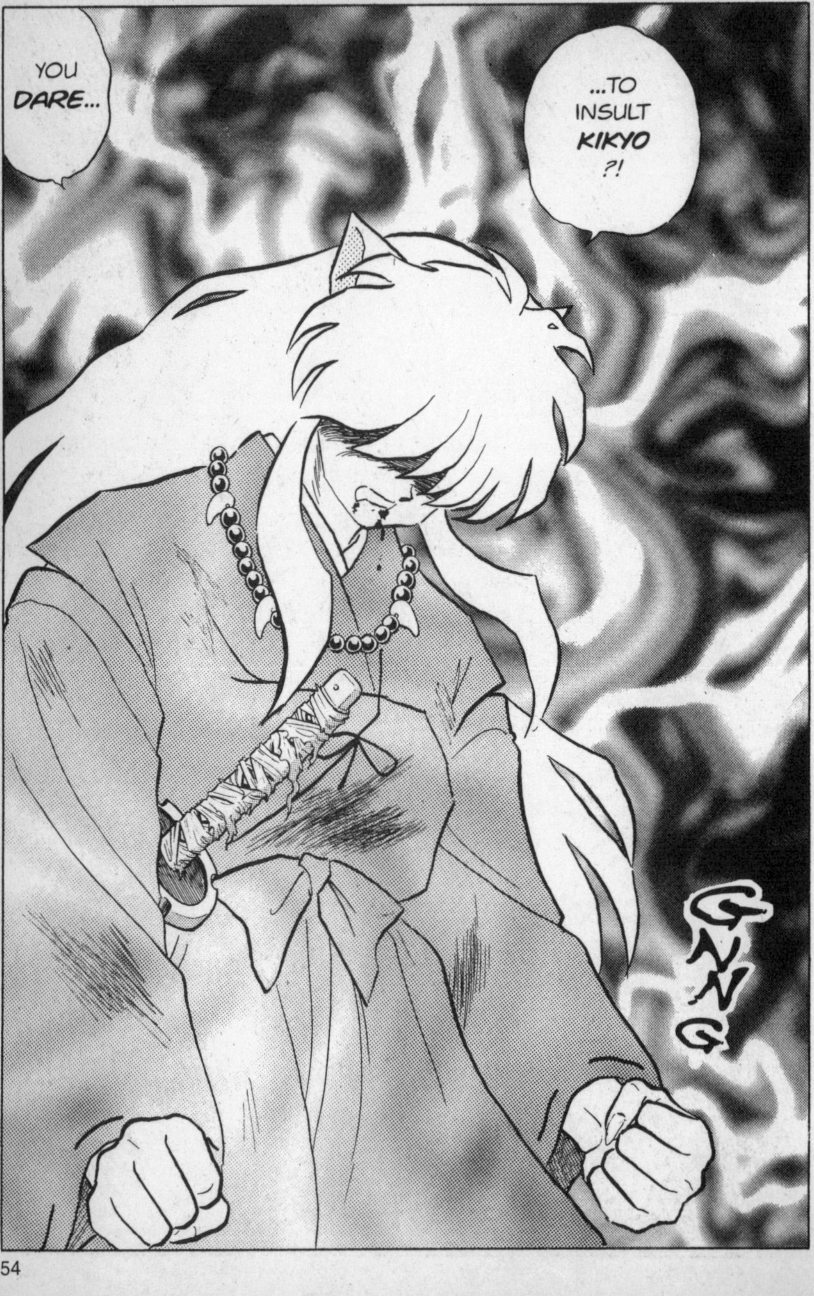
YOU DARE...
...TO INSULT KIKYO ?!
GNNG

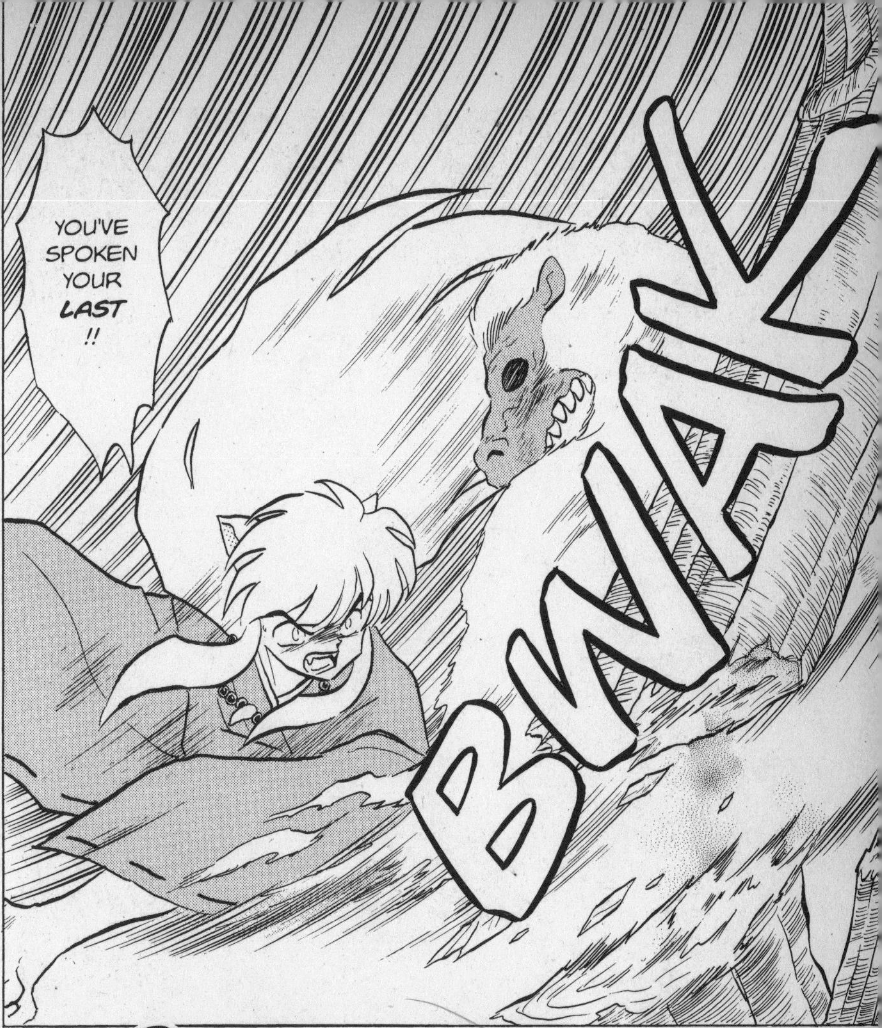
YOU'VE SPOKEN YOUR **LAST** !!
BWAK
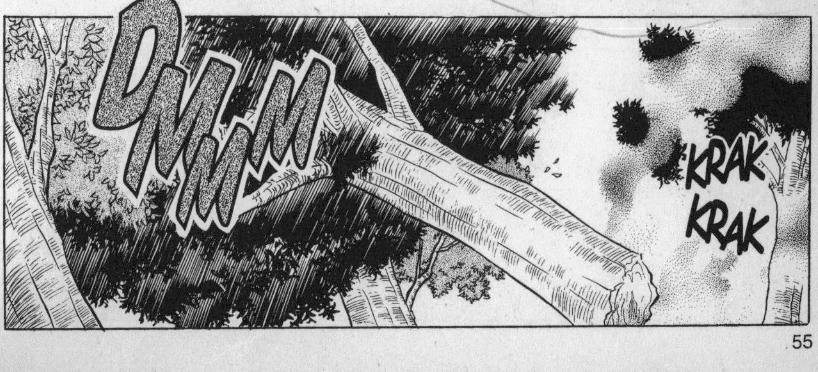
DMMM
KRAK KRAK

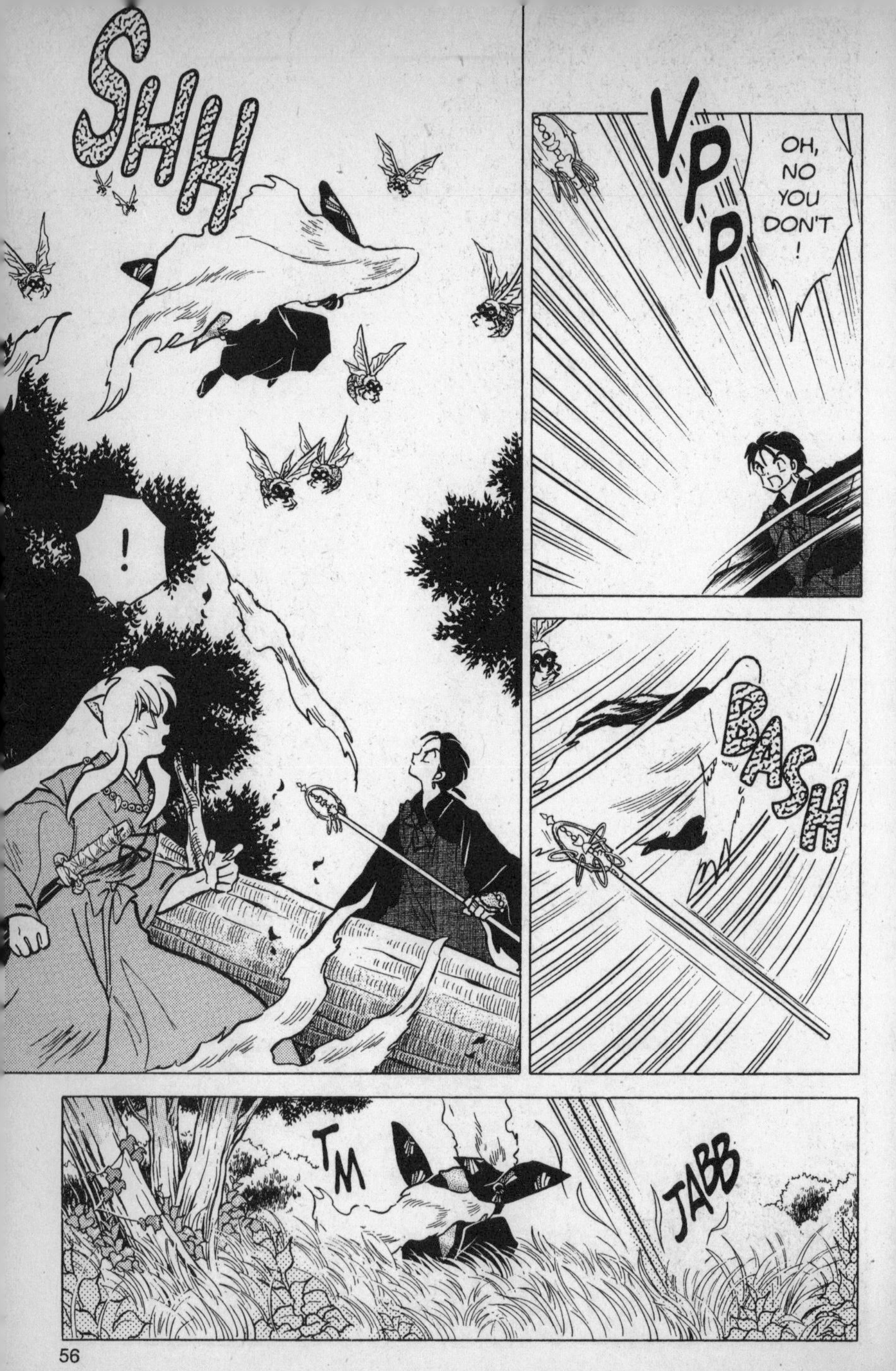
SHH
!
VPP
OH, NO YOU DON'T!
BASH
TM
JABB

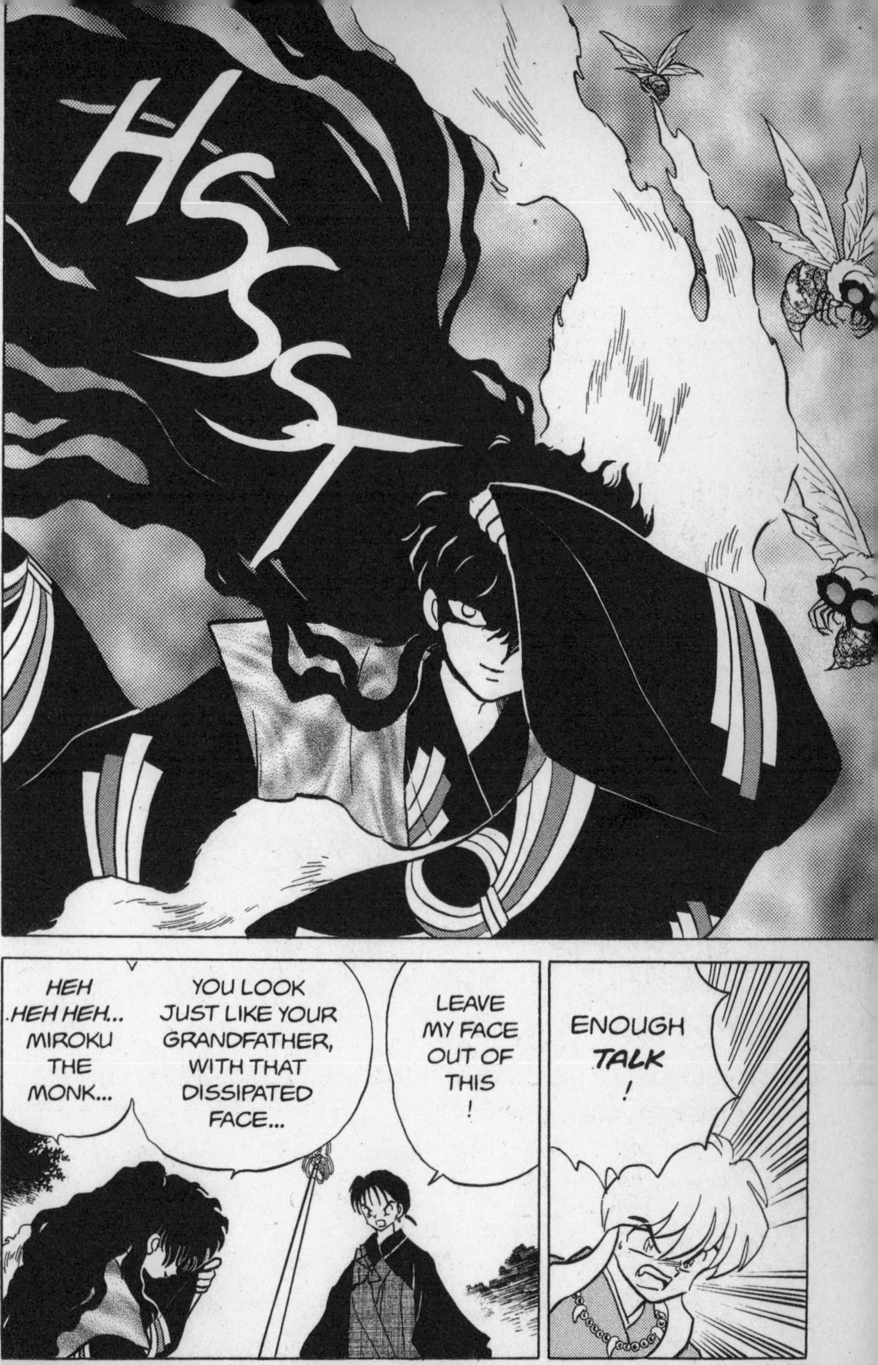
HSST
HEH HEH HEH... MIROKU THE MONK...
YOU LOOK JUST LIKE YOUR GRANDFATHER, WITH THAT DISSIPATED FACE...
LEAVE MY FACE OUT OF THIS!
ENOUGH TALK!

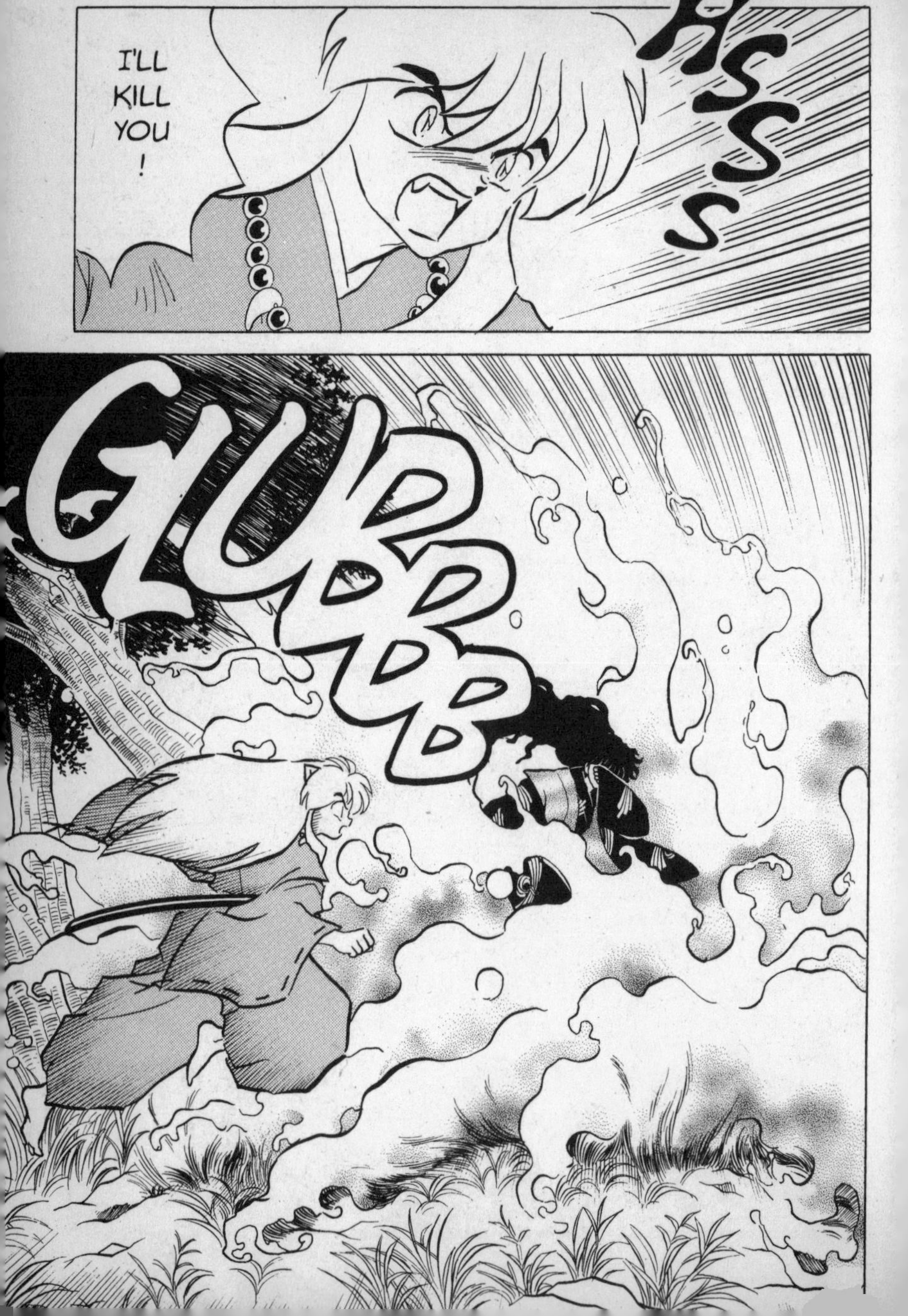
I'LL KILL YOU!
HSSS
GLUBBB

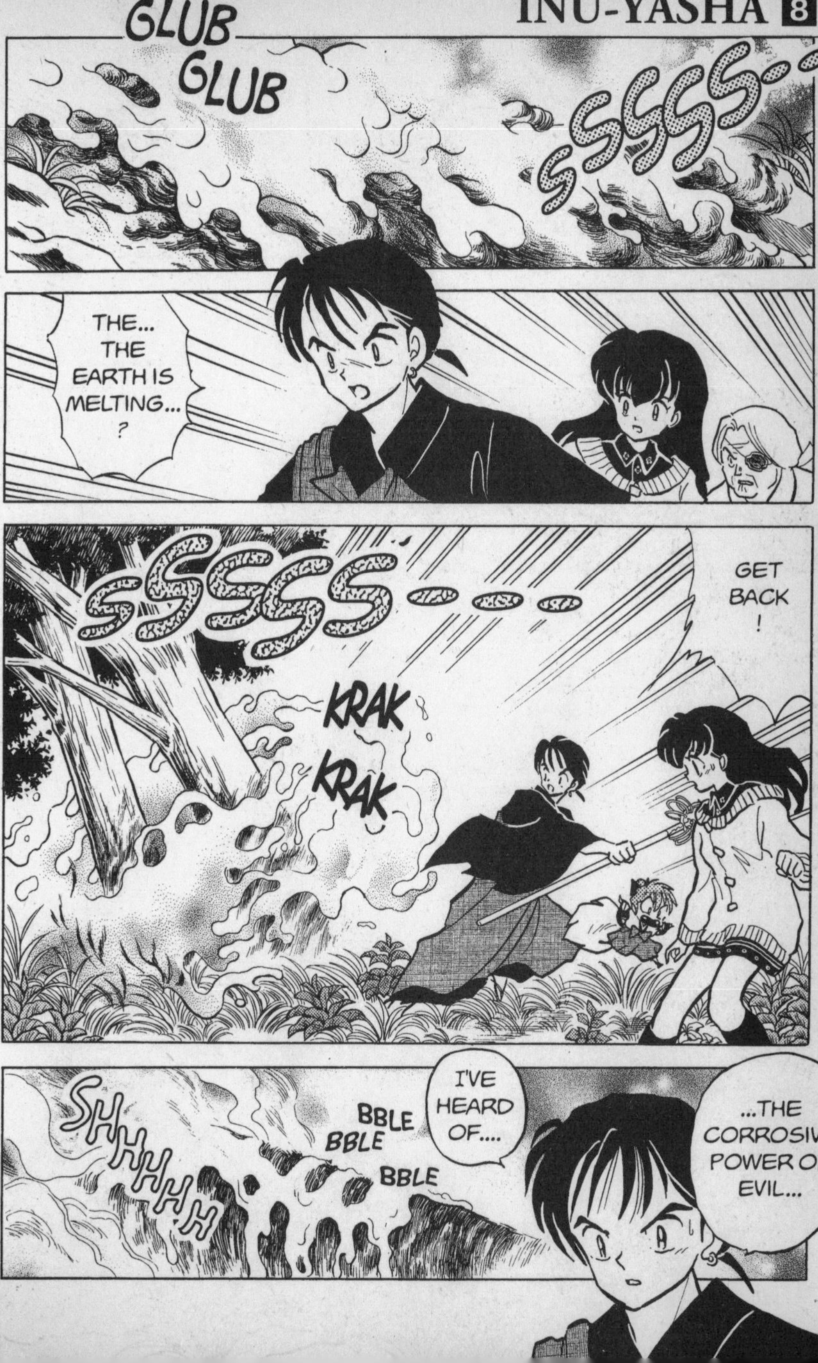
GLUB
GLUB
SSSSS-···
THE... THE EARTH IS MELTING... ?
SSSSS-···
GET BACK !
KRAK
KRAK
SHHHHH
BBLE
BBLE
BBLE
I'VE HEARD OF....
...THE CORROSIVE POWER OF EVIL...

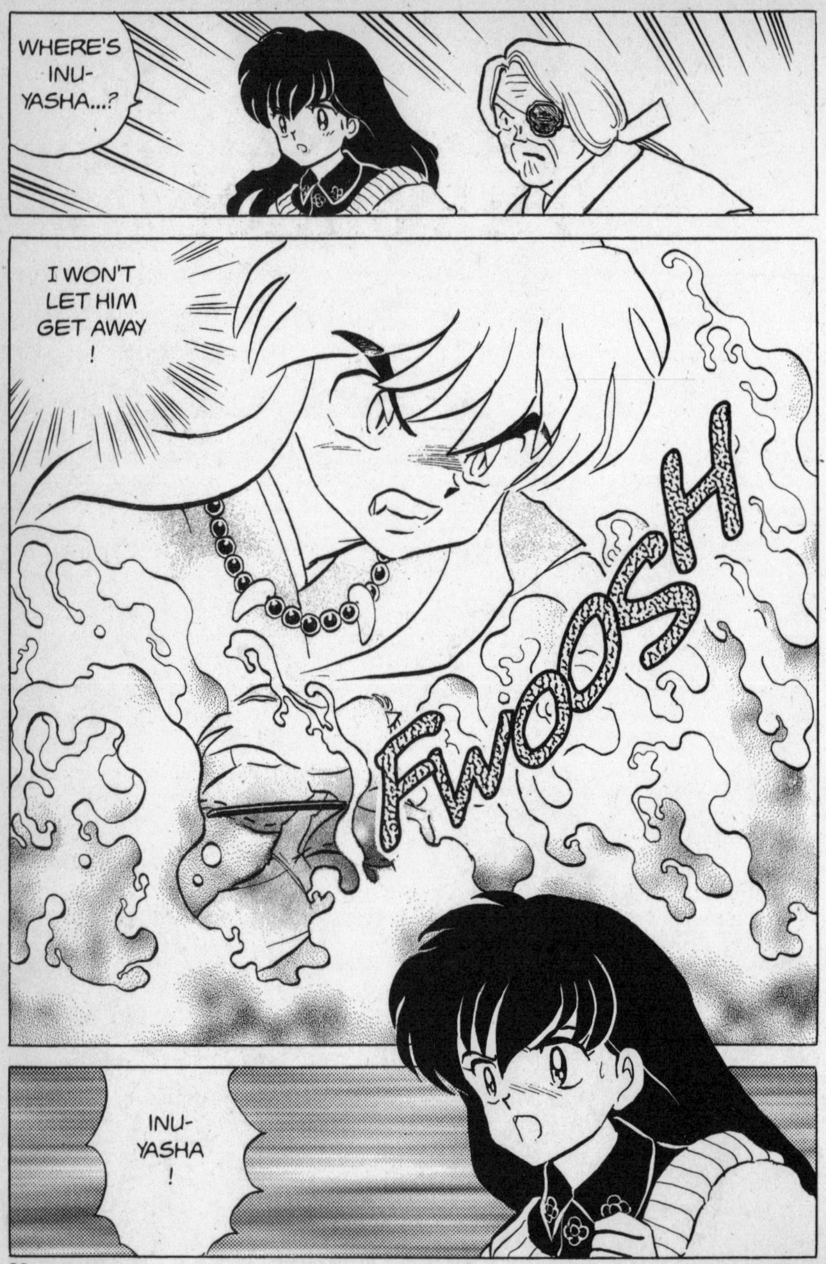
WHERE'S INU-YASHA...?
I WON'T LET HIM GET AWAY!
FWOOSH
INU-YASHA!

SCROLL FOUR
THE MARK

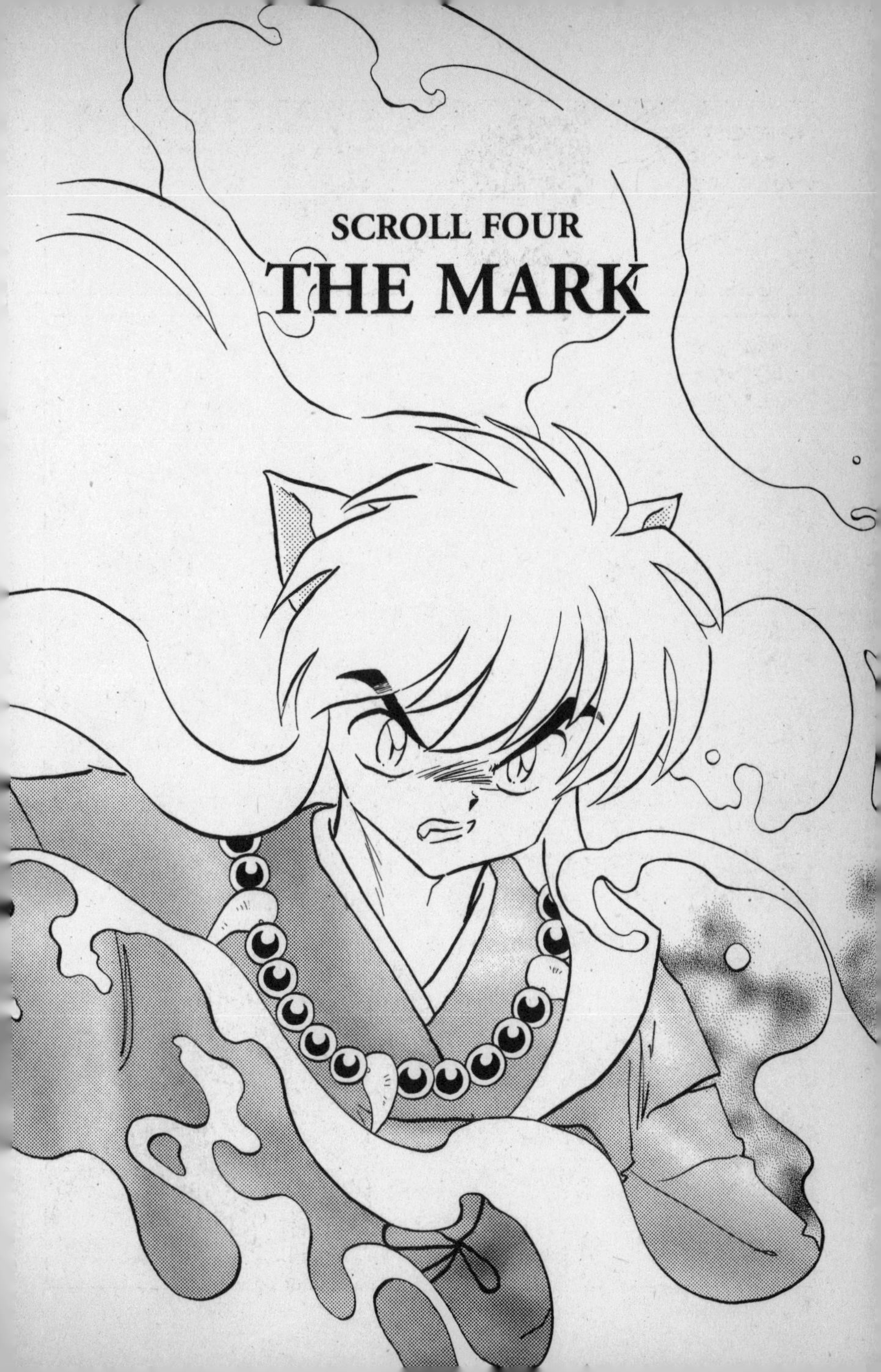

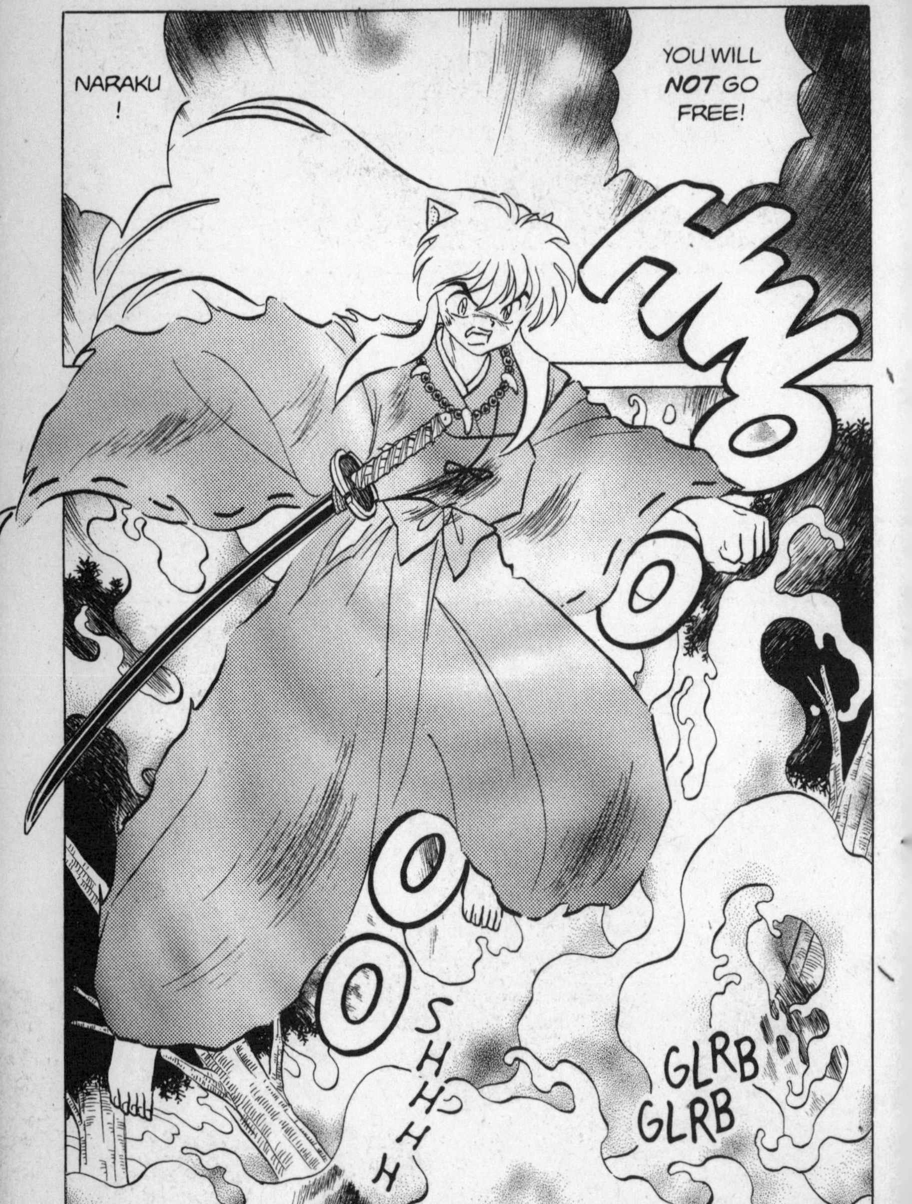
NARAKU
!
YOU WILL NOT GO FREE!
HWOOOO
SHHHH
GLRB GLRB

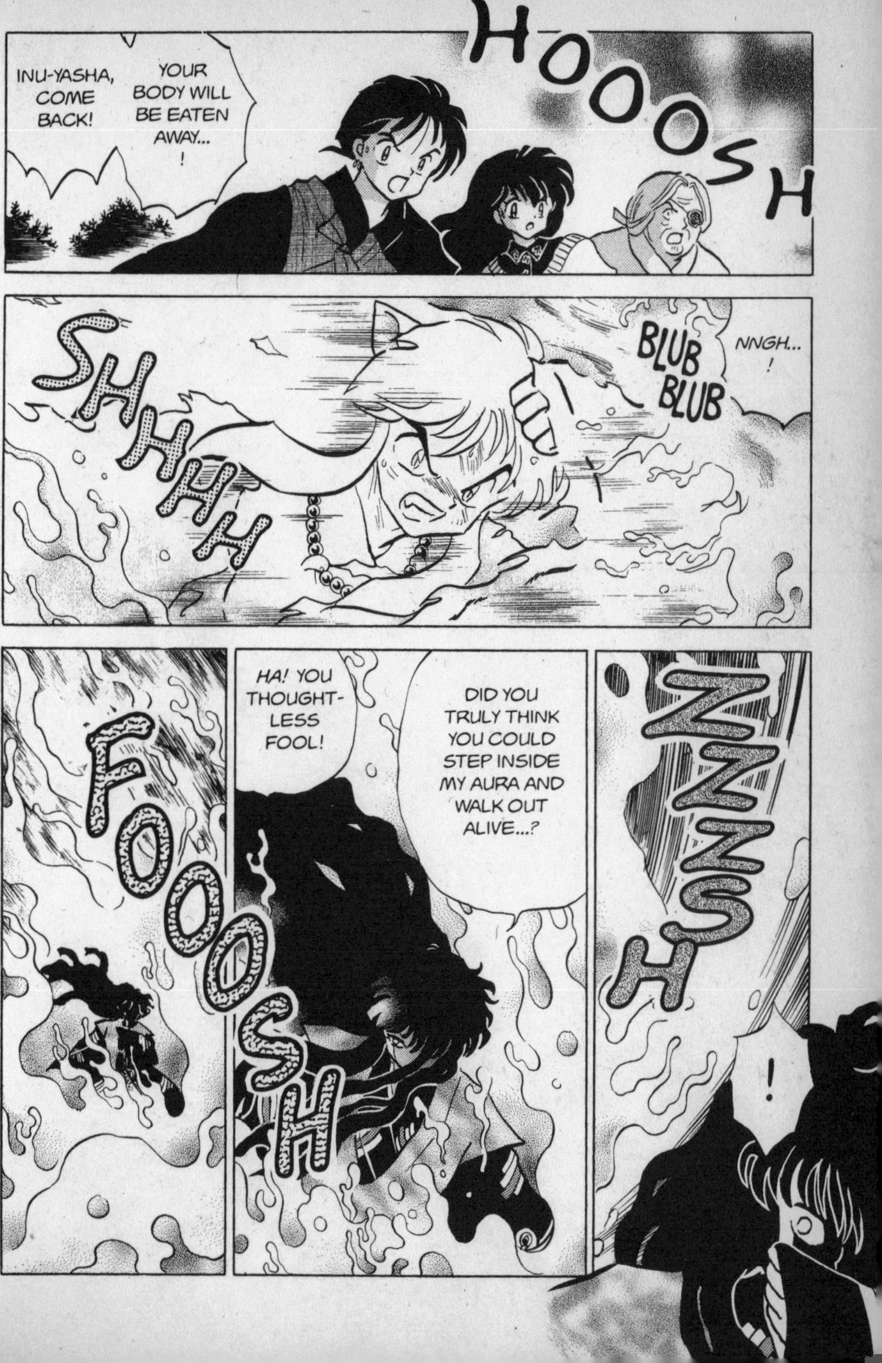
INU-YASHA, COME BACK!
YOUR BODY WILL BE EATEN AWAY... !
HOOOOSH
SHHHHH
BLUB BLUB
NNGH... !
FOOOOSH
HA! YOU THOUGHT-LESS FOOL!
DID YOU TRULY THINK YOU COULD STEP INSIDE MY AURA AND WALK OUT ALIVE...?
ZZZSH
!

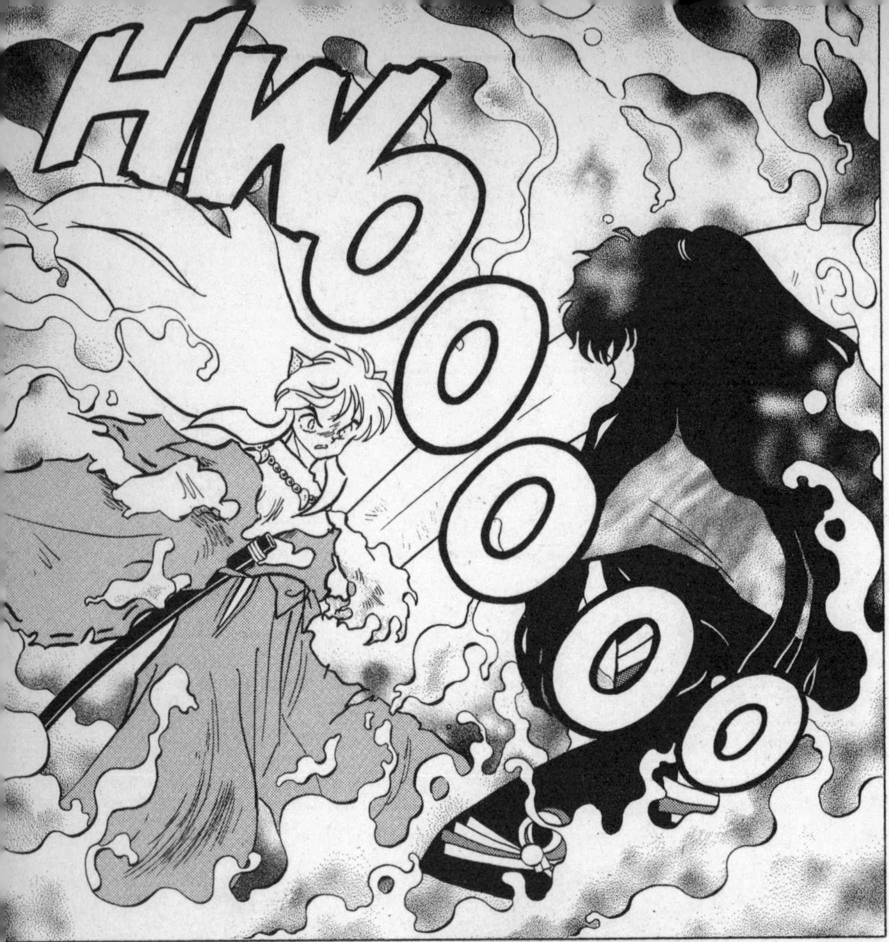
HWOOOOOO

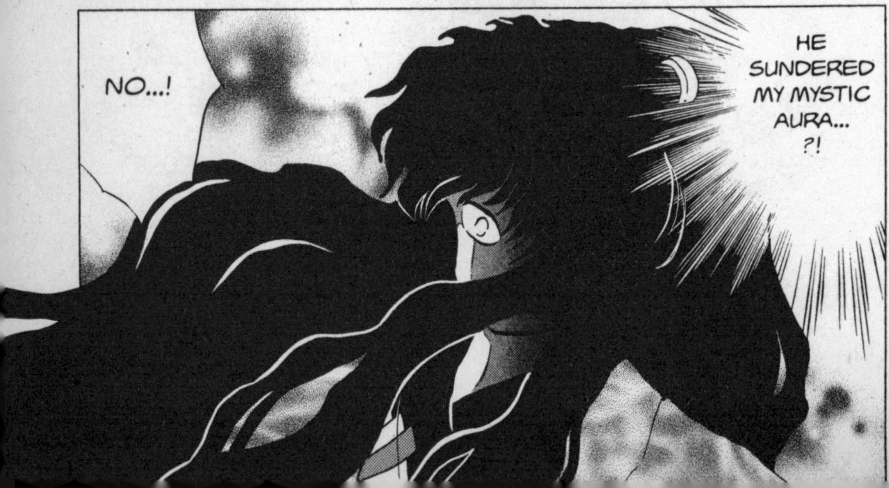
NO...!
HE SUNDERED MY MYSTIC AURA...?!

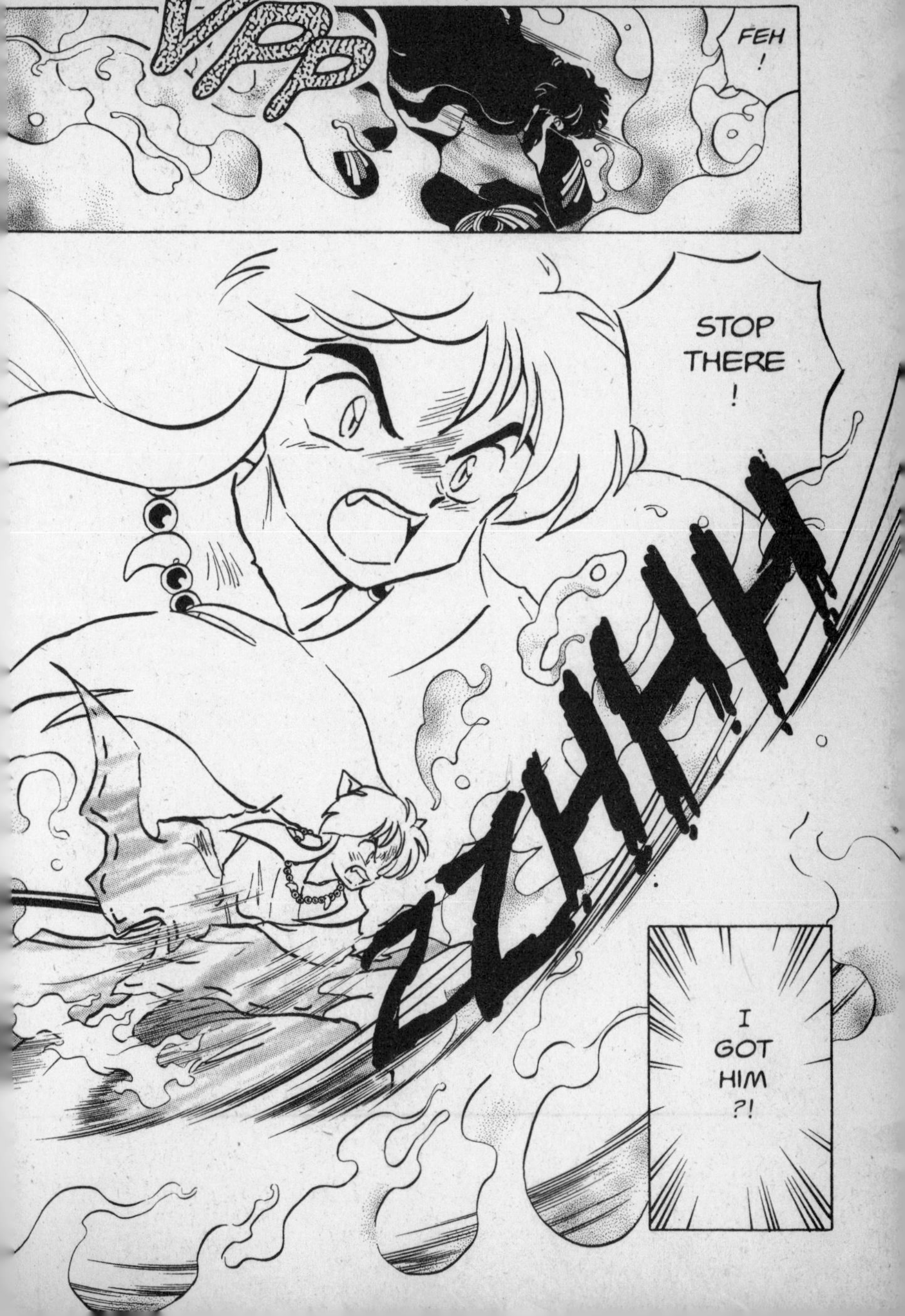
VPP
FEH!
STOP THERE!
ZZHHHH
I GOT HIM?!

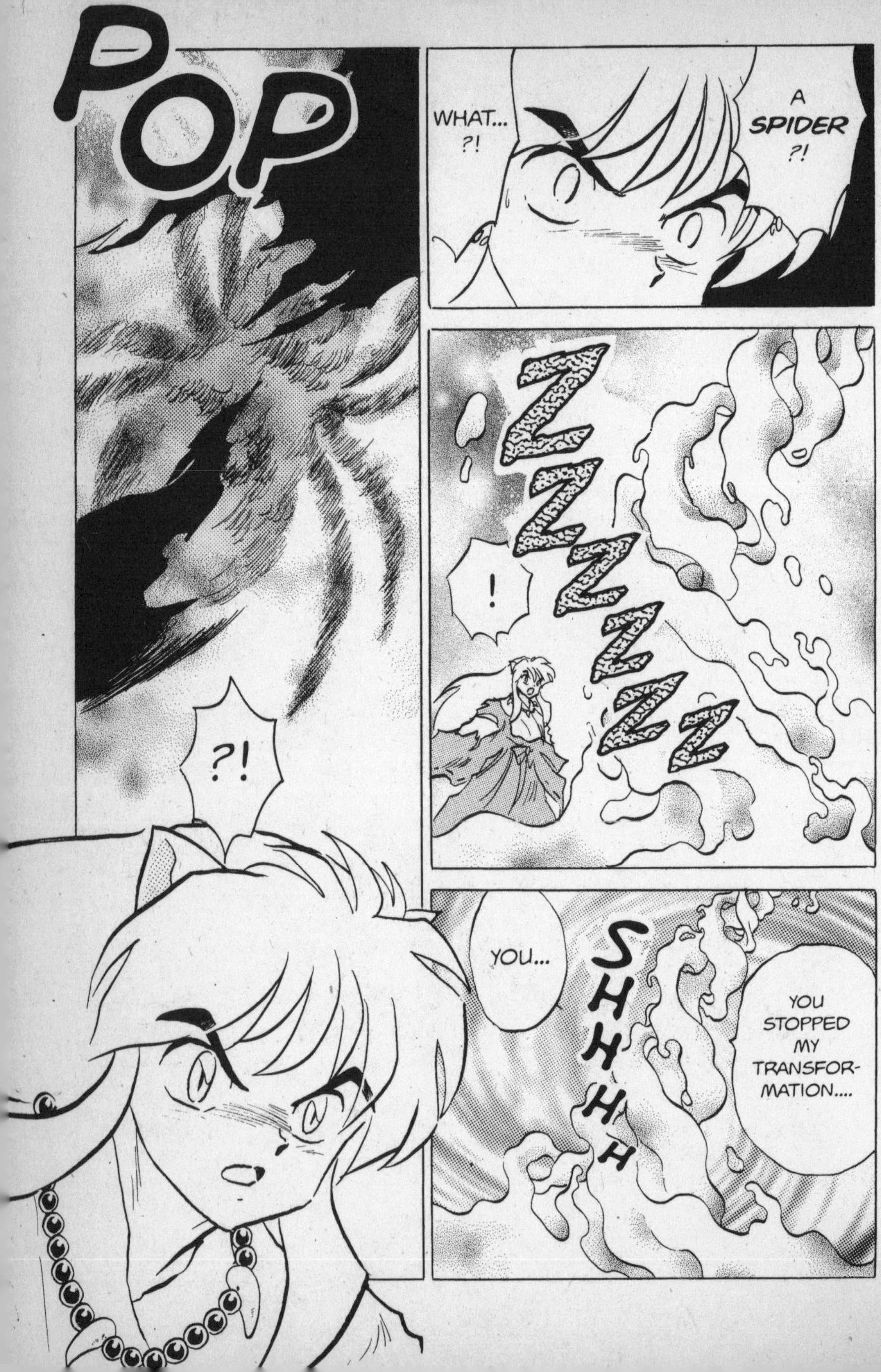

WHAT... ?!
A SPIDER ?!
ZZZZZZZ
!
YOU...
SHHHH
YOU STOPPED MY TRANSFORMATION....
POP
?!

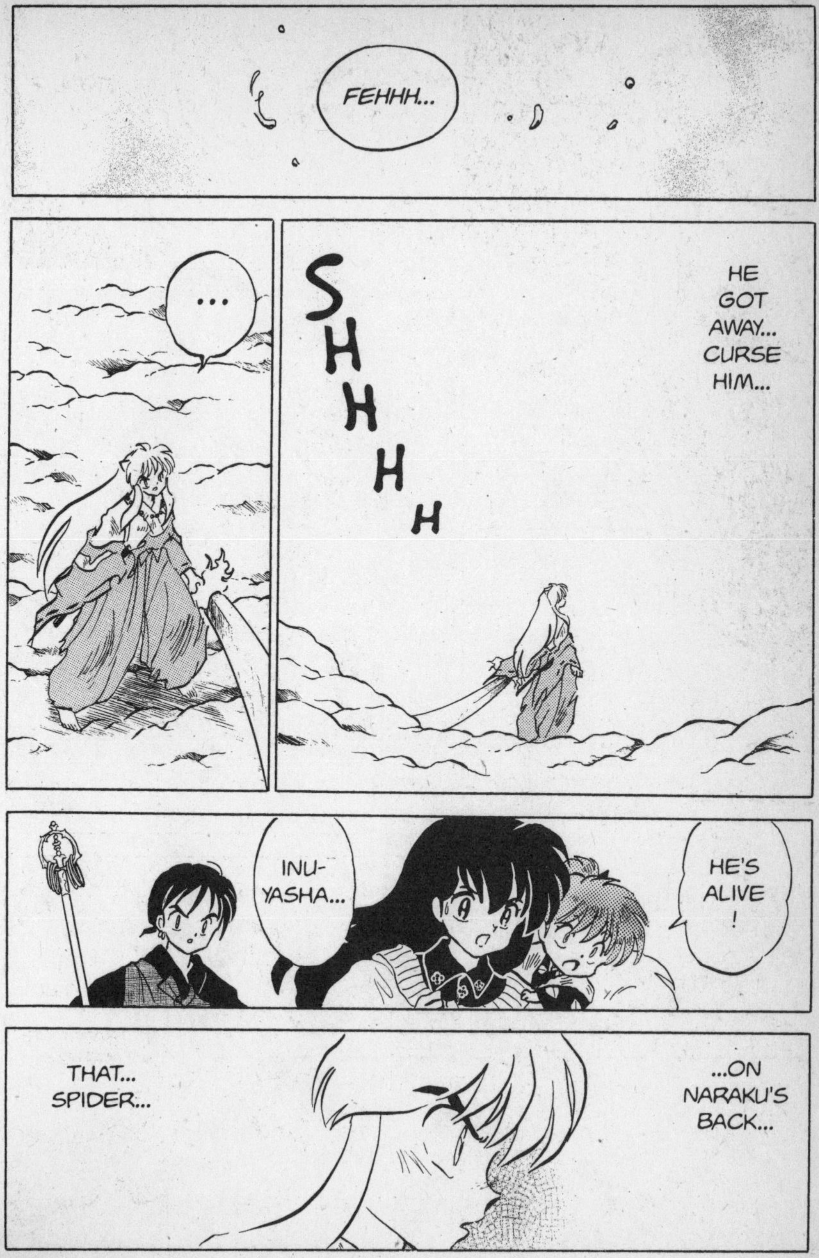
FEHHH...
...
SHHHH
HE GOT AWAY... CURSE HIM...
INU-YASHA...
HE'S ALIVE!
THAT... SPIDER...
...ON NARAKU'S BACK...

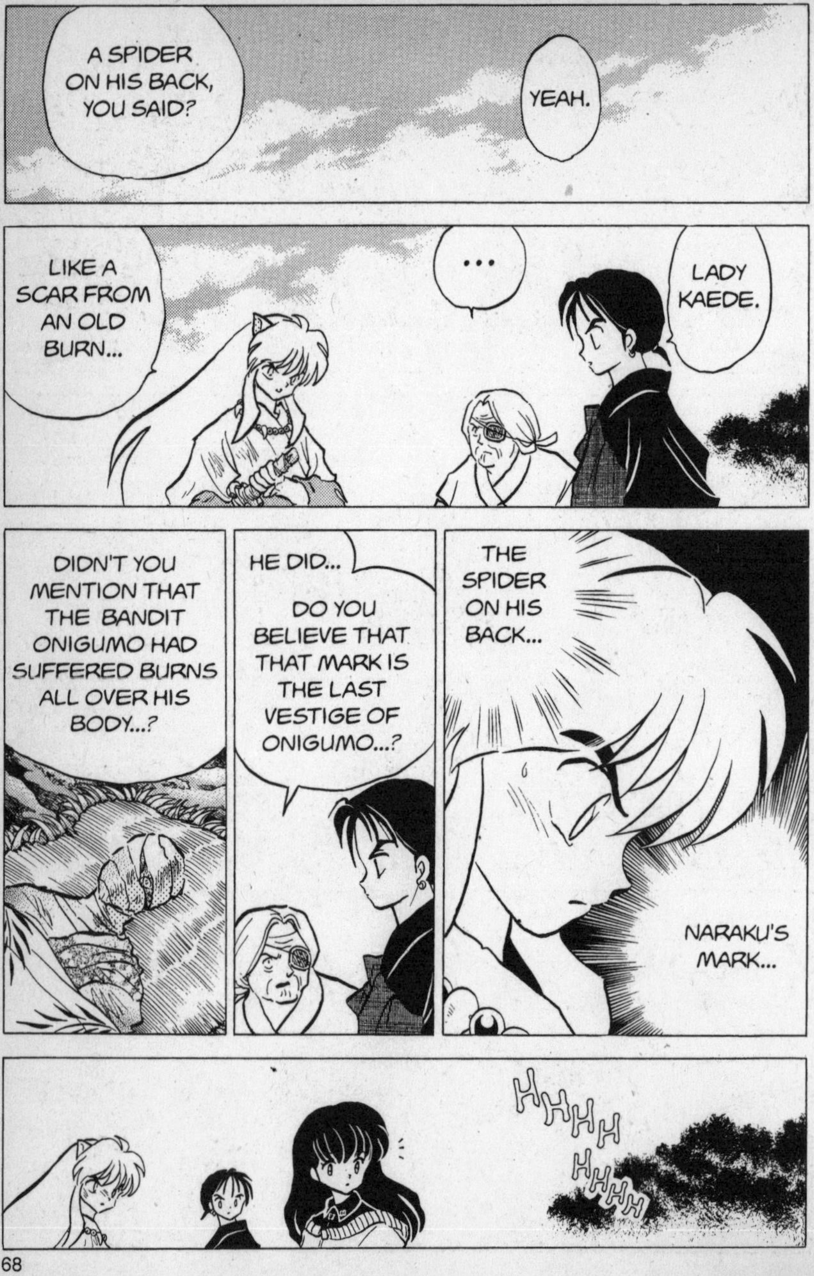
A SPIDER ON HIS BACK, YOU SAID?
YEAH.
LIKE A SCAR FROM AN OLD BURN...
...
LADY KAEDE.
DIDN'T YOU MENTION THAT THE BANDIT ONIGUMO HAD SUFFERED BURNS ALL OVER HIS BODY...?
HE DID...
DO YOU BELIEVE THAT THAT MARK IS THE LAST VESTIGE OF ONIGUMO...?
THE SPIDER ON HIS BACK...
NARAKU'S MARK...
HHHHH
HHHHH

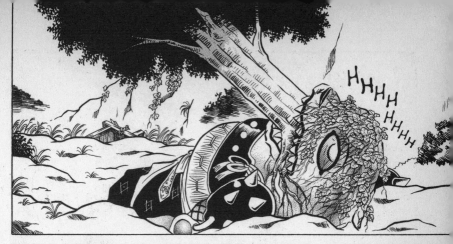

HHHHHHHHHH

CHOMP
CHOMP
CHOMP

ROYAKAN...

H-HE'S STILL ALIVE!

TOOOM

MY... HEAD...!

KRAK

IT'S SPLITTTTTING--!

MWRIII
MWRIII
MWRIII

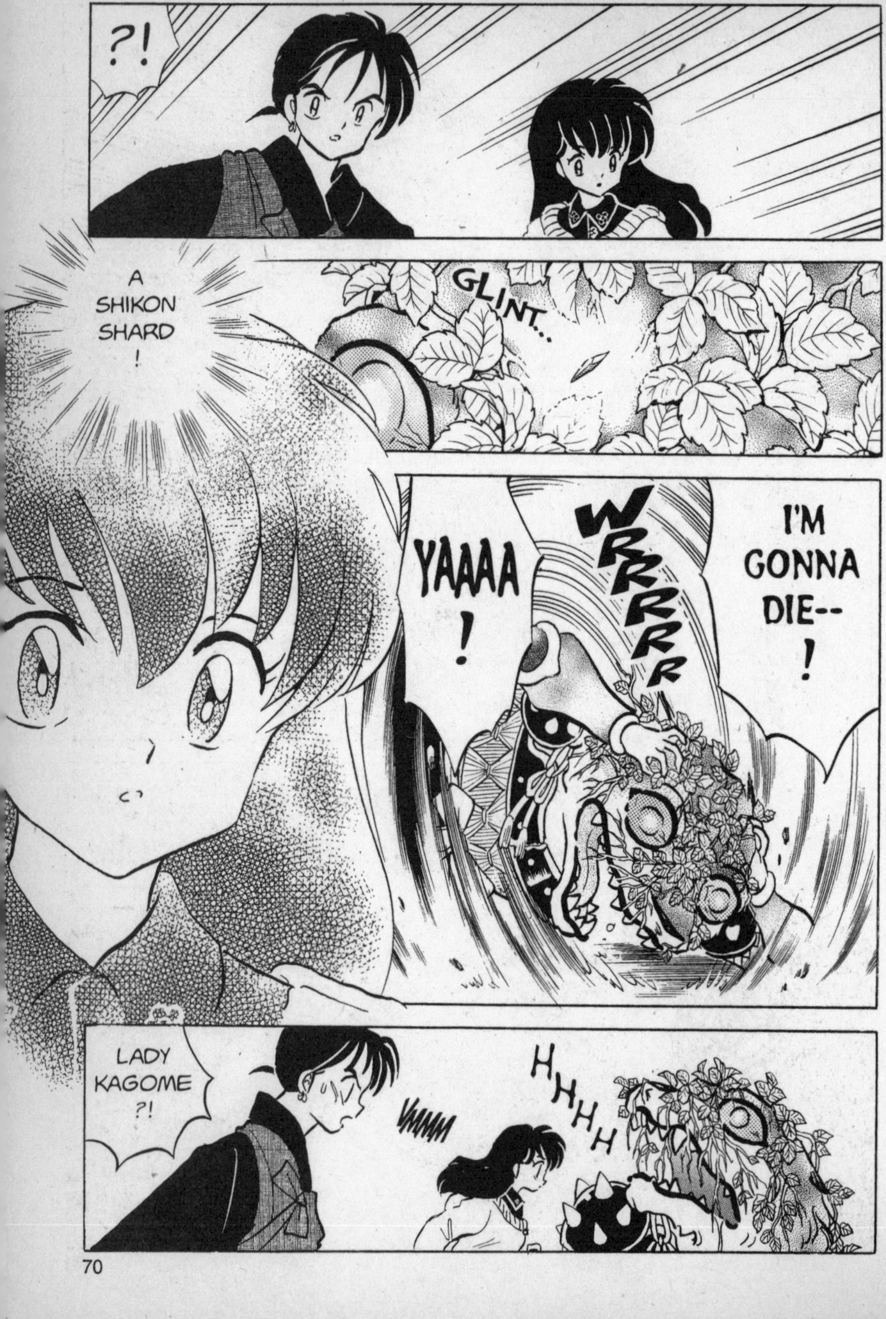
?!
A SHIKON SHARD !
GLINT...
YAAAA !
WRRRRR
I'M GONNA DIE-- !
LADY KAGOME ?!
HHHHH

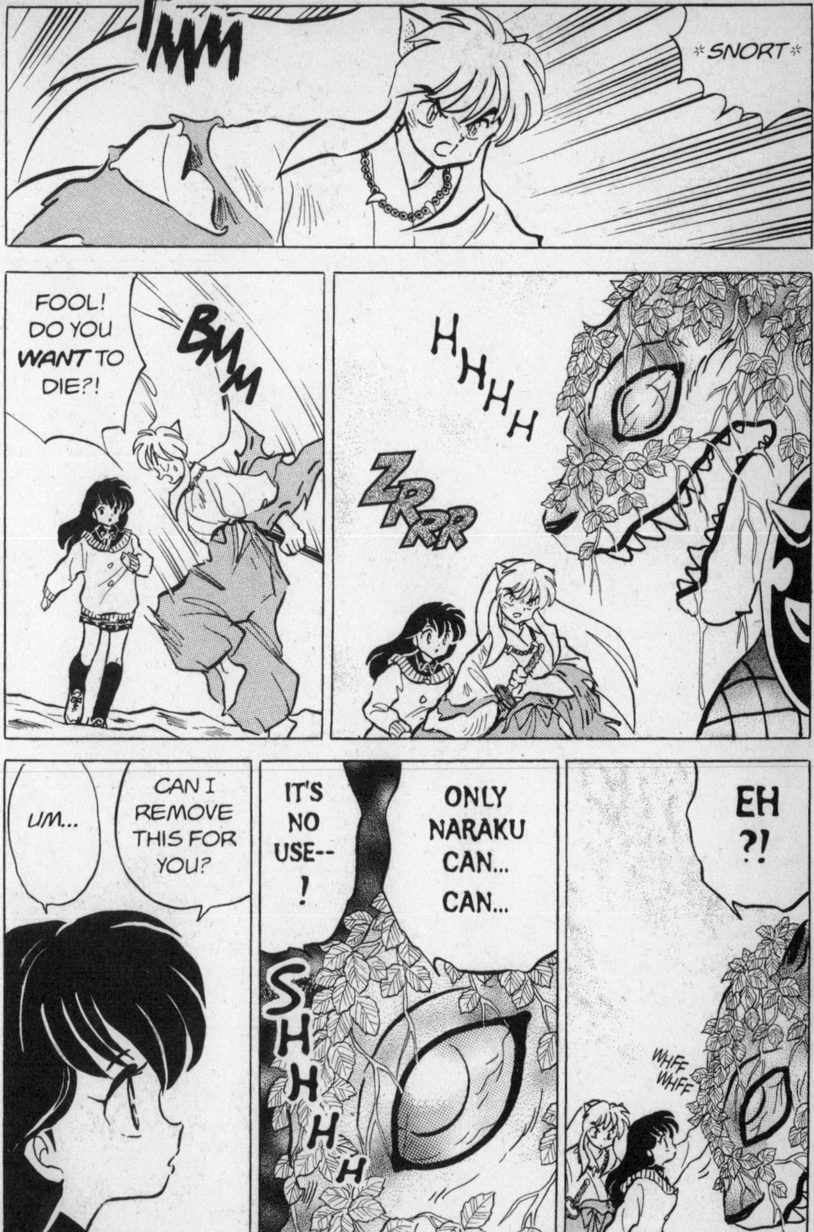
TMM
SNORT
FOOL! DO YOU WANT TO DIE?!
BMM
HHHHH
ZRRR
UM...
CAN I REMOVE THIS FOR YOU?
IT'S NO USE--!
ONLY NARAKU CAN... CAN...
SHHHH
EH?!
WHFF WHFF

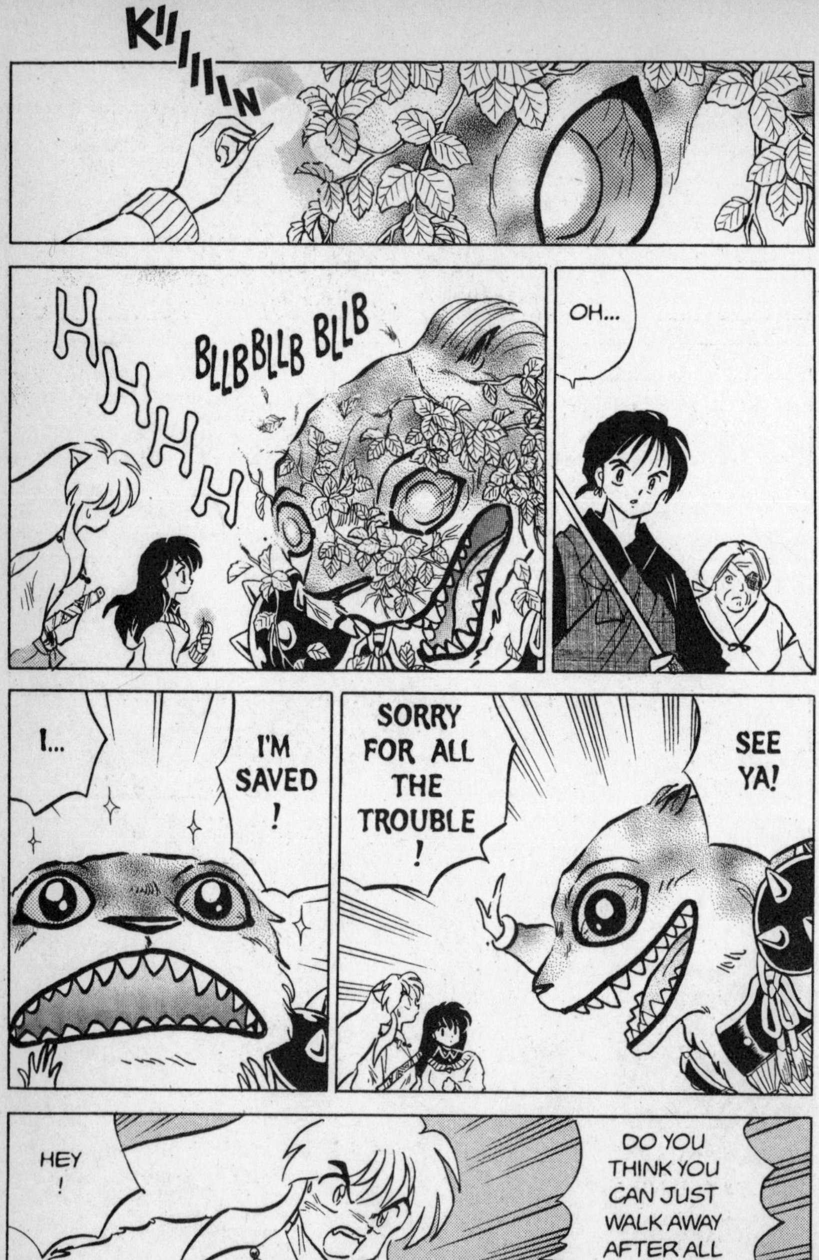
KIIIIIN
HHHHH
BLLBBLLB BLLB
OH...
I...
I'M SAVED!
SORRY FOR ALL THE TROUBLE!
SEE YA!
HEY!
DO YOU THINK YOU CAN JUST WALK AWAY AFTER ALL THAT?!

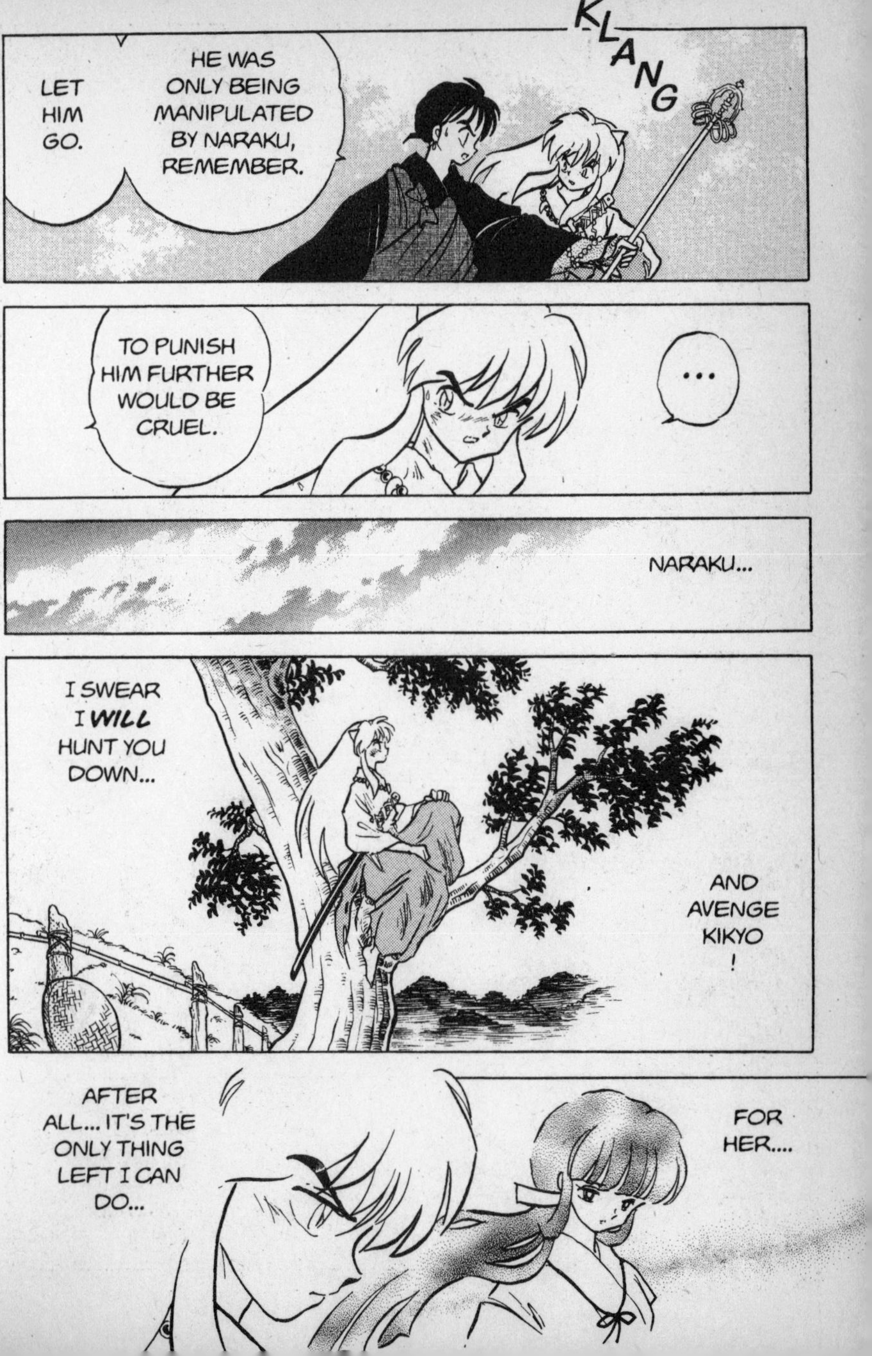
LET HIM GO.
HE WAS ONLY BEING MANIPULATED BY NARAKU, REMEMBER.
KLANG
TO PUNISH HIM FURTHER WOULD BE CRUEL.
...
NARAKU...
I SWEAR I WILL HUNT YOU DOWN...
AND AVENGE KIKYO!
AFTER ALL... IT'S THE ONLY THING LEFT I CAN DO...
FOR HER....

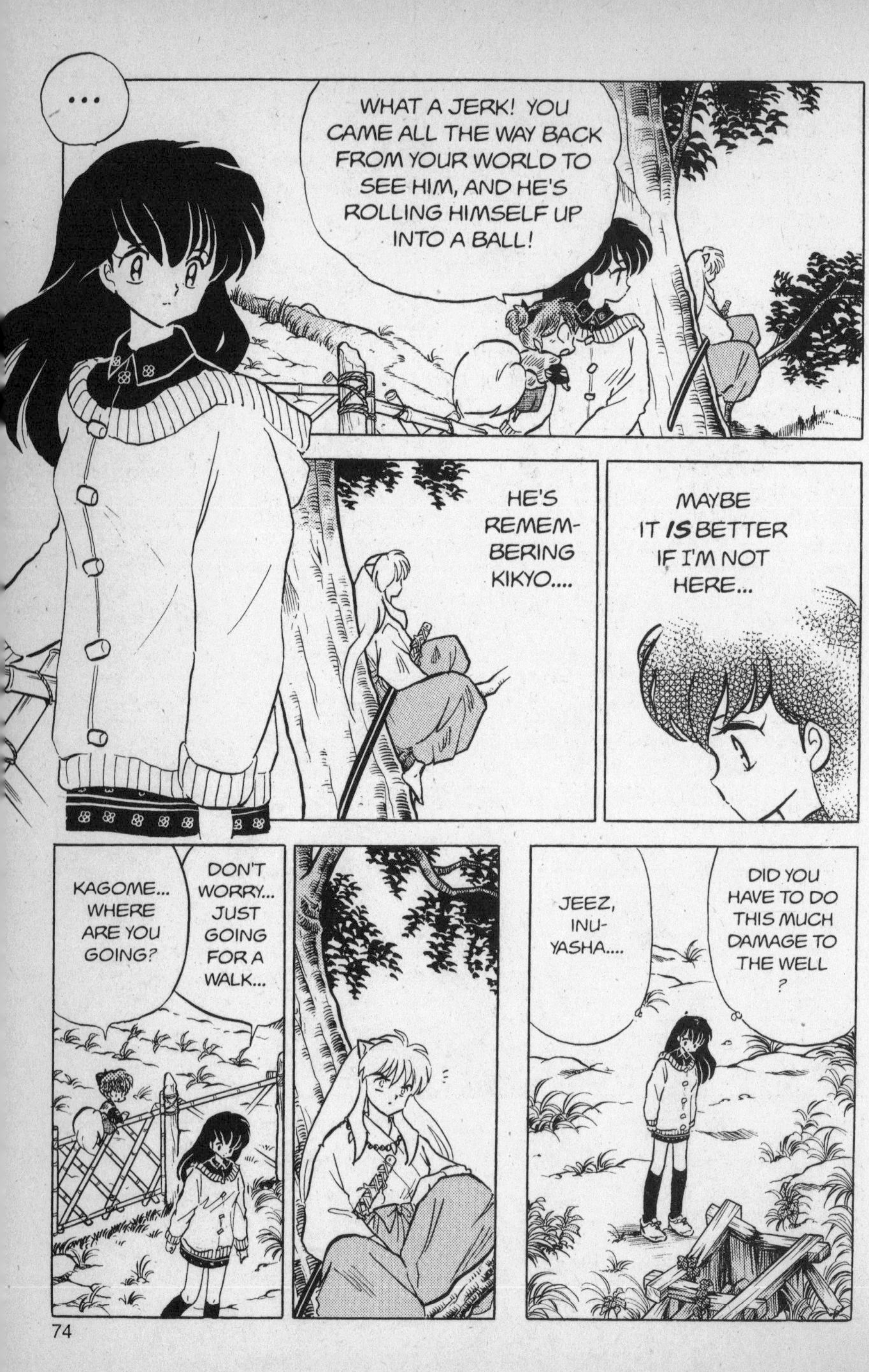
...
WHAT A JERK! YOU CAME ALL THE WAY BACK FROM YOUR WORLD TO SEE HIM, AND HE'S ROLLING HIMSELF UP INTO A BALL!
HE'S REMEM-BERING KIKYO....
MAYBE IT *IS* BETTER IF I'M NOT HERE...
KAGOME... WHERE ARE YOU GOING?
DON'T WORRY... JUST GOING FOR A WALK...
JEEZ, INU-YASHA....
DID YOU HAVE TO DO THIS MUCH DAMAGE TO THE WELL?

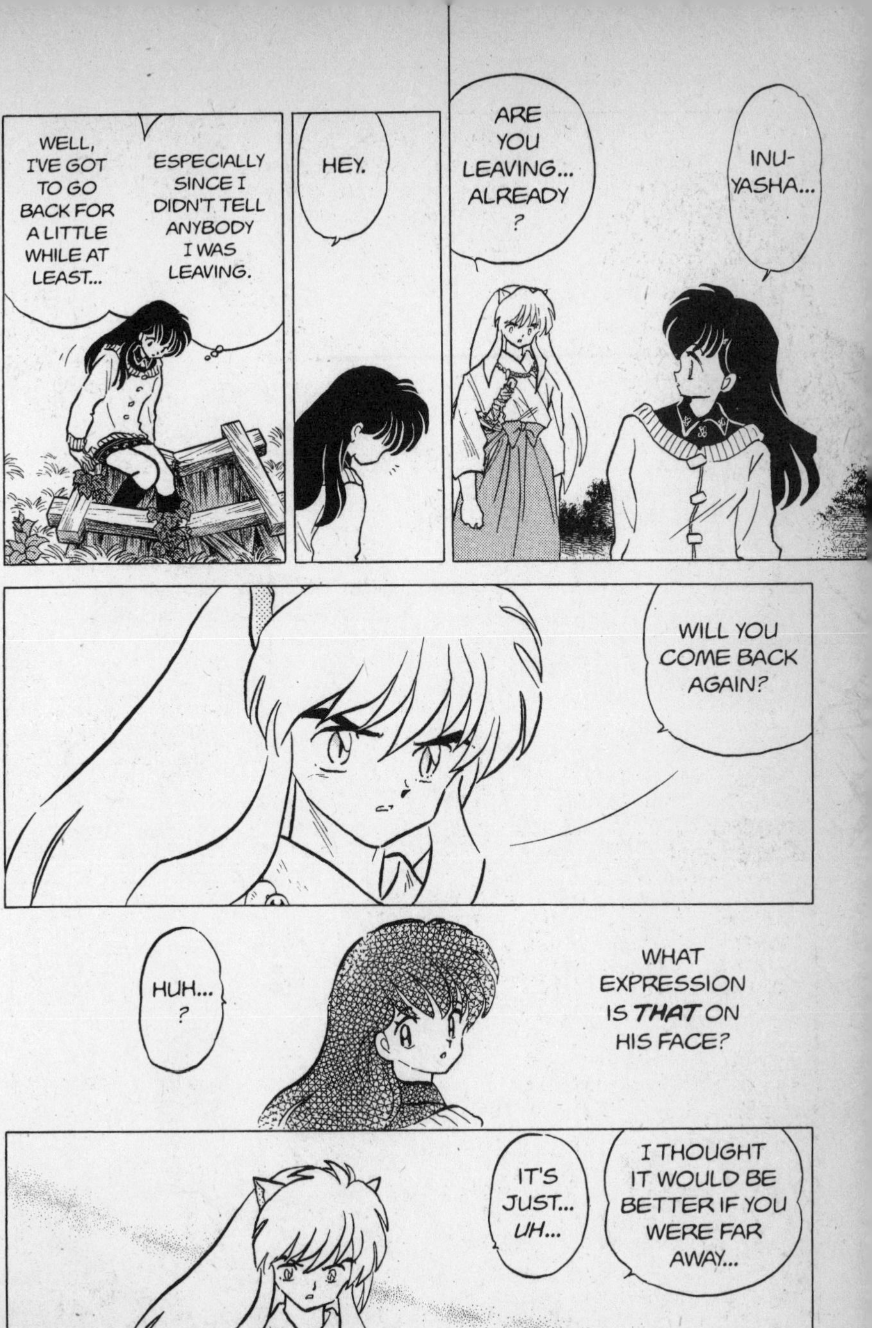
WELL, I'VE GOT TO GO BACK FOR A LITTLE WHILE AT LEAST...
ESPECIALLY SINCE I DIDN'T TELL ANYBODY I WAS LEAVING.
HEY.
ARE YOU LEAVING... ALREADY?
INU-YASHA...
WILL YOU COME BACK AGAIN?
HUH...?
WHAT EXPRESSION IS *THAT* ON HIS FACE?
IT'S JUST... *UH*...
I THOUGHT IT WOULD BE BETTER IF YOU WERE FAR AWAY...

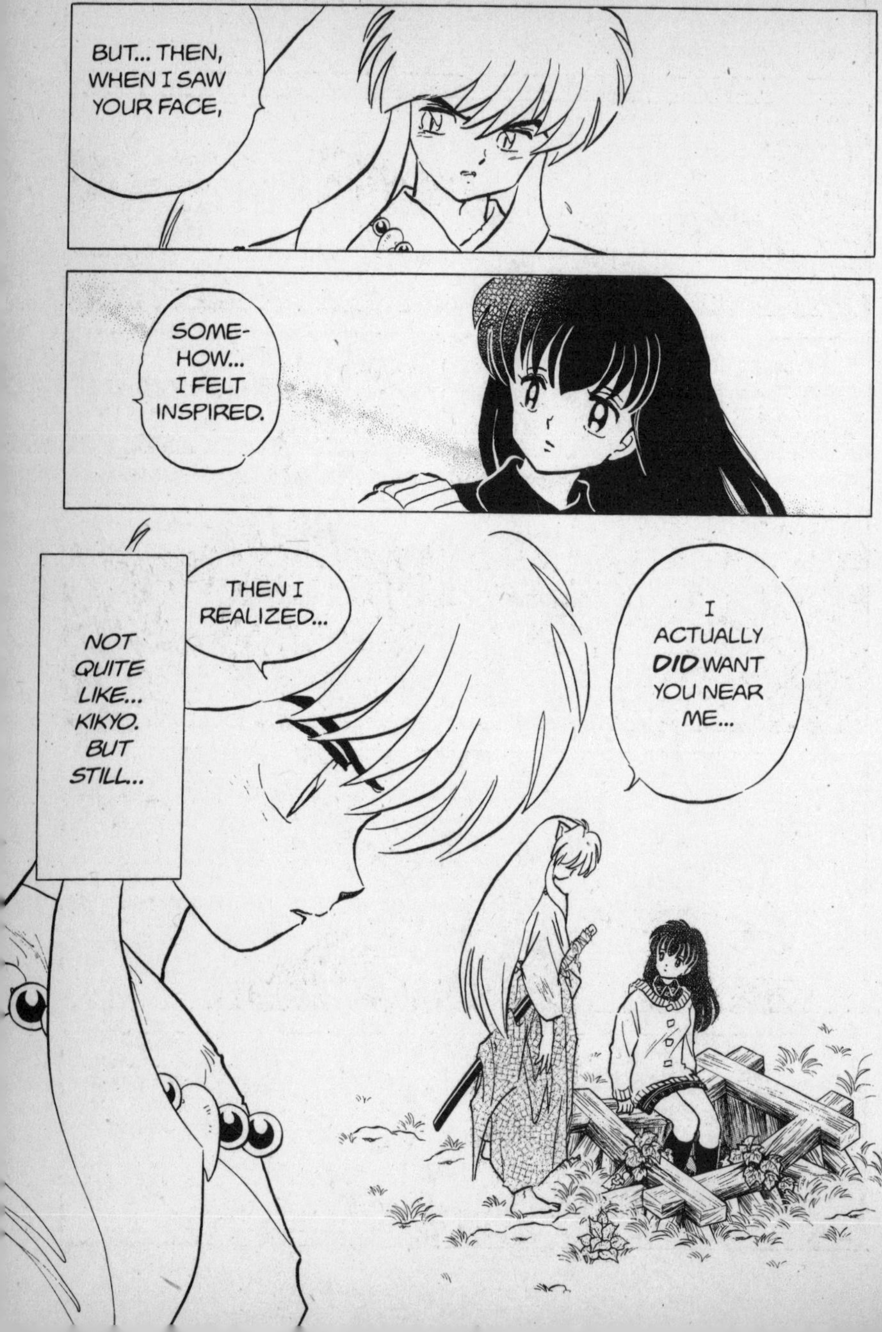
BUT... THEN, WHEN I SAW YOUR FACE,
SOME-HOW... I FELT INSPIRED.
NOT QUITE LIKE... KIKYO. BUT STILL...
THEN I REALIZED...
I ACTUALLY DID WANT YOU NEAR ME...

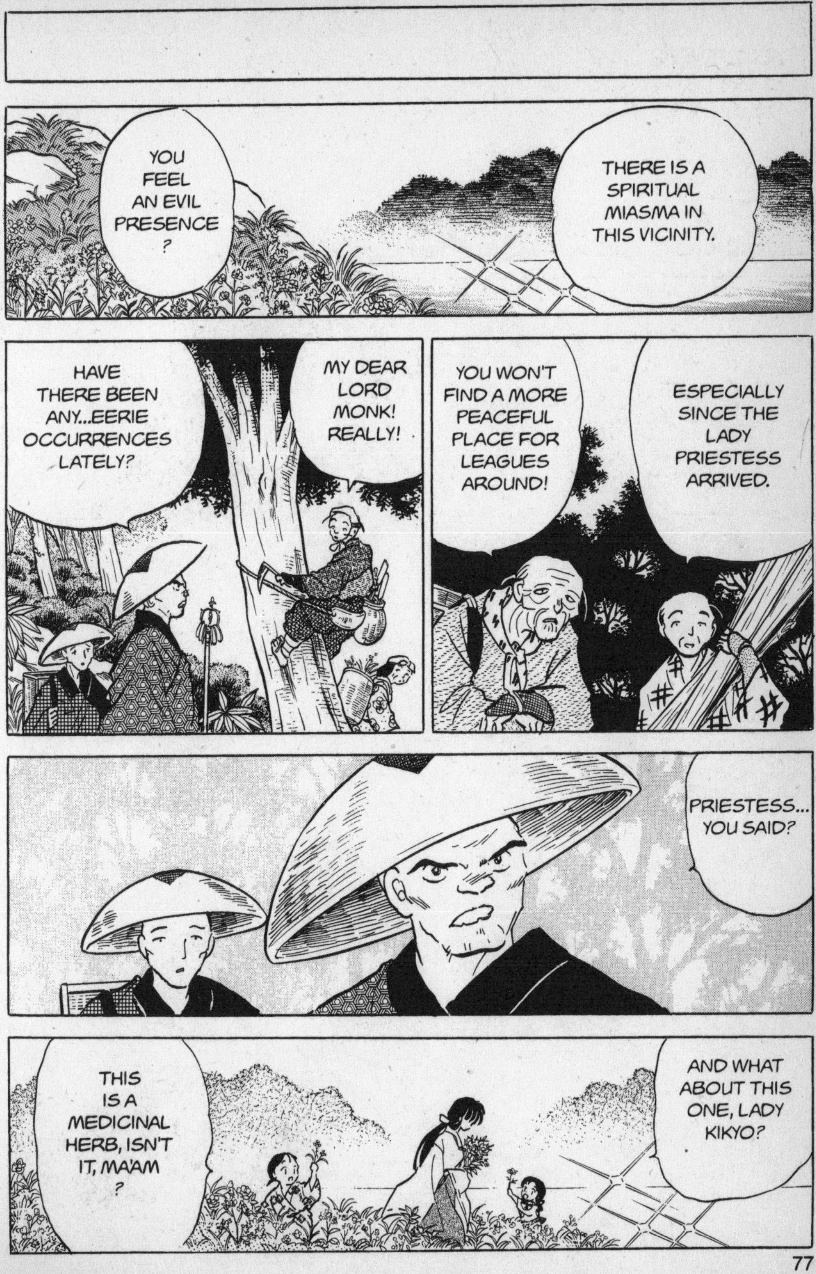
YOU FEEL AN EVIL PRESENCE?
THERE IS A SPIRITUAL MIASMA IN THIS VICINITY.
HAVE THERE BEEN ANY...EERIE OCCURRENCES LATELY?
MY DEAR LORD MONK! REALLY!
YOU WON'T FIND A MORE PEACEFUL PLACE FOR LEAGUES AROUND!
ESPECIALLY SINCE THE LADY PRIESTESS ARRIVED.
PRIESTESS... YOU SAID?
THIS IS A MEDICINAL HERB, ISN'T IT, MA'AM?
AND WHAT ABOUT THIS ONE, LADY KIKYO?

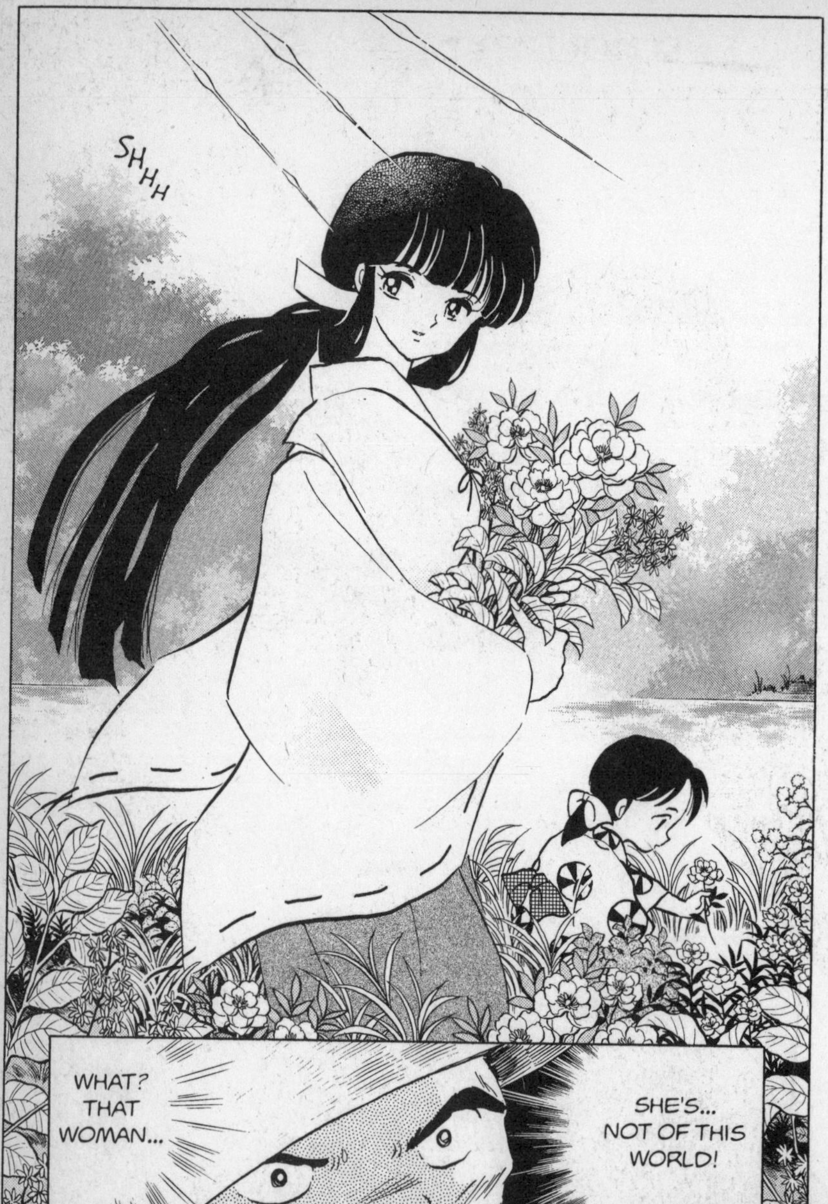
SHHH
WHAT? THAT WOMAN...
SHE'S... NOT OF THIS WORLD!

SCROLL FIVE

YOUNG SOULS

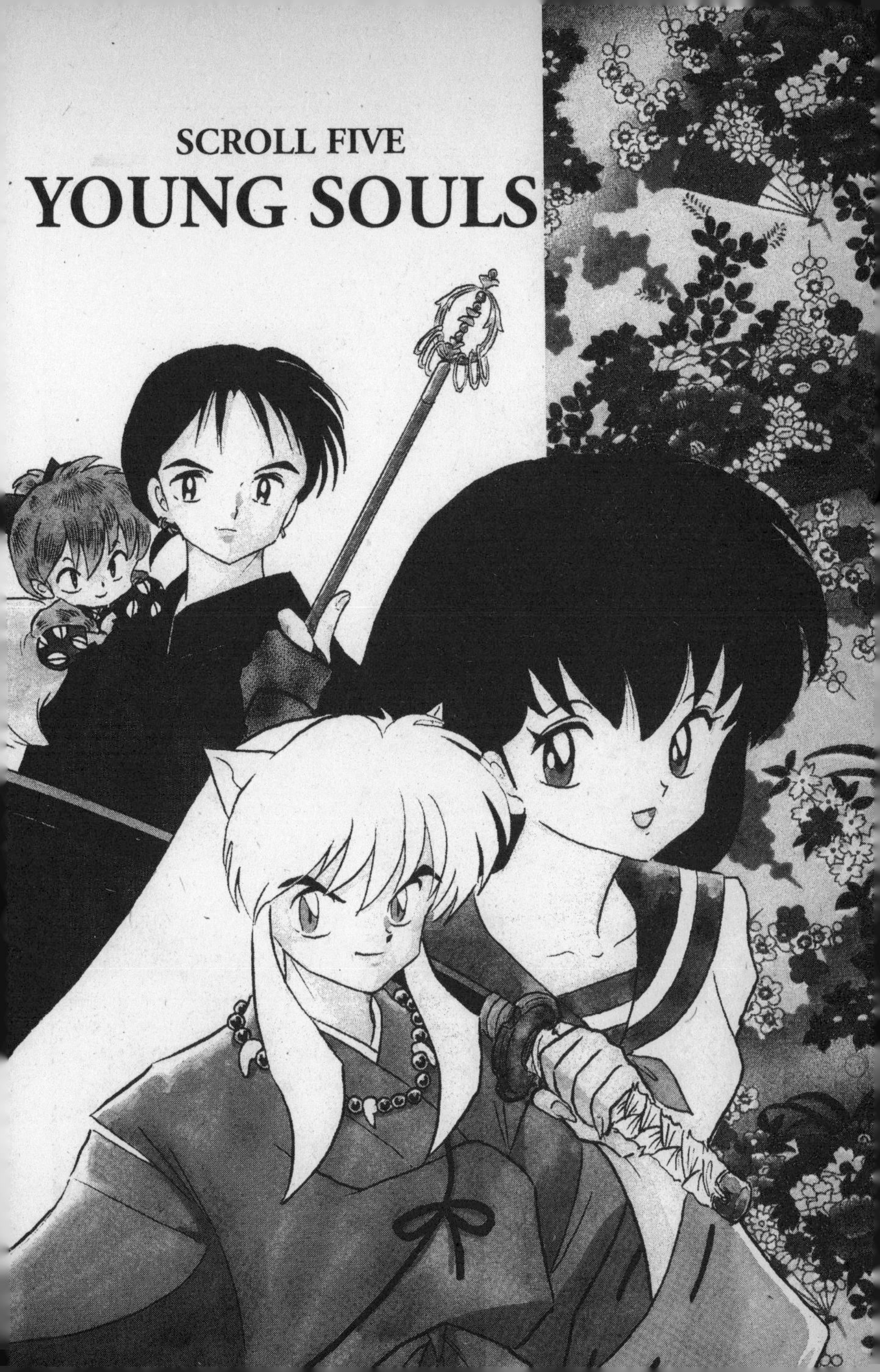

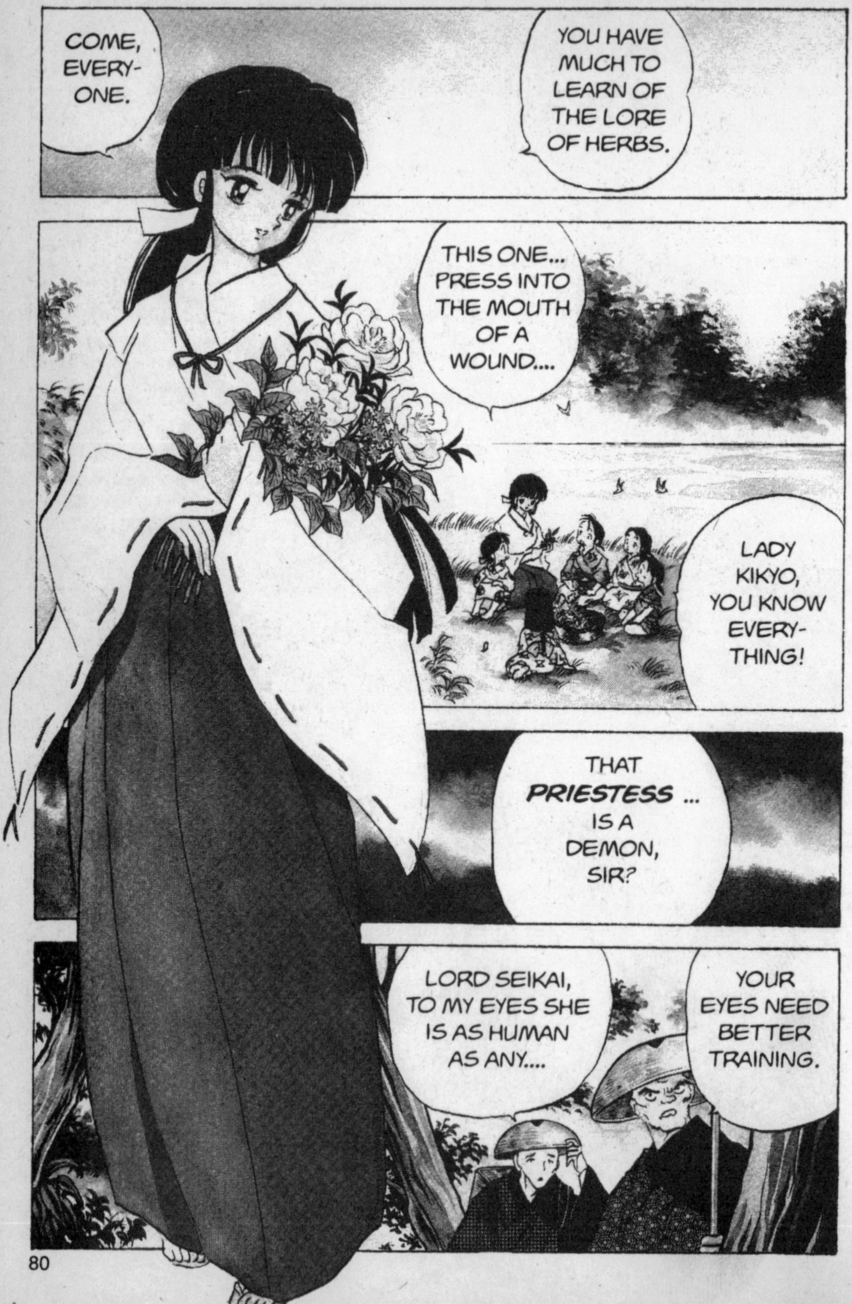
COME, EVERY-ONE.
YOU HAVE MUCH TO LEARN OF THE LORE OF HERBS.
THIS ONE... PRESS INTO THE MOUTH OF A WOUND....
LADY KIKYO, YOU KNOW EVERY-THING!
THAT PRIESTESS ... IS A DEMON, SIR?
LORD SEIKAI, TO MY EYES SHE IS AS HUMAN AS ANY....
YOUR EYES NEED BETTER TRAINING.

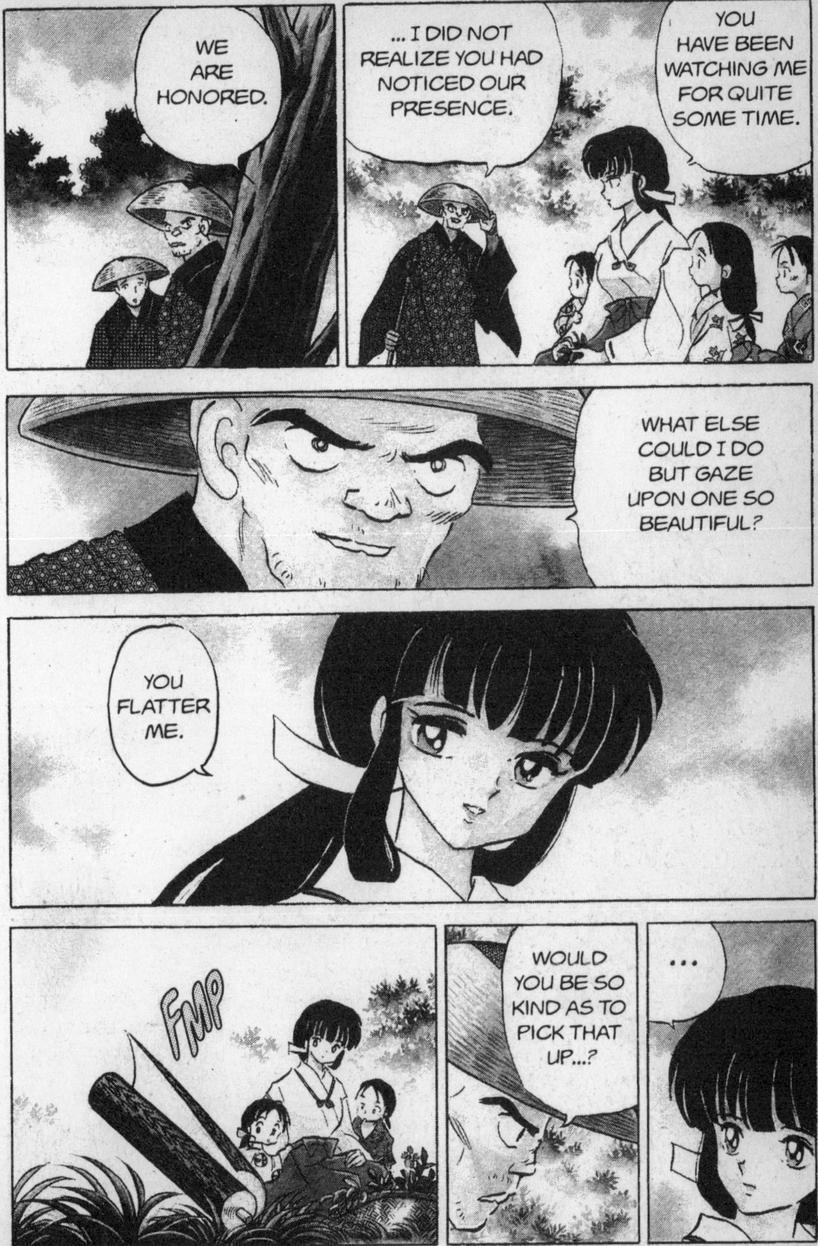
WE ARE HONORED.
...I DID NOT REALIZE YOU HAD NOTICED OUR PRESENCE.
YOU HAVE BEEN WATCHING ME FOR QUITE SOME TIME.
WHAT ELSE COULD I DO BUT GAZE UPON ONE SO BEAUTIFUL?
YOU FLATTER ME.
FMP
WOULD YOU BE SO KIND AS TO PICK THAT UP...?
...

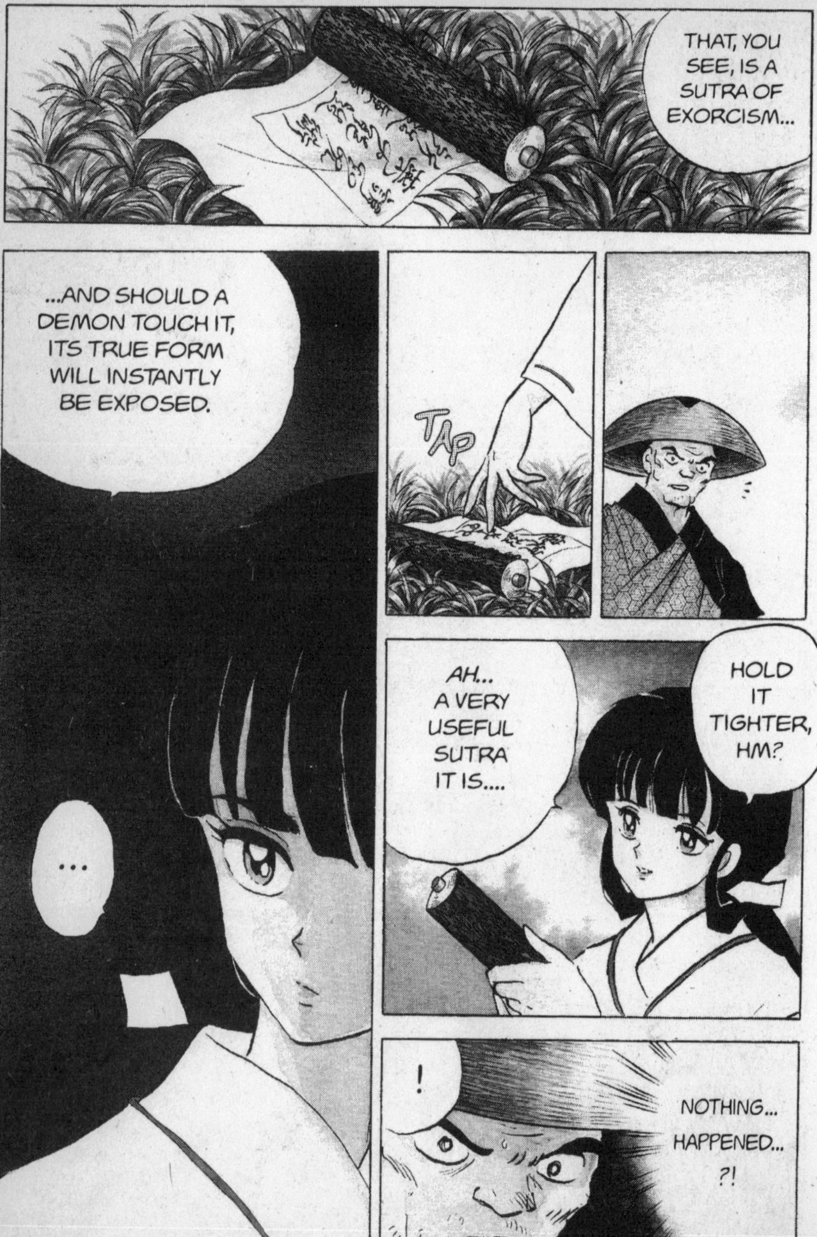
THAT, YOU SEE, IS A SUTRA OF EXORCISM...
...AND SHOULD A DEMON TOUCH IT, ITS TRUE FORM WILL INSTANTLY BE EXPOSED.
...
TAP
AH... A VERY USEFUL SUTRA IT IS....
HOLD IT TIGHTER, HM?
!
NOTHING... HAPPENED... ?!

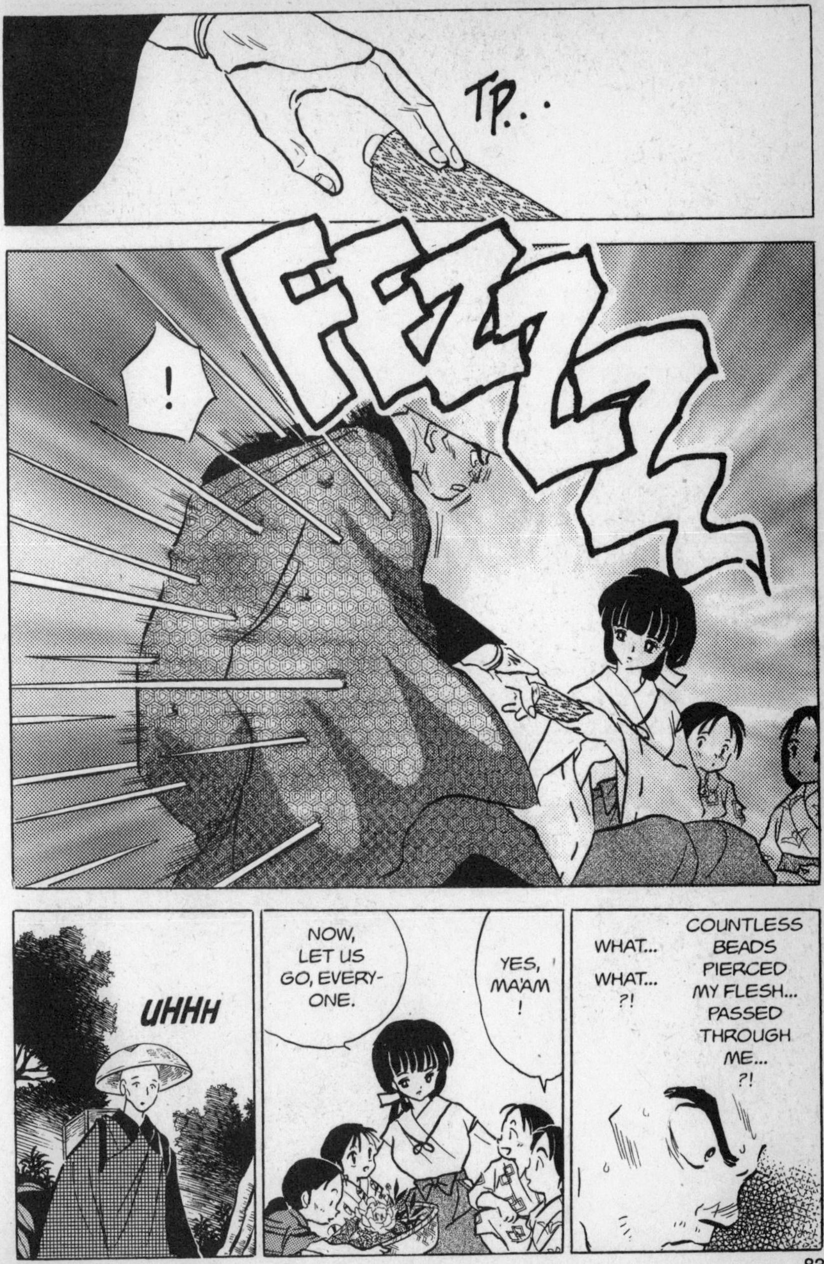
TP...
FZZZ
!
UHHH
NOW, LET US GO, EVERY-ONE.
YES, MA'AM!
WHAT... WHAT...?!
COUNTLESS BEADS PIERCED MY FLESH... PASSED THROUGH ME...?!

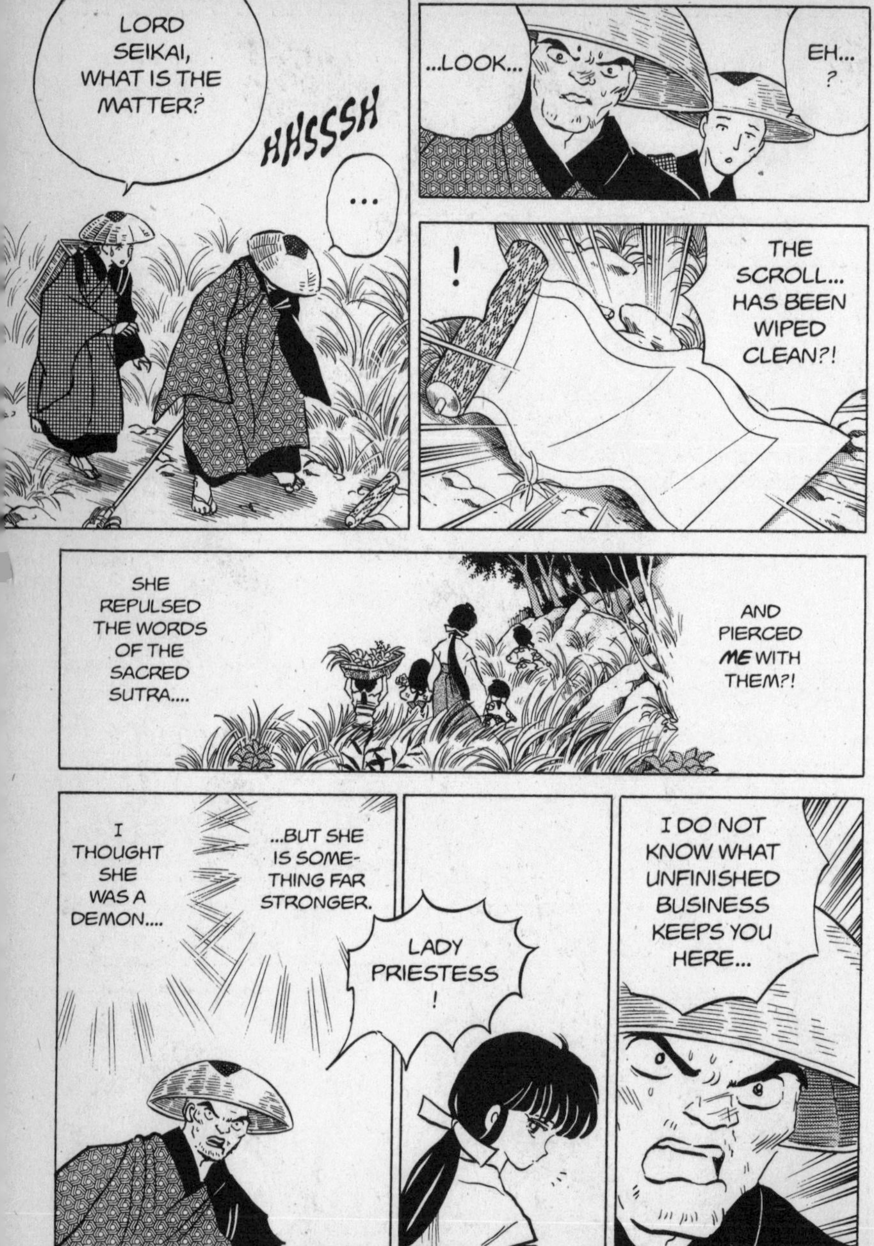
LORD SEIKAI, WHAT IS THE MATTER?
HHSSSH
...
...LOOK...
EH... ?
!
THE SCROLL... HAS BEEN WIPED CLEAN?!
SHE REPULSED THE WORDS OF THE SACRED SUTRA....
AND PIERCED ME WITH THEM?!
I THOUGHT SHE WAS A DEMON....
...BUT SHE IS SOMETHING FAR STRONGER.
LADY PRIESTESS !
I DO NOT KNOW WHAT UNFINISHED BUSINESS KEEPS YOU HERE...

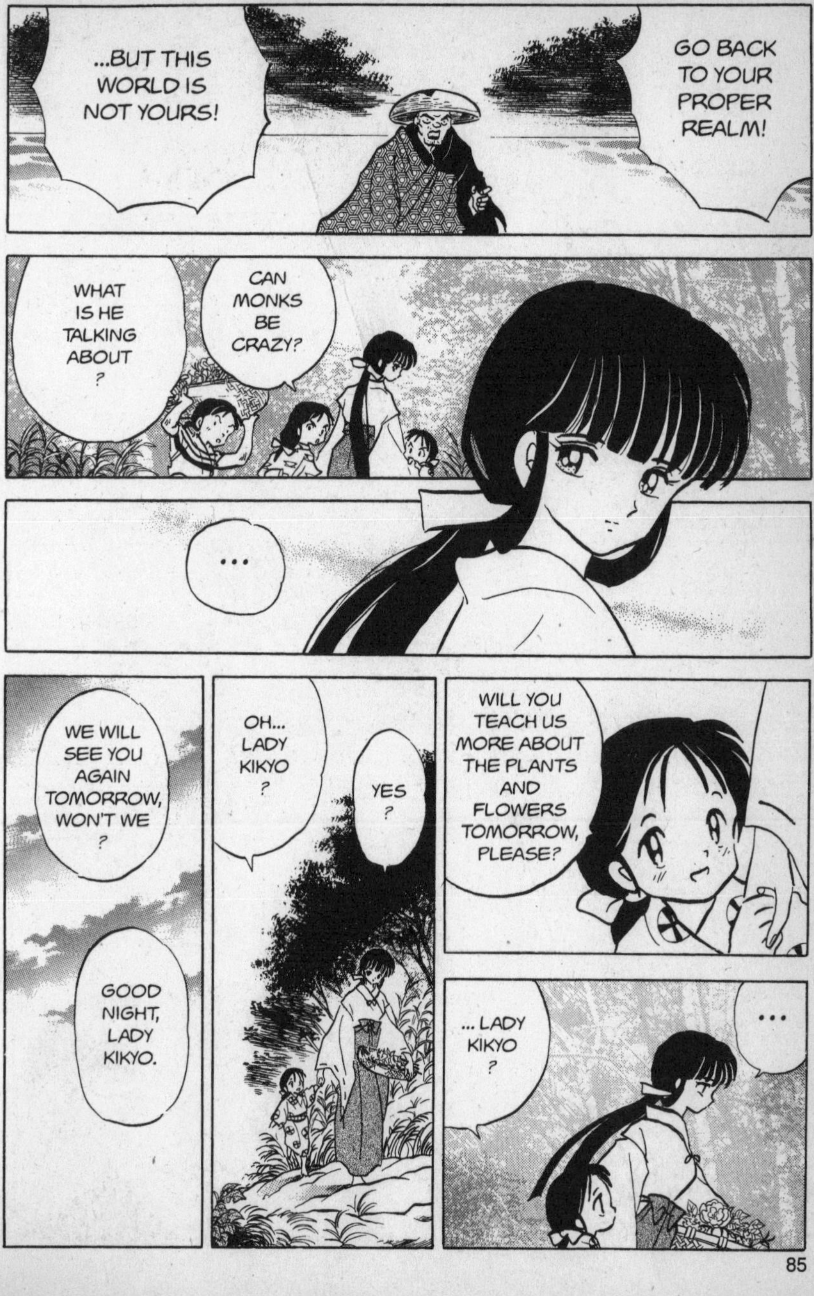
...BUT THIS WORLD IS NOT YOURS!
GO BACK TO YOUR PROPER REALM!
WHAT IS HE TALKING ABOUT ?
CAN MONKS BE CRAZY?
...
WE WILL SEE YOU AGAIN TOMORROW, WON'T WE ?
GOOD NIGHT, LADY KIKYO.
OH... LADY KIKYO ?
YES ?
WILL YOU TEACH US MORE ABOUT THE PLANTS AND FLOWERS TOMORROW, PLEASE?
... LADY KIKYO ?
...

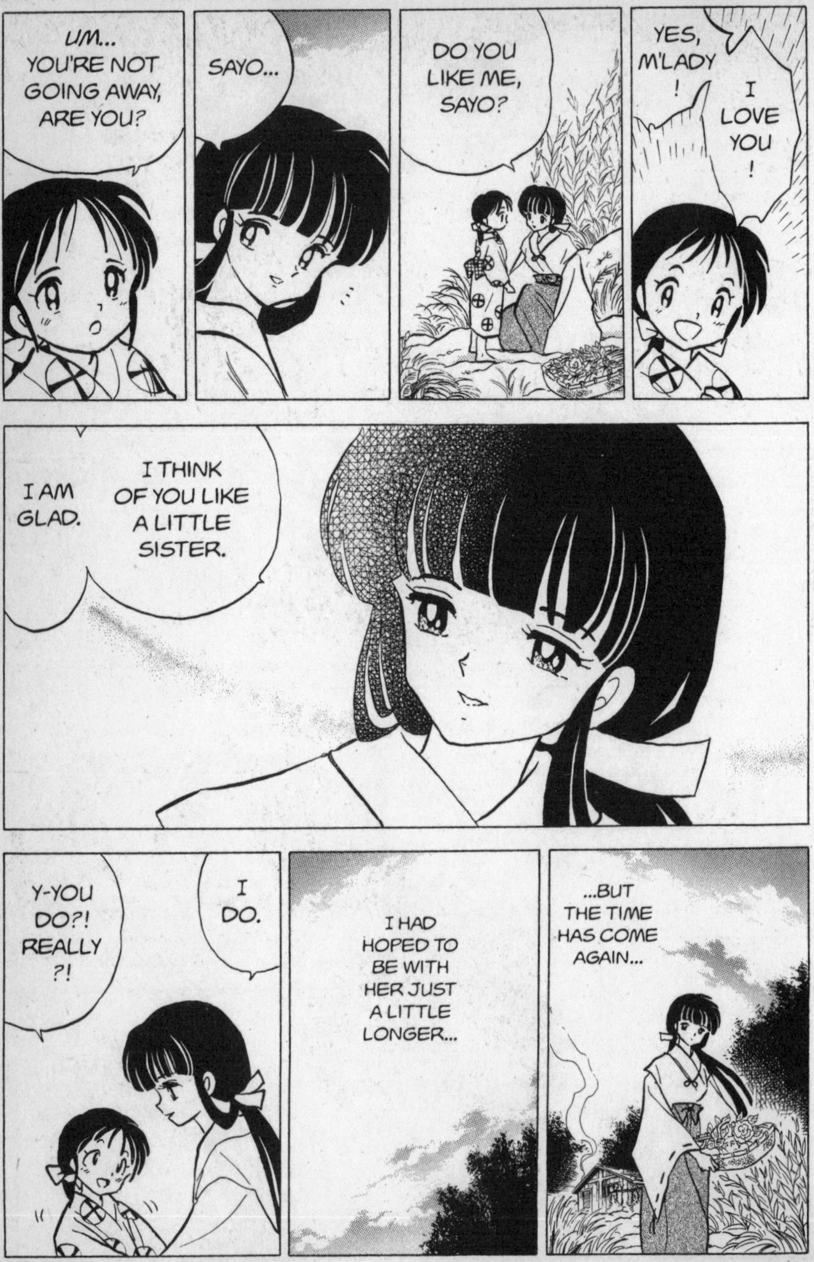
UM... YOU'RE NOT GOING AWAY, ARE YOU?
SAYO...
DO YOU LIKE ME, SAYO?
YES, M'LADY !
I LOVE YOU !
I AM GLAD.
I THINK OF YOU LIKE A LITTLE SISTER.
Y-YOU DO?! REALLY ?!
I DO.
I HAD HOPED TO BE WITH HER JUST A LITTLE LONGER...
...BUT THE TIME HAS COME AGAIN...

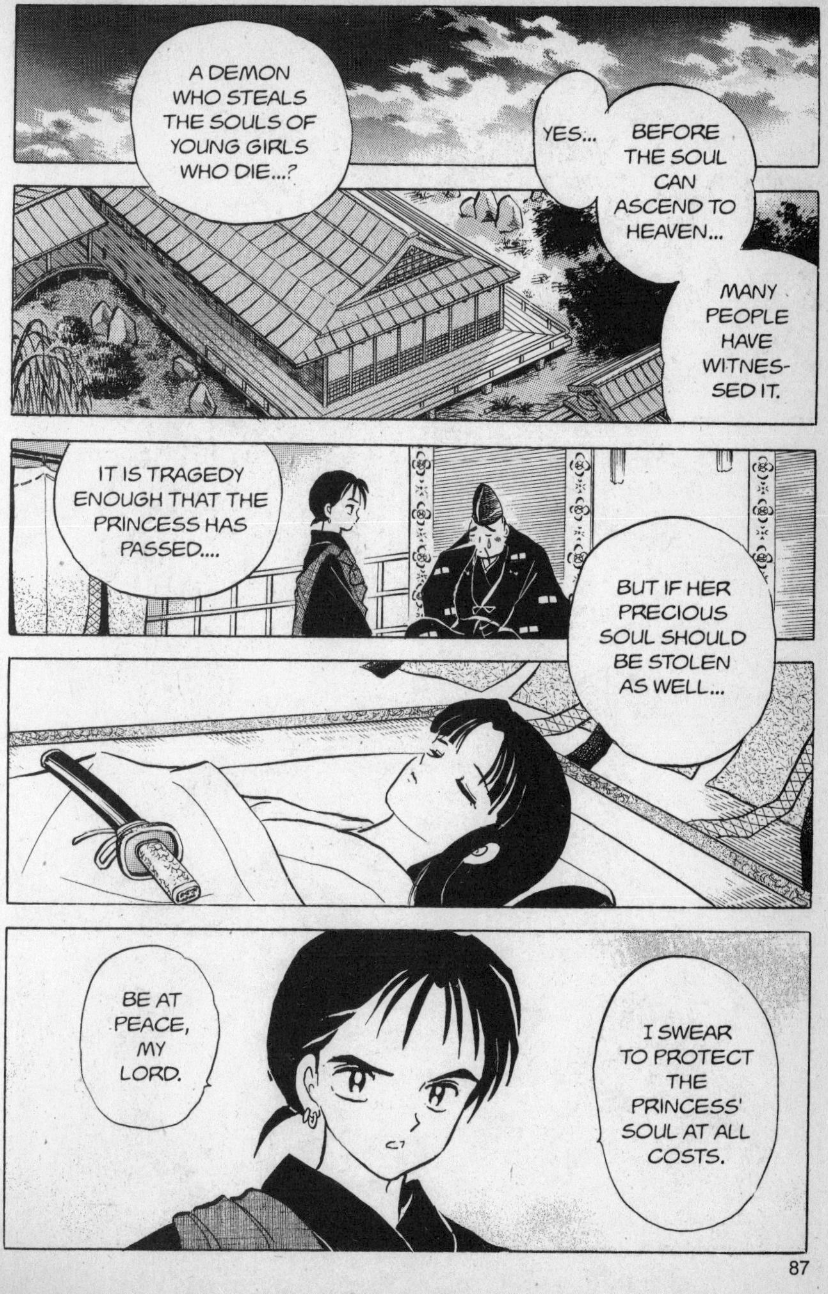
A DEMON WHO STEALS THE SOULS OF YOUNG GIRLS WHO DIE...?
YES...
BEFORE THE SOUL CAN ASCEND TO HEAVEN...
MANY PEOPLE HAVE WITNES-SED IT.
IT IS TRAGEDY ENOUGH THAT THE PRINCESS HAS PASSED....
BUT IF HER PRECIOUS SOUL SHOULD BE STOLEN AS WELL...
BE AT PEACE, MY LORD.
I SWEAR TO PROTECT THE PRINCESS' SOUL AT ALL COSTS.

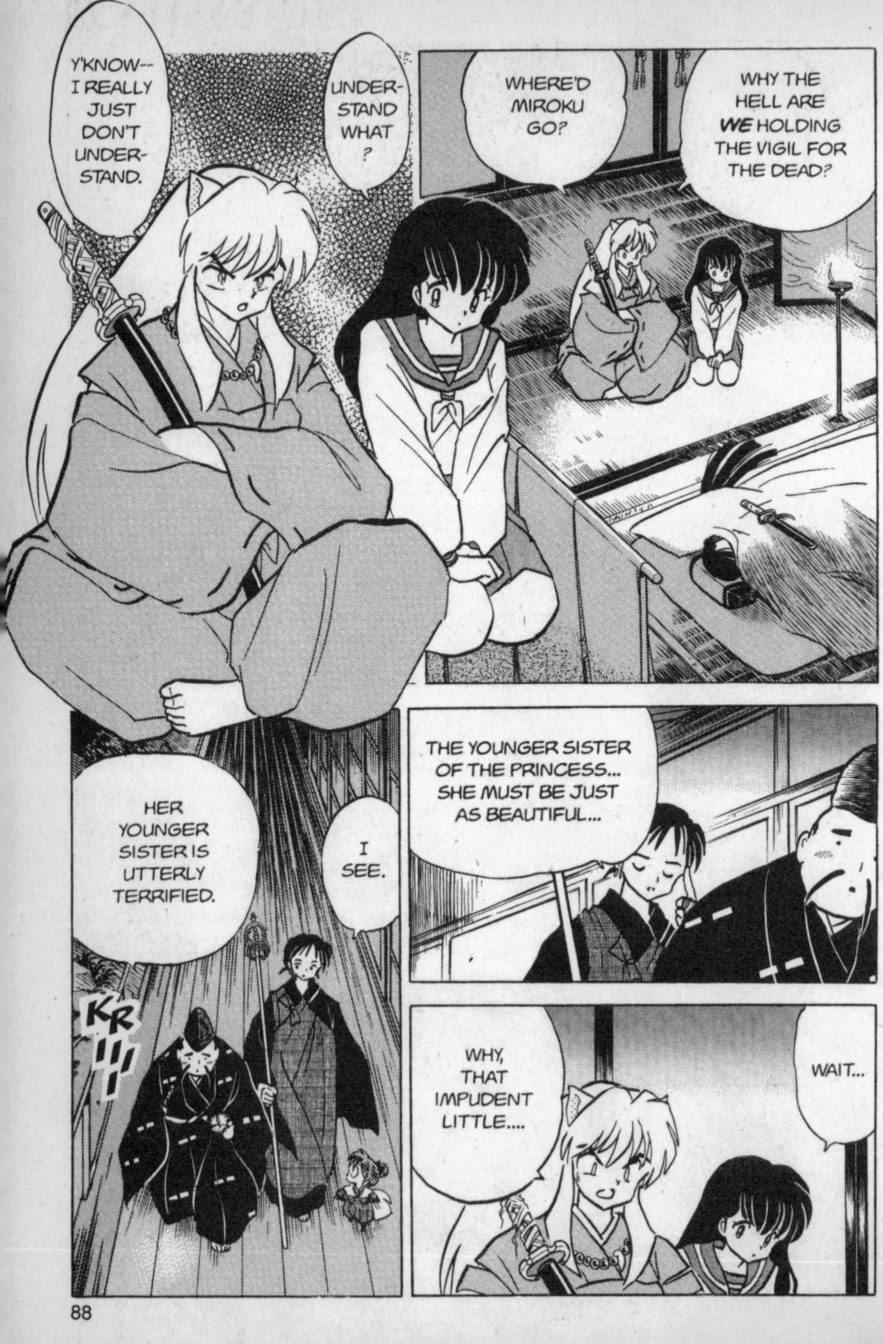

Y'KNOW-- I REALLY JUST DON'T UNDER-STAND.
UNDER-STAND WHAT ?
WHERE'D MIROKU GO?
WHY THE HELL ARE *WE* HOLDING THE VIGIL FOR THE DEAD?
HER YOUNGER SISTER IS UTTERLY TERRIFIED.
I SEE.
KR
THE YOUNGER SISTER OF THE PRINCESS... SHE MUST BE JUST AS BEAUTIFUL...
WHY, THAT IMPUDENT LITTLE....
WAIT...

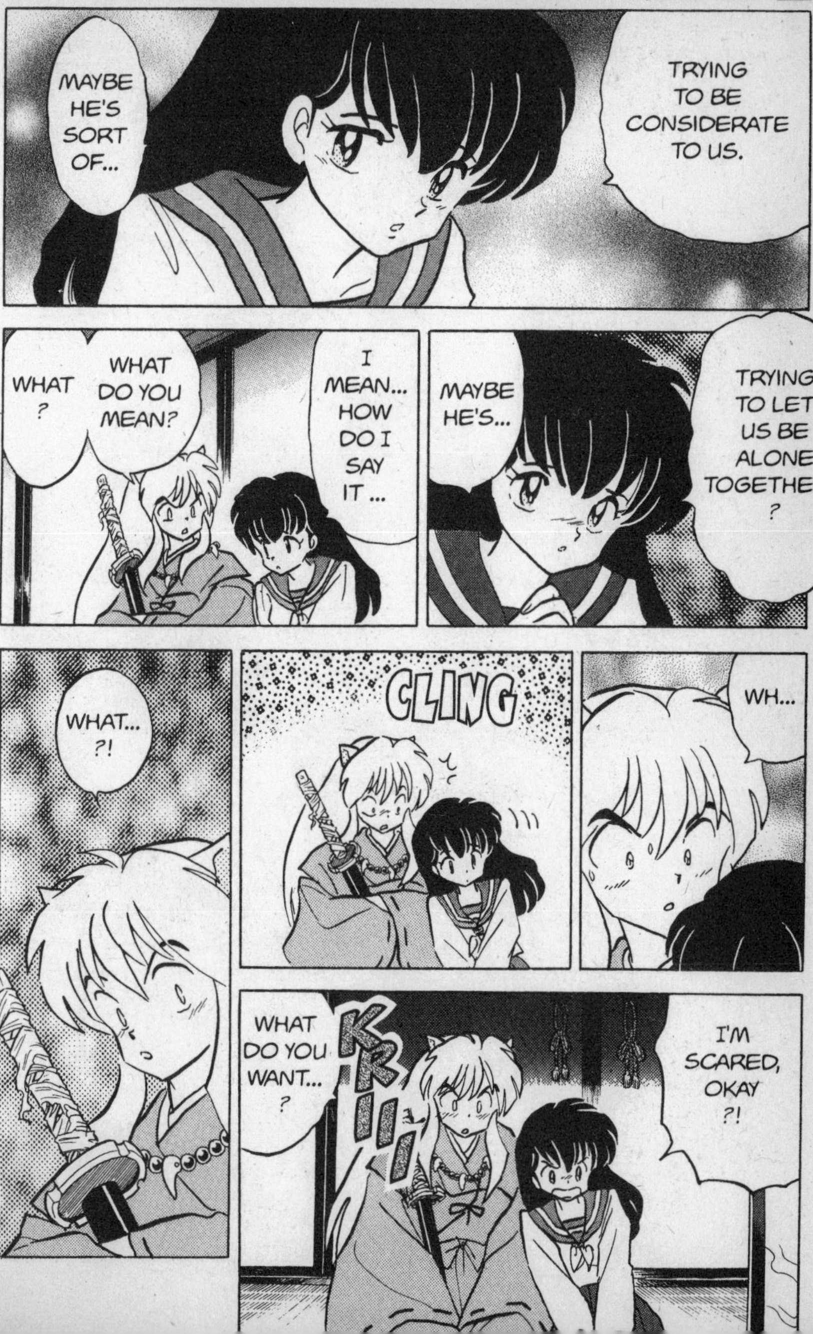
MAYBE HE'S SORT OF...
TRYING TO BE CONSIDERATE TO US.
WHAT ?
WHAT DO YOU MEAN?
I MEAN... HOW DO I SAY IT ...
MAYBE HE'S...
TRYING TO LET US BE ALONE TOGETHER... ?
WHAT... ?!
CLING
WH...
WHAT DO YOU WANT... ?
KRIII
I'M SCARED, OKAY ?!

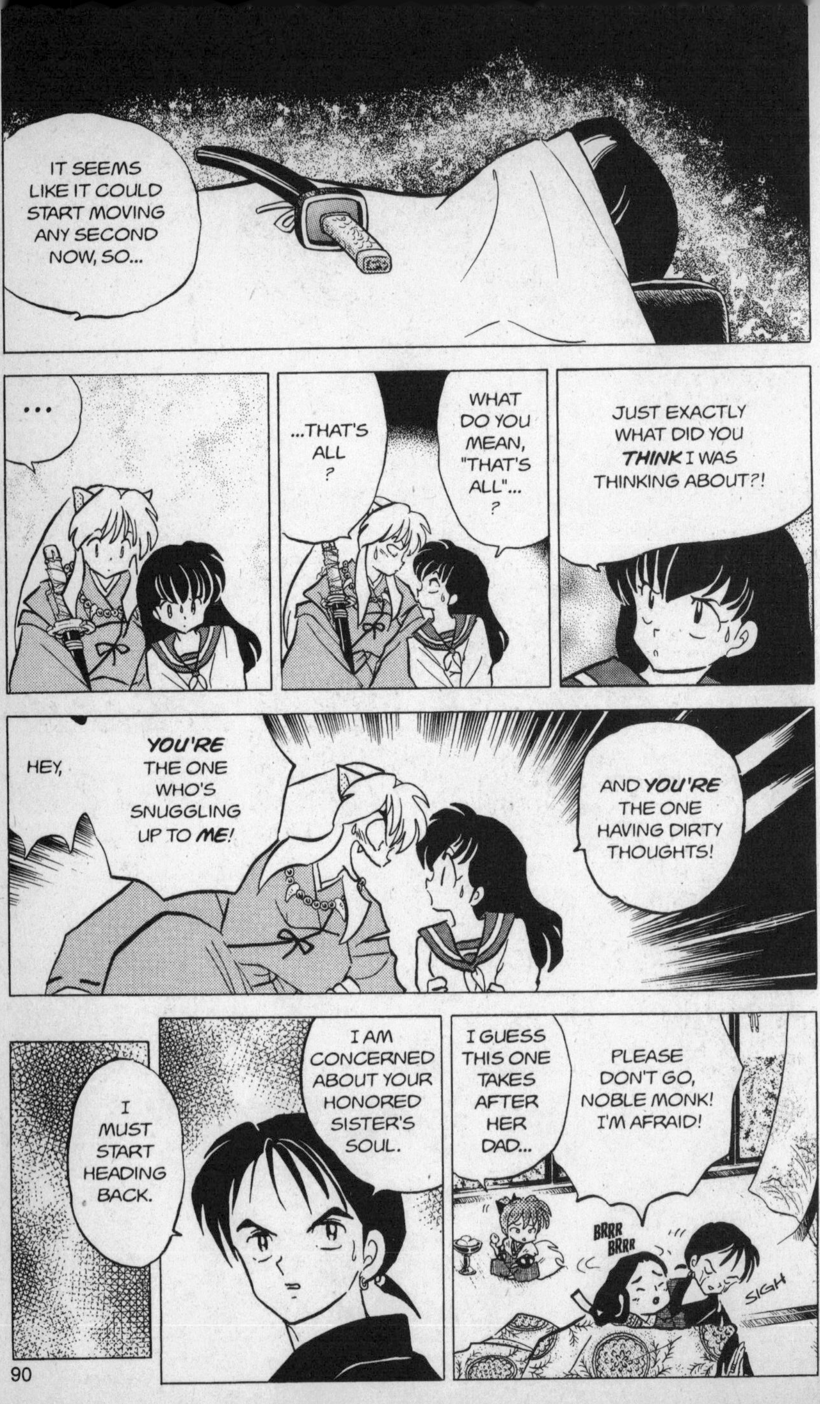
IT SEEMS LIKE IT COULD START MOVING ANY SECOND NOW, SO...
...
...THAT'S ALL ?
WHAT DO YOU MEAN, "THAT'S ALL"... ?
JUST EXACTLY WHAT DID YOU THINK I WAS THINKING ABOUT?!
HEY,
YOU'RE THE ONE WHO'S SNUGGLING UP TO ME!
AND YOU'RE THE ONE HAVING DIRTY THOUGHTS!
I MUST START HEADING BACK.
I AM CONCERNED ABOUT YOUR HONORED SISTER'S SOUL.
I GUESS THIS ONE TAKES AFTER HER DAD...
PLEASE DON'T GO, NOBLE MONK! I'M AFRAID!
BRRR BRRR
SIGH

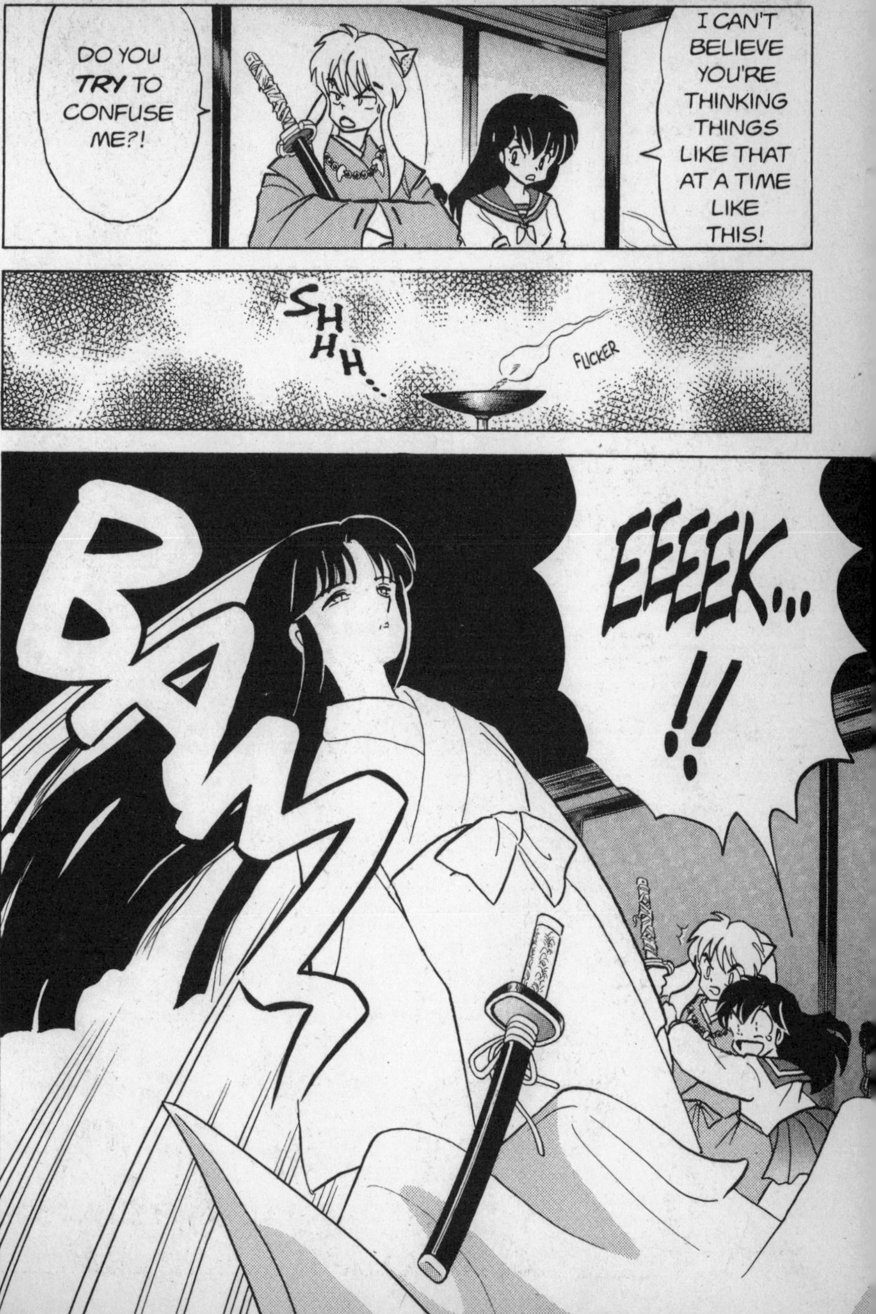
DO YOU *TRY* TO CONFUSE ME?!
I CAN'T BELIEVE YOU'RE THINKING THINGS LIKE THAT AT A TIME LIKE THIS!
SHHH...
FLICKER
BAM
EEEEK... !!

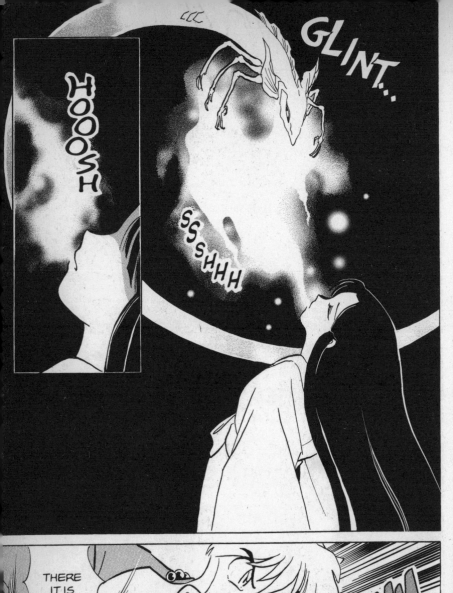

GLINT...

HOOOSH

SSSHHH

THERE IT IS AT LAST!

VNNMM

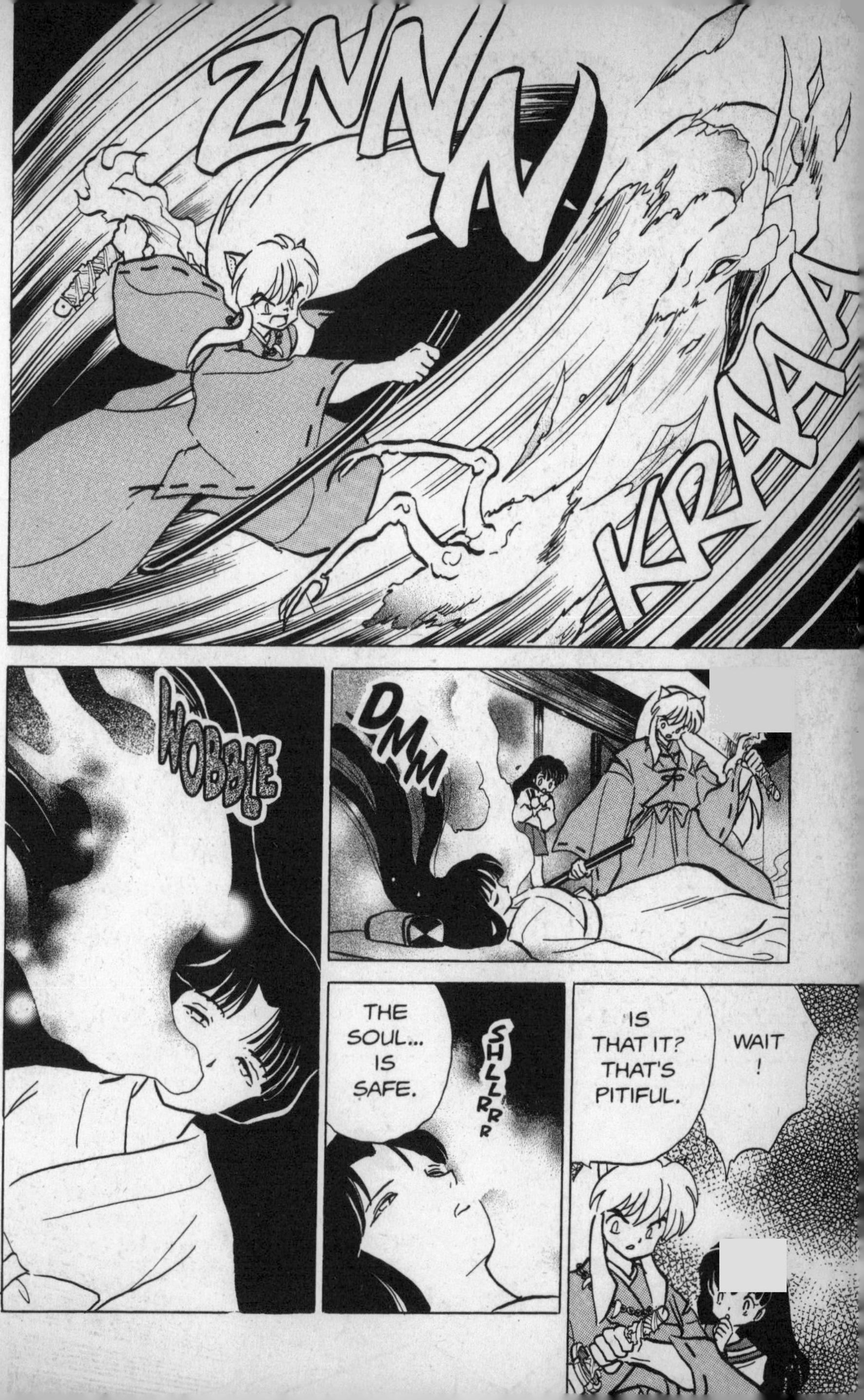
ZNNN
KRAAA
WOBBLE
DMM
THE SOUL... IS SAFE.
SHLLRRR
IS THAT IT? THAT'S PITIFUL.
WAIT!

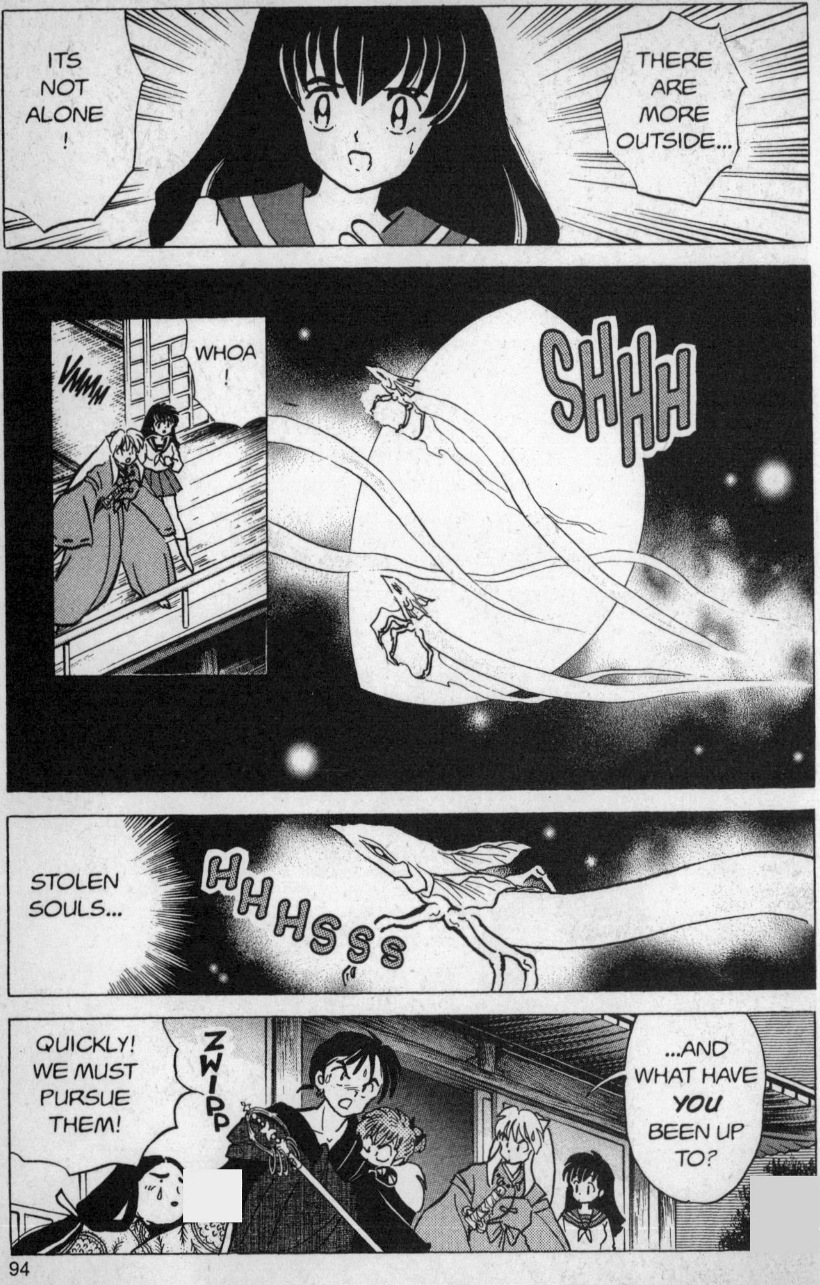
ITS NOT ALONE !
THERE ARE MORE OUTSIDE...
VMMM
WHOA !
SHHH
STOLEN SOULS...
HHHSSSS
QUICKLY! WE MUST PURSUE THEM!
ZWIPP
...AND WHAT HAVE *YOU* BEEN UP TO?

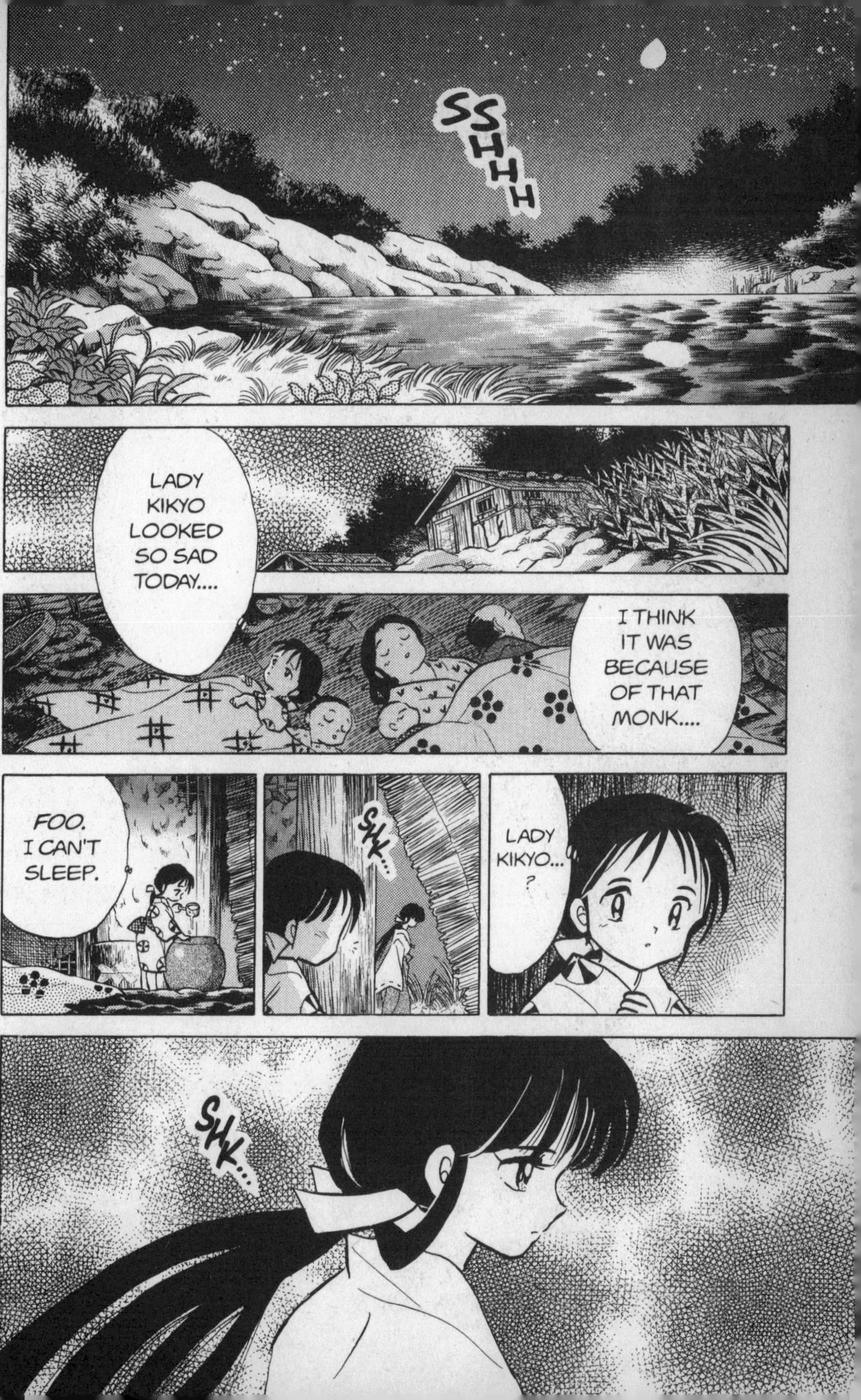
SSHHH
LADY KIKYO LOOKED SO SAD TODAY....
I THINK IT WAS BECAUSE OF THAT MONK....
FOO. I CAN'T SLEEP.
SHK...
LADY KIKYO... ?
SHK...

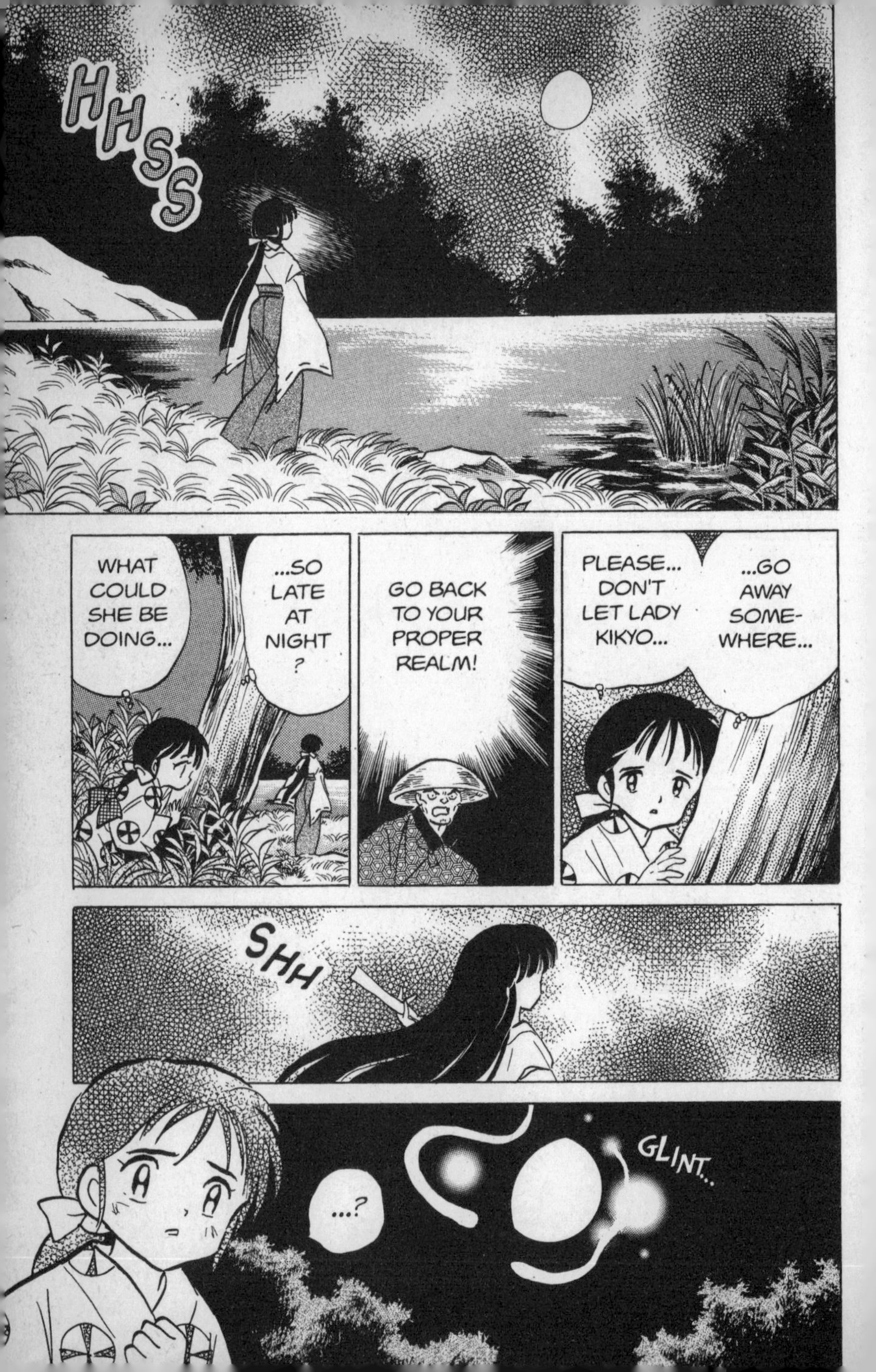
HHSS
WHAT COULD SHE BE DOING...
...SO LATE AT NIGHT?
GO BACK TO YOUR PROPER REALM!
PLEASE... DON'T LET LADY KIKYO...
...GO AWAY SOMEWHERE...
SHH
...?
GLINT...

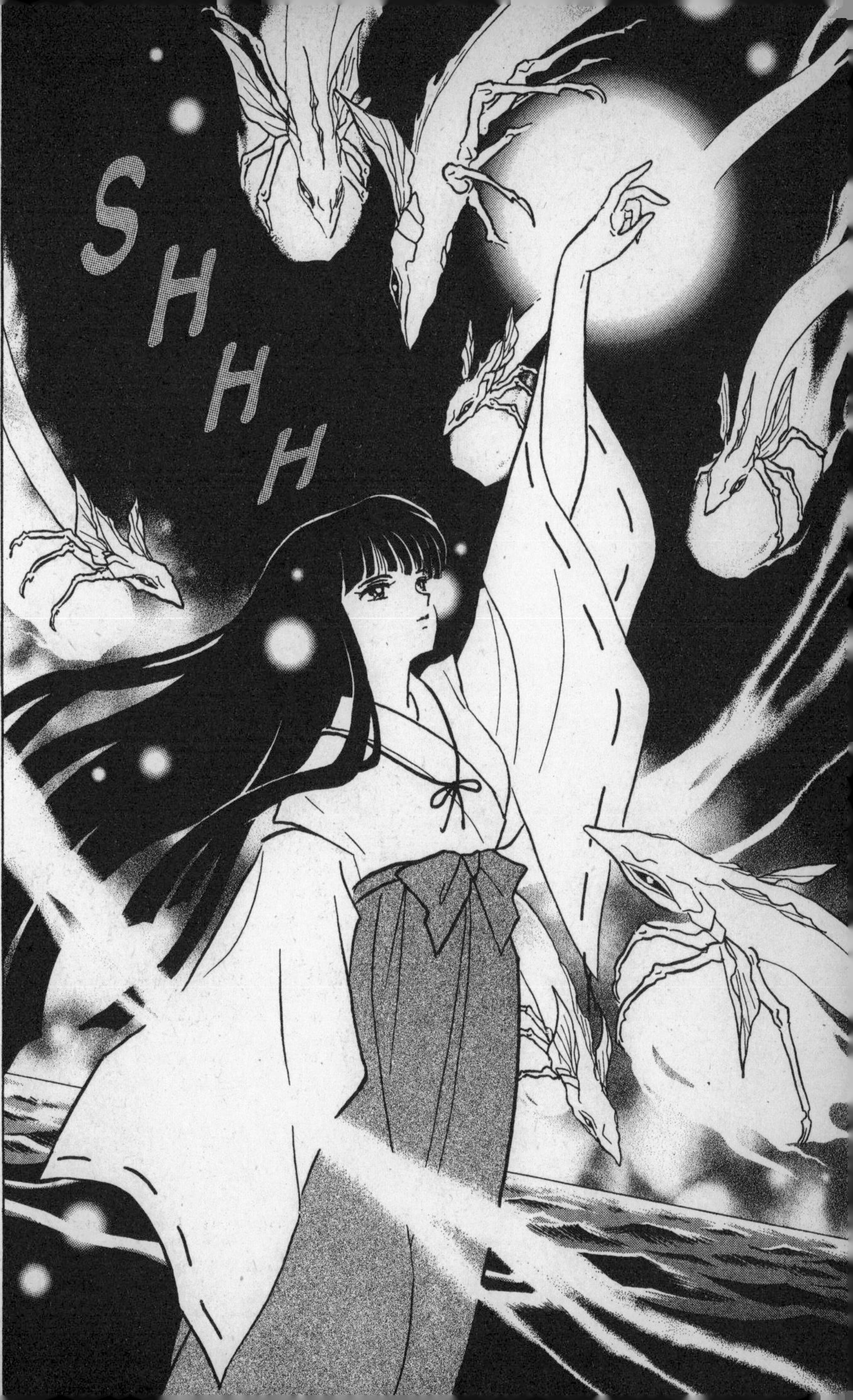
SHHH

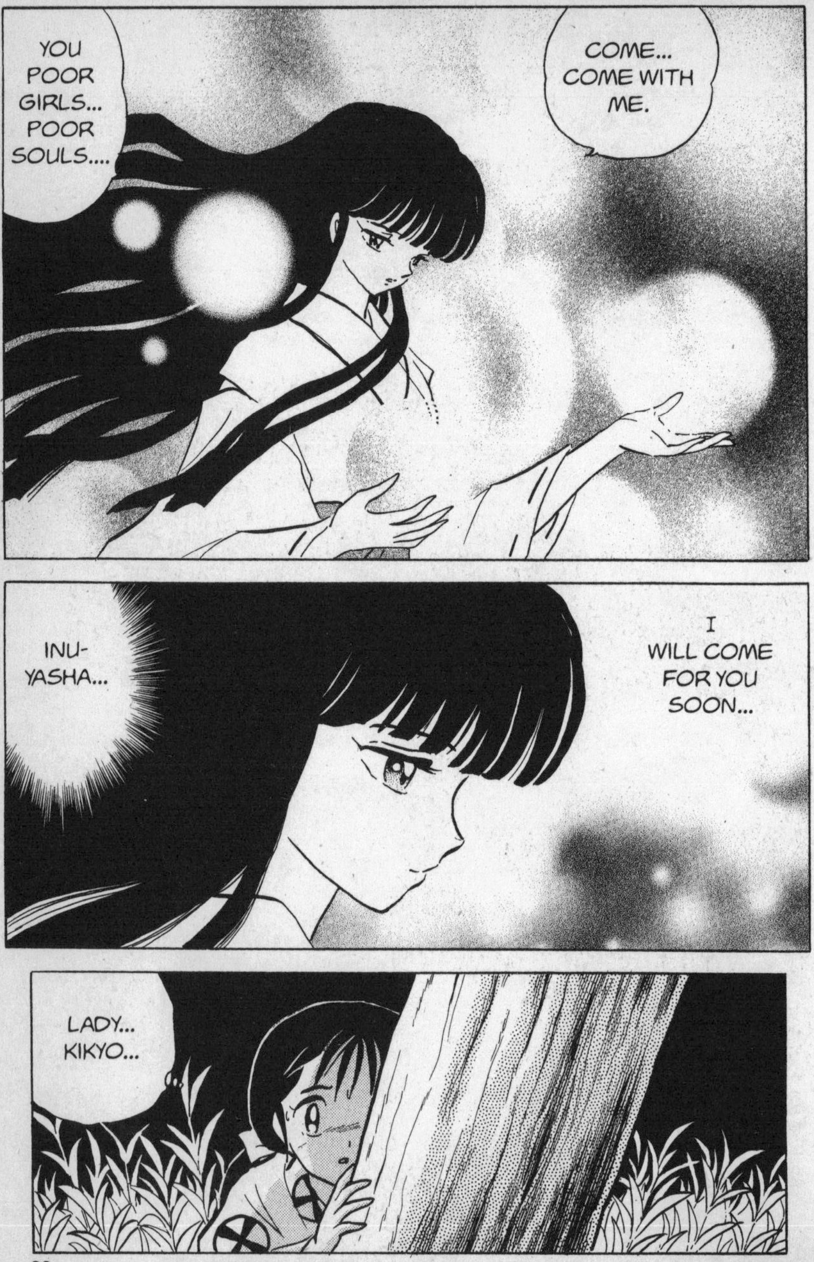
YOU POOR GIRLS... POOR SOULS....
COME... COME WITH ME.
INU-YASHA...
I WILL COME FOR YOU SOON...
LADY... KIKYO...

SCROLL SIX

THE SOUL PAST SAVING

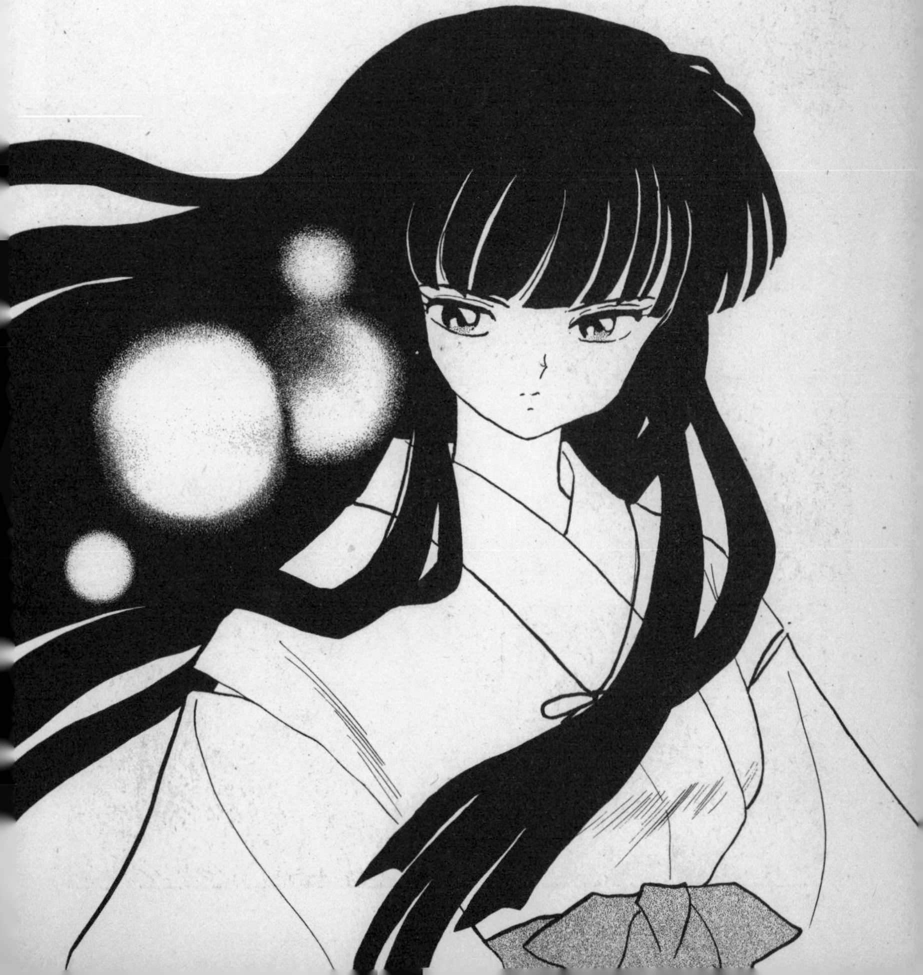

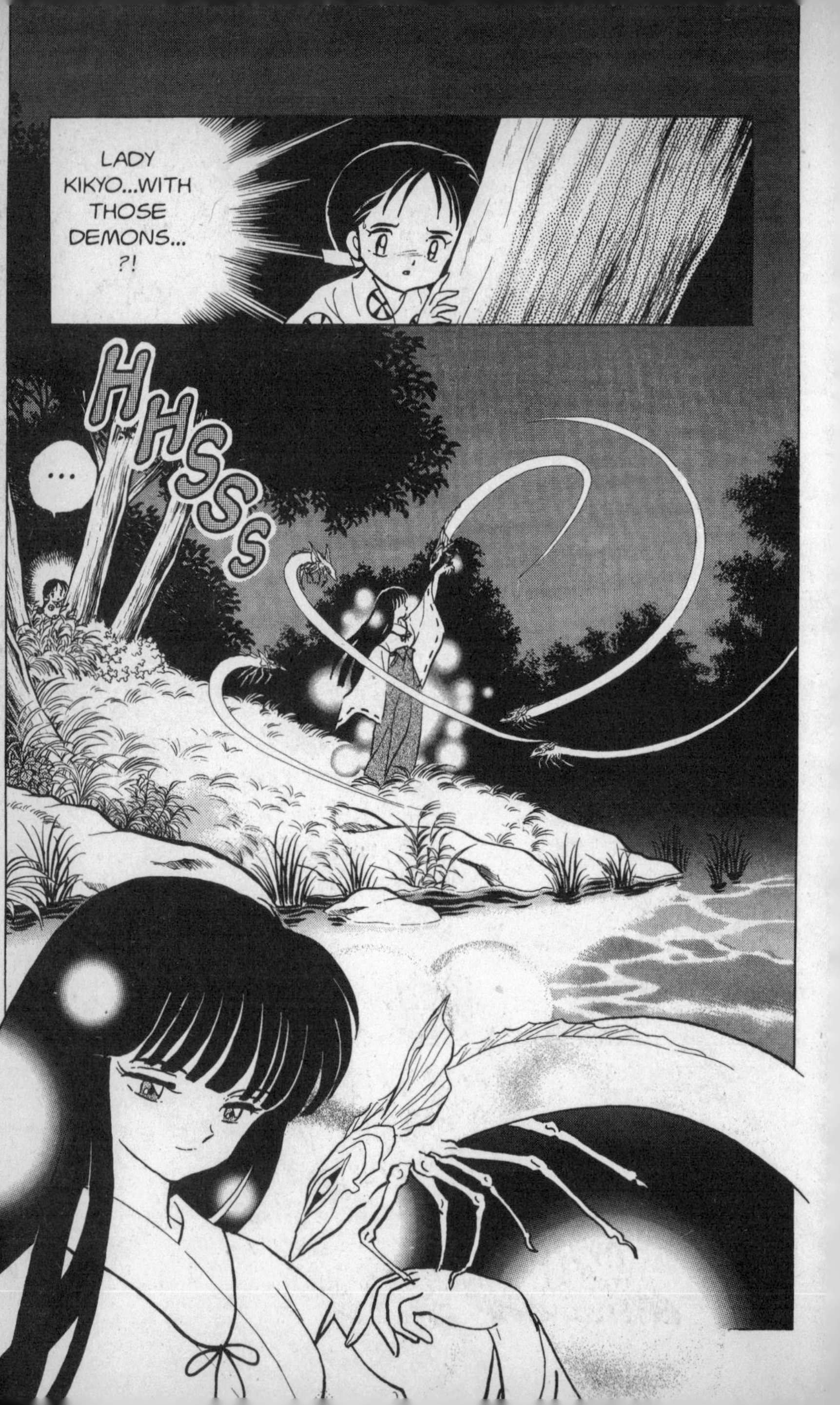
LADY KIKYO...WITH THOSE DEMONS... ?!
HHSSSS
...

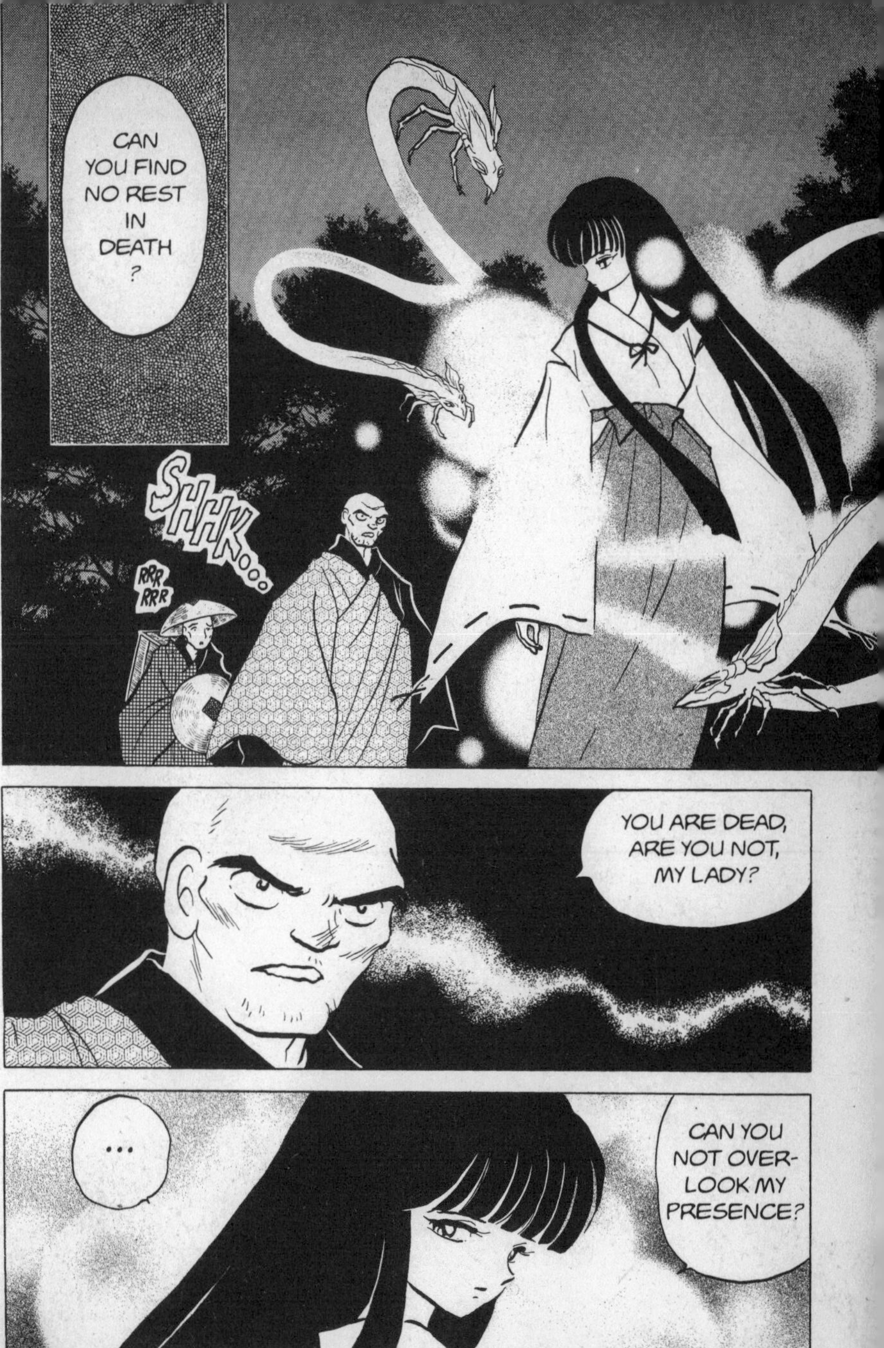

CAN YOU FIND NO REST IN DEATH ?
SHHK...
RRR RRR
YOU ARE DEAD, ARE YOU NOT, MY LADY?
...
CAN YOU NOT OVER-LOOK MY PRESENCE?

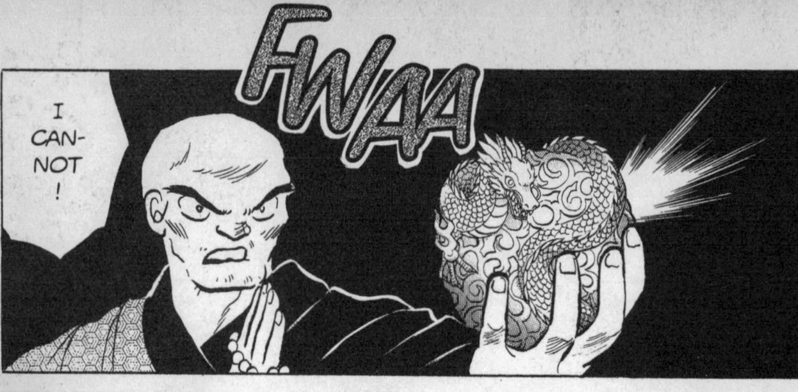
FWAA
I CAN-NOT!
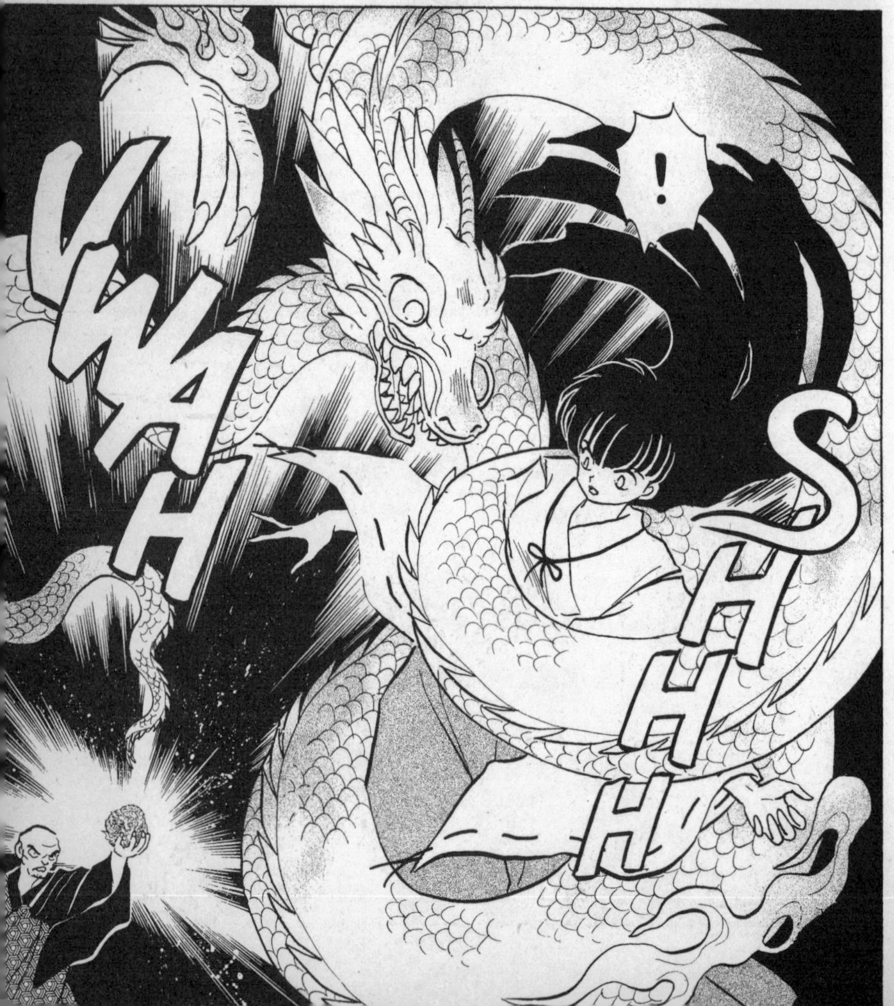
WAH
!
SHHHH

LADY KIKYO...!

YOU CANNOT ESCAPE FROM THIS SOUL-BOND! I SHALL LAY YOU TO REST!

GRRN GRRN GRRN GRRN

NKH...

GRRN

SLEEP, NOW! FIND PEACE!

I SHALL SAVE YOUR SOUL!

GNNNG

SAVE... MY SOUL, YOU SAY...?

A LITTLE MONK... LIKE YOU...

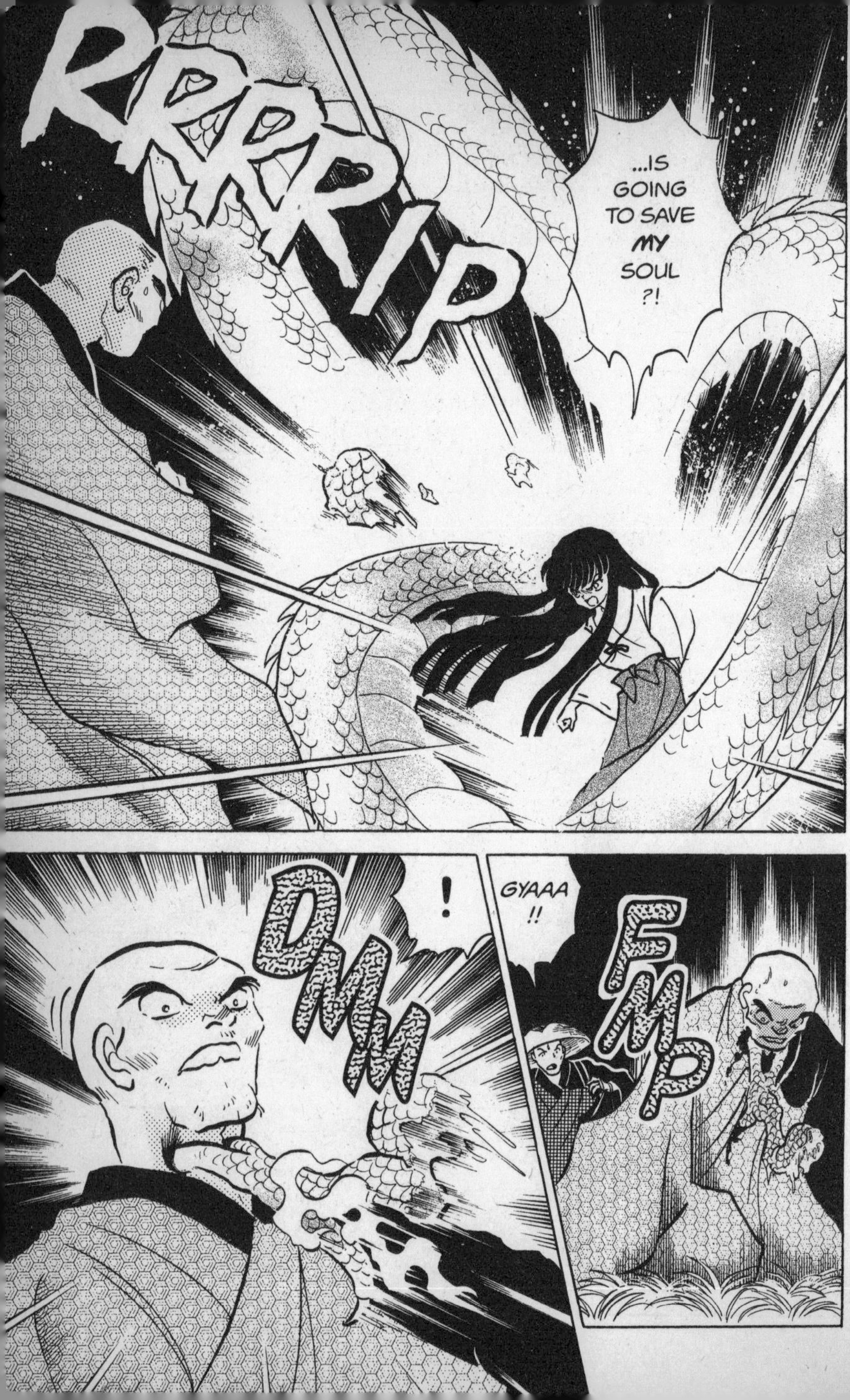
RPPRIP
...IS GOING TO SAVE MY SOUL ?!
DMM
!
GYAAA !!
FMP

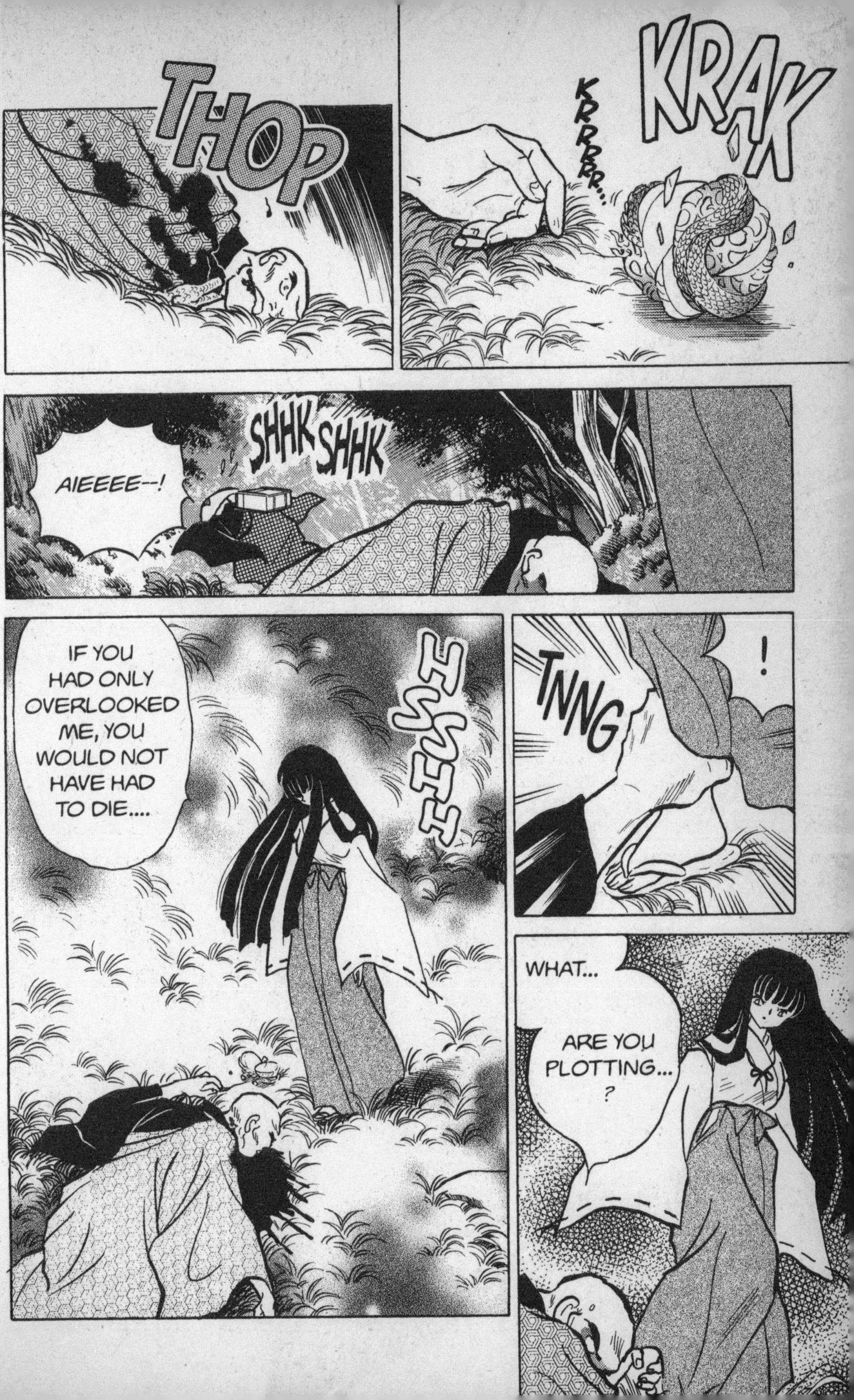
THOP
KRRRRR...
KRAK
AIEEEE--!
SHHK SHHK
IF YOU HAD ONLY OVERLOOKED ME, YOU WOULD NOT HAVE HAD TO DIE....
HISSSS
TNNG
!
WHAT...
ARE YOU PLOTTING...?

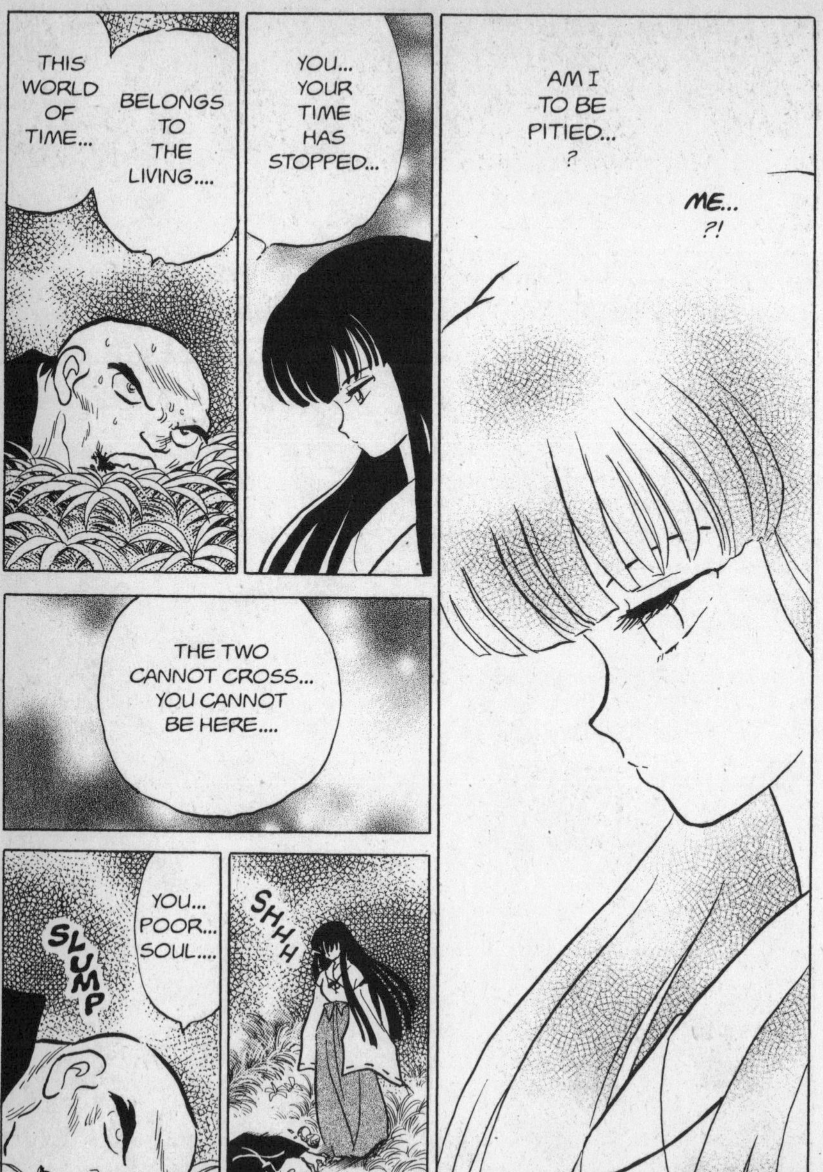
THIS WORLD OF TIME...
BELONGS TO THE LIVING....
YOU... YOUR TIME HAS STOPPED...
THE TWO CANNOT CROSS... YOU CANNOT BE HERE....
SLUMP
YOU... POOR... SOUL....
SHHH
AM I TO BE PITIED...?
ME...?!

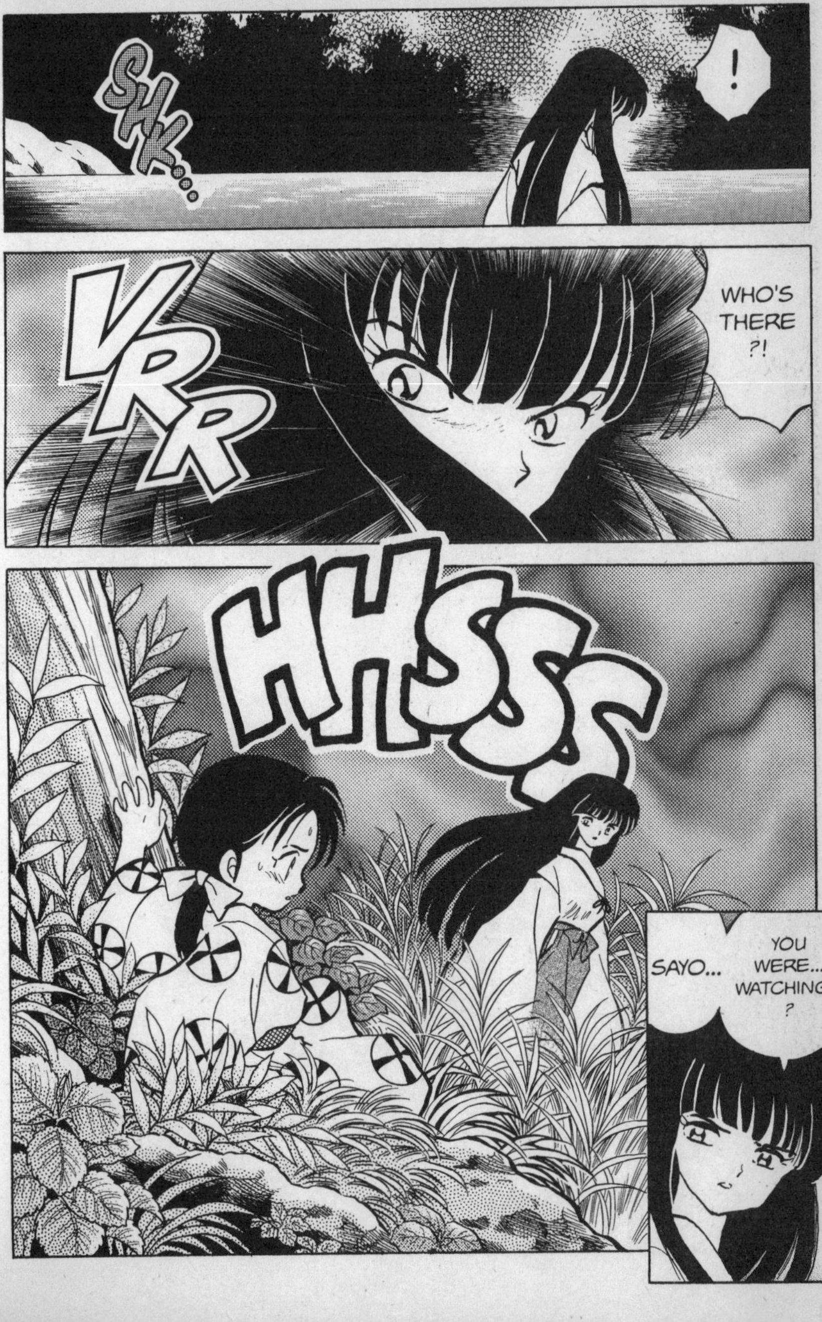
SHK...
!
VRR
WHO'S THERE ?!
HHSSS
SAYO... YOU WERE... WATCHING... ?

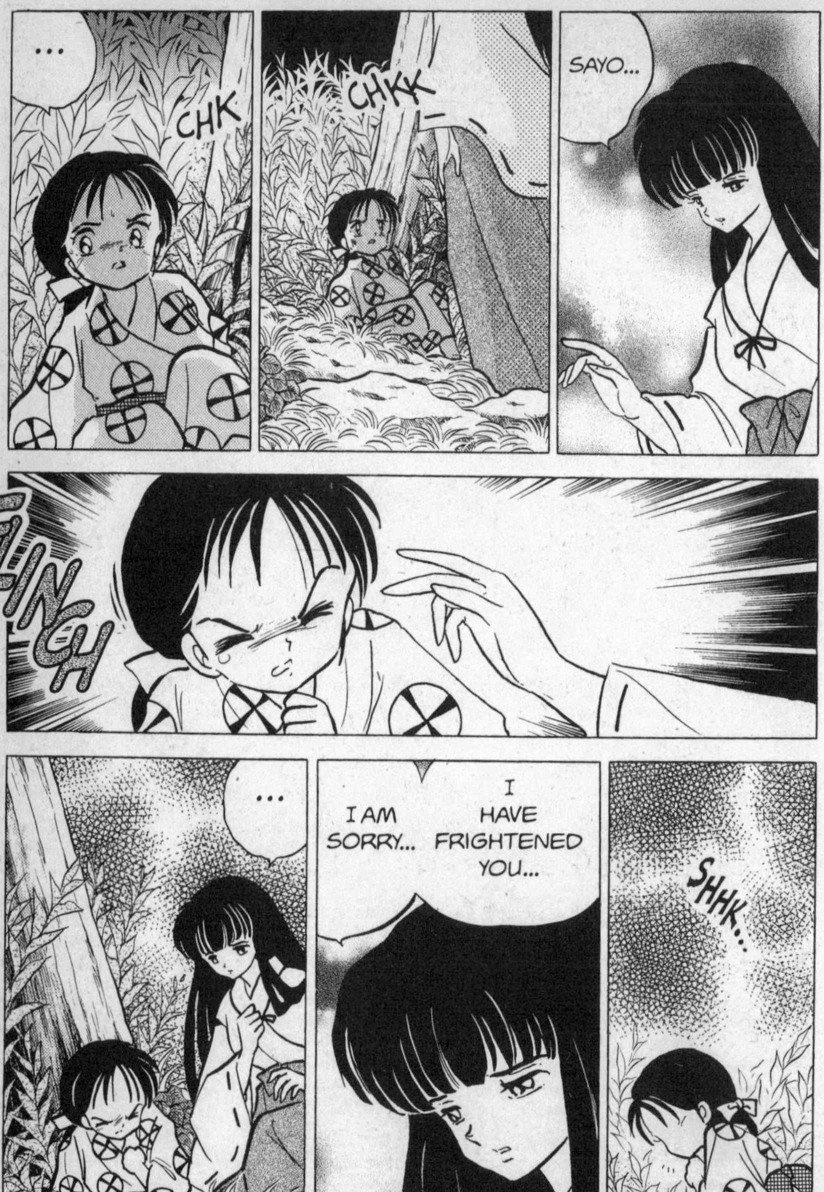
...
CHK
CHKK
SAYO...
FLINCH
...
I AM SORRY...
I HAVE FRIGHTENED YOU...
SHHK...

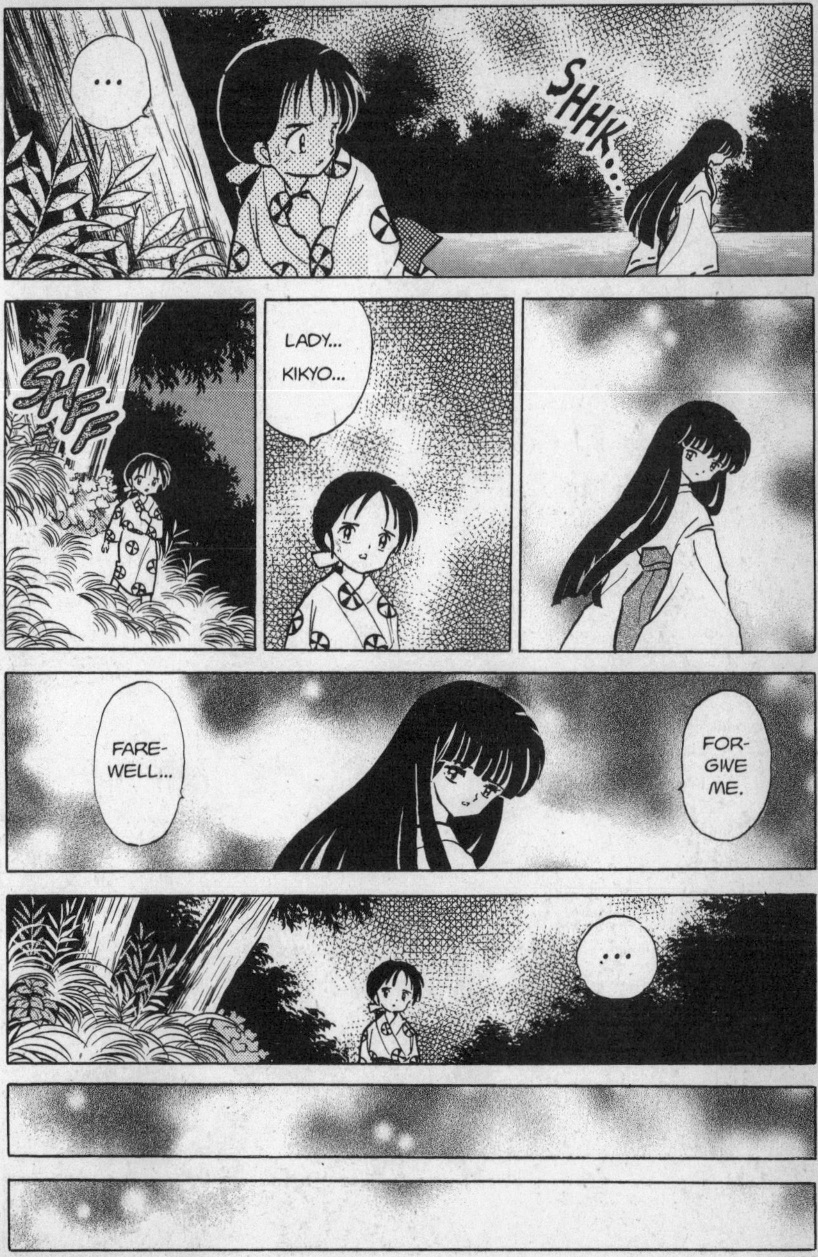
...
SHHK...
SHFF
LADY... KIKYO...
FARE-WELL...
FOR-GIVE ME.
...

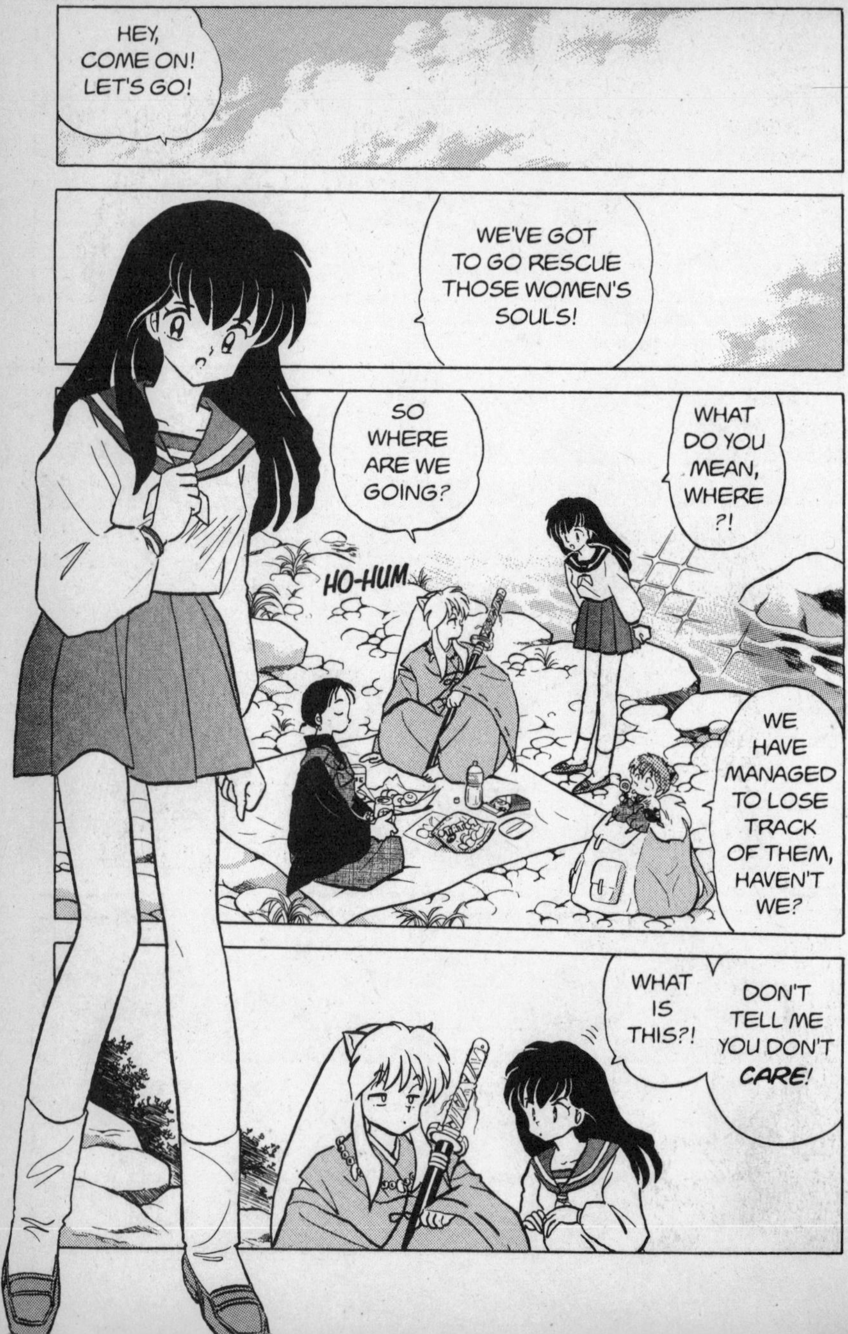
HEY, COME ON! LET'S GO!
WE'VE GOT TO GO RESCUE THOSE WOMEN'S SOULS!
HO-HUM
SO WHERE ARE WE GOING?
WHAT DO YOU MEAN, WHERE ?!
WE HAVE MANAGED TO LOSE TRACK OF THEM, HAVEN'T WE?
WHAT IS THIS?!
DON'T TELL ME YOU DON'T CARE!

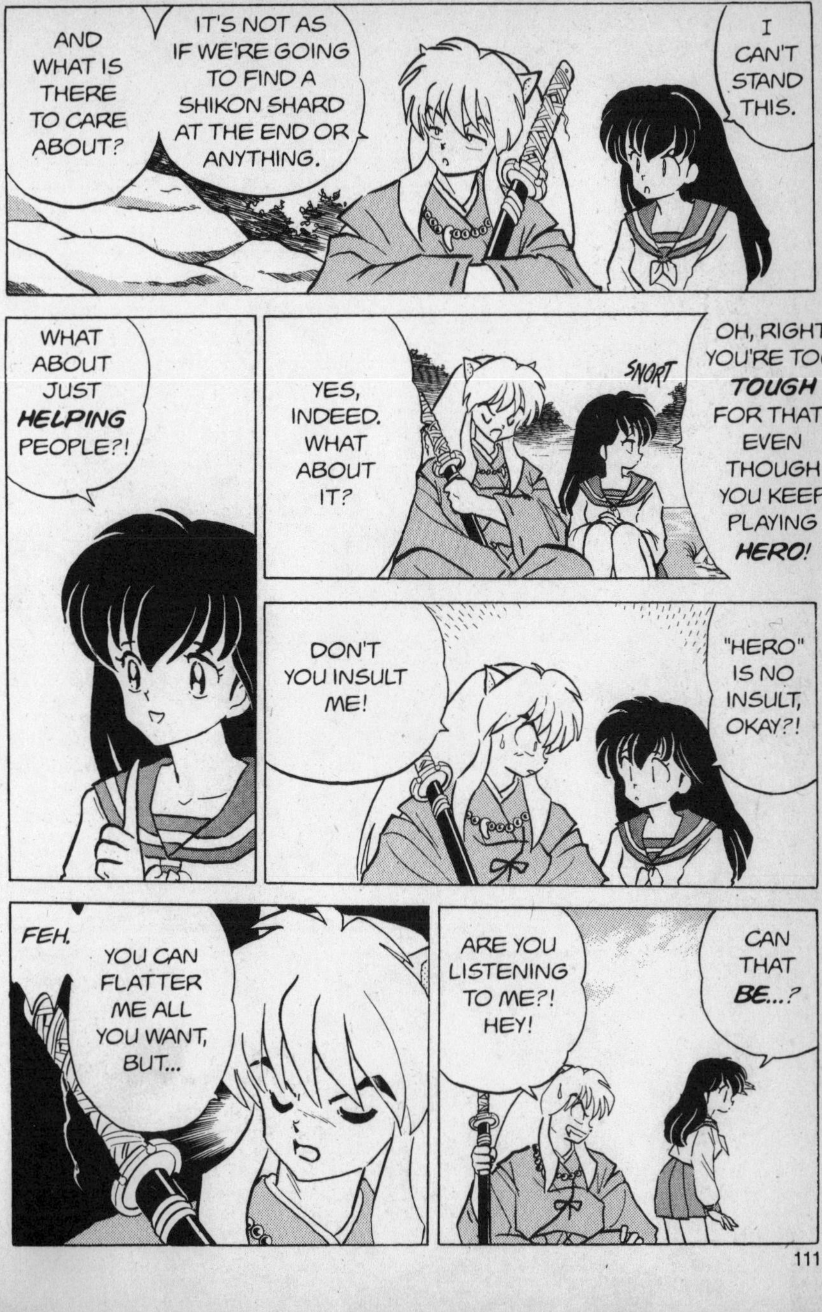
AND WHAT IS THERE TO CARE ABOUT?
IT'S NOT AS IF WE'RE GOING TO FIND A SHIKON SHARD AT THE END OR ANYTHING.
I CAN'T STAND THIS.
WHAT ABOUT JUST **HELPING** PEOPLE?!
YES, INDEED. WHAT ABOUT IT?
SNORT
OH, RIGHT, YOU'RE TOO **TOUGH** FOR THAT! EVEN THOUGH YOU KEEP PLAYING **HERO**!
DON'T YOU INSULT ME!
"HERO" IS NO INSULT, OKAY?!
FEH.
YOU CAN FLATTER ME ALL YOU WANT, BUT...
ARE YOU LISTENING TO ME?! HEY!
CAN THAT **BE**...?

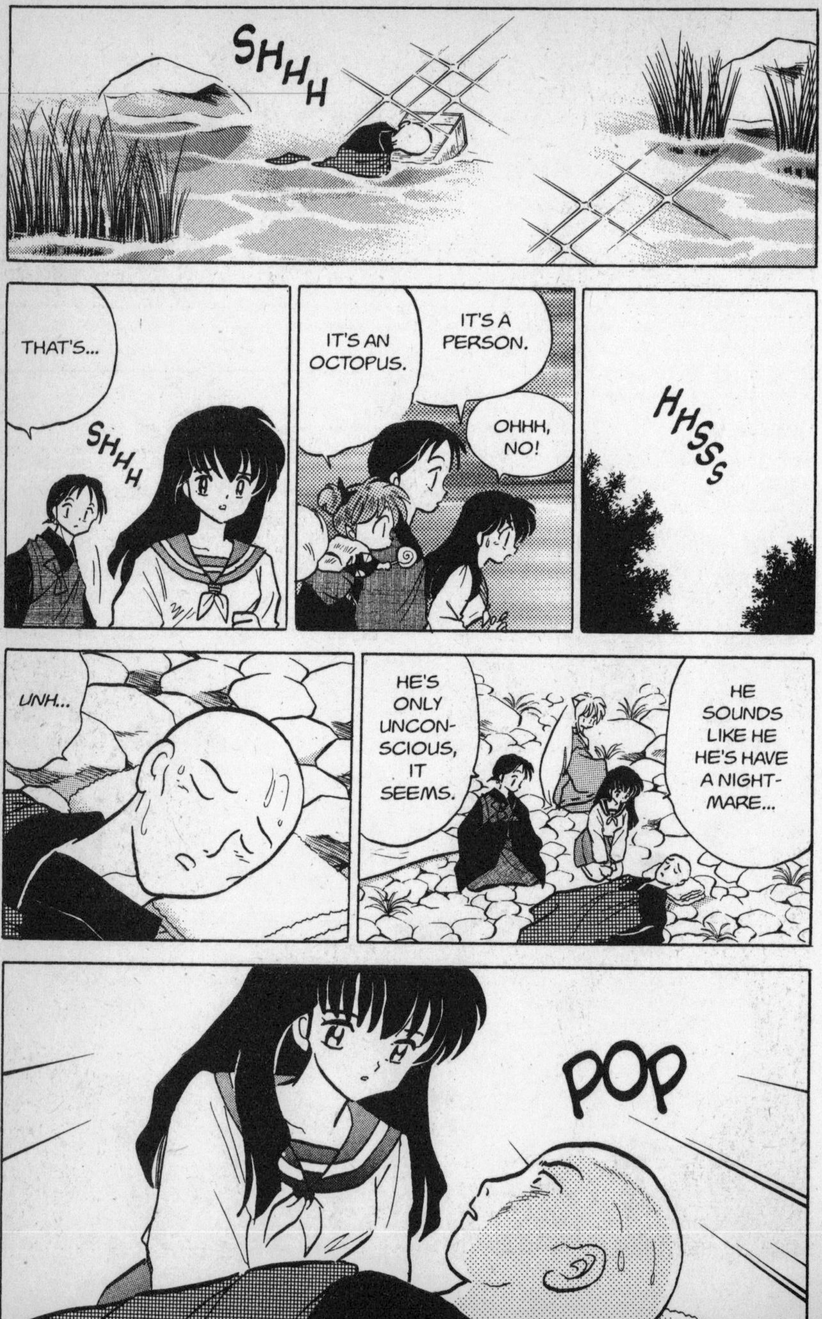
SHHH
THAT'S...
SHHH
IT'S AN OCTOPUS.
IT'S A PERSON.
OHHH, NO!
HHSSS
UNH...
HE'S ONLY UNCON-SCIOUS, IT SEEMS.
HE SOUNDS LIKE HE HE'S HAVE A NIGHT-MARE...
POP

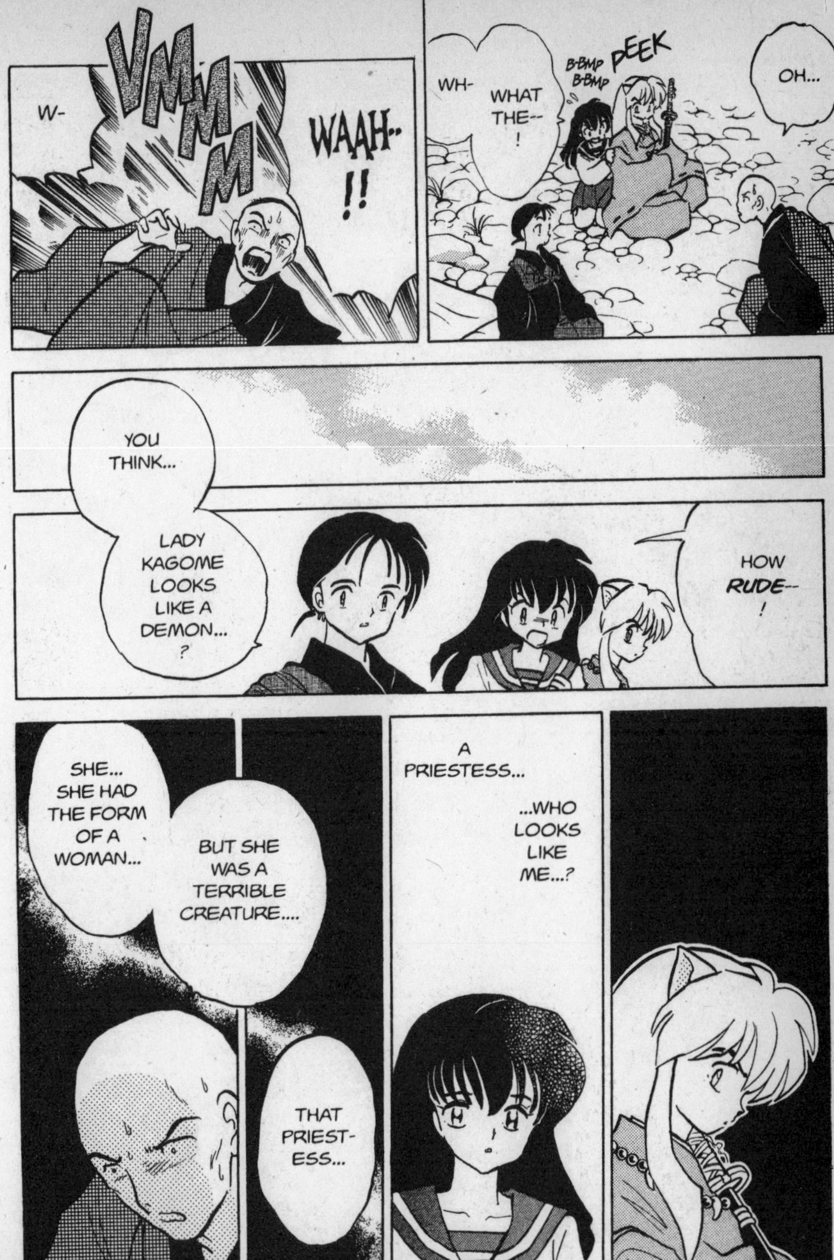
VMMM
W-
WAAH--!!
WH-
WHAT THE--!
B-BMP B-BMP
PEEK
OH...
YOU THINK...
LADY KAGOME LOOKS LIKE A DEMON...?
HOW RUDE--!
SHE... SHE HAD THE FORM OF A WOMAN...
BUT SHE WAS A TERRIBLE CREATURE....
THAT PRIEST-ESS...
A PRIESTESS...
...WHO LOOKS LIKE ME...?

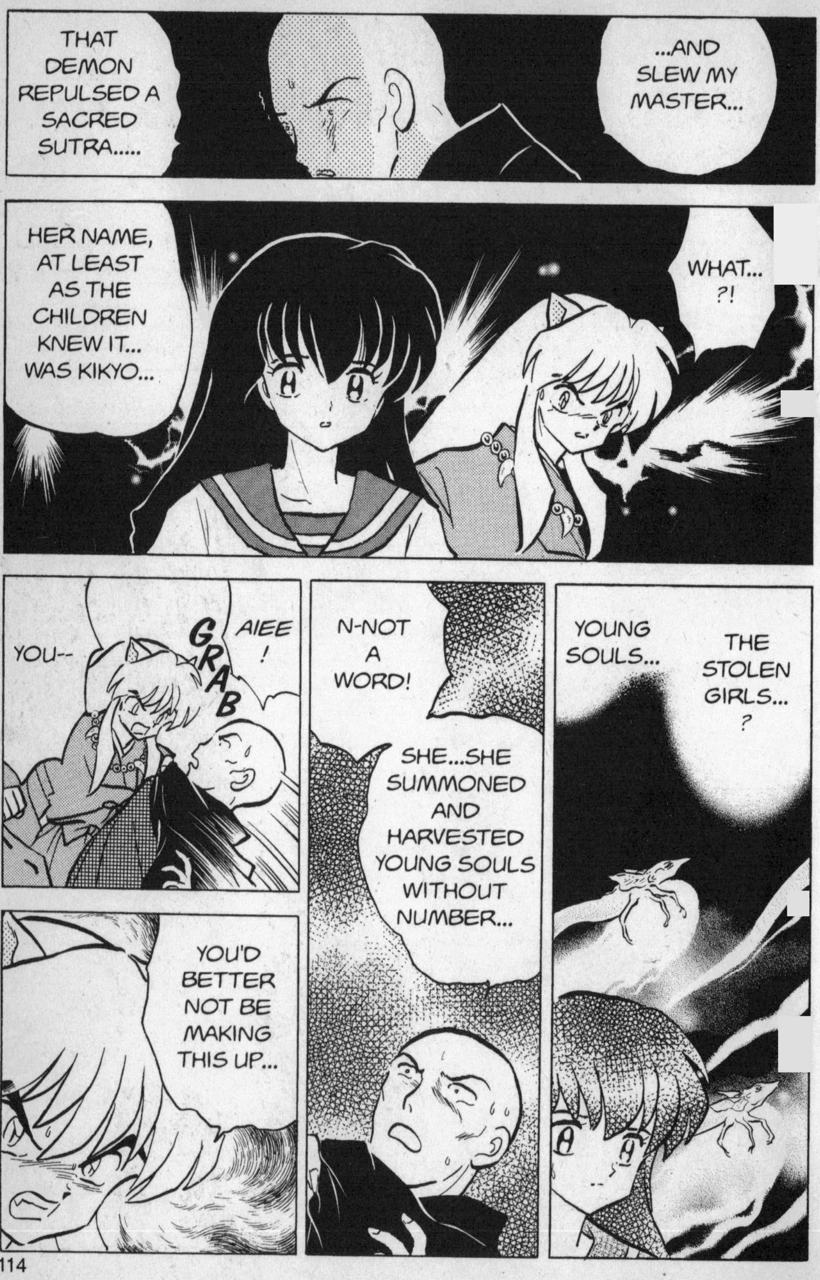
THAT DEMON REPULSED A SACRED SUTRA.....
...AND SLEW MY MASTER...
HER NAME, AT LEAST AS THE CHILDREN KNEW IT... WAS KIKYO...
WHAT... ?!
YOU--
GRAB
AIEE !
YOU'D BETTER NOT BE MAKING THIS UP...
N-NOT A WORD!
SHE...SHE SUMMONED AND HARVESTED YOUNG SOULS WITHOUT NUMBER...
YOUNG SOULS...
THE STOLEN GIRLS... ?

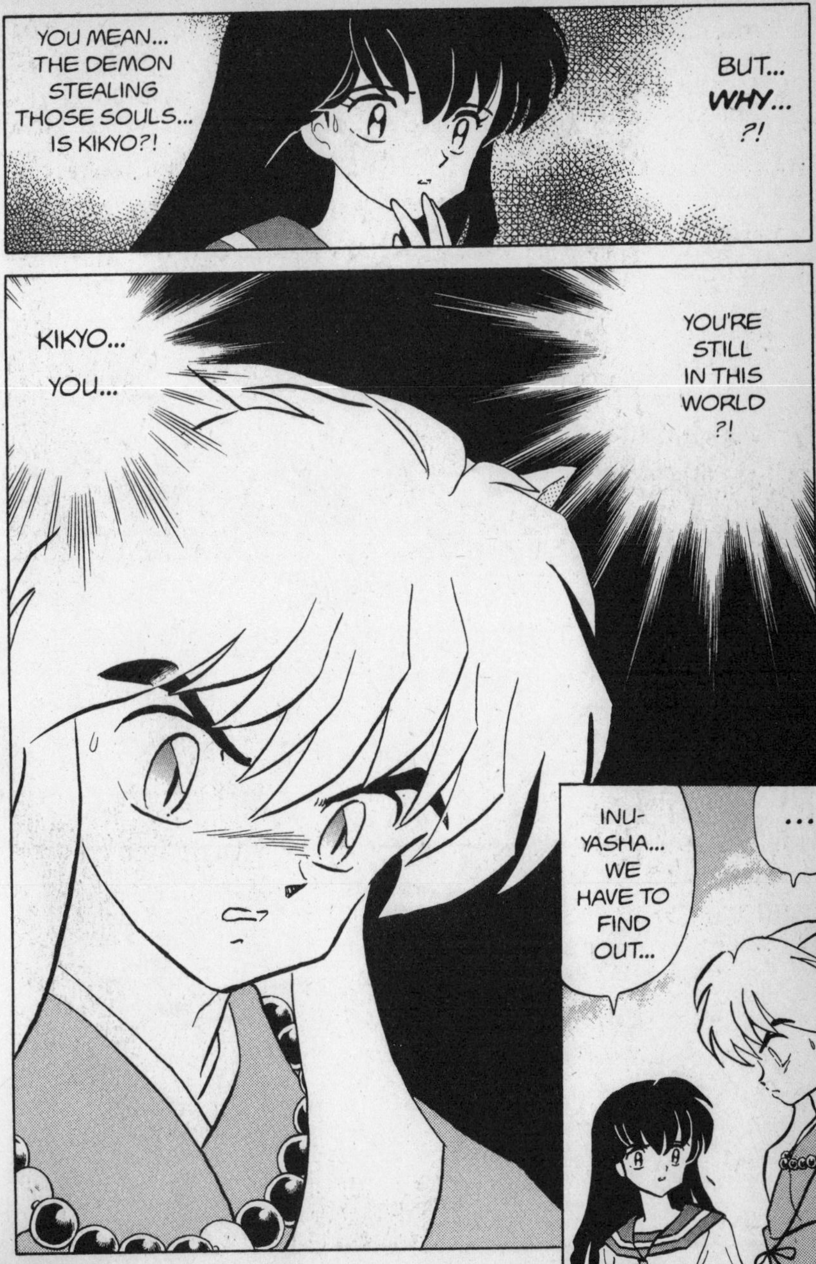
YOU MEAN... THE DEMON STEALING THOSE SOULS... IS KIKYO?!
BUT... WHY... ?!
KIKYO...
YOU...
YOU'RE STILL IN THIS WORLD ?!
INU-YASHA... WE HAVE TO FIND OUT...
...

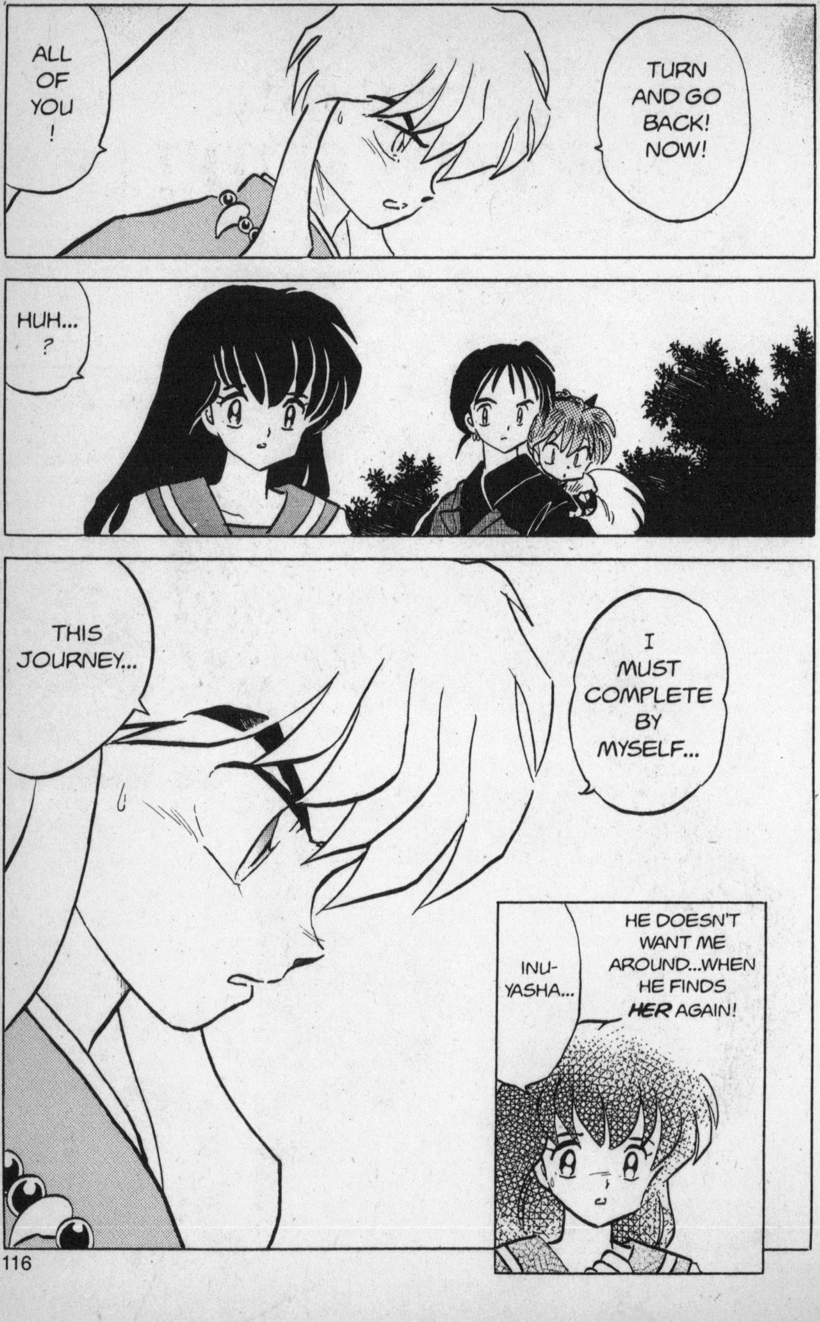
ALL OF YOU !
TURN AND GO BACK! NOW!
HUH... ?
THIS JOURNEY...
I MUST COMPLETE BY MYSELF...
INU-YASHA...
HE DOESN'T WANT ME AROUND...WHEN HE FINDS **HER** AGAIN!

SCROLL SEVEN
KIKYO'S SHIELD

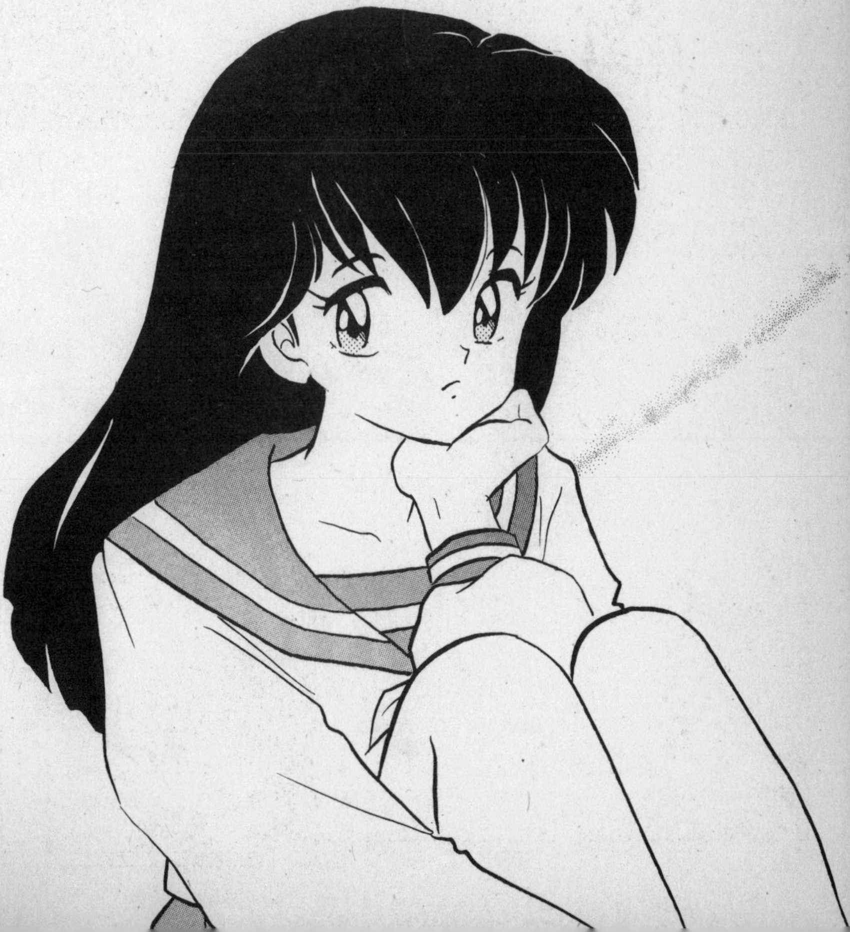

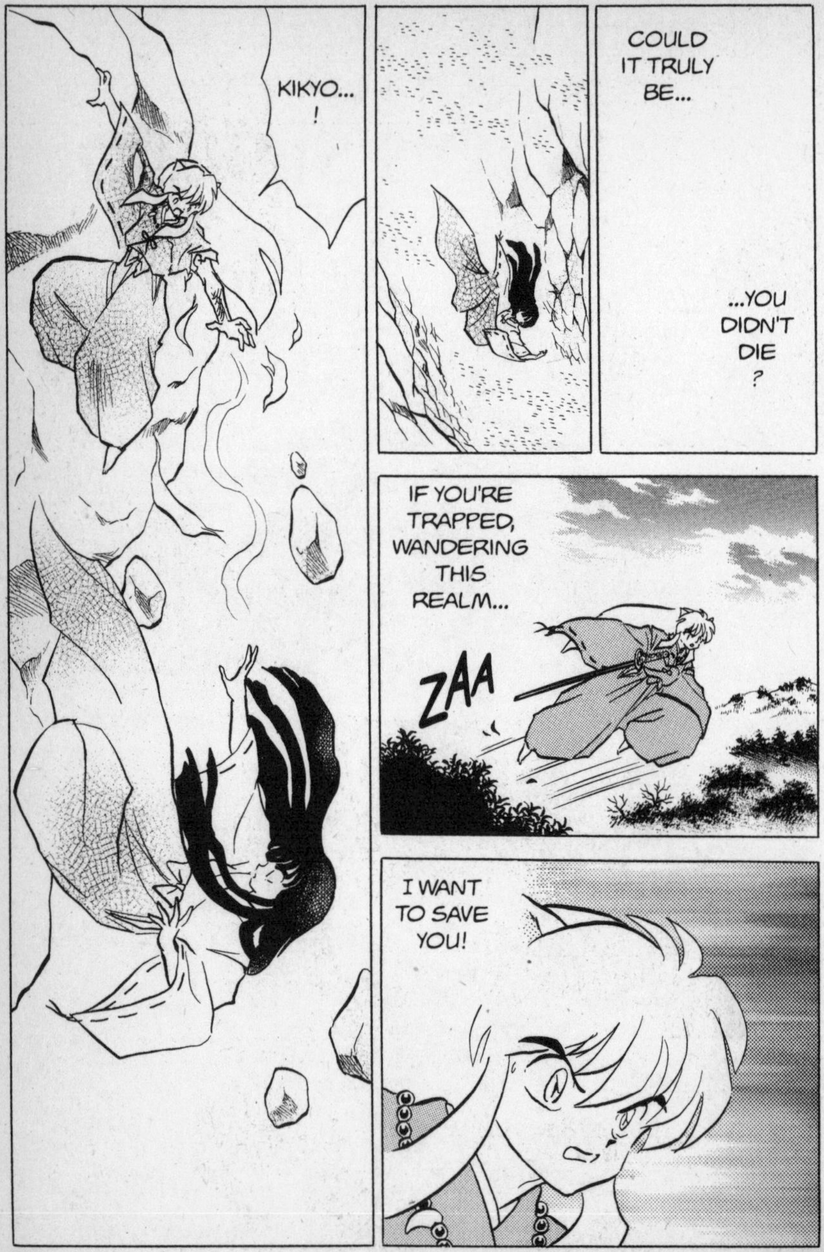
KIKYO... !
COULD IT TRULY BE...
...YOU DIDN'T DIE?
IF YOU'RE TRAPPED, WANDERING THIS REALM...
ZAA
I WANT TO SAVE YOU!

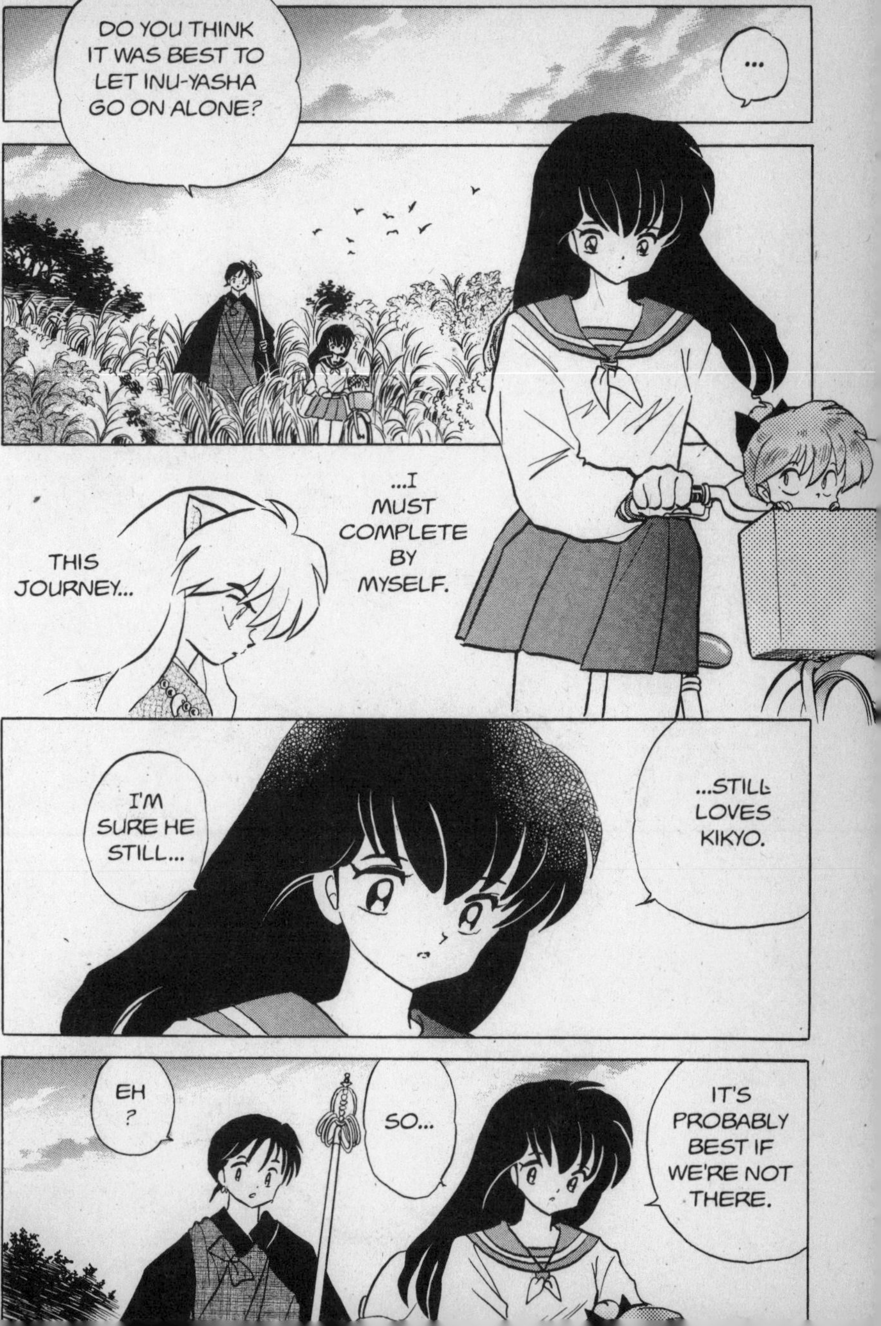
DO YOU THINK IT WAS BEST TO LET INU-YASHA GO ON ALONE?
...
THIS JOURNEY...
...I MUST COMPLETE BY MYSELF.
I'M SURE HE STILL...
...STILL LOVES KIKYO.
EH ?
SO...
IT'S PROBABLY BEST IF WE'RE NOT THERE.

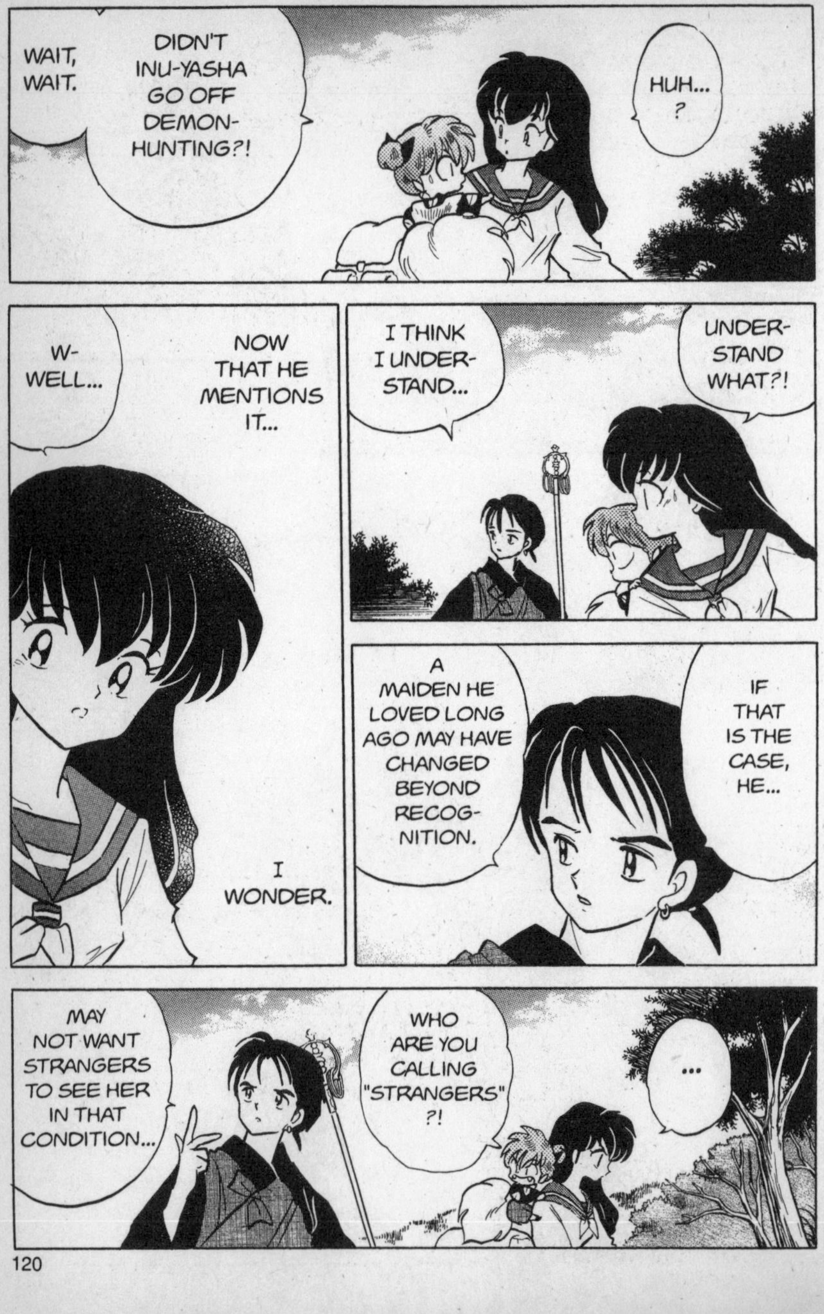
WAIT, WAIT.
DIDN'T INU-YASHA GO OFF DEMON-HUNTING?!
HUH...?
W-WELL...
NOW THAT HE MENTIONS IT...
I WONDER.
I THINK I UNDER-STAND...
UNDER-STAND WHAT?!
A MAIDEN HE LOVED LONG AGO MAY HAVE CHANGED BEYOND RECOG-NITION.
IF THAT IS THE CASE, HE...
MAY NOT WANT STRANGERS TO SEE HER IN THAT CONDITION...
WHO ARE YOU CALLING "STRANGERS"?!
...

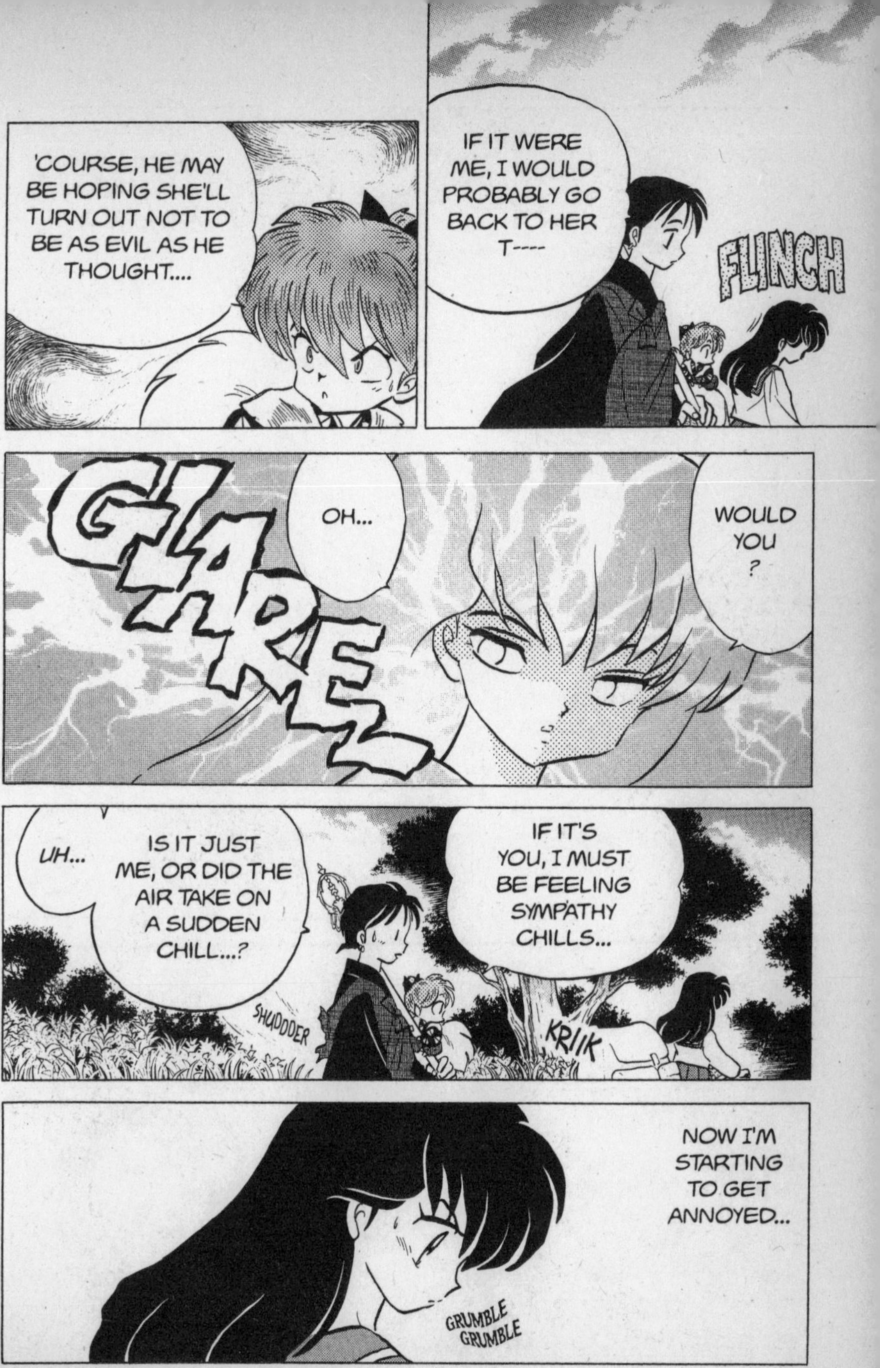
'COURSE, HE MAY BE HOPING SHE'LL TURN OUT NOT TO BE AS EVIL AS HE THOUGHT....
IF IT WERE ME, I WOULD PROBABLY GO BACK TO HER T----
FLINCH
GLARE
OH...
WOULD YOU ?
UH...
IS IT JUST ME, OR DID THE AIR TAKE ON A SUDDEN CHILL...?
SHUDDDER
IF IT'S YOU, I MUST BE FEELING SYMPATHY CHILLS...
KRIIK
NOW I'M STARTING TO GET ANNOYED...
GRUMBLE GRUMBLE

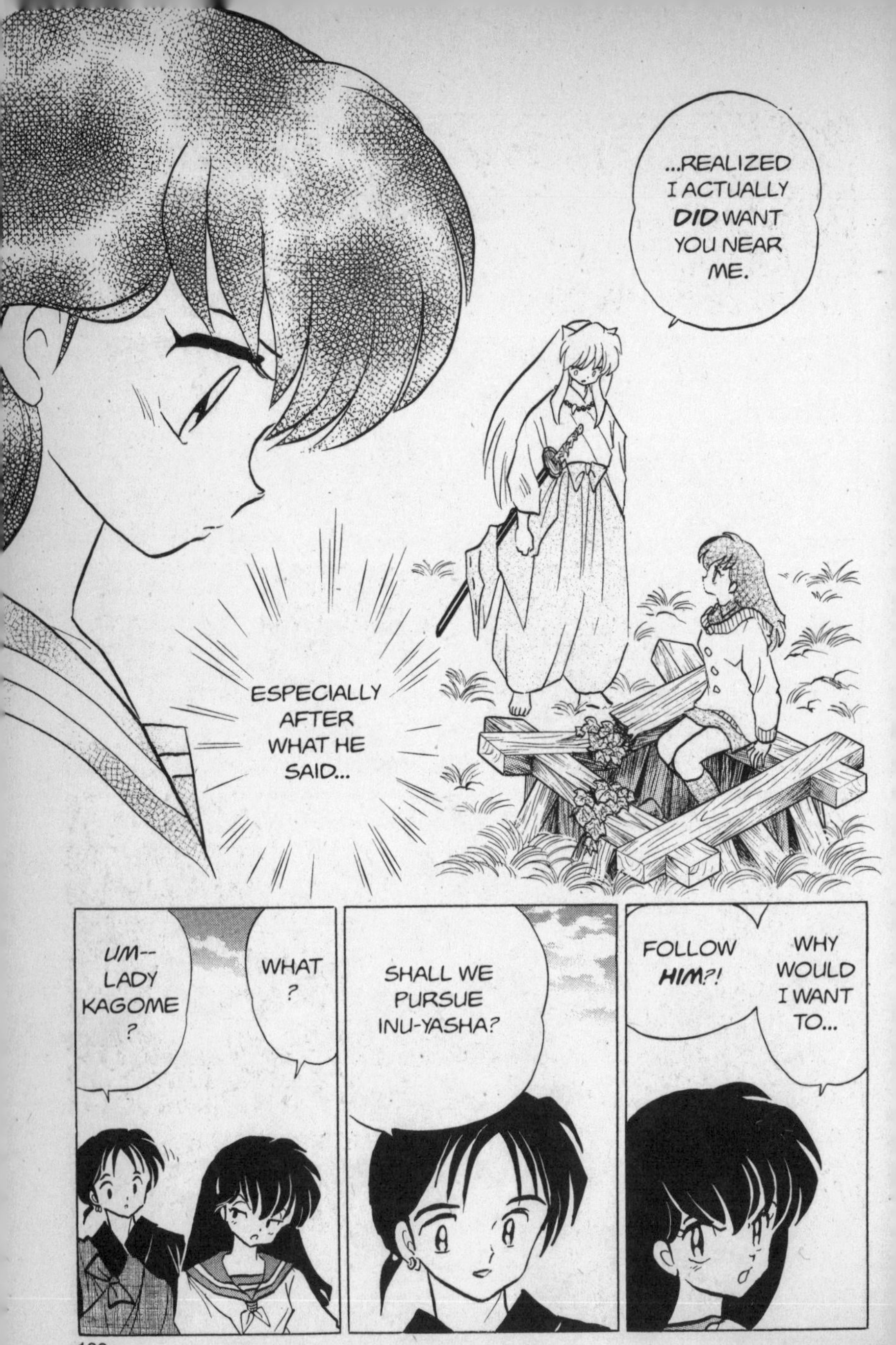
...REALIZED I ACTUALLY DID WANT YOU NEAR ME.
ESPECIALLY AFTER WHAT HE SAID...
UM-- LADY KAGOME?
WHAT?
SHALL WE PURSUE INU-YASHA?
FOLLOW HIM?!
WHY WOULD I WANT TO...

THIS IS... DEMON ENERGY ?!

SSHH...

GLINT...

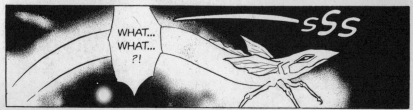

WHAT... WHAT... ?!

sSS

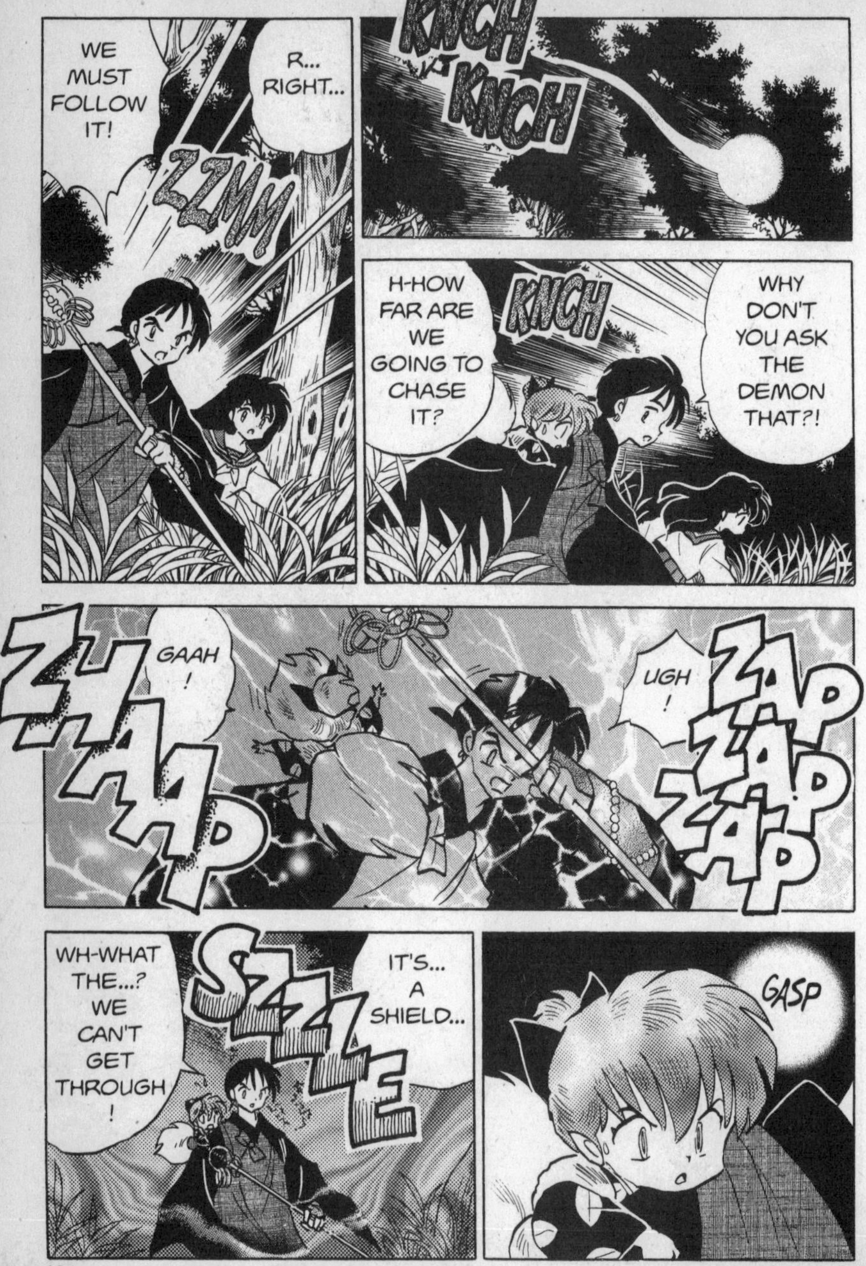
WE MUST FOLLOW IT!
R... RIGHT...
ZZMM
KNCH KNCH
H-HOW FAR ARE WE GOING TO CHASE IT?
KNCH
WHY DON'T YOU ASK THE DEMON THAT?!
ZHAAP
GAAH!
UGH!
ZAP ZAP ZAP
WH-WHAT THE...? WE CAN'T GET THROUGH!
SZZZLE
IT'S... A SHIELD...
GASP

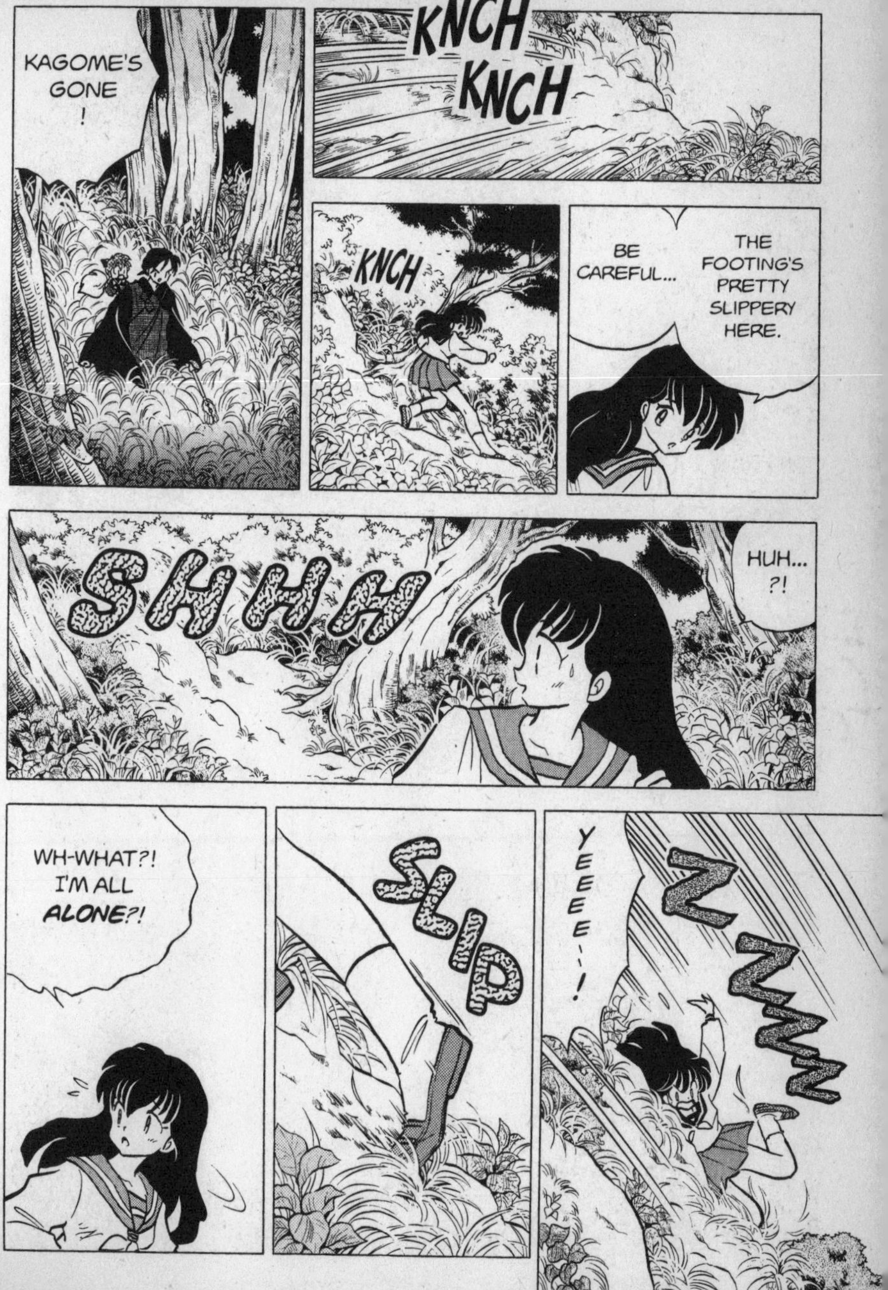
KAGOME'S GONE !
KNCH KNCH
KNCH
BE CAREFUL...
THE FOOTING'S PRETTY SLIPPERY HERE.
SHHH
HUH... ?!
WH-WHAT?! I'M ALL ***ALONE***?!
SLIP
YEEEE...!
ZZZZ

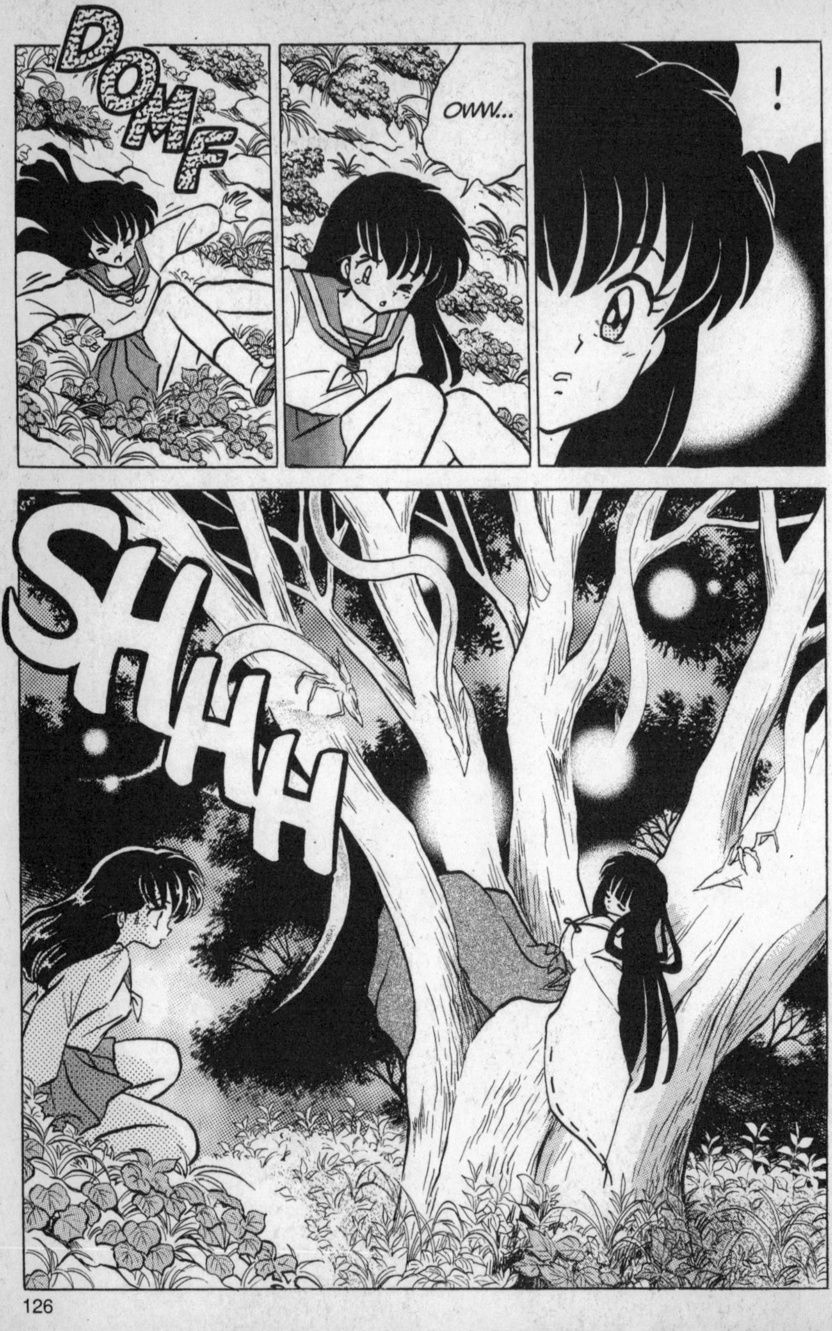
DOMF
OWW...
!
SHHHH

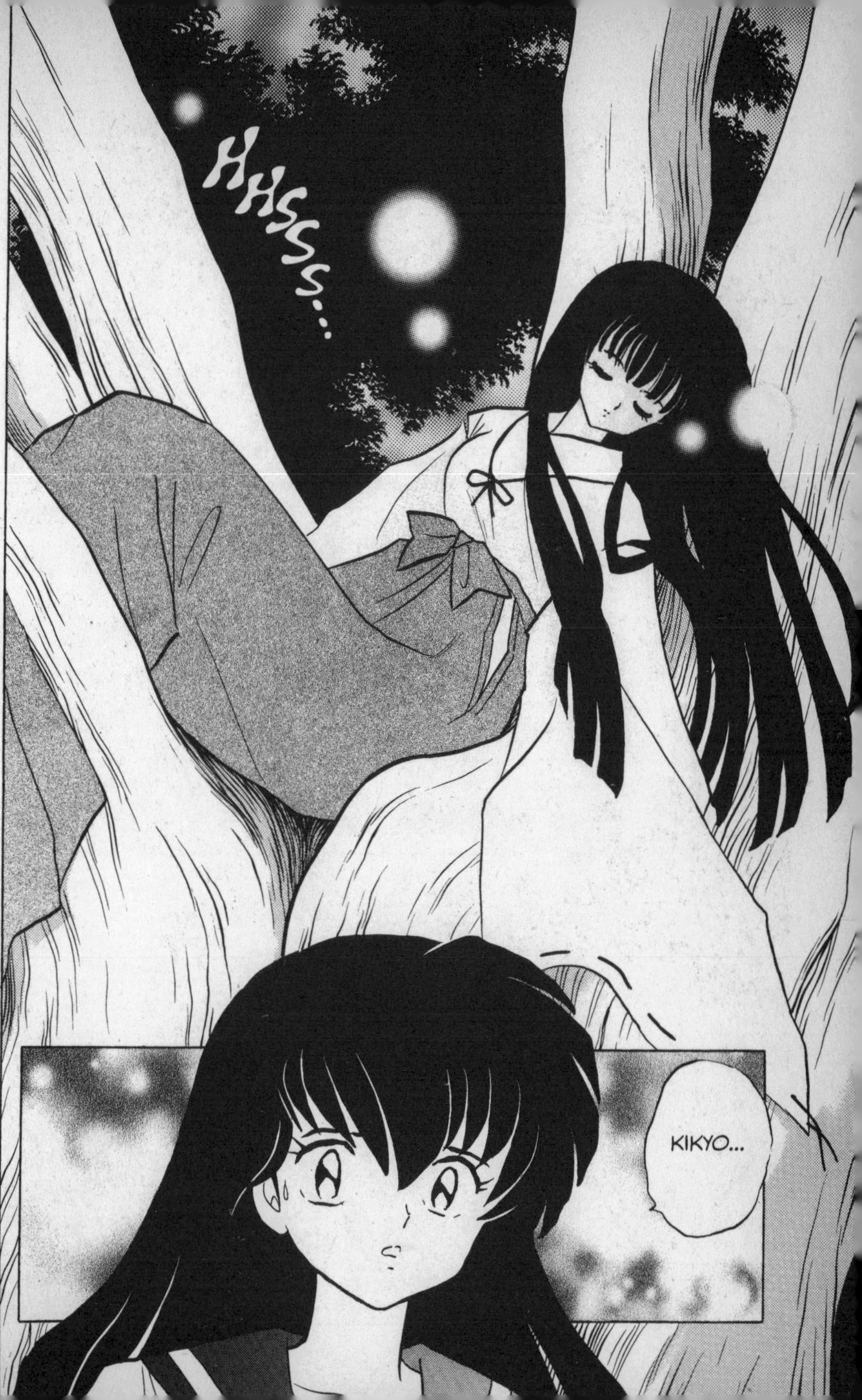
HHSSS...
KIKYO...

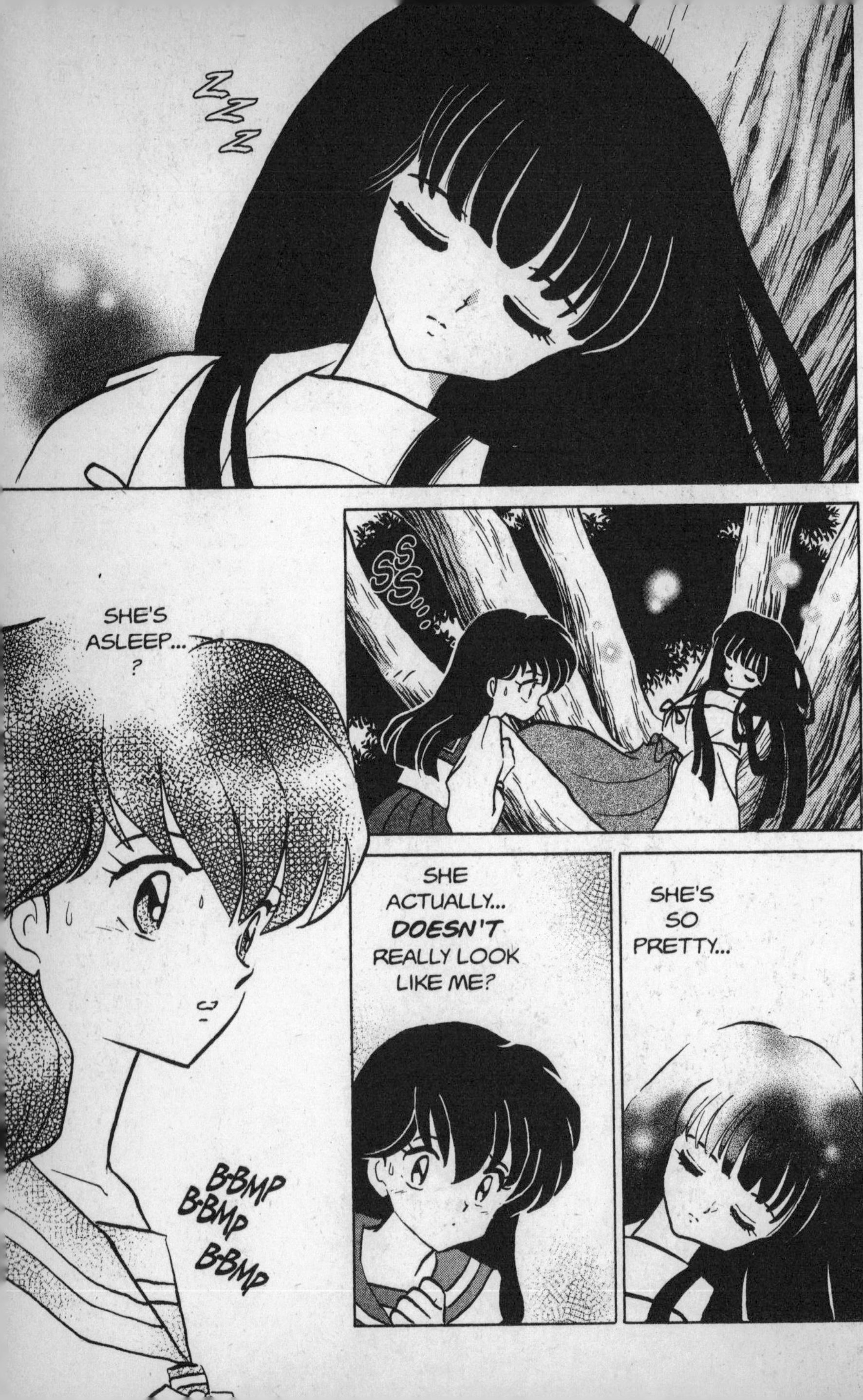
ZZZ
SHE'S ASLEEP...?
B-BMP B-BMP B-BMP
SSS...
SHE ACTUALLY... DOESN'T REALLY LOOK LIKE ME?
SHE'S SO PRETTY...

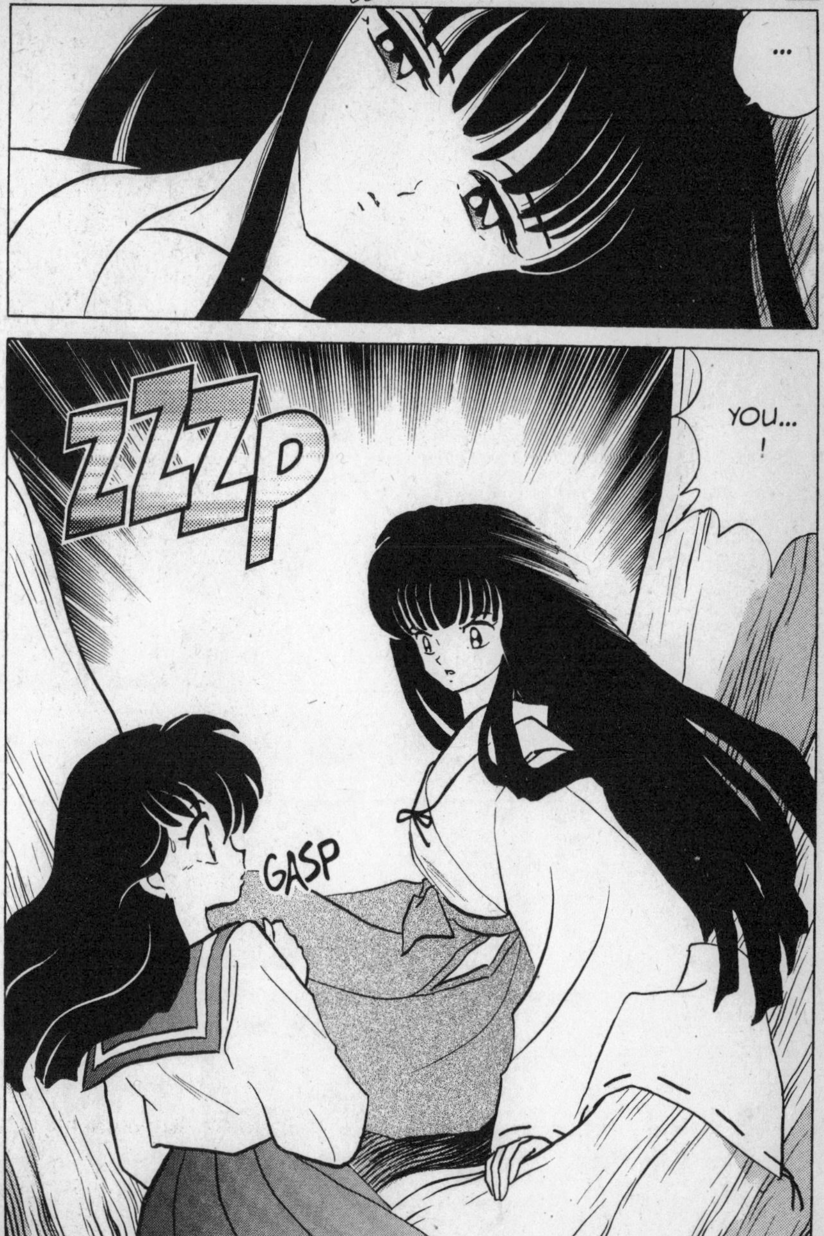
BLINK
...
ZZZP
YOU... !
GASP

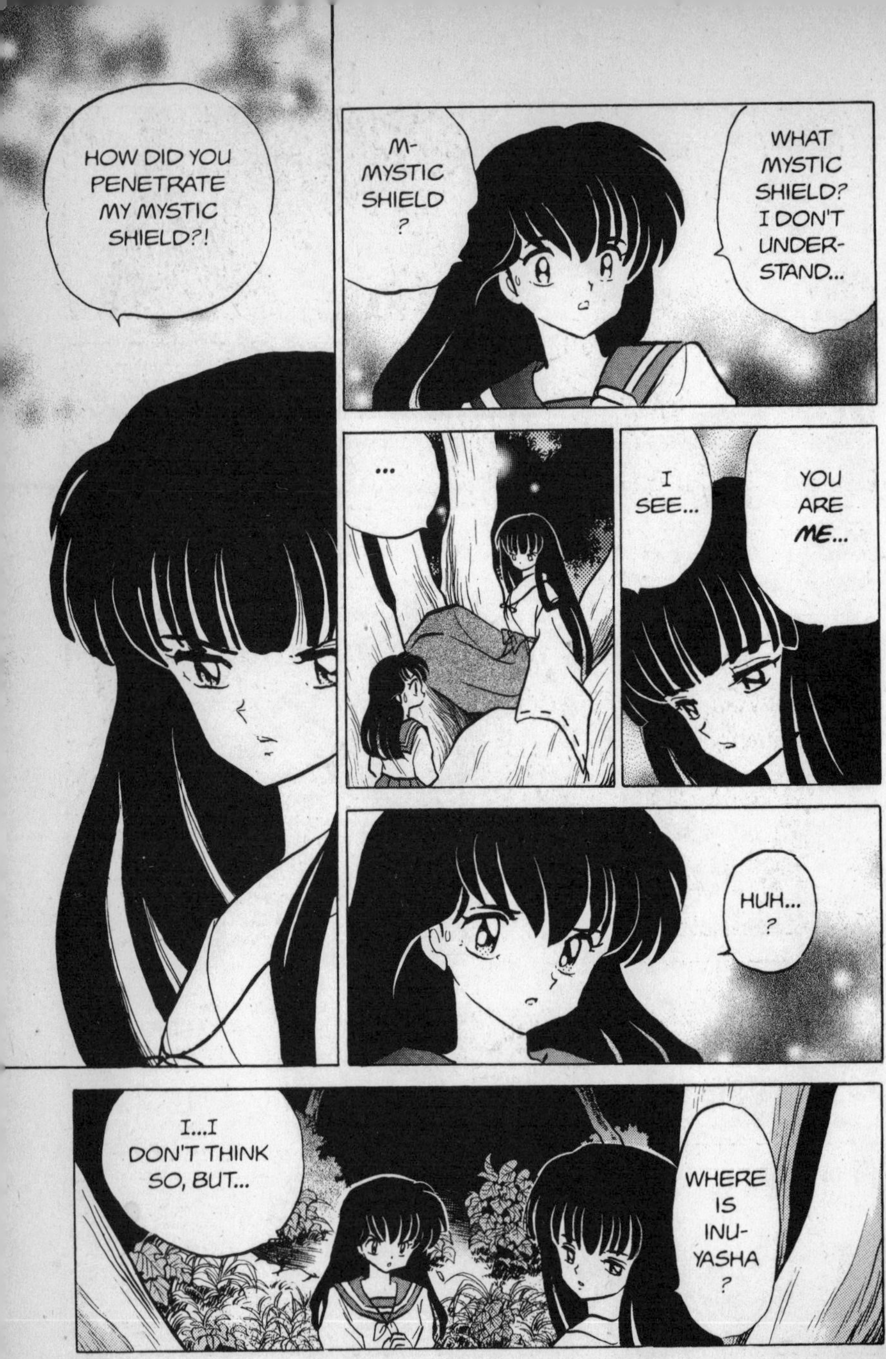
HOW DID YOU PENETRATE MY MYSTIC SHIELD?!
M- MYSTIC SHIELD ?
WHAT MYSTIC SHIELD? I DON'T UNDER- STAND...
...
I SEE...
YOU ARE *ME*...
HUH... ?
I...I DON'T THINK SO, BUT...
WHERE IS INU- YASHA ?

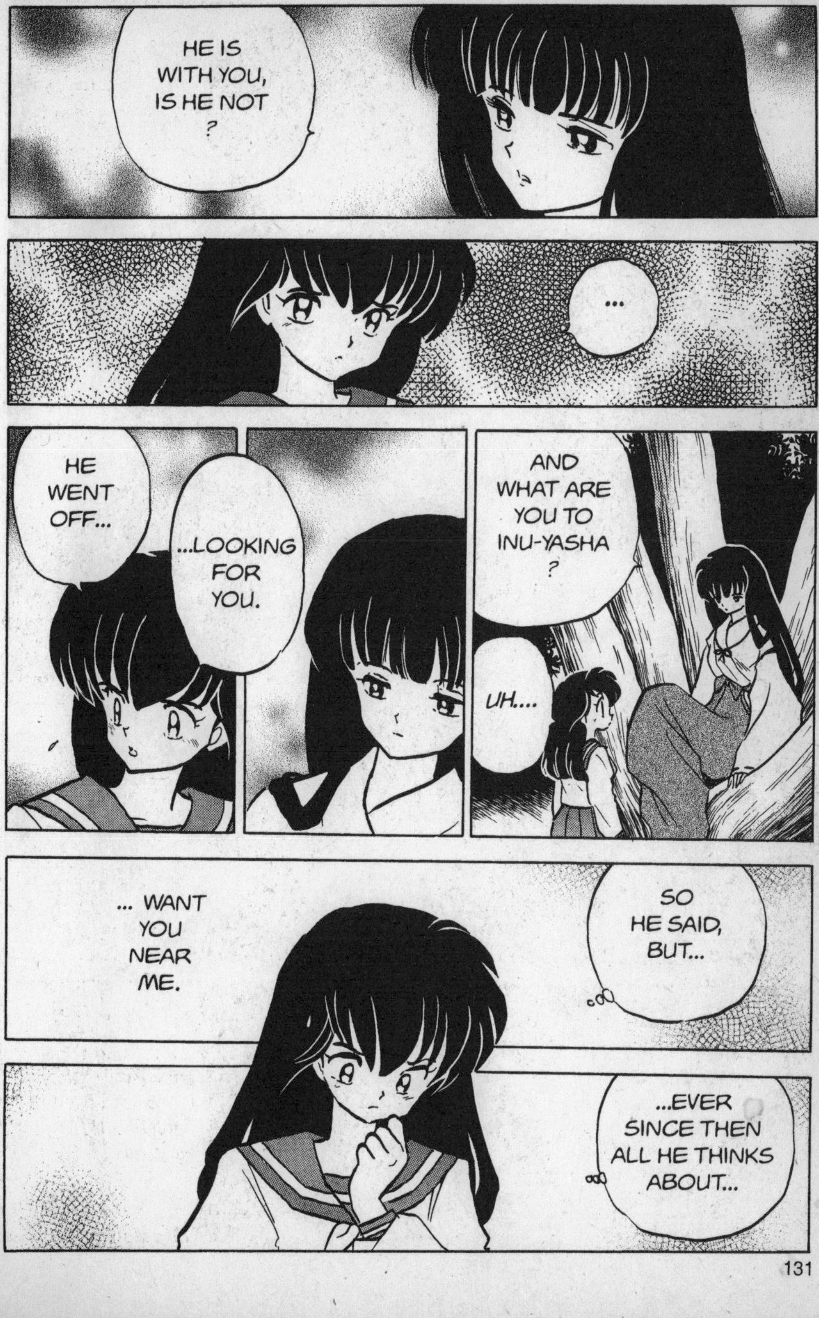
HE IS WITH YOU, IS HE NOT ?
...
HE WENT OFF...
...LOOKING FOR YOU.
AND WHAT ARE YOU TO INU-YASHA ?
UH....
... WANT YOU NEAR ME.
SO HE SAID, BUT...
...EVER SINCE THEN ALL HE THINKS ABOUT...

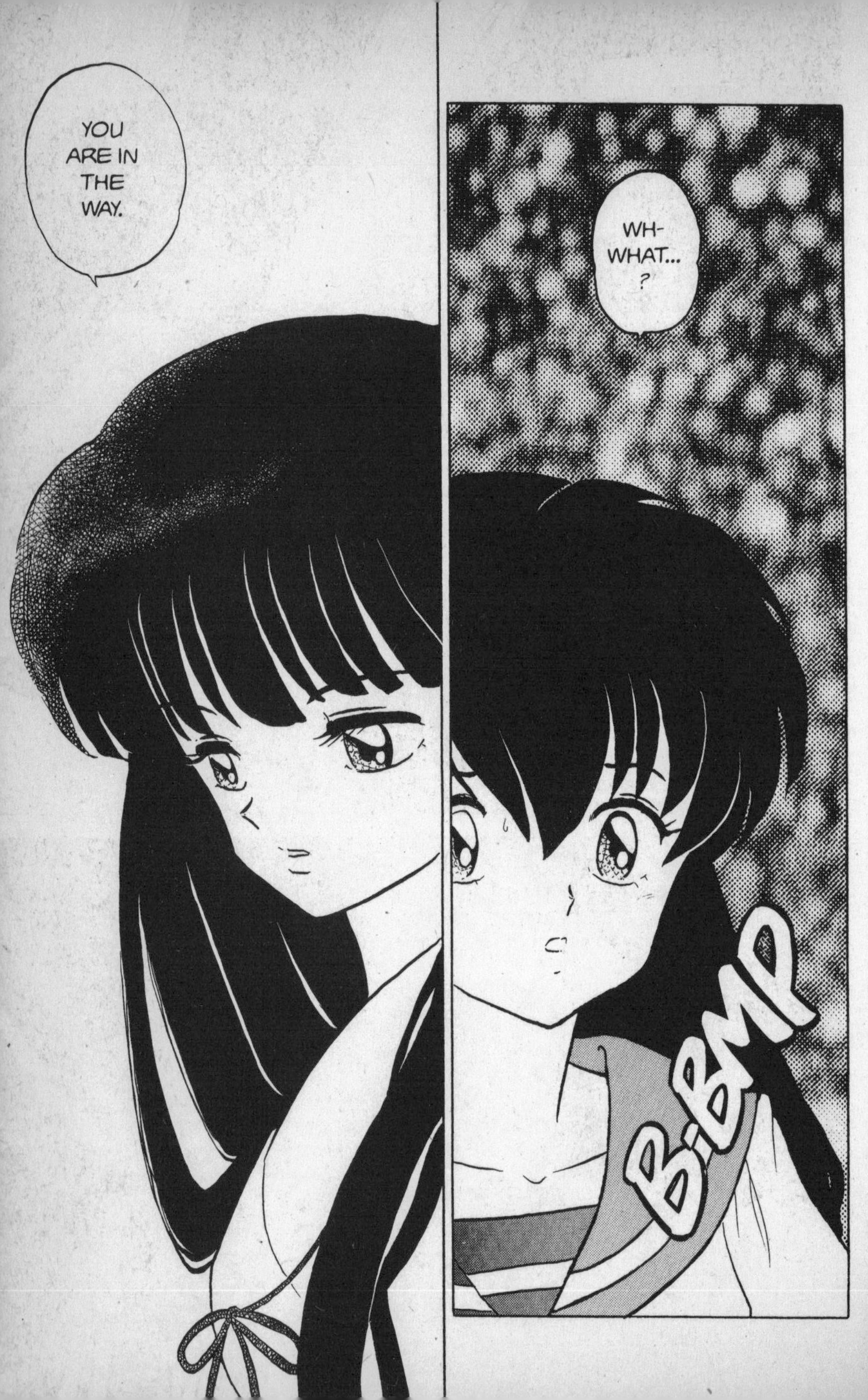
YOU ARE IN THE WAY.
WH- WHAT...?
B-BMP

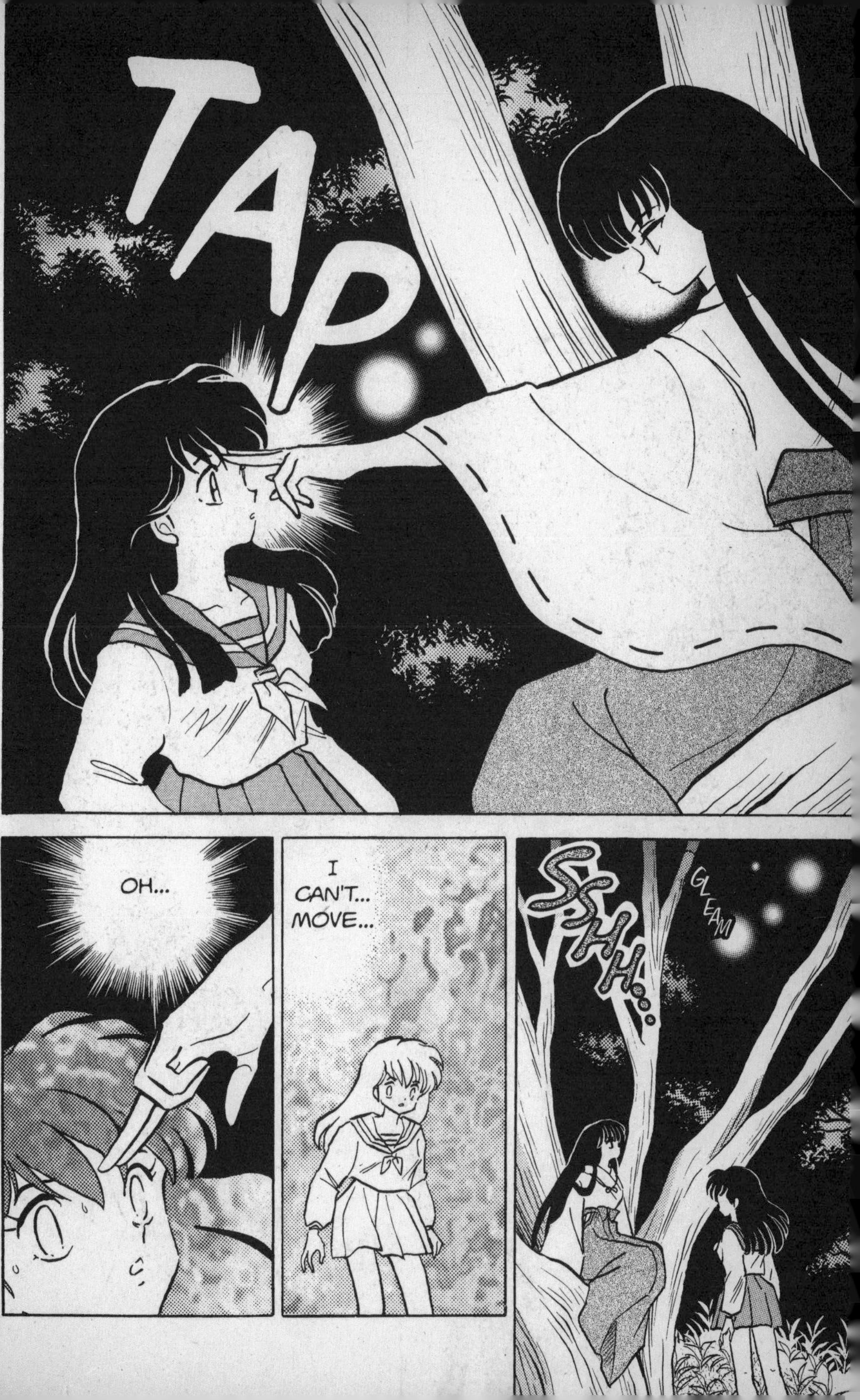
TAP
OH...
I CAN'T... MOVE...
SSHH...
GLEAM

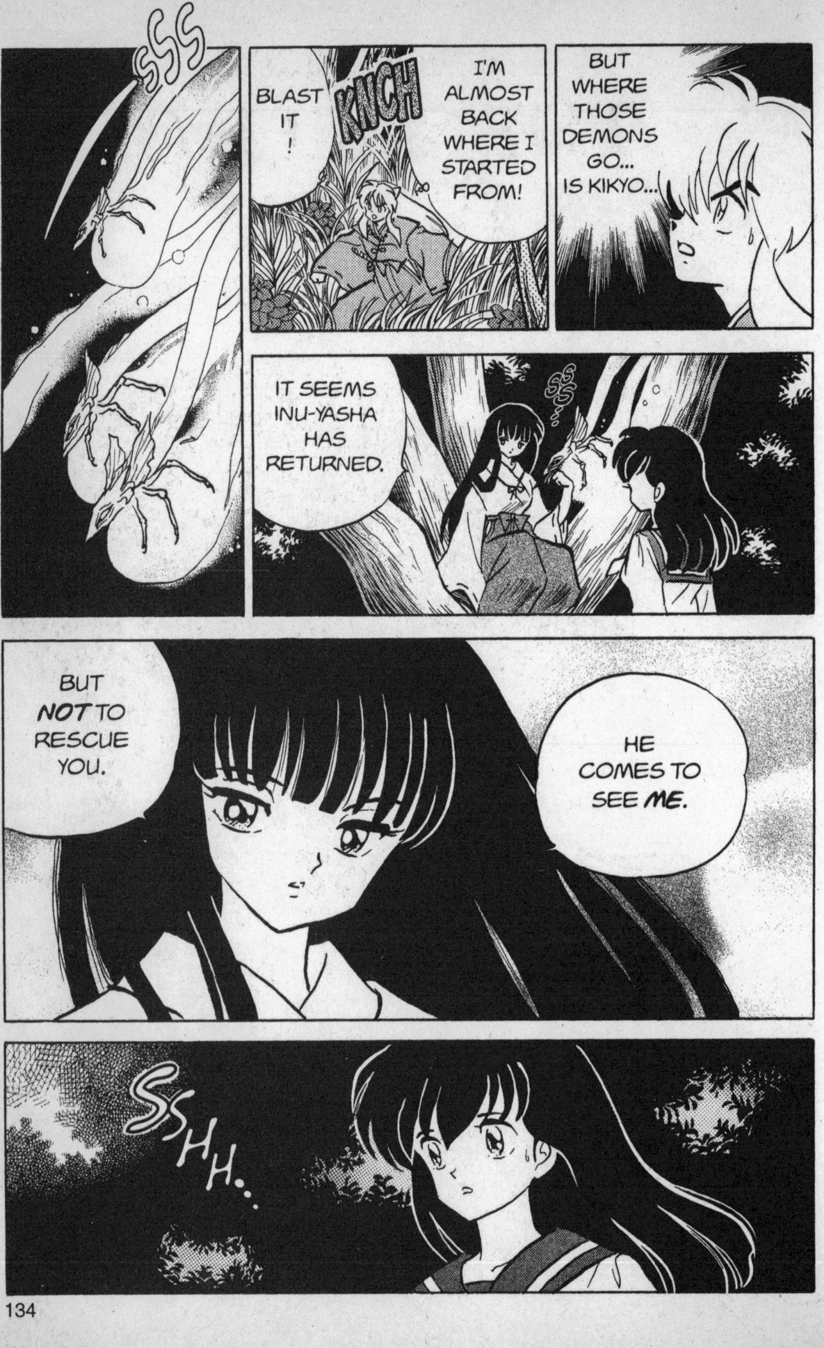
SSS
BLAST IT!
KNCH
I'M ALMOST BACK WHERE I STARTED FROM!
BUT WHERE THOSE DEMONS GO... IS KIKYO...
IT SEEMS INU-YASHA HAS RETURNED.
SSS
BUT *NOT* TO RESCUE YOU.
HE COMES TO SEE *ME*.
SSHH...

SCROLL EIGHT

THE SMELL OF DEATH

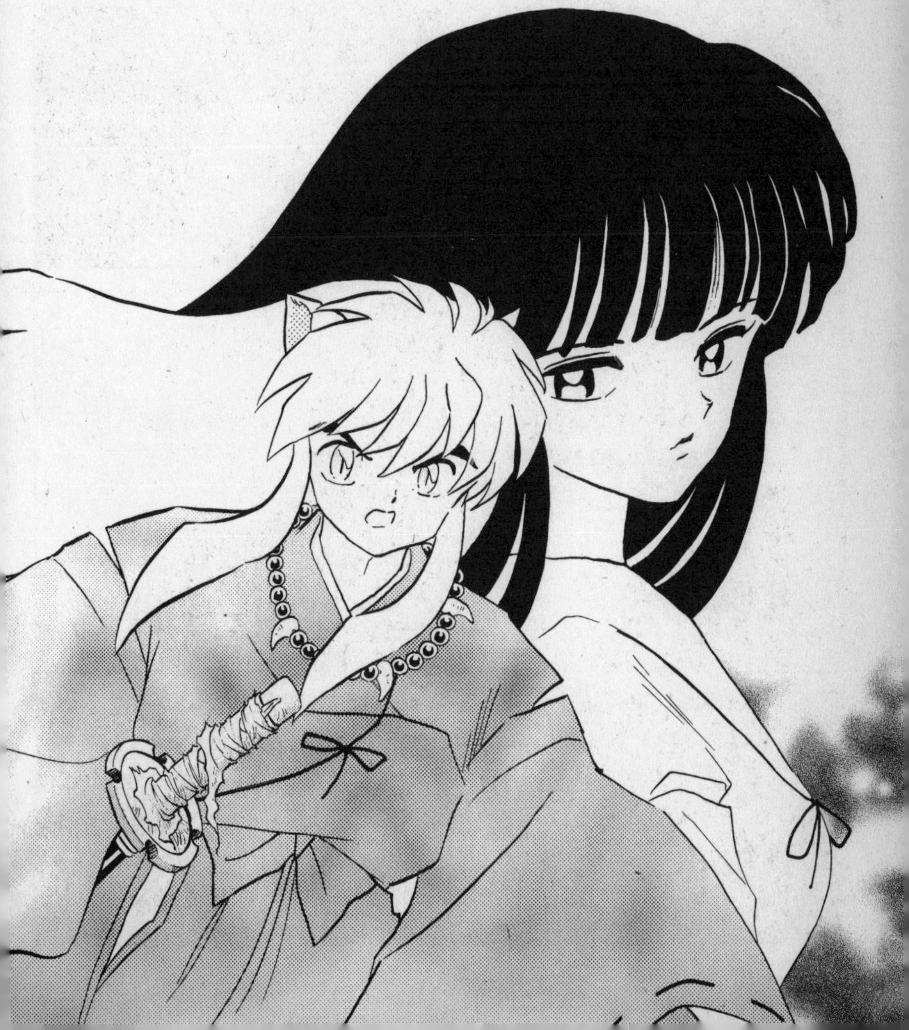

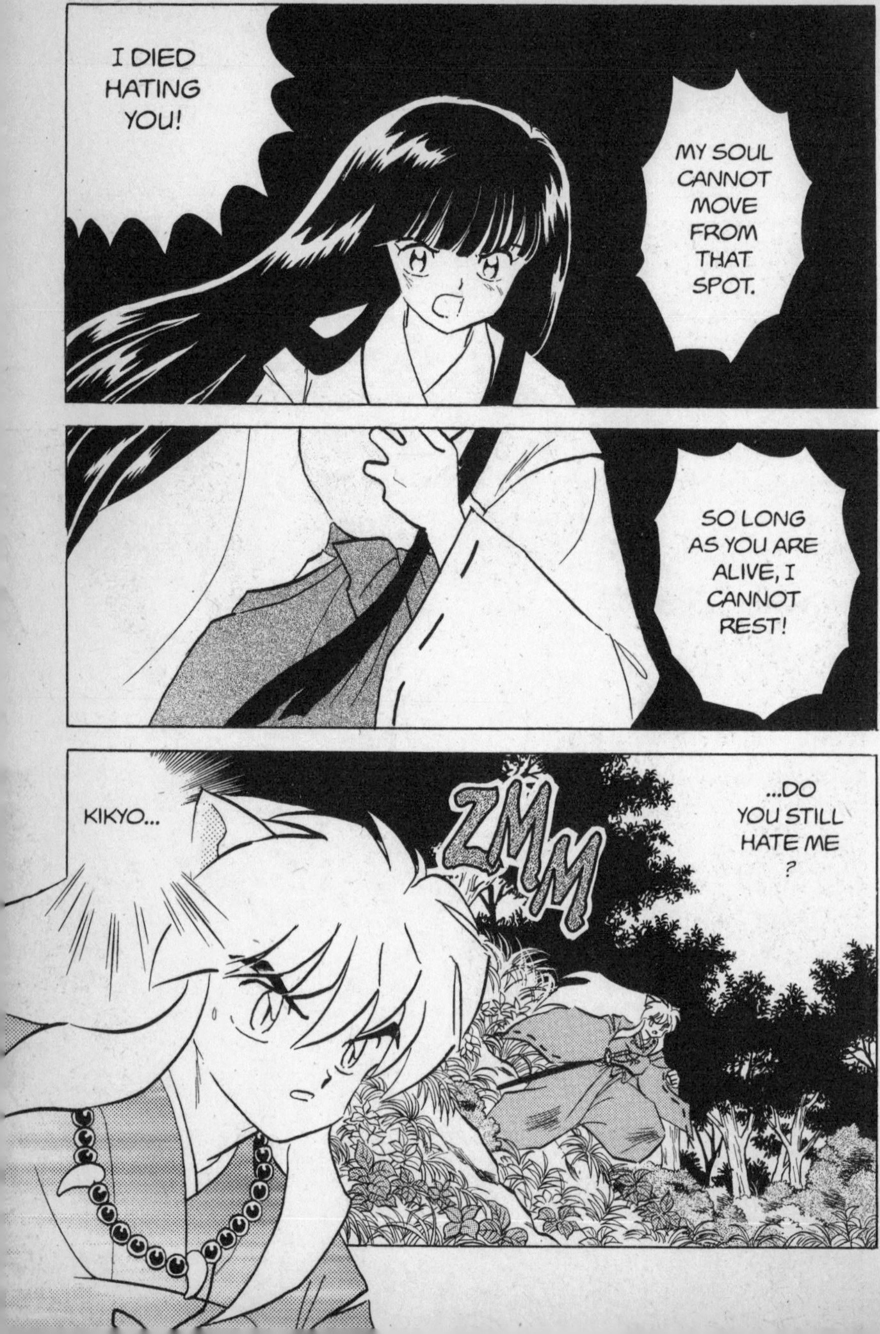
I DIED HATING YOU!
MY SOUL CANNOT MOVE FROM THAT SPOT.
SO LONG AS YOU ARE ALIVE, I CANNOT REST!
KIKYO...
ZMM
...DO YOU STILL HATE ME ?

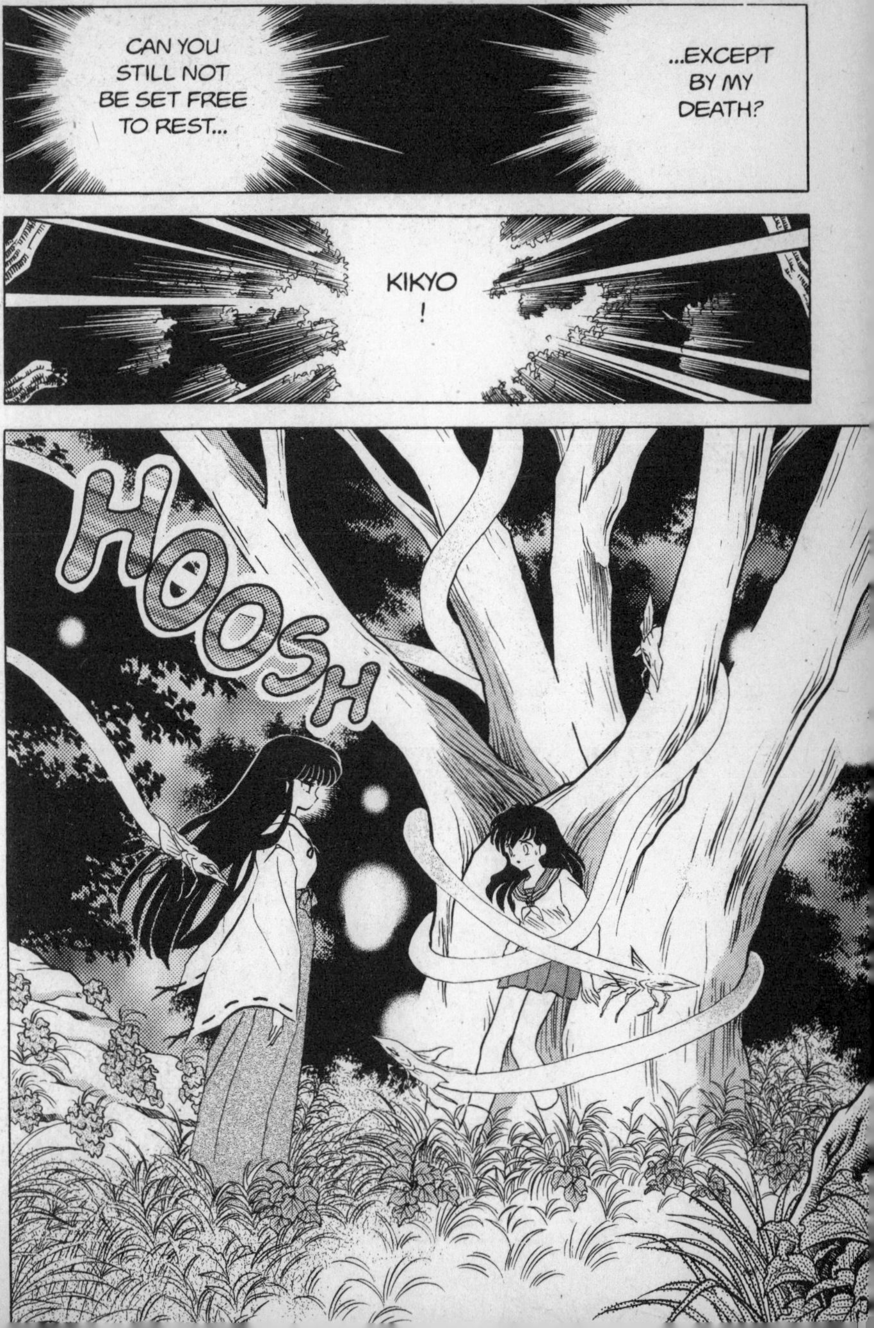
CAN YOU STILL NOT BE SET FREE TO REST...
...EXCEPT BY MY DEATH?
KIKYO !
HOOSH

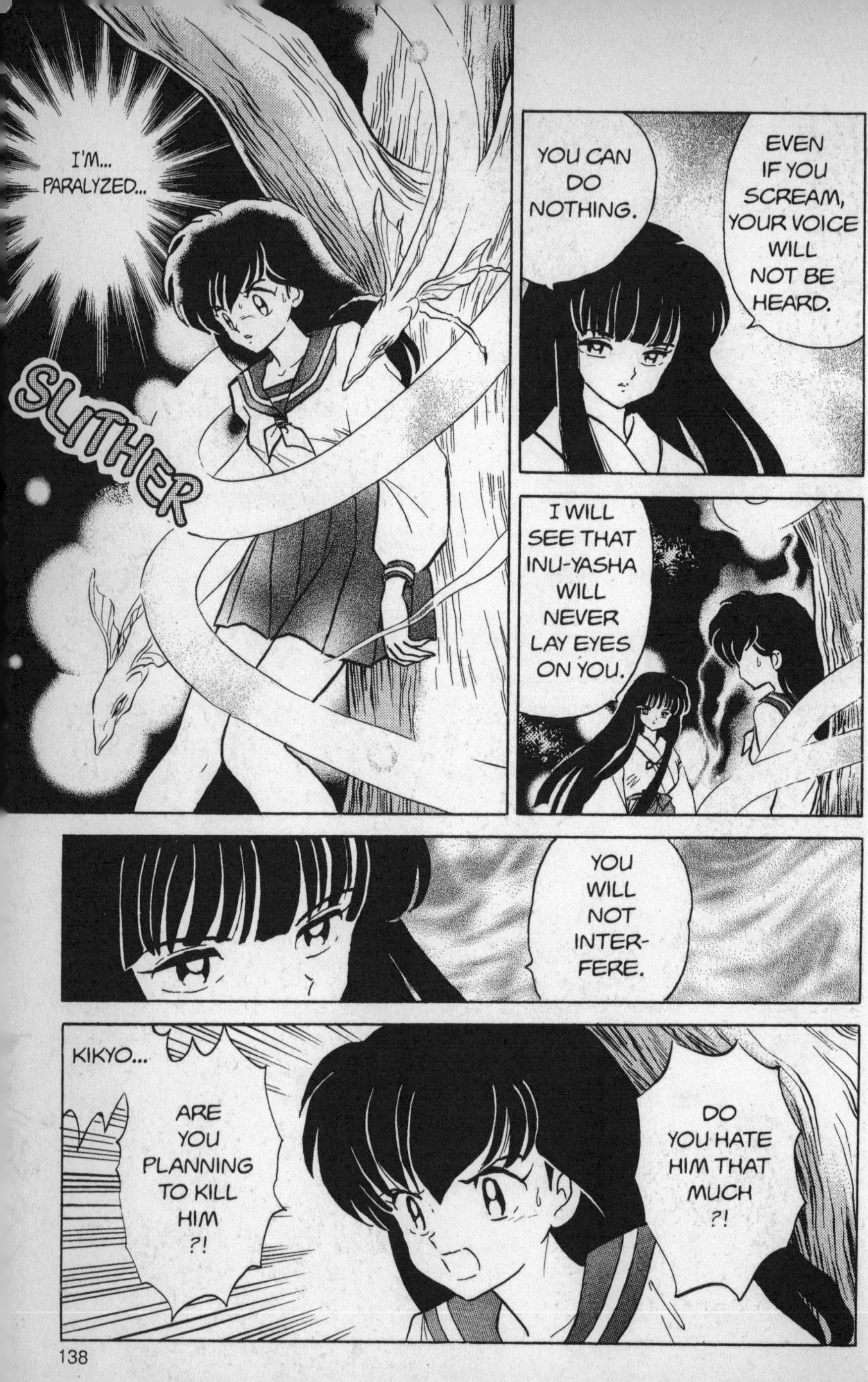
I'M... PARALYZED...
SLITHER
YOU CAN DO NOTHING.
EVEN IF YOU SCREAM, YOUR VOICE WILL NOT BE HEARD.
I WILL SEE THAT INU-YASHA WILL NEVER LAY EYES ON YOU.
YOU WILL NOT INTER-FERE.
KIKYO...
ARE YOU PLANNING TO KILL HIM ?!
DO YOU HATE HIM THAT MUCH ?!

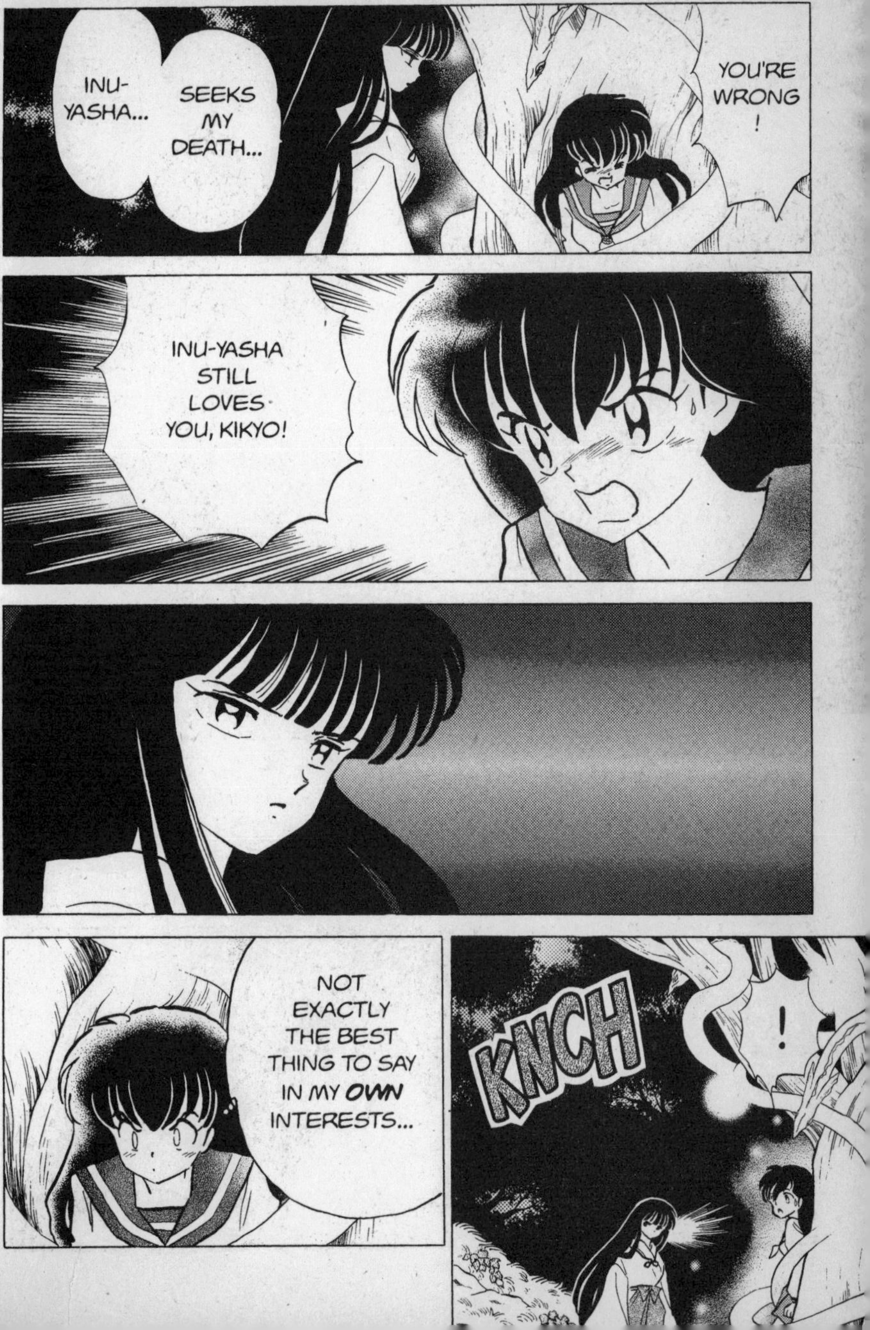
INU-YASHA...
SEEKS MY DEATH...
YOU'RE WRONG !
INU-YASHA STILL LOVES YOU, KIKYO!
NOT EXACTLY THE BEST THING TO SAY IN MY OWN INTERESTS...
KNCH
!

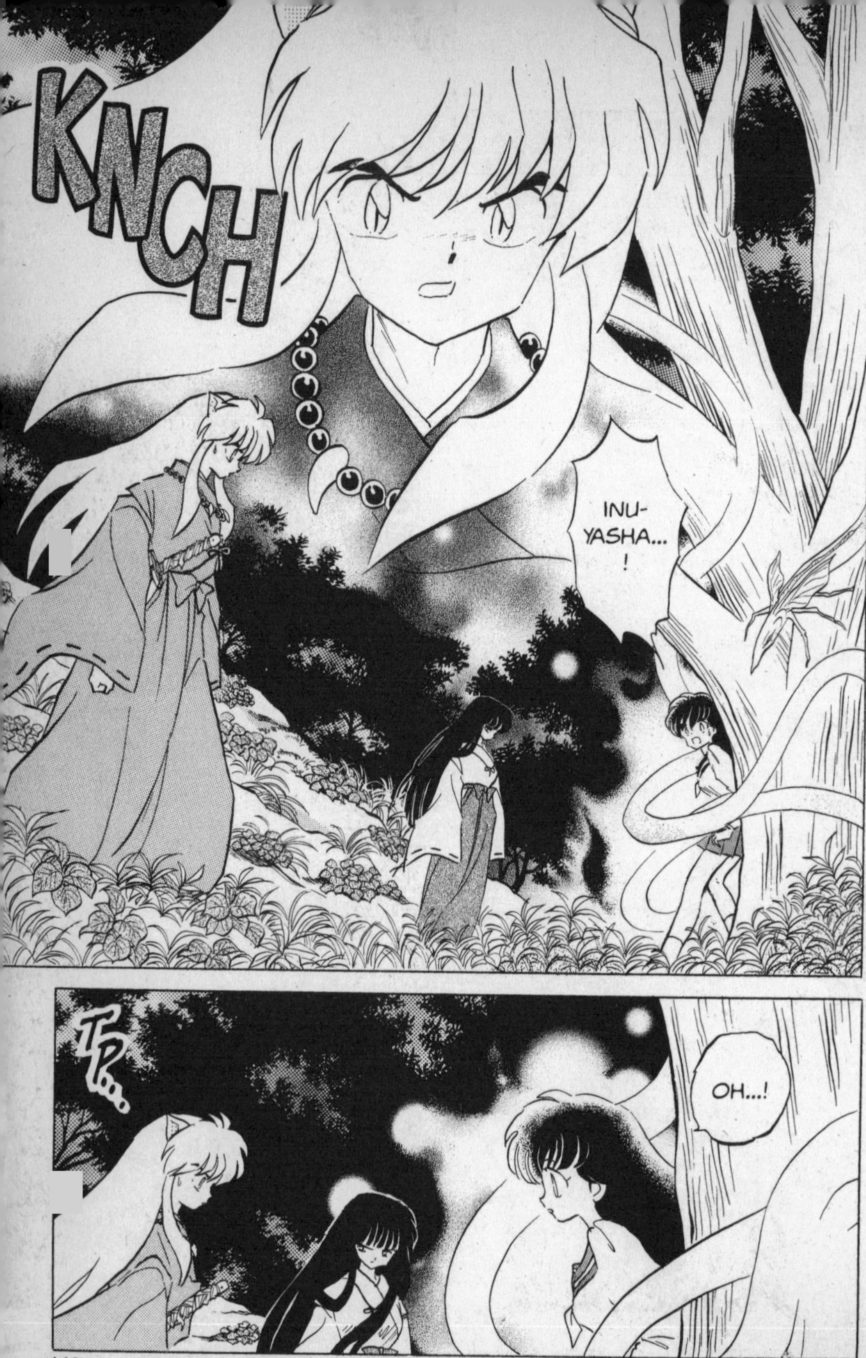
KNCH
INU-YASHA...!
TP...
OH...!

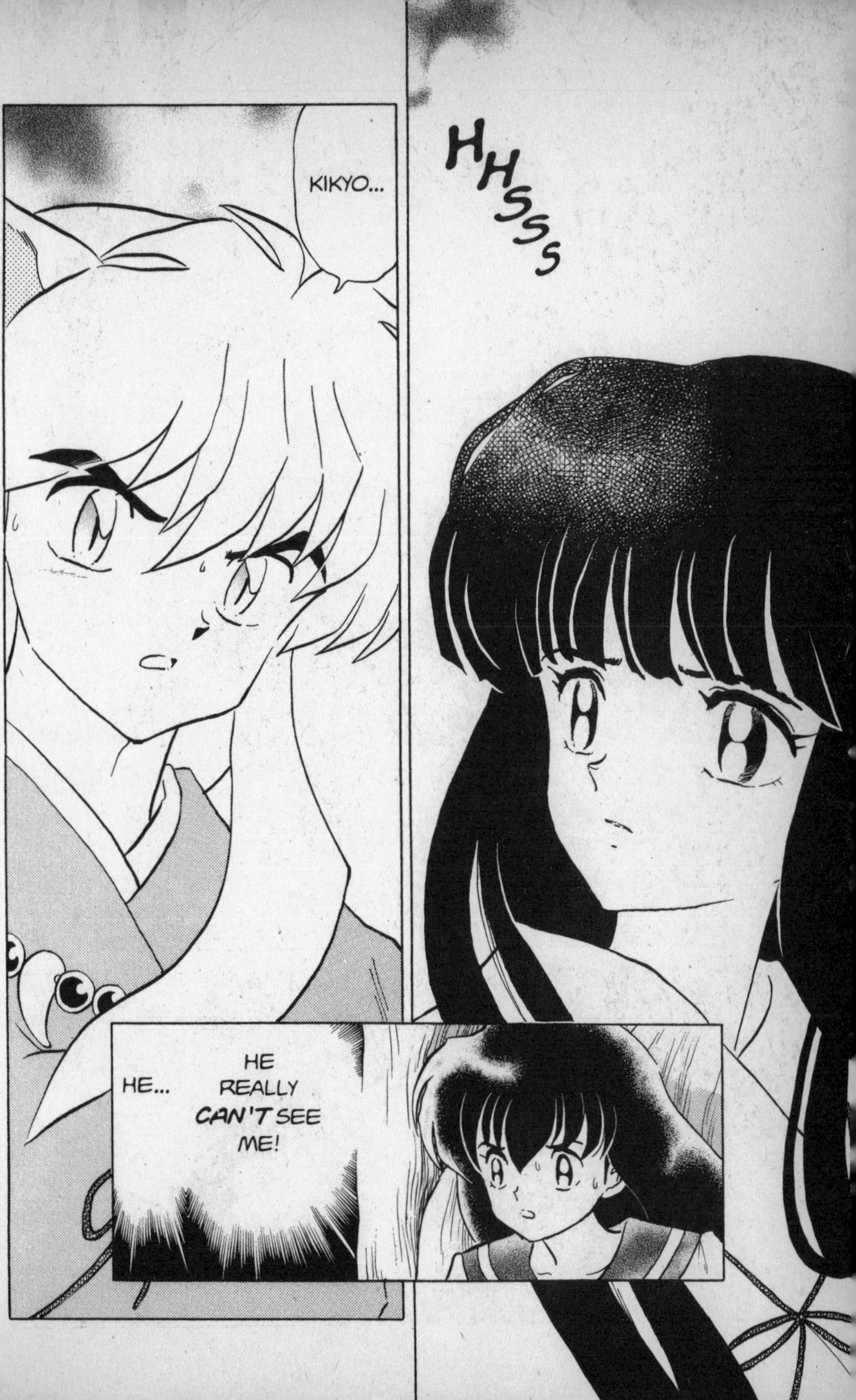
KIKYO...
HHSSSS
HE...
HE REALLY *CAN'T* SEE ME!

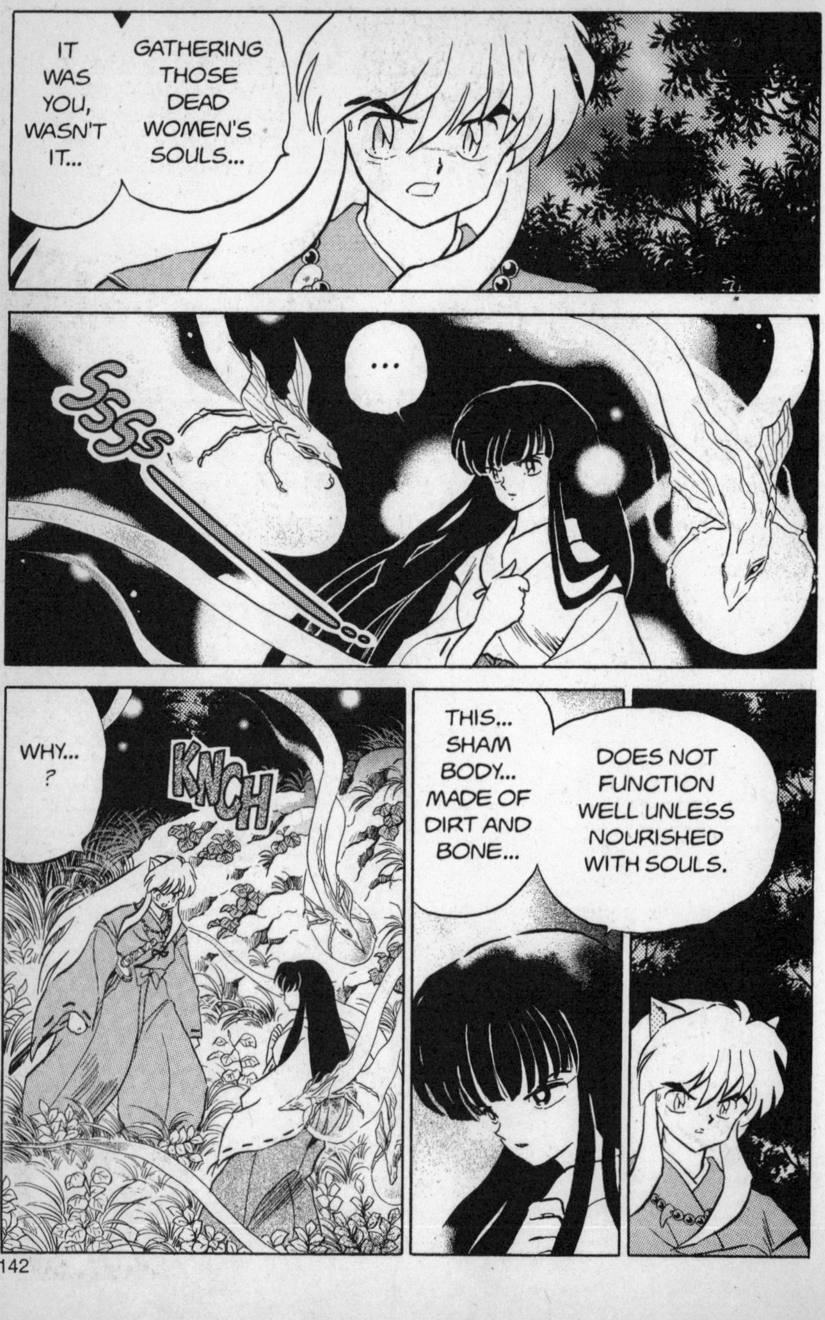
IT WAS YOU, WASN'T IT...
GATHERING THOSE DEAD WOMEN'S SOULS...
...
SSSSS
WHY... ?
KNCH
THIS... SHAM BODY... MADE OF DIRT AND BONE...
DOES NOT FUNCTION WELL UNLESS NOURISHED WITH SOULS.

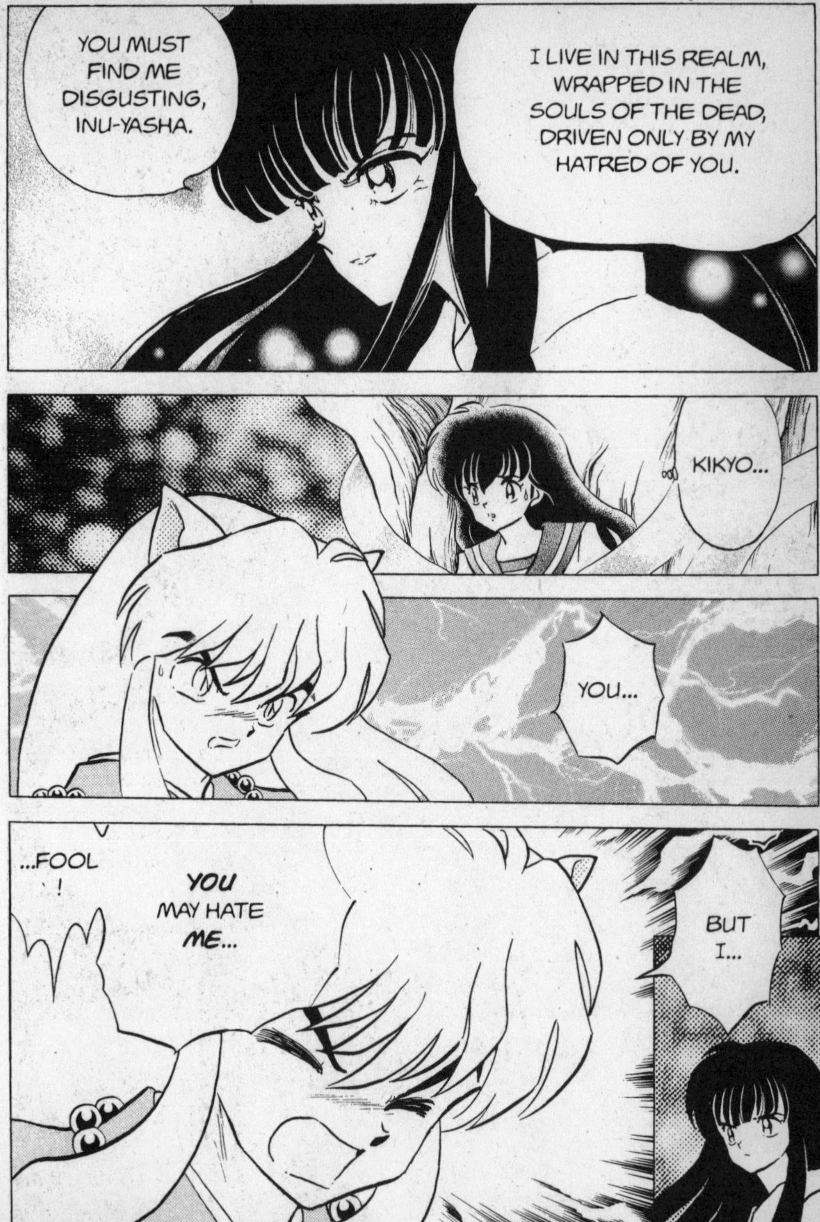
YOU MUST FIND ME DISGUSTING, INU-YASHA.
I LIVE IN THIS REALM, WRAPPED IN THE SOULS OF THE DEAD, DRIVEN ONLY BY MY HATRED OF YOU.
KIKYO...
YOU...
...FOOL!
YOU MAY HATE ME...
BUT I...

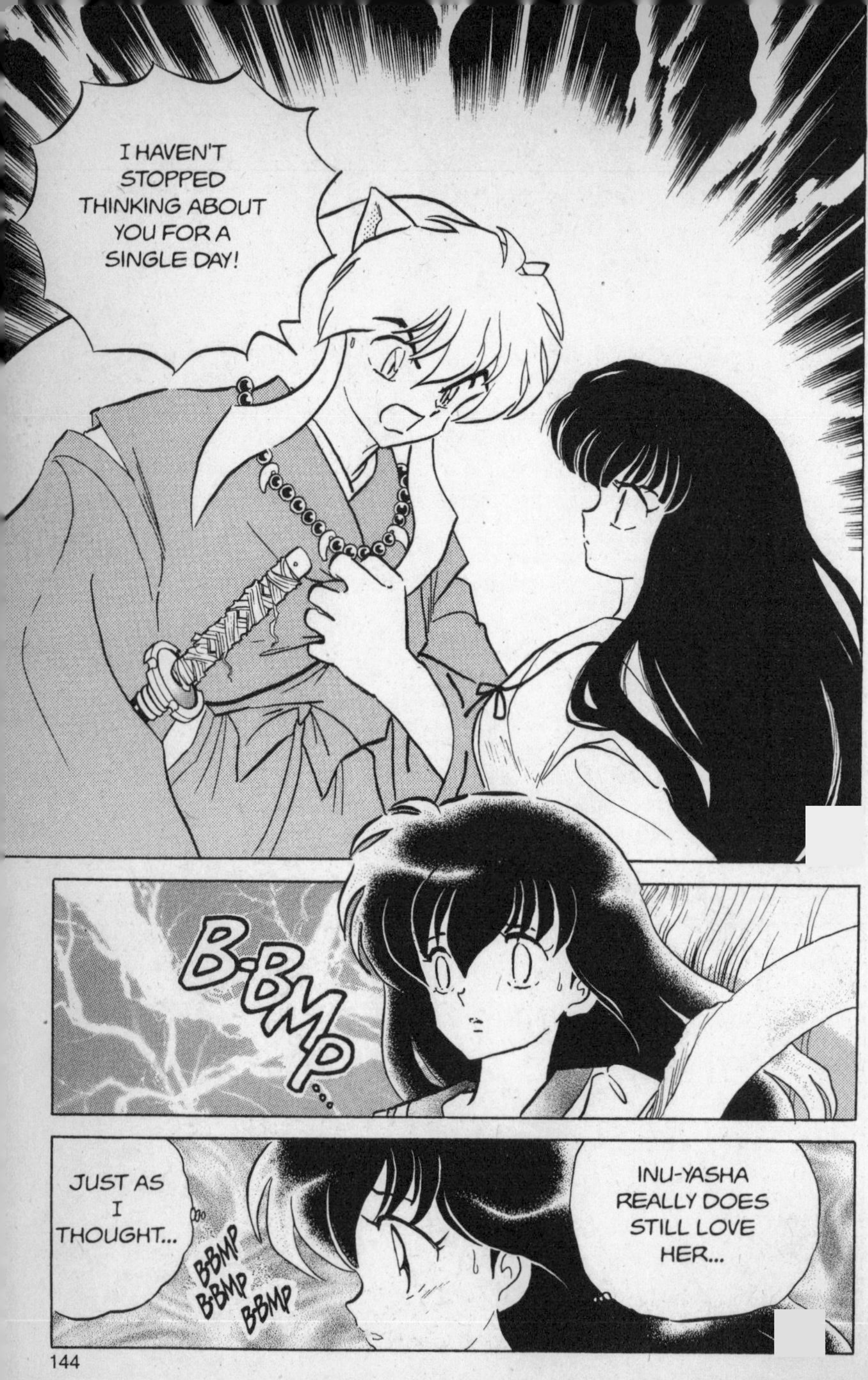
I HAVEN'T STOPPED THINKING ABOUT YOU FOR A SINGLE DAY!
B-BMP...
JUST AS I THOUGHT...
B-BMP B-BMP B-BMP
INU-YASHA REALLY DOES STILL LOVE HER...

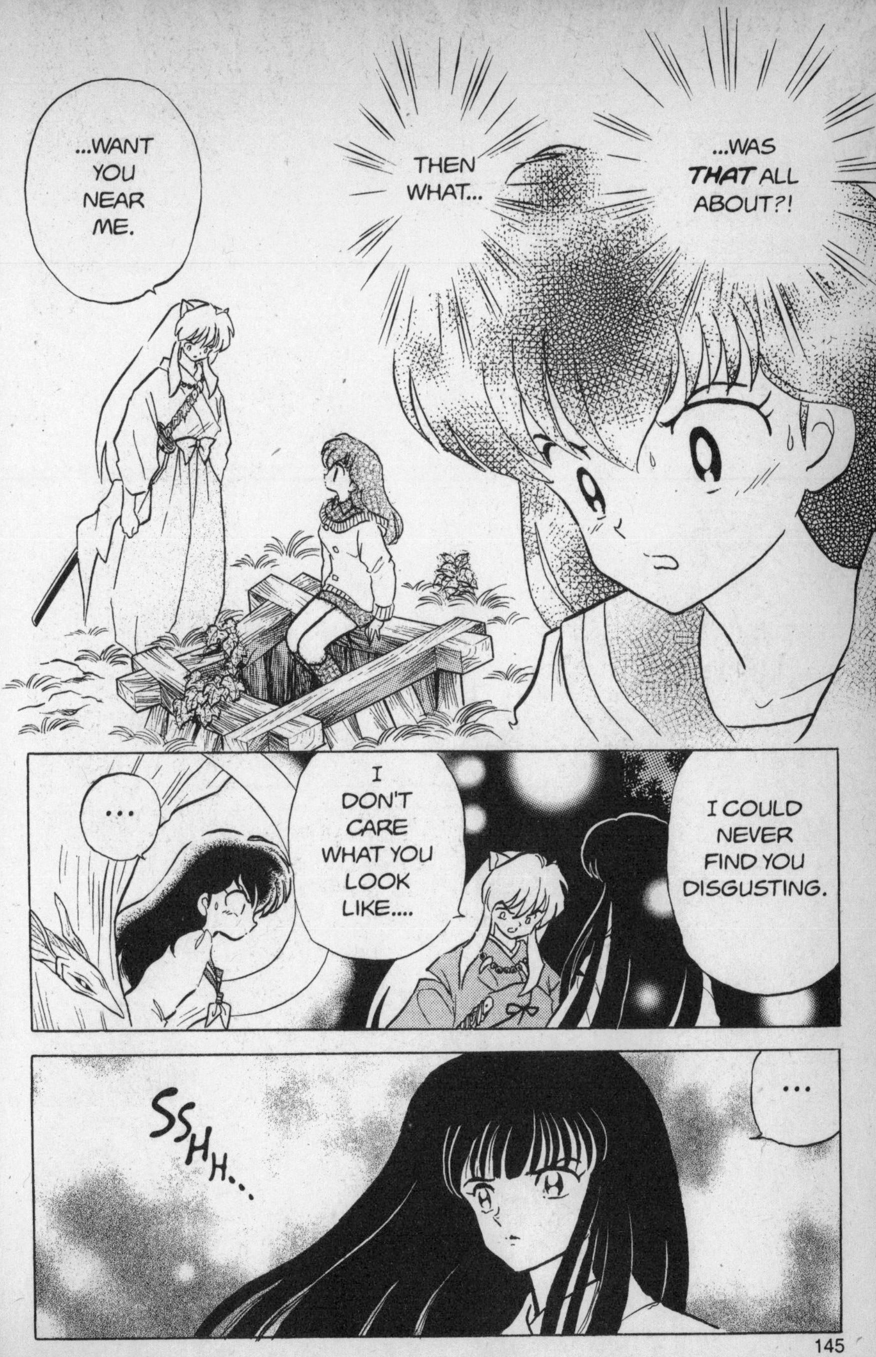

...WANT YOU NEAR ME.
THEN WHAT...
...WAS **THAT** ALL ABOUT?!
...
I DON'T CARE WHAT YOU LOOK LIKE....
I COULD NEVER FIND YOU DISGUSTING.
SSHH...
...

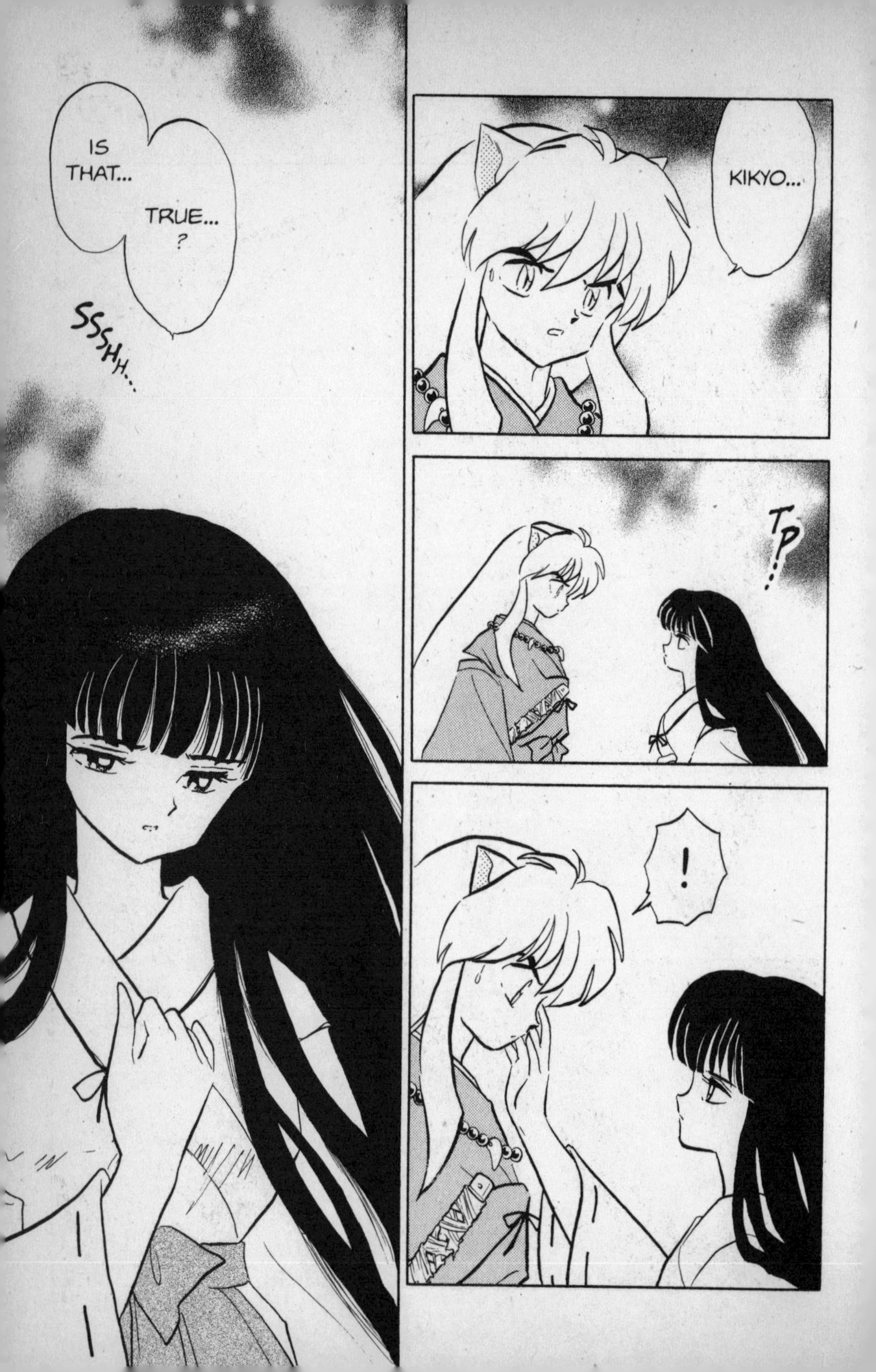
IS THAT... TRUE... ?
SSSHH...
KIKYO...
TP...
!

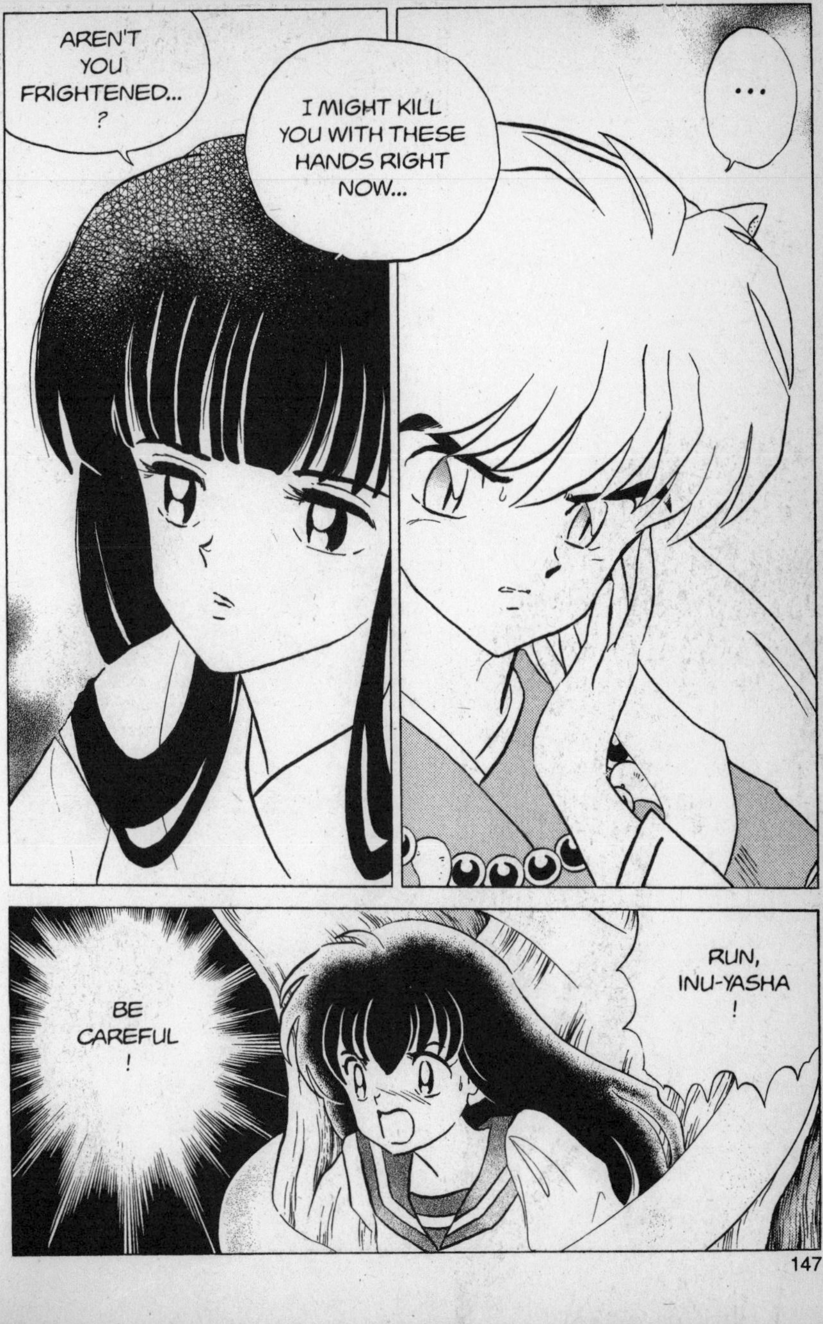
AREN'T YOU FRIGHTENED... ?
I MIGHT KILL YOU WITH THESE HANDS RIGHT NOW...
...
BE CAREFUL !
RUN, INU-YASHA !

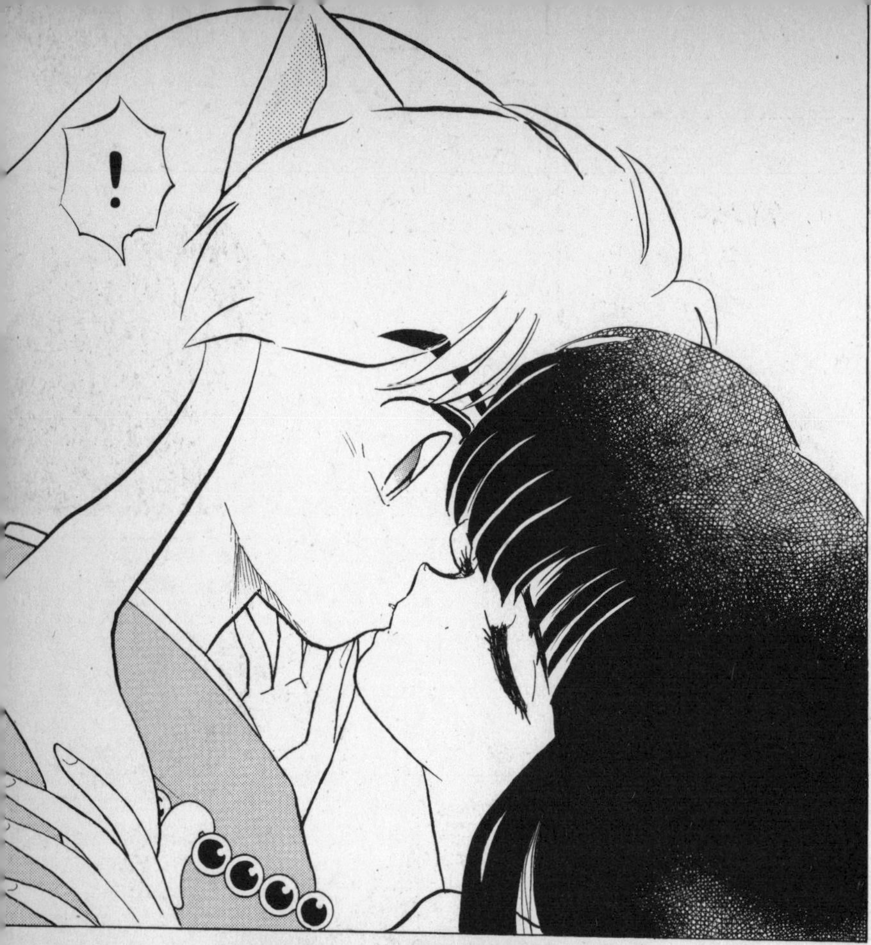
!
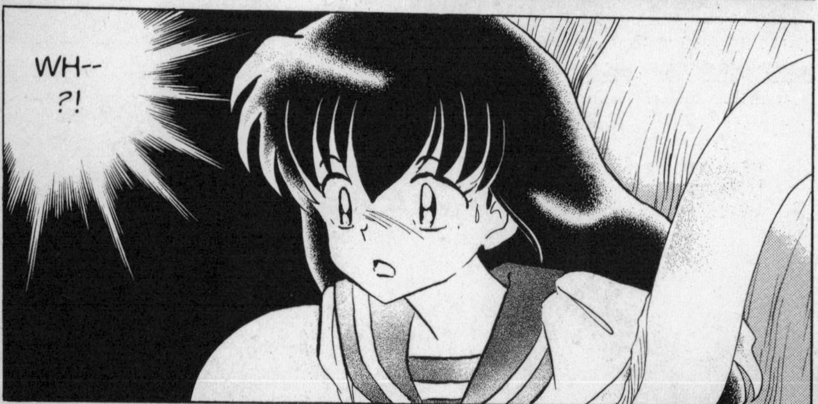
WH--
?!

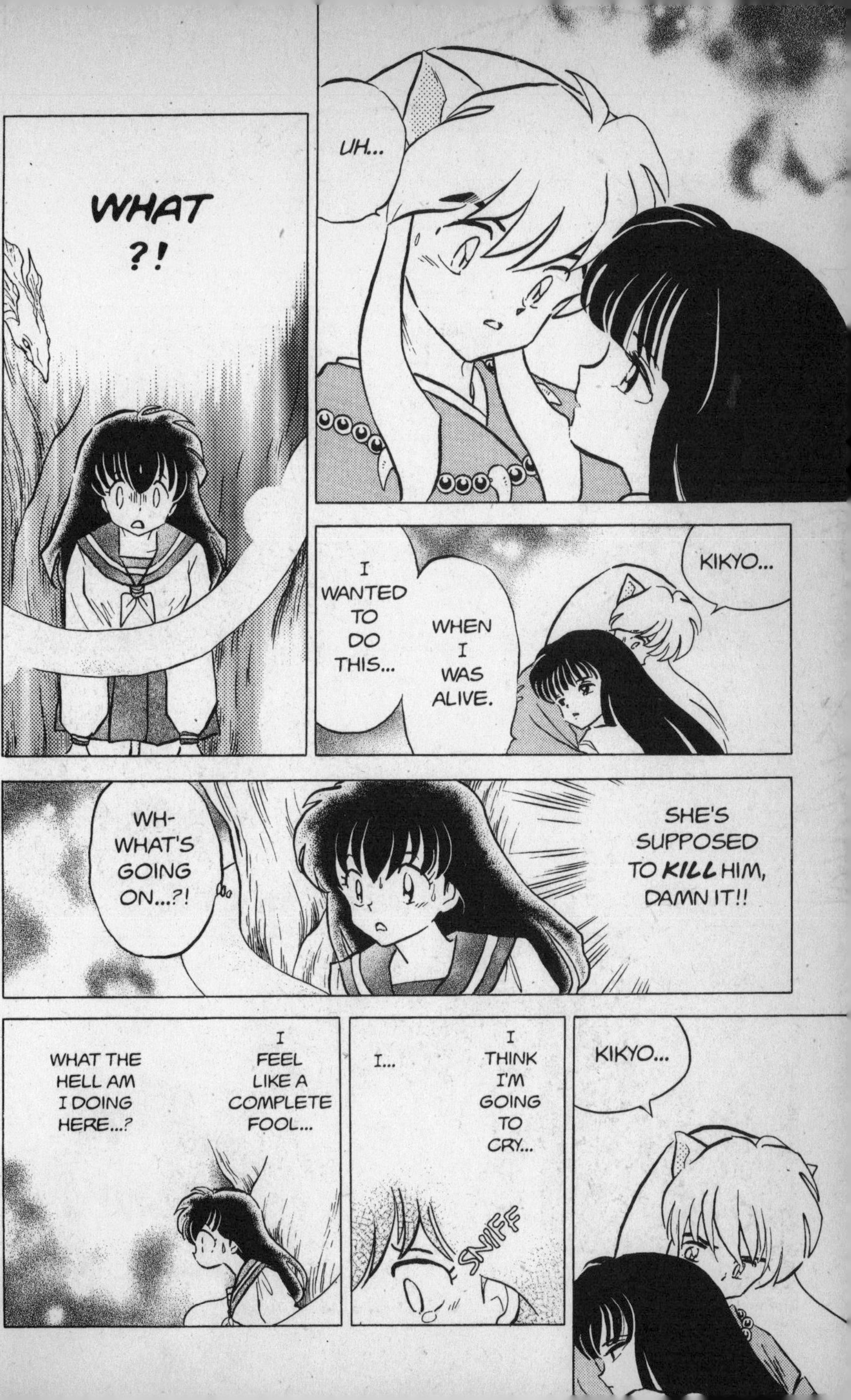
WHAT ?!
UH...
I WANTED TO DO THIS...
WHEN I WAS ALIVE.
KIKYO...
WH- WHAT'S GOING ON...?!
SHE'S SUPPOSED TO **KILL** HIM, DAMN IT!!
WHAT THE HELL AM I DOING HERE...?
I FEEL LIKE A COMPLETE FOOL...
I...
I THINK I'M GOING TO CRY...
SNIFF
KIKYO...

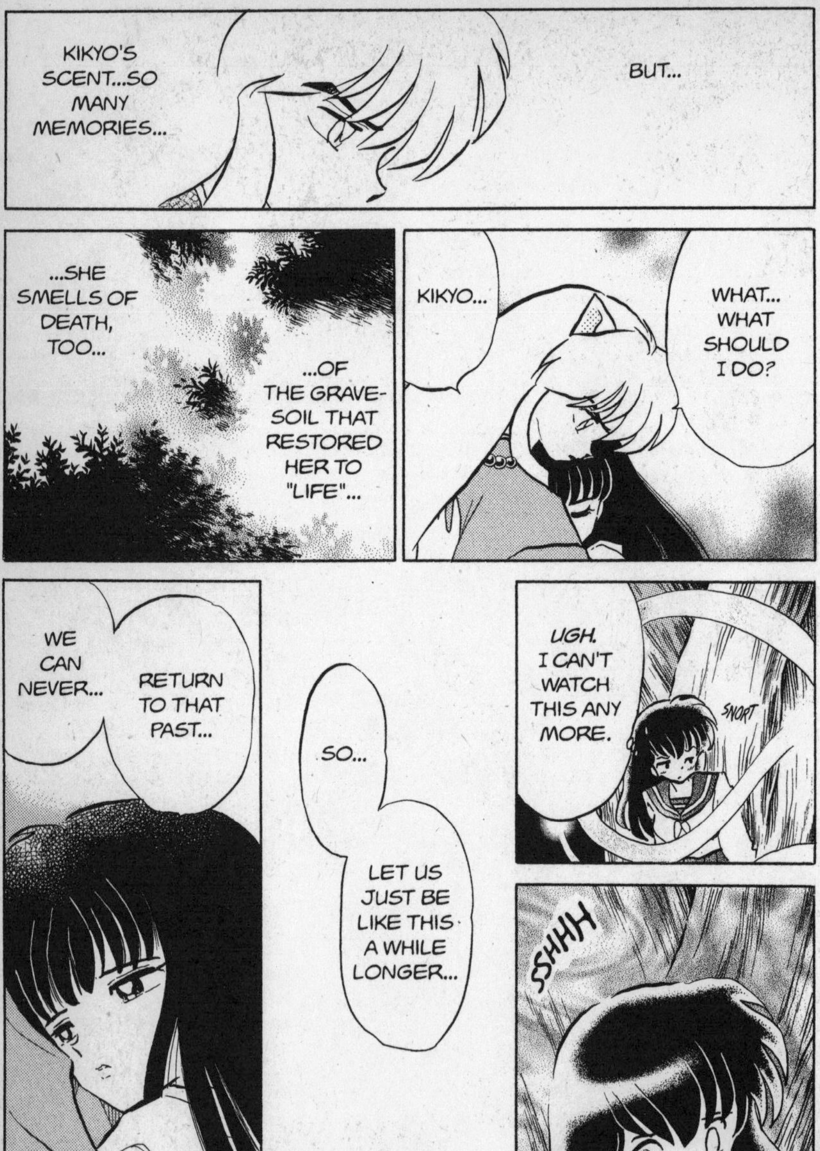
KIKYO'S SCENT...SO MANY MEMORIES...
BUT...
...SHE SMELLS OF DEATH, TOO...
...OF THE GRAVE-SOIL THAT RESTORED HER TO "LIFE"...
KIKYO...
WHAT... WHAT SHOULD I DO?
WE CAN NEVER...
RETURN TO THAT PAST...
SO...
LET US JUST BE LIKE THIS A WHILE LONGER...
UGH. I CAN'T WATCH THIS ANY MORE.
SNORT
SHHH

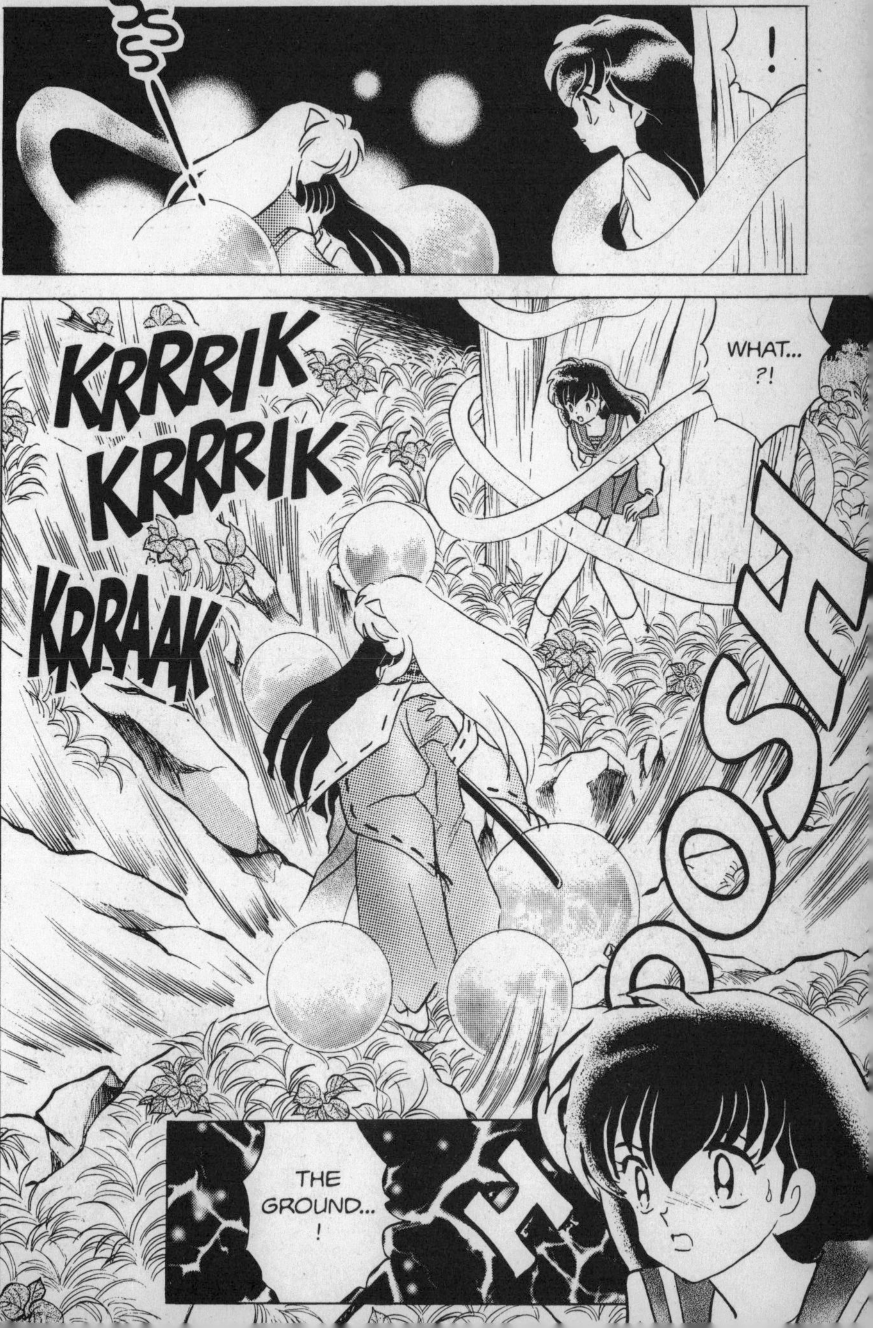
SSS
!
KRRRIK
KRRRIK
KRRAAK
WHAT... ?!
DOOSH
THE GROUND... !

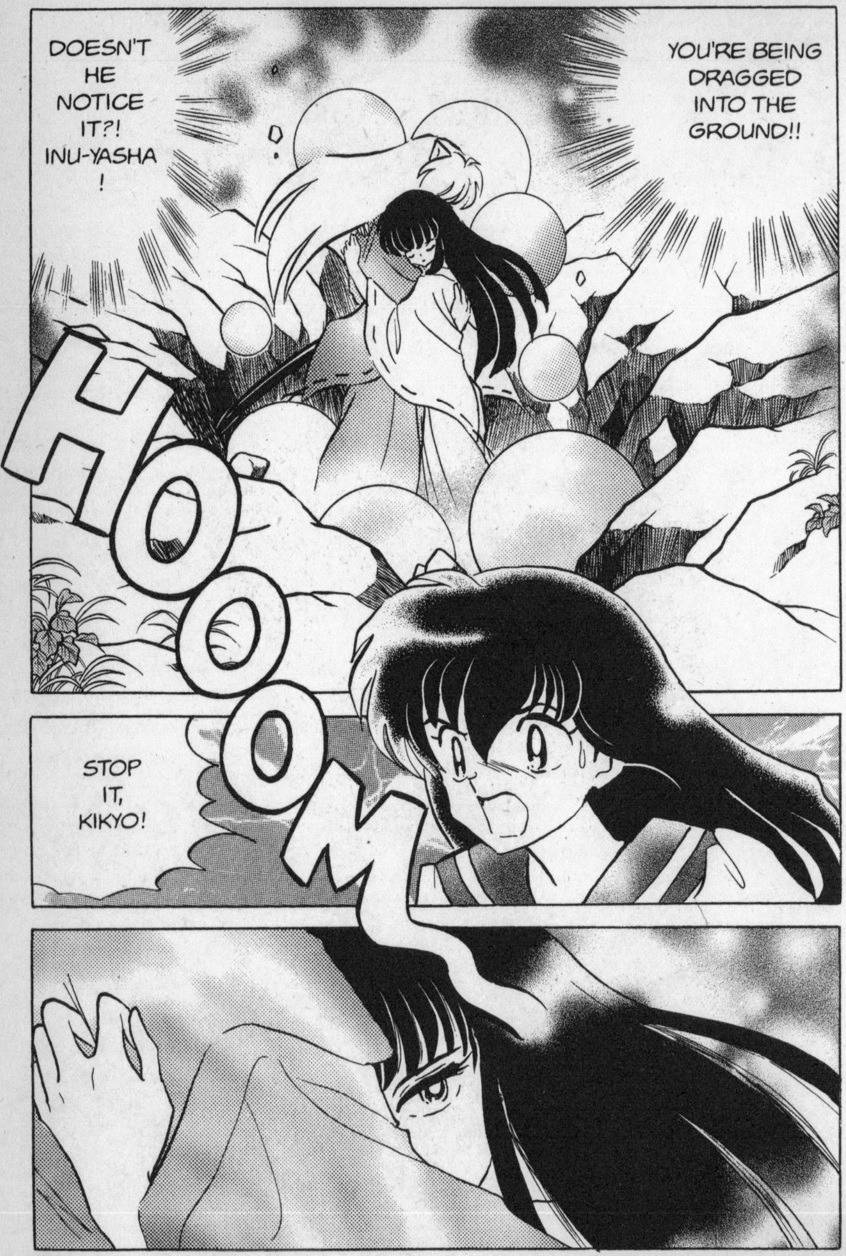

DOESN'T HE NOTICE IT?! INU-YASHA!
YOU'RE BEING DRAGGED INTO THE GROUND!!
HOOOOOM
STOP IT, KIKYO!

SCROLL NINE
KAGOME'S VOICE

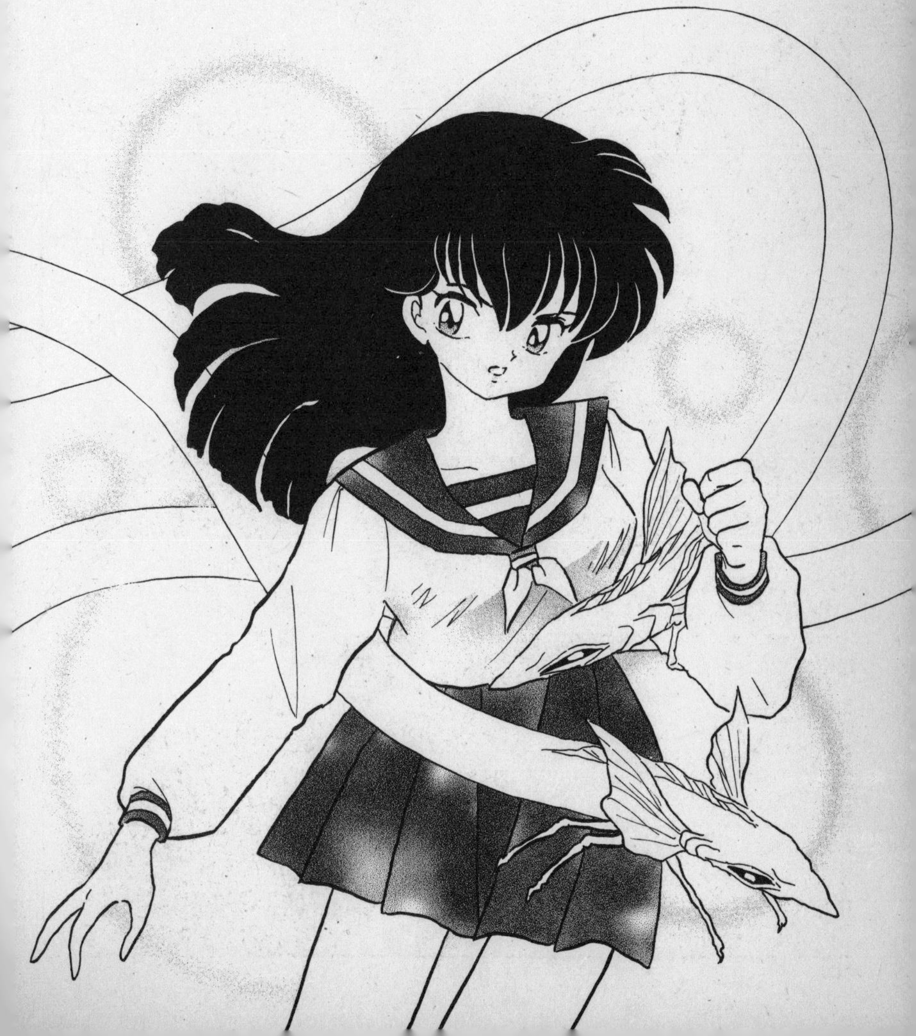

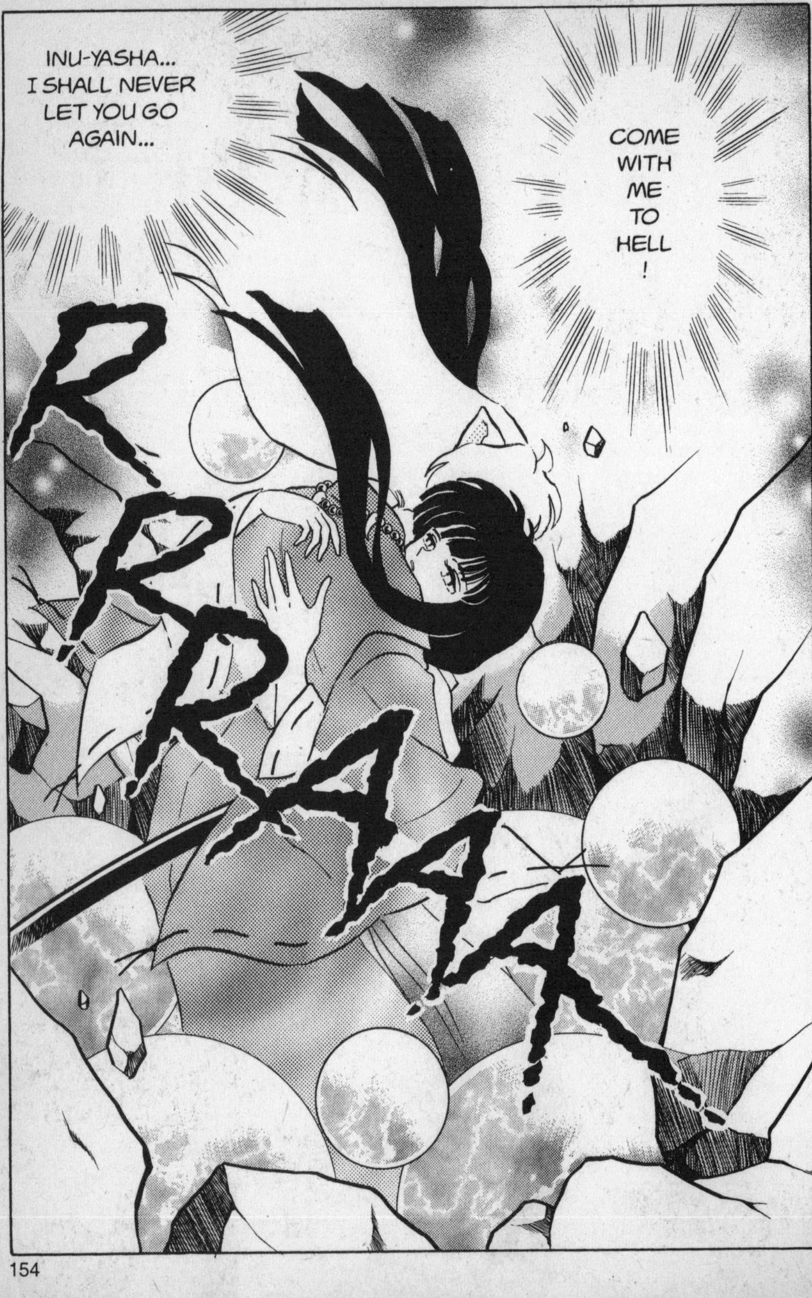
INU-YASHA... I SHALL NEVER LET YOU GO AGAIN...
COME WITH ME TO HELL!
RRAAA!

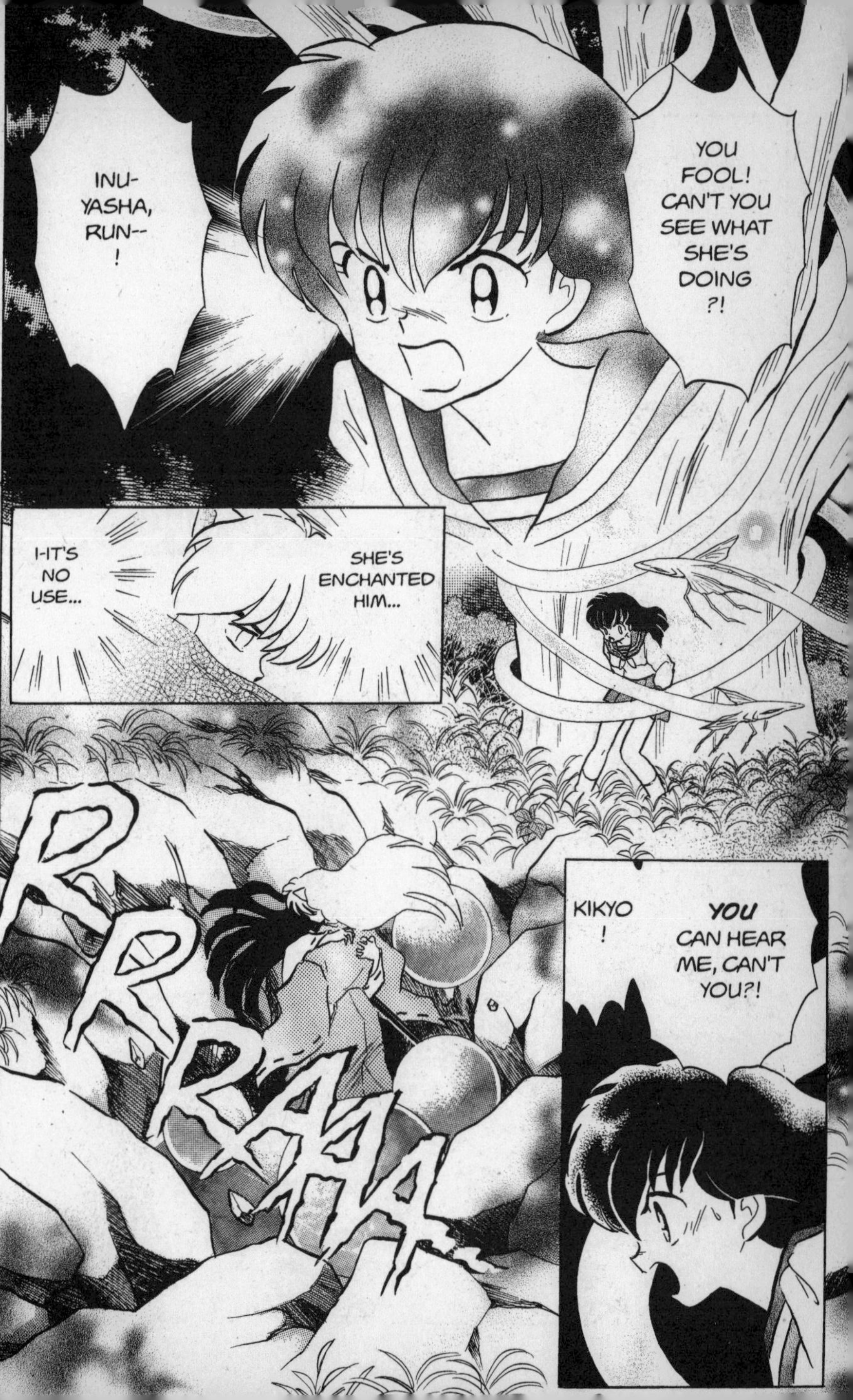
INU-YASHA, RUN--!
YOU FOOL! CAN'T YOU SEE WHAT SHE'S DOING?!
I-IT'S NO USE...
SHE'S ENCHANTED HIM...
RRRAAA
KIKYO!
YOU CAN HEAR ME, CAN'T YOU?!

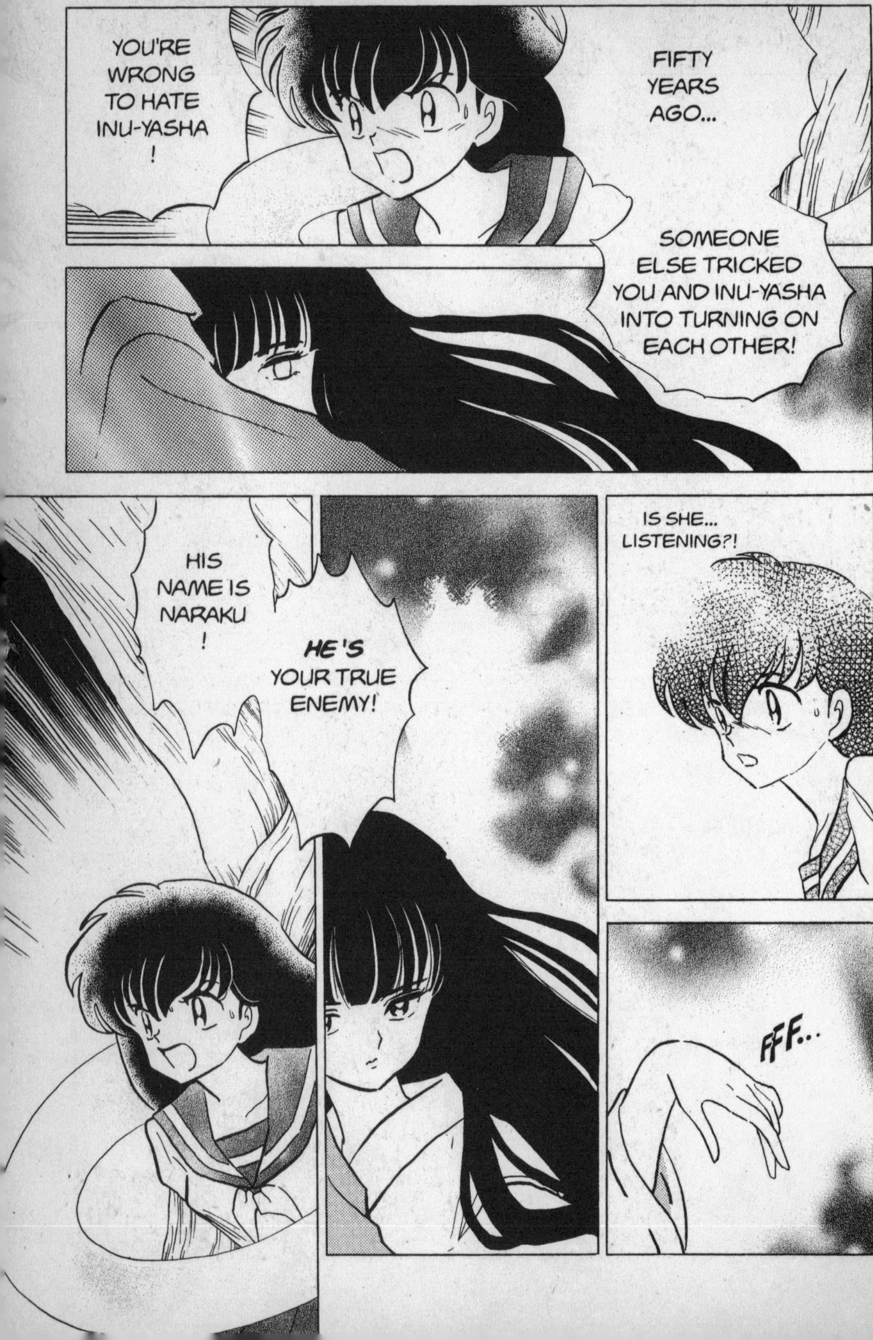
YOU'RE WRONG TO HATE INU-YASHA !
FIFTY YEARS AGO...
SOMEONE ELSE TRICKED YOU AND INU-YASHA INTO TURNING ON EACH OTHER!
HIS NAME IS NARAKU !
HE'S YOUR TRUE ENEMY!
IS SHE... LISTENING?!
FFF...

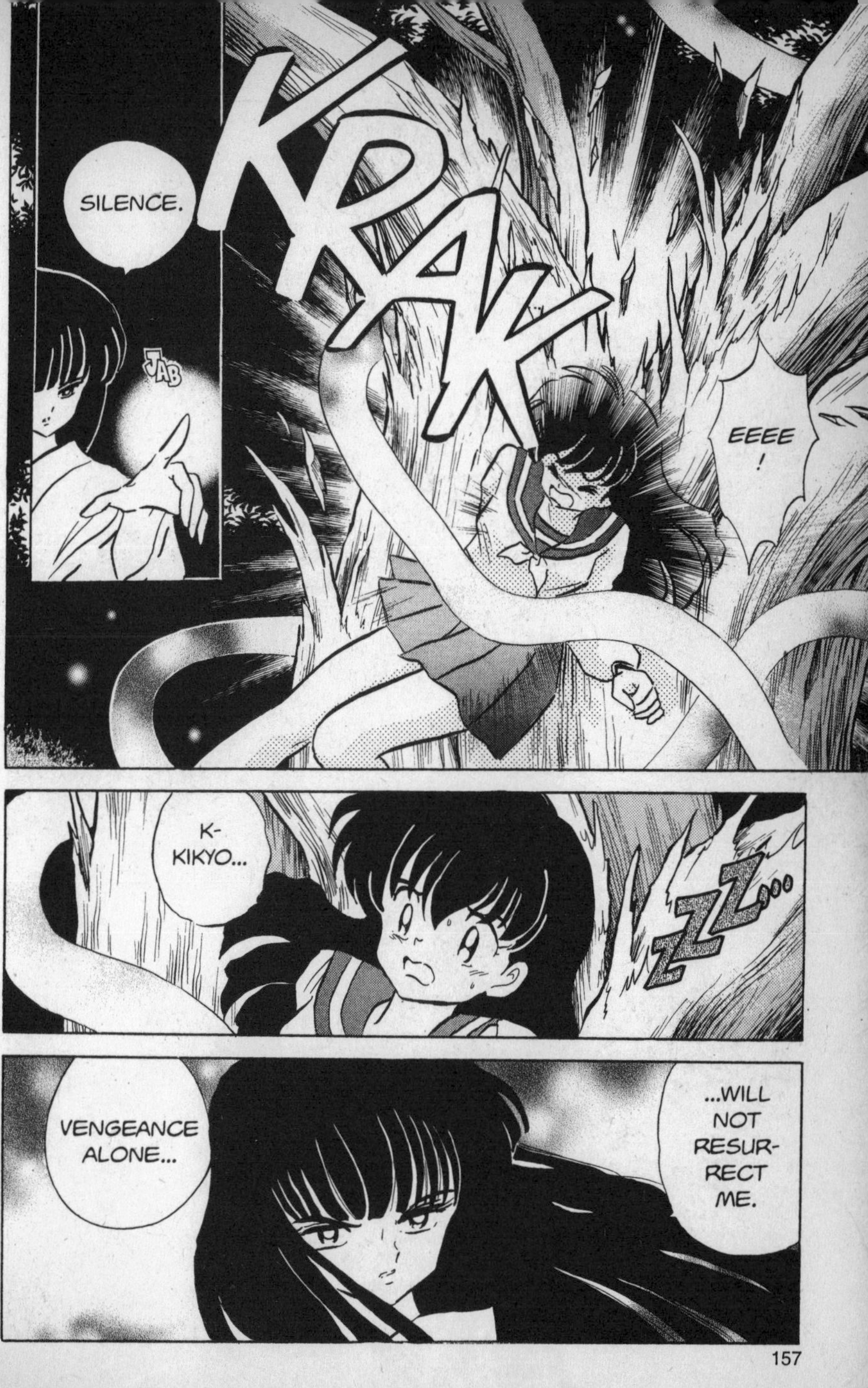
SILENCE.
JAB
KRAK
EEEE!
K-KIKYO...
ZZZ...
VENGEANCE ALONE...
...WILL NOT RESURRECT ME.

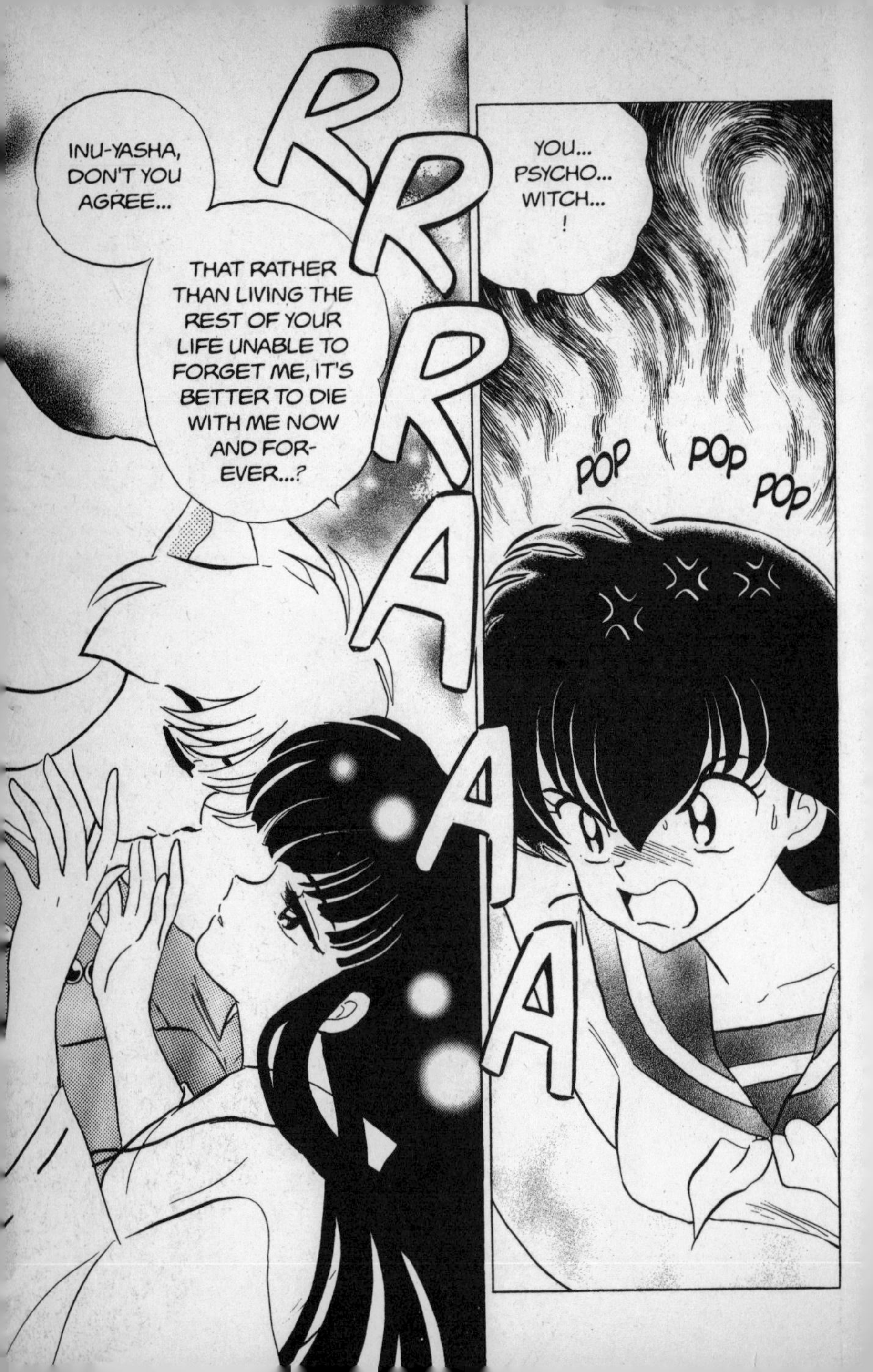
INU-YASHA, DON'T YOU AGREE...
THAT RATHER THAN LIVING THE REST OF YOUR LIFE UNABLE TO FORGET ME, IT'S BETTER TO DIE WITH ME NOW AND FOR-EVER...?
RRRRAAA
YOU... PSYCHO... WITCH... !
POP POP POP

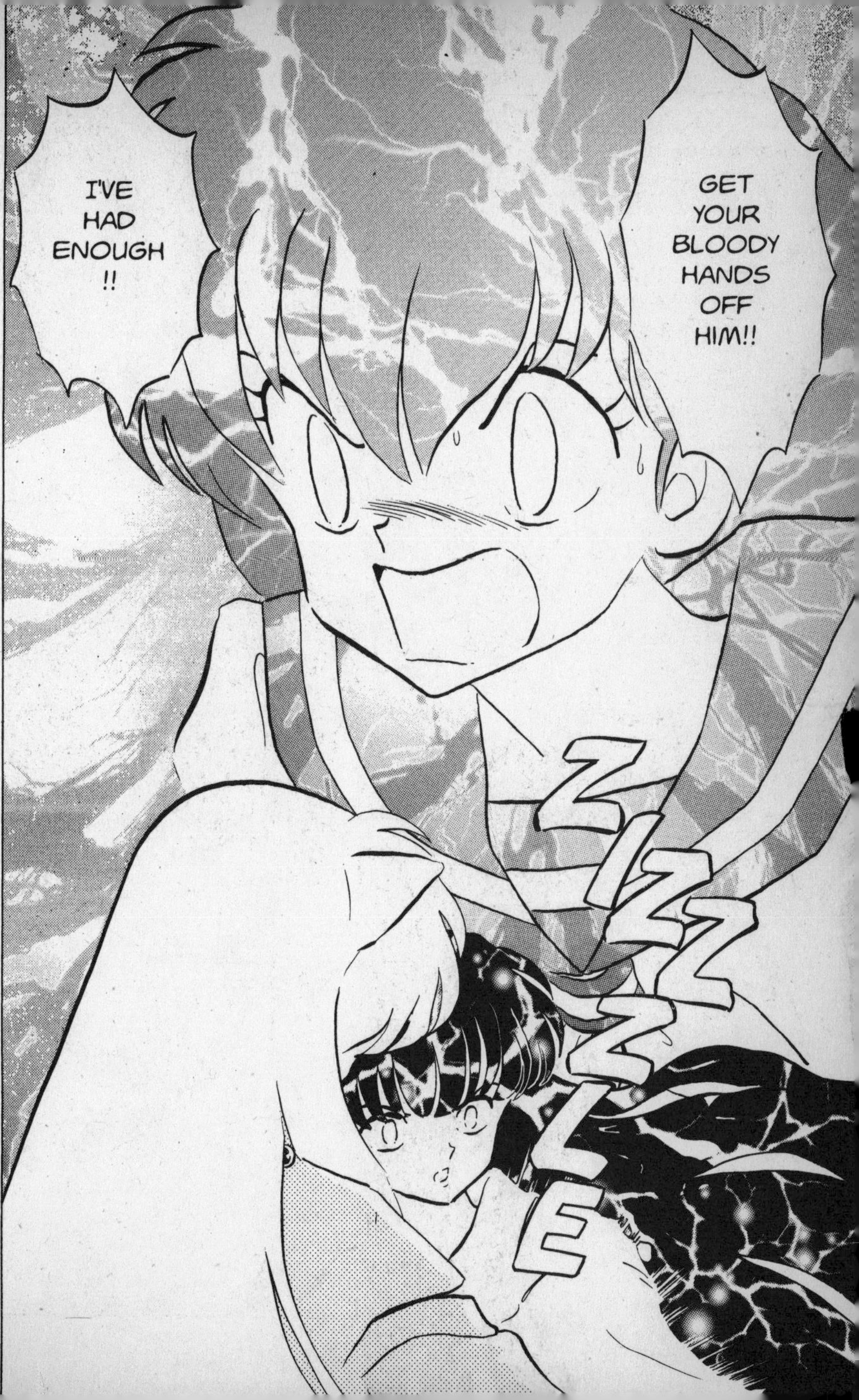
I'VE HAD ENOUGH !!
GET YOUR BLOODY HANDS OFF HIM!!
ZIZZZZZLE

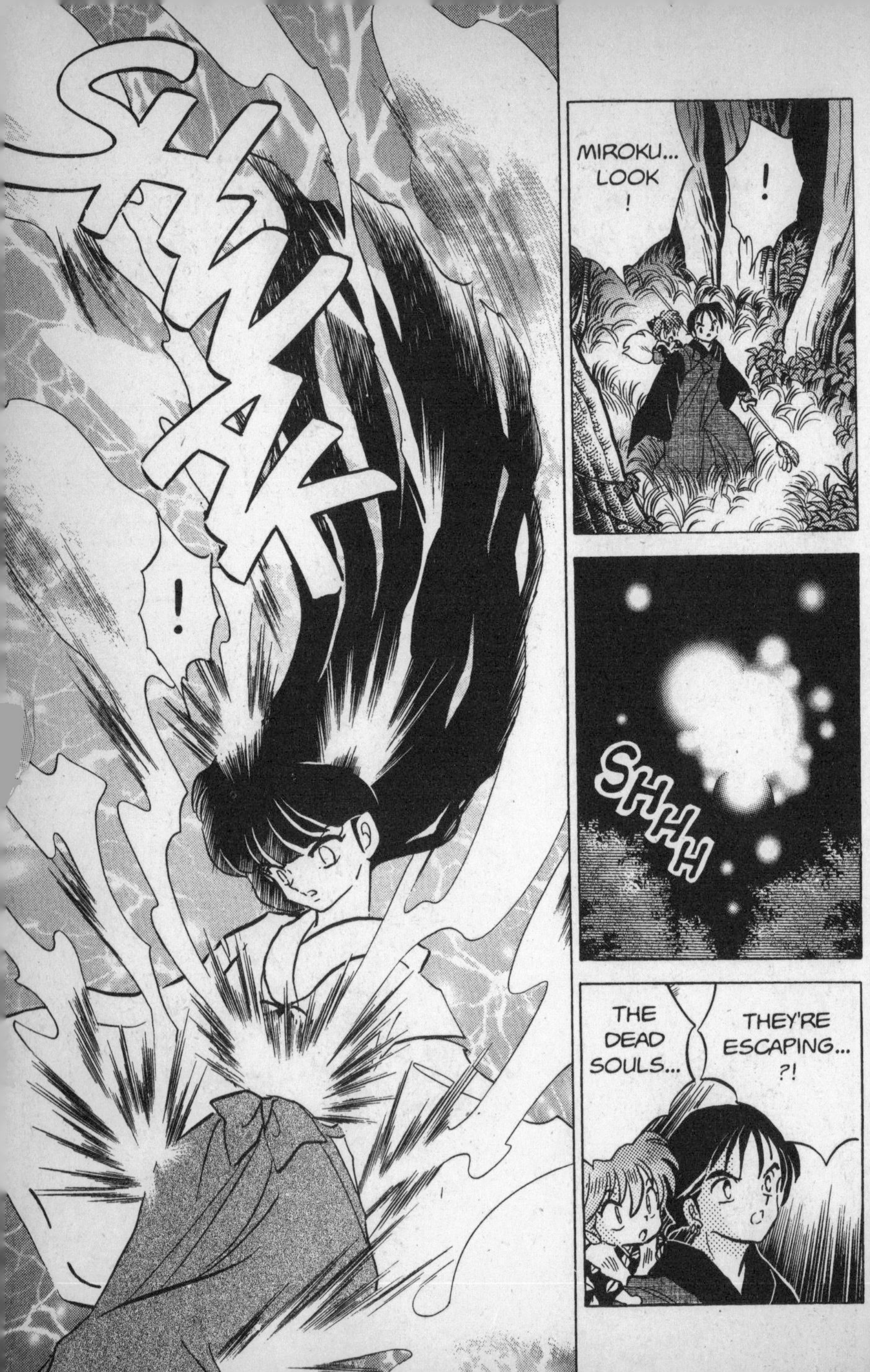
SHAK
!
MIROKU... LOOK !
!
SHHHH
THE DEAD SOULS...
THEY'RE ESCAPING... ?!

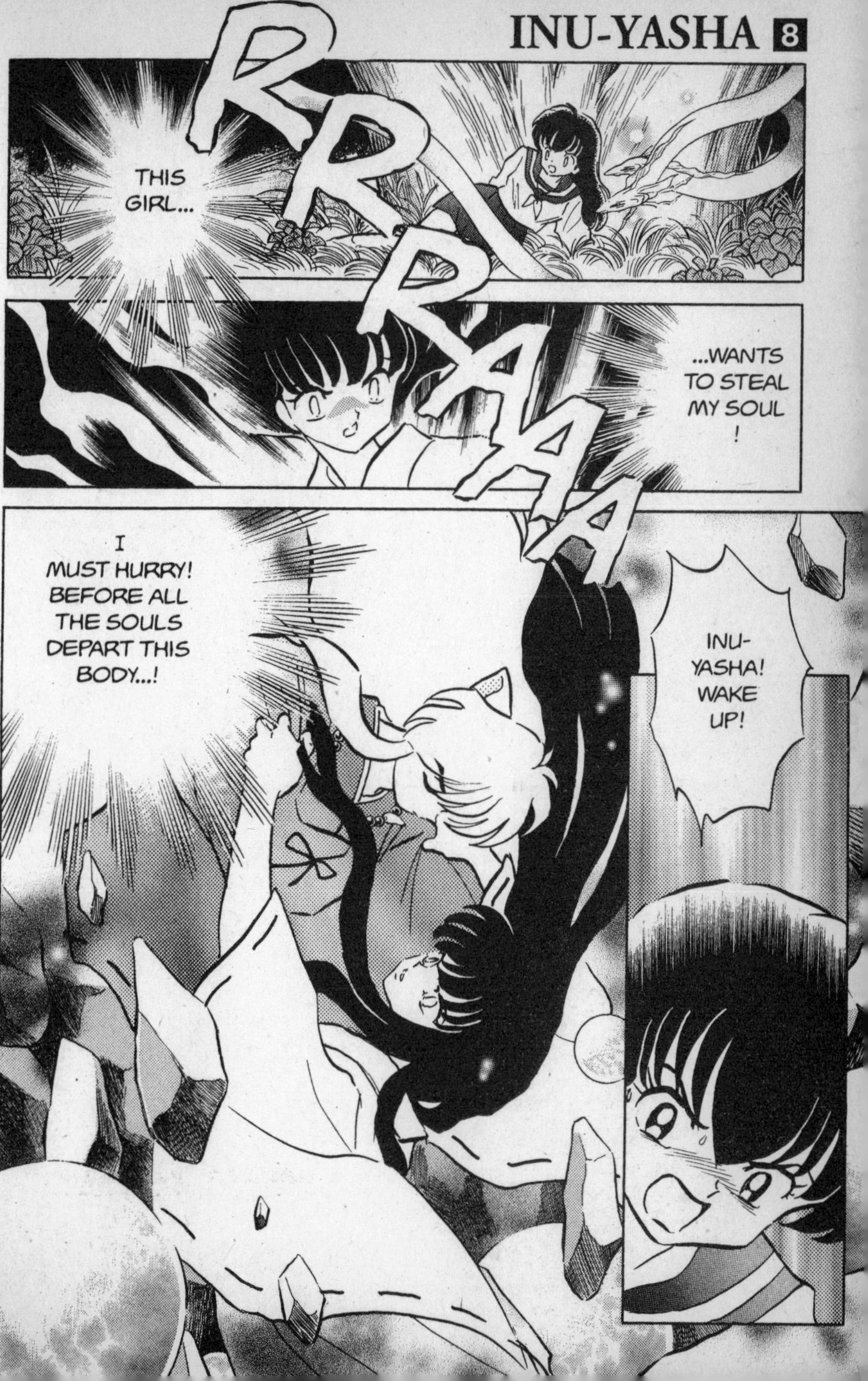
RRRAAAA
THIS GIRL...
...WANTS TO STEAL MY SOUL !
I MUST HURRY! BEFORE ALL THE SOULS DEPART THIS BODY...!
INU-YASHA! WAKE UP!

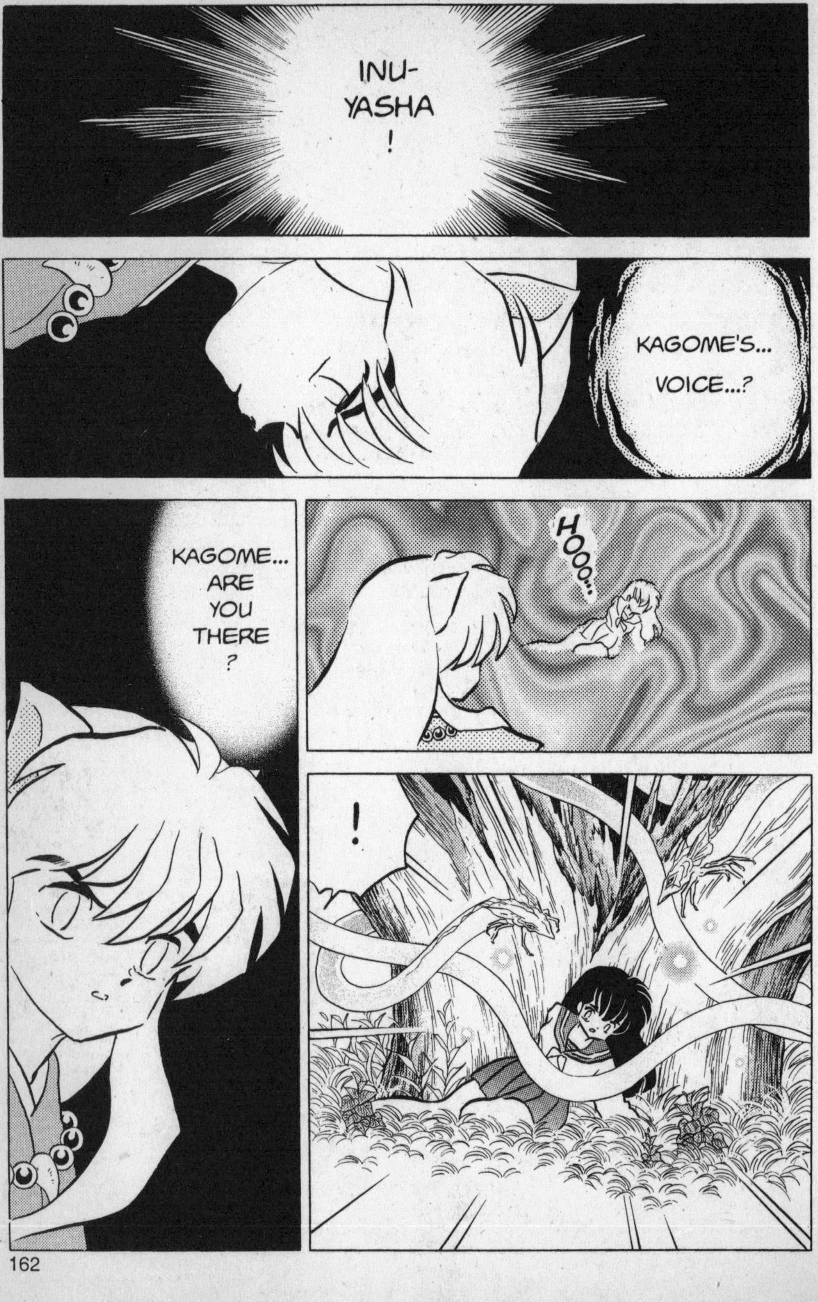
INU-YASHA !
KAGOME'S... VOICE...?
KAGOME... ARE YOU THERE ?
HOOO...
!

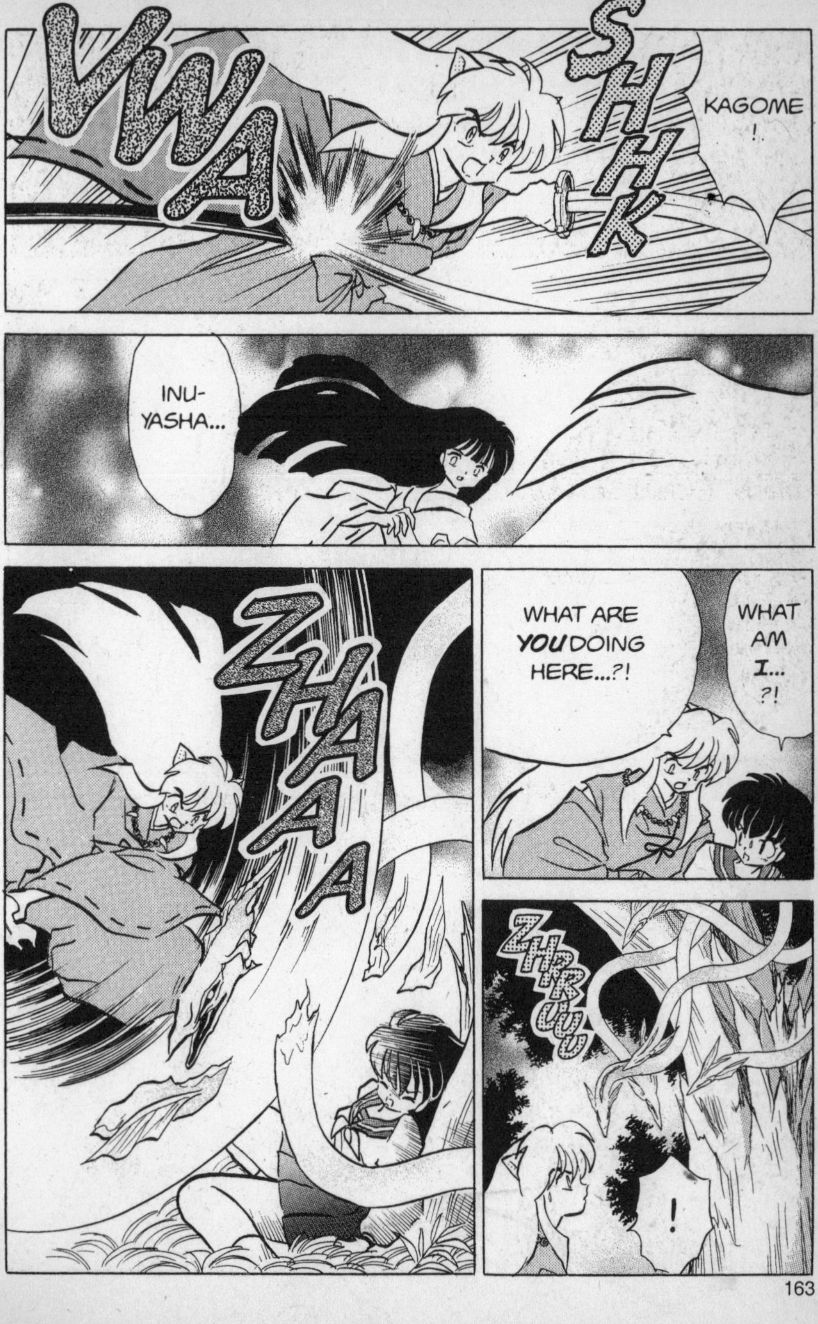
VWA
SHHK
KAGOME
!
INU-YASHA...
ZHAAAA
WHAT ARE **YOU** DOING HERE...?!
WHAT AM I...?!
ZHRRUU
!

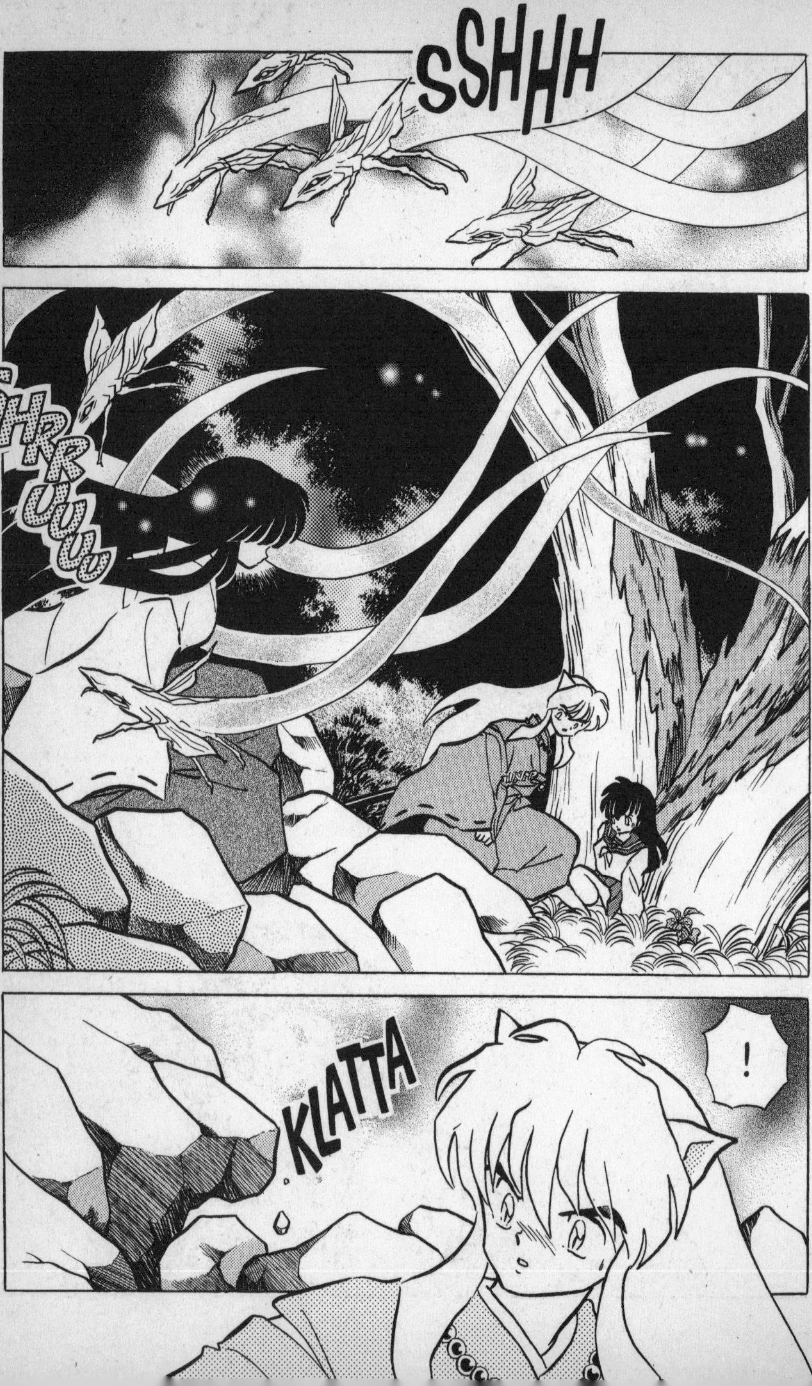
SSHHH
SHRRUUUU
KLATTA
!

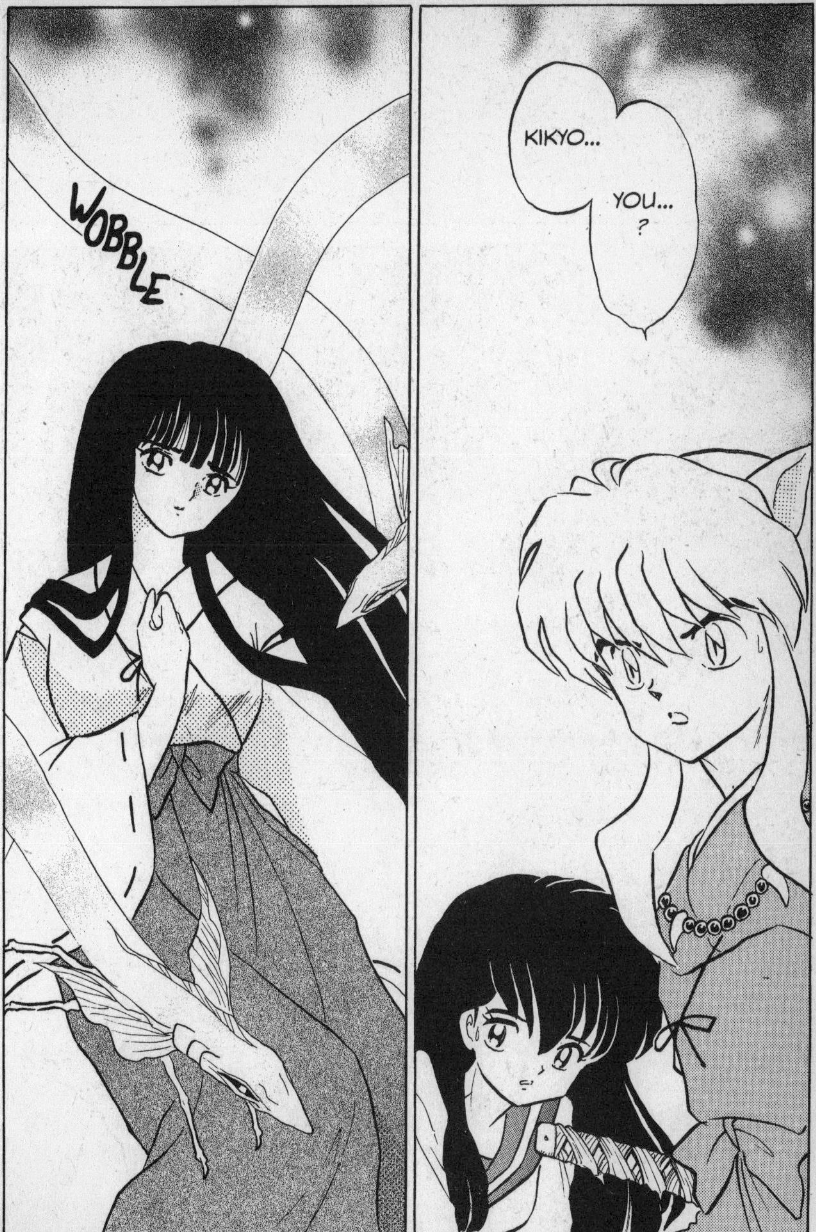
WOBBLE
KIKYO...
YOU...
?

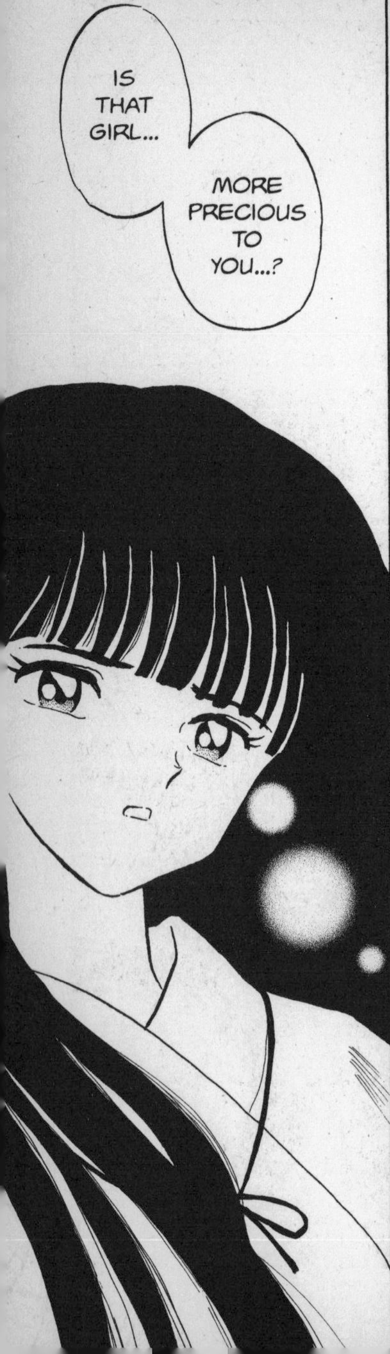
IS THAT GIRL...
MORE PRECIOUS TO YOU...?

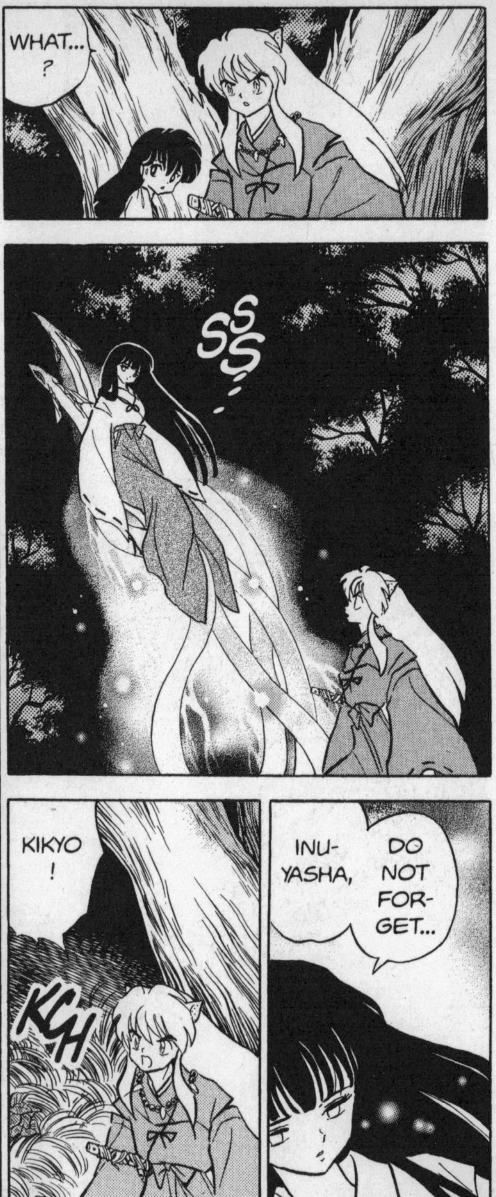
WHAT...?
SSS
KIKYO!
KCH
INU-YASHA,
DO NOT FOR-GET...

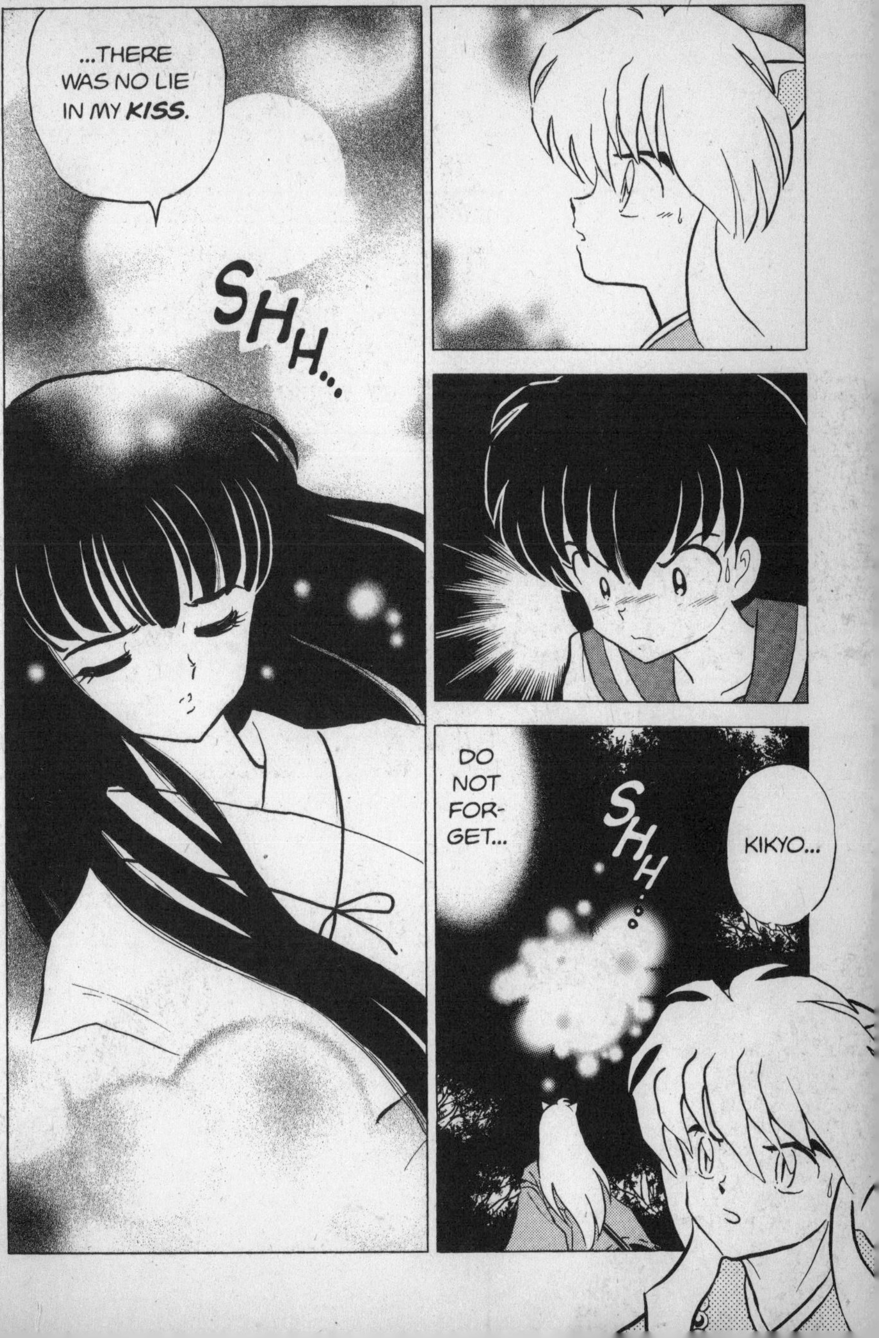
...THERE WAS NO LIE IN MY KISS.
SHH...
DO NOT FORGET...
SHH...
KIKYO...

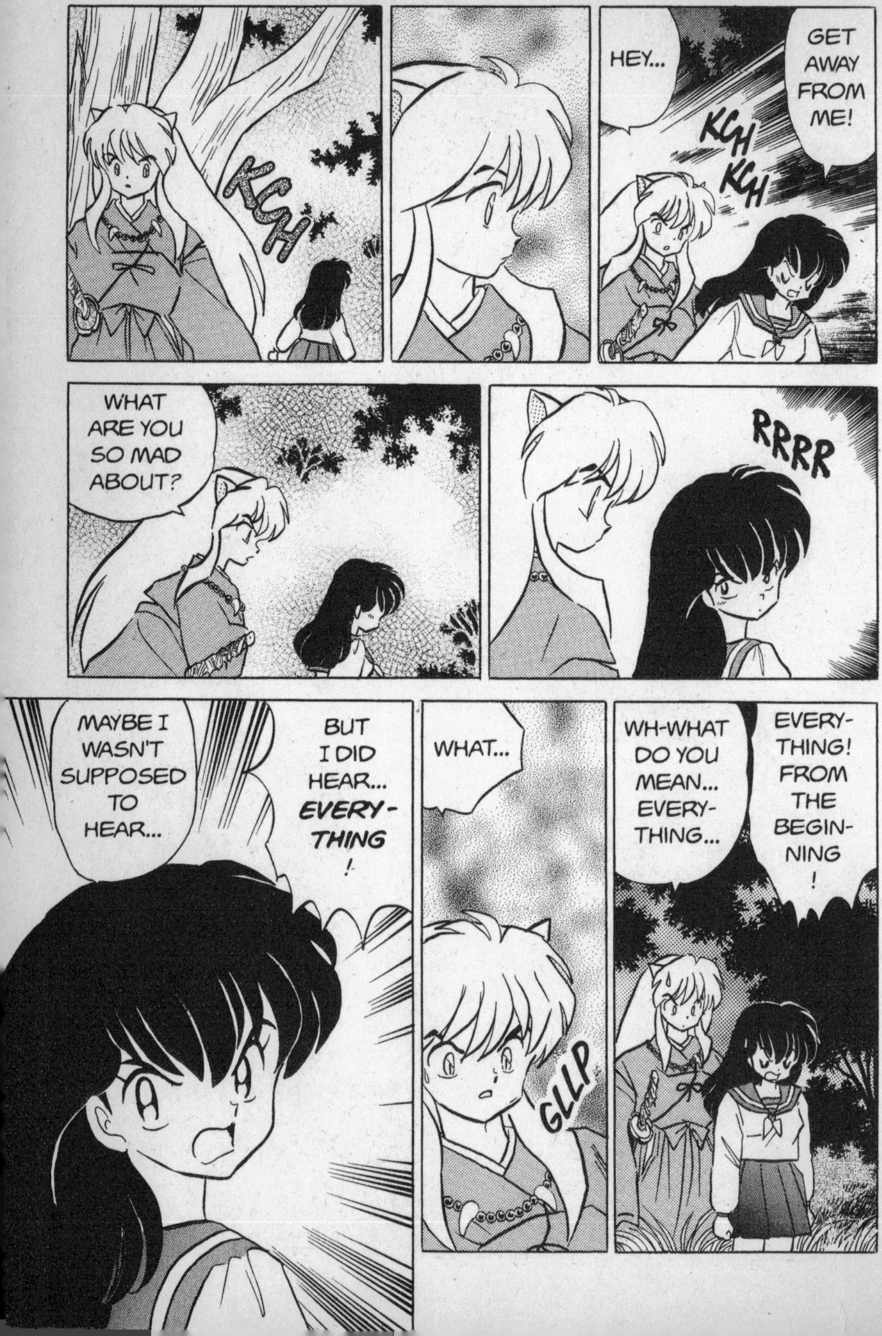
KCH
HEY...
GET AWAY FROM ME!
KCH KCH
WHAT ARE YOU SO MAD ABOUT?
RRRR
MAYBE I WASN'T SUPPOSED TO HEAR...
BUT I DID HEAR... **EVERYTHING**!
WHAT...
GLLP
WH-WHAT DO YOU MEAN... EVERYTHING...
EVERYTHING! FROM THE BEGINNING!

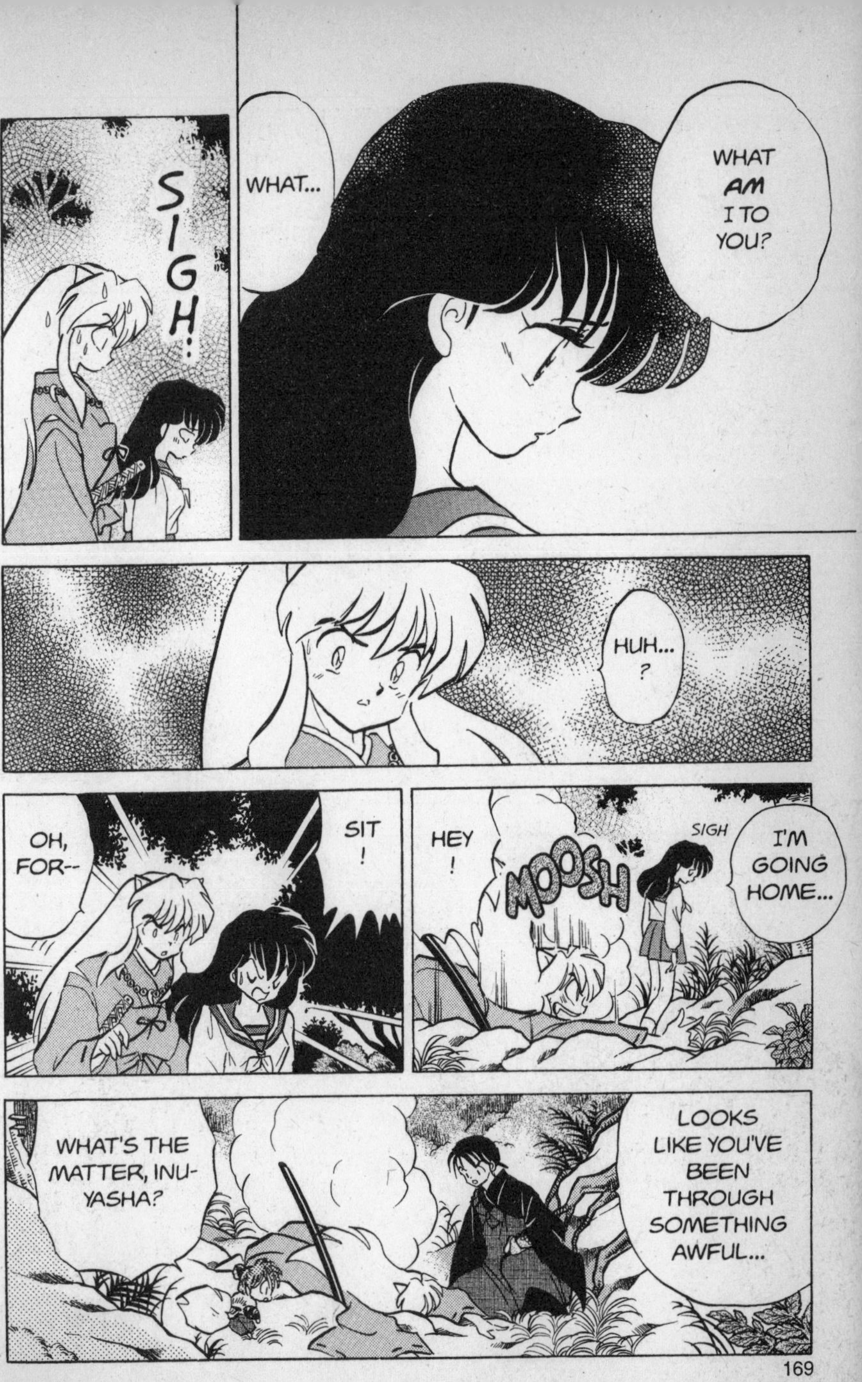
SIGH!!
WHAT...
WHAT AM I TO YOU?
HUH... ?
OH, FOR--
SIT!
HEY!
MOOSH
SIGH
I'M GOING HOME...
WHAT'S THE MATTER, INU-YASHA?
LOOKS LIKE YOU'VE BEEN THROUGH SOMETHING AWFUL...

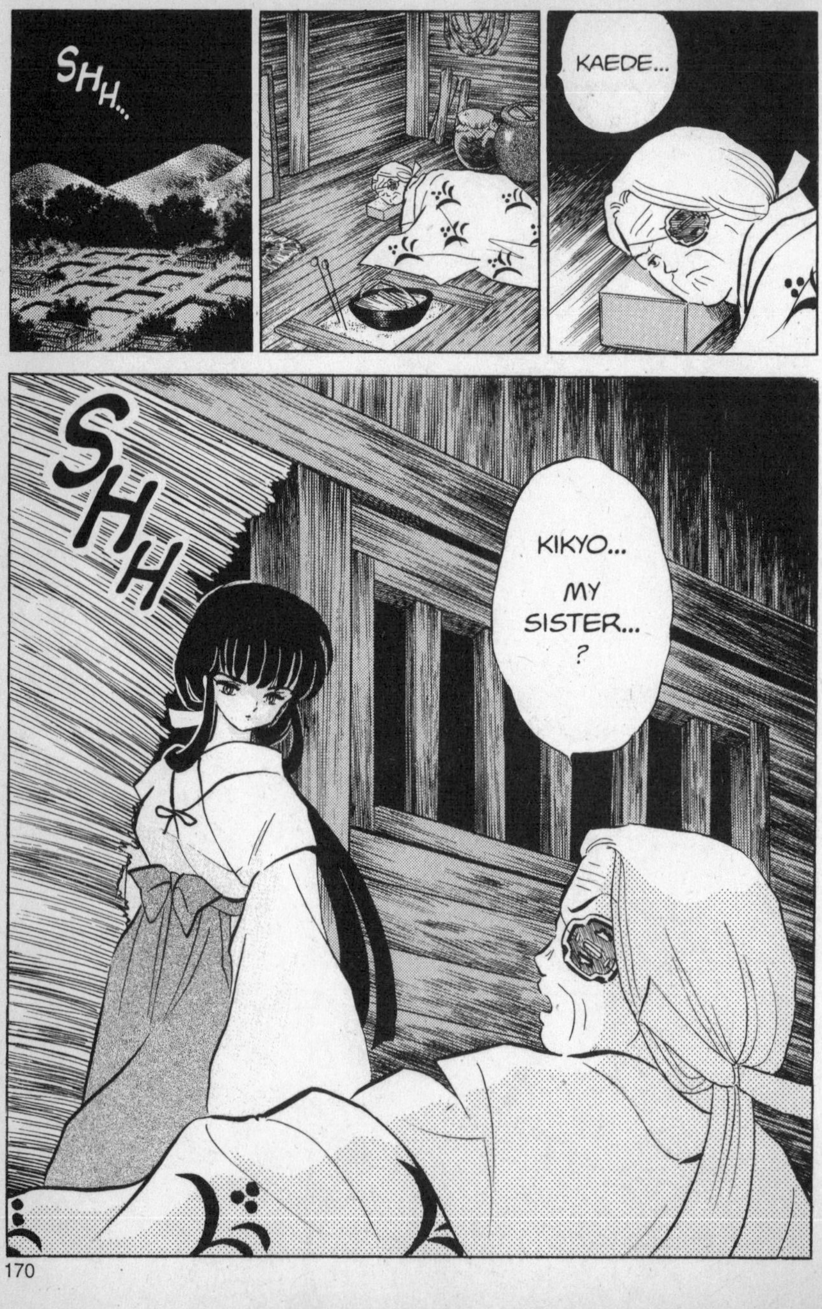
SHH...
KAEDE...
SHH
KIKYO... MY SISTER... ?

SCROLL TEN

A GENTLE SCENT

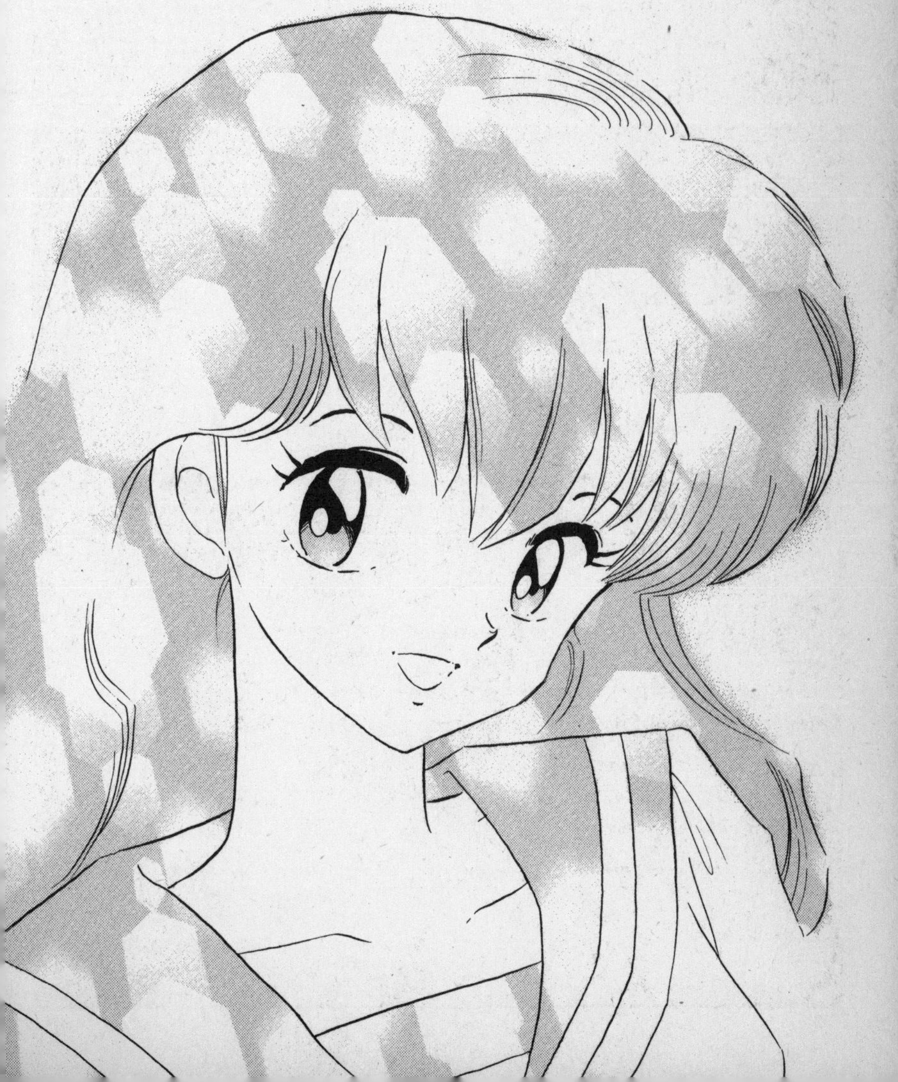

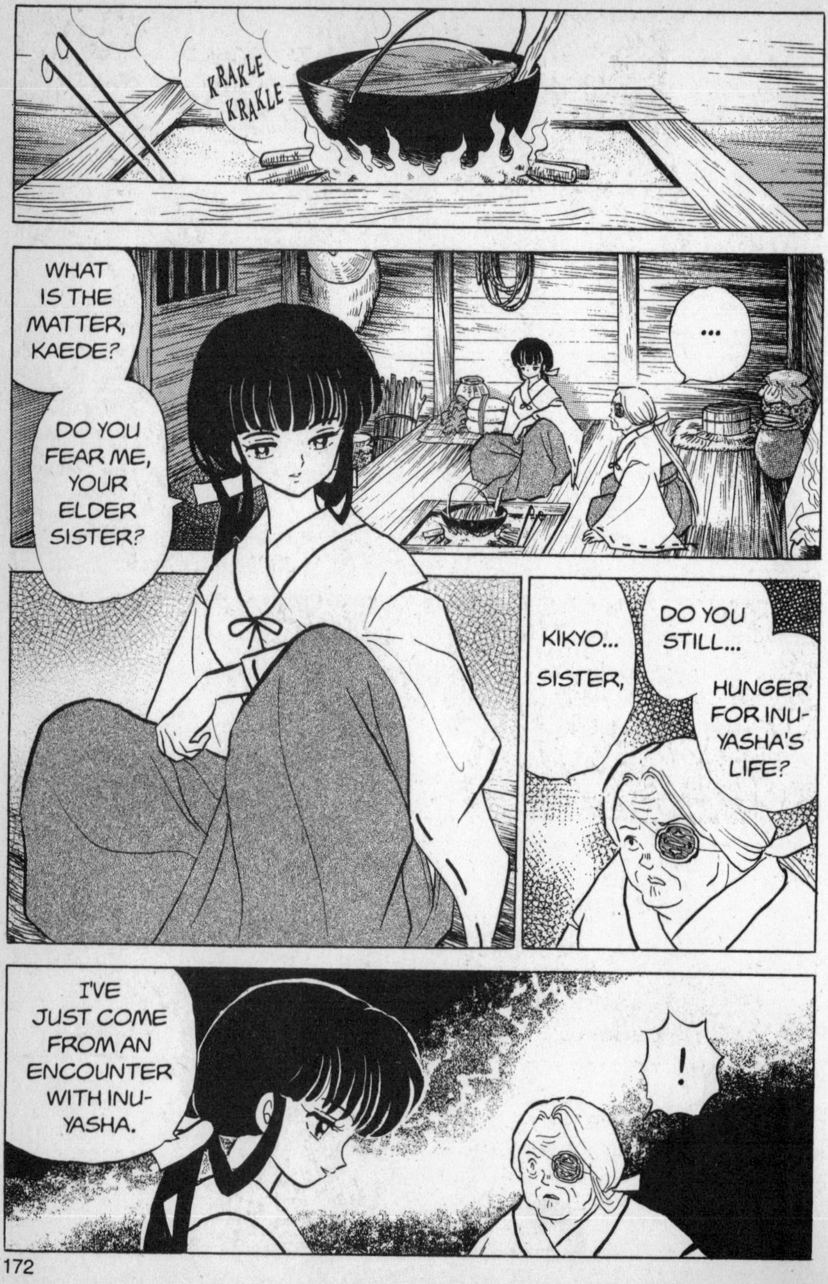
KRAKLE KRAKLE
WHAT IS THE MATTER, KAEDE?
DO YOU FEAR ME, YOUR ELDER SISTER?
...
KIKYO... SISTER,
DO YOU STILL...
HUNGER FOR INU-YASHA'S LIFE?
I'VE JUST COME FROM AN ENCOUNTER WITH INU-YASHA.
!

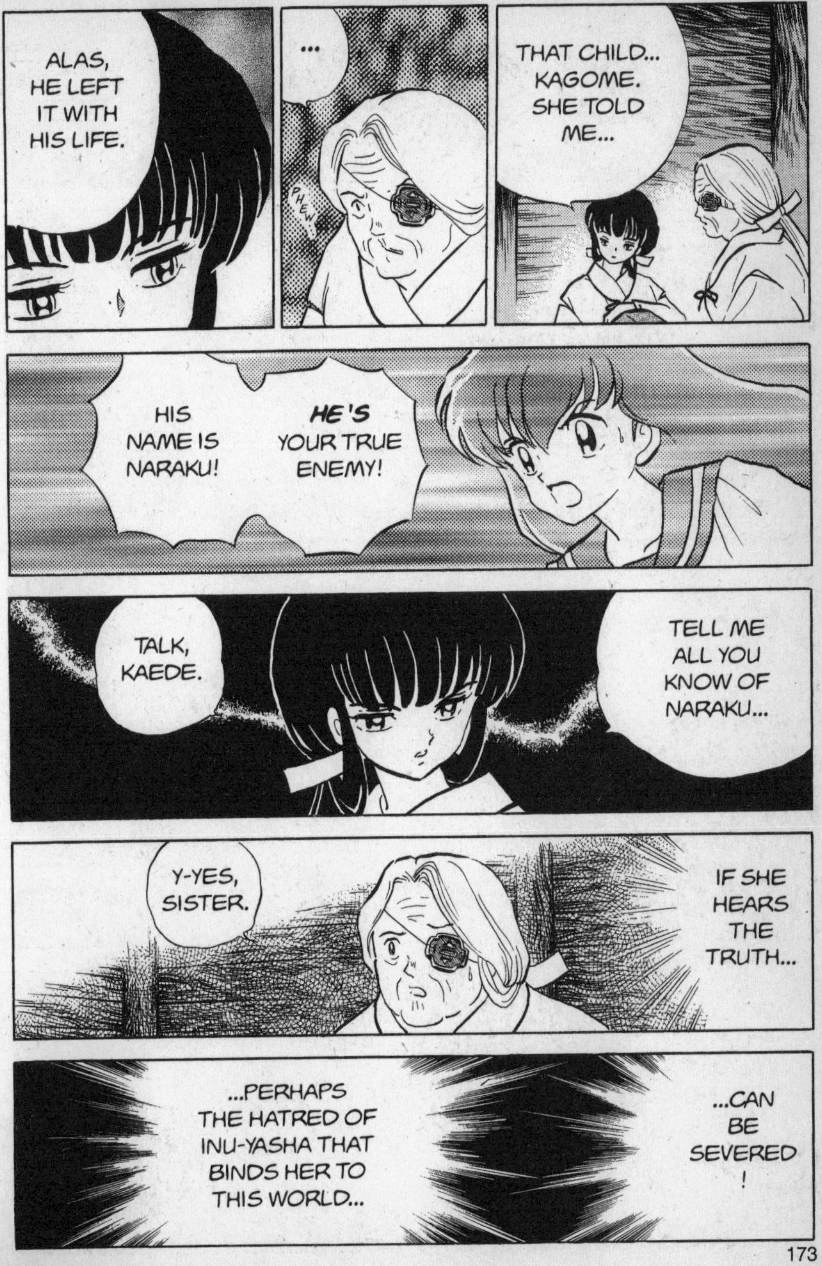
ALAS, HE LEFT IT WITH HIS LIFE.
...
PHEW
THAT CHILD... KAGOME. SHE TOLD ME...
HIS NAME IS NARAKU!
HE'S YOUR TRUE ENEMY!
TALK, KAEDE.
TELL ME ALL YOU KNOW OF NARAKU...
Y-YES, SISTER.
IF SHE HEARS THE TRUTH...
...PERHAPS THE HATRED OF INU-YASHA THAT BINDS HER TO THIS WORLD...
...CAN BE SEVERED!

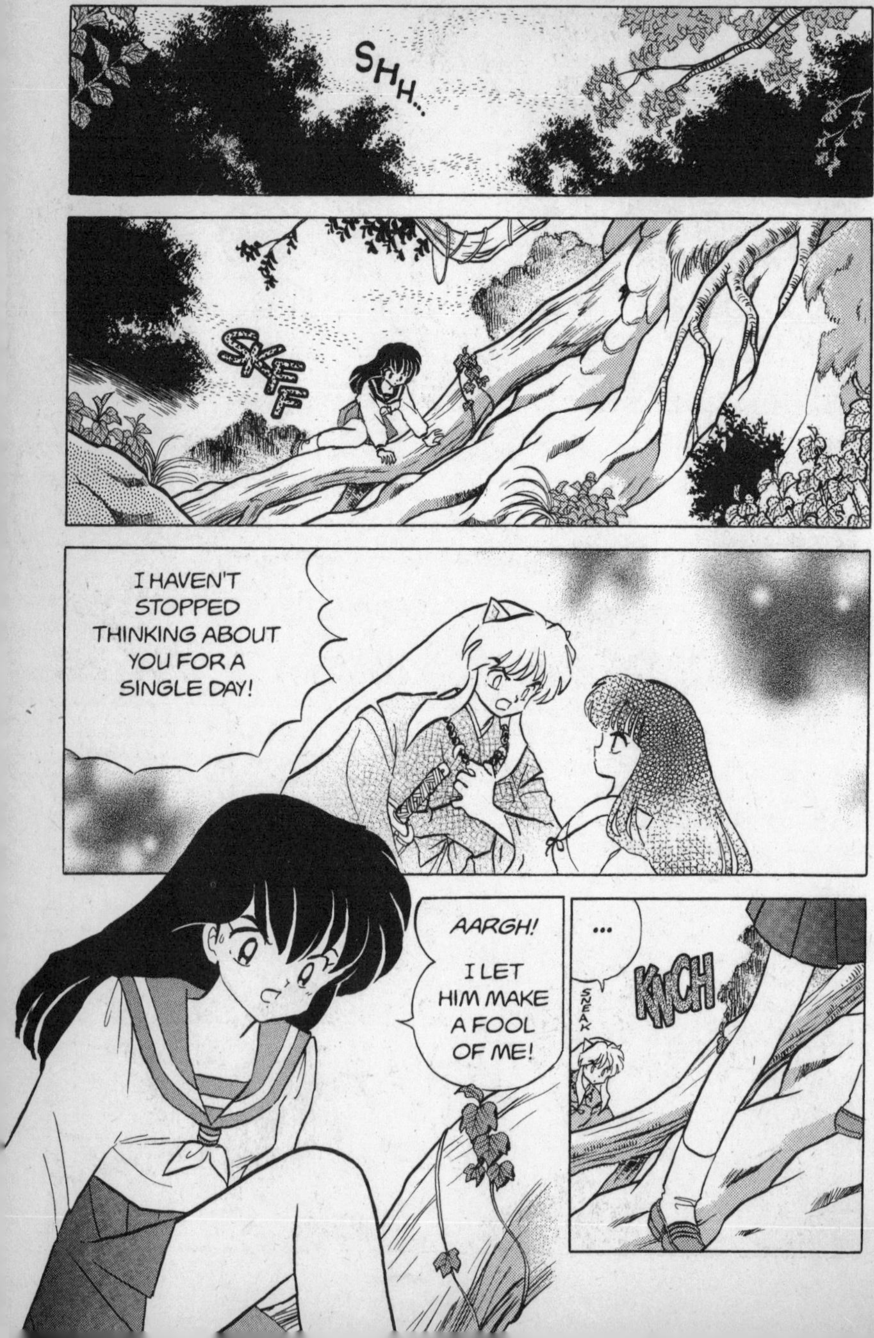
SHH...
SKFF
I HAVEN'T STOPPED THINKING ABOUT YOU FOR A SINGLE DAY!
AARGH!
I LET HIM MAKE A FOOL OF ME!
...
SNEAK
KNCH

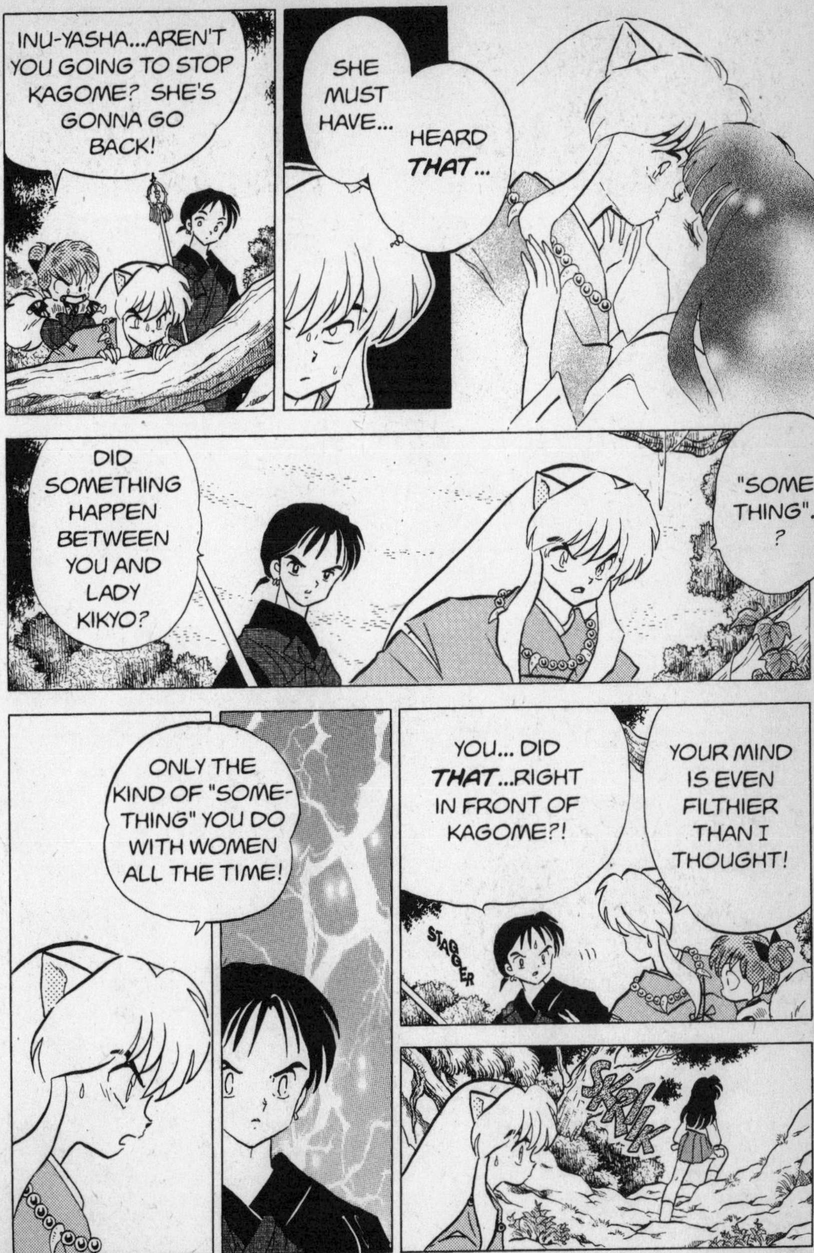
INU-YASHA...AREN'T YOU GOING TO STOP KAGOME? SHE'S GONNA GO BACK!
SHE MUST HAVE...
HEARD *THAT*...
DID SOMETHING HAPPEN BETWEEN YOU AND LADY KIKYO?
"SOME-THING"...?
ONLY THE KIND OF "SOME-THING" YOU DO WITH WOMEN ALL THE TIME!
YOU... DID *THAT*...RIGHT IN FRONT OF KAGOME?!
YOUR MIND IS EVEN FILTHIER THAN I THOUGHT!
STAGGER

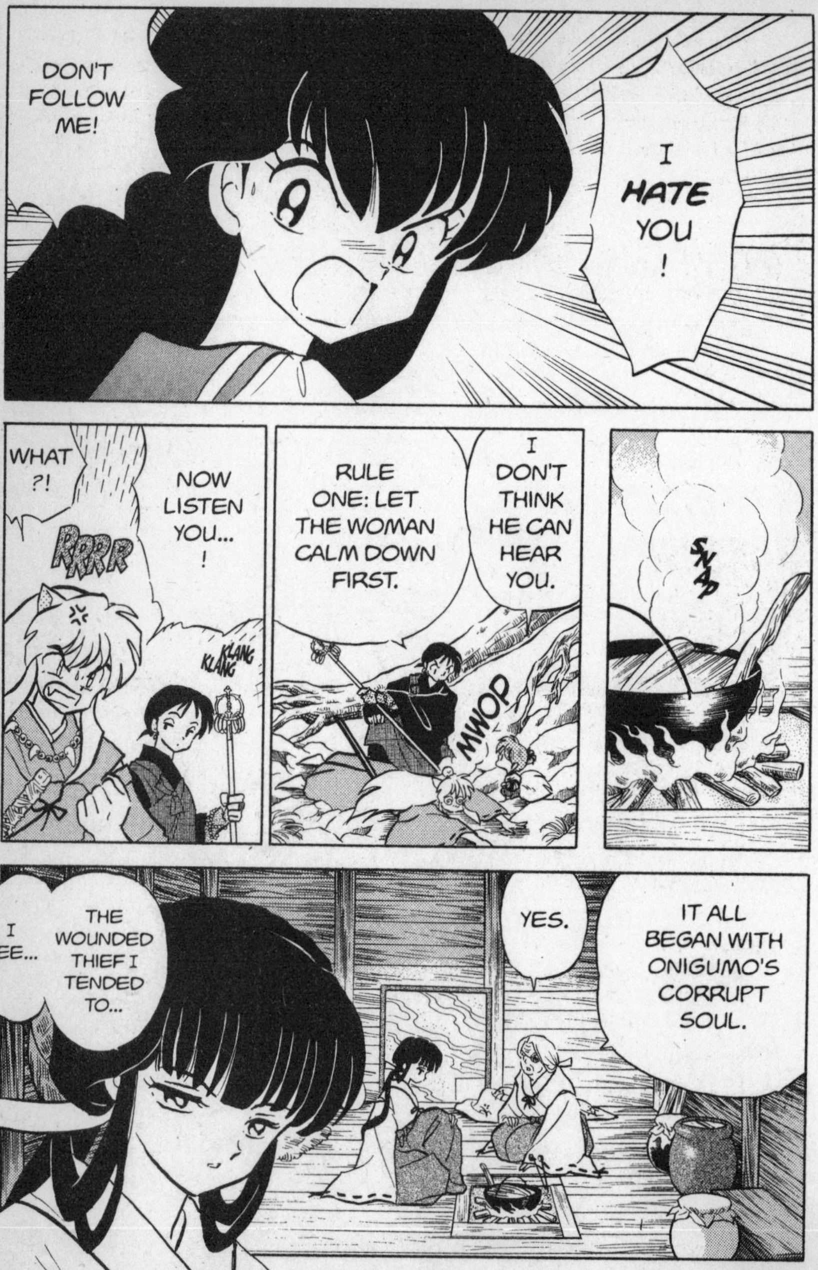
DON'T FOLLOW ME!
I HATE YOU!
WHAT?!
RRRR
NOW LISTEN YOU...!
KLANG KLANG
RULE ONE: LET THE WOMAN CALM DOWN FIRST.
I DON'T THINK HE CAN HEAR YOU.
MWOP
SNAP
I SEE...
THE WOUNDED THIEF I TENDED TO...
YES.
IT ALL BEGAN WITH ONIGUMO'S CORRUPT SOUL.

HE WAS DEVOURED BY HORDES OF THE VERY DEMONS THAT HE HIMSELF HAD SUMMONED TO HIS SIDE.

FROM THAT DEVOURING, THE DEMON NARAKU WAS BORN.

MY SISTER...

INU-YASHA HIMSELF WAS ALSO DEEPLY SCARRED BY NARAKU'S WEB OF DECEIT.

SISTER...?

SHH...

AT FIRST...

I ONLY WANTED TO KNOW THE REASON I DIED.

KAEDE. INU-YASHA HAS CHANGED, HASN'T HE?

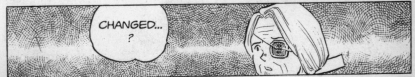

CHANGED...?

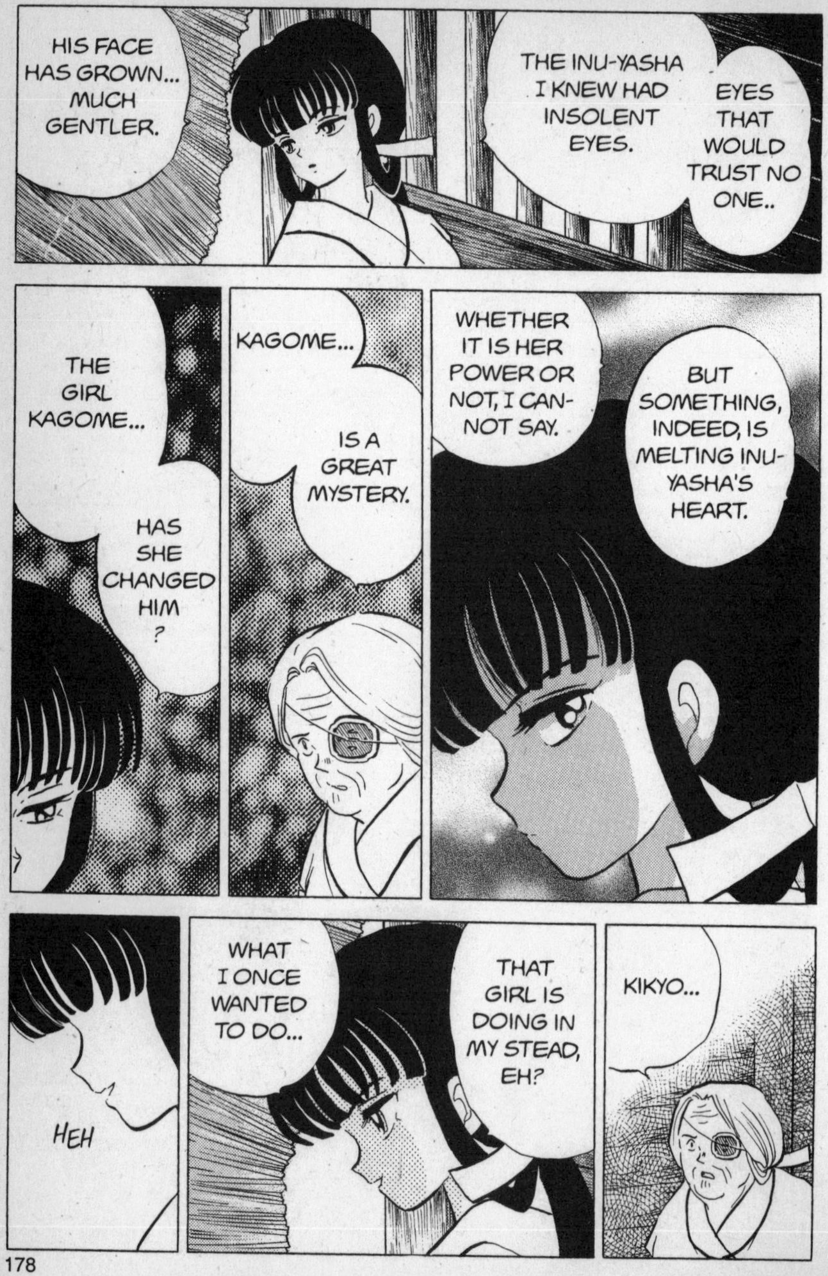
HIS FACE HAS GROWN... MUCH GENTLER.
THE INU-YASHA I KNEW HAD INSOLENT EYES.
EYES THAT WOULD TRUST NO ONE..
THE GIRL KAGOME...
HAS SHE CHANGED HIM ?
KAGOME...
IS A GREAT MYSTERY.
WHETHER IT IS HER POWER OR NOT, I CAN-NOT SAY.
BUT SOMETHING, INDEED, IS MELTING INU-YASHA'S HEART.
HEH
WHAT I ONCE WANTED TO DO...
THAT GIRL IS DOING IN MY STEAD, EH?
KIKYO...

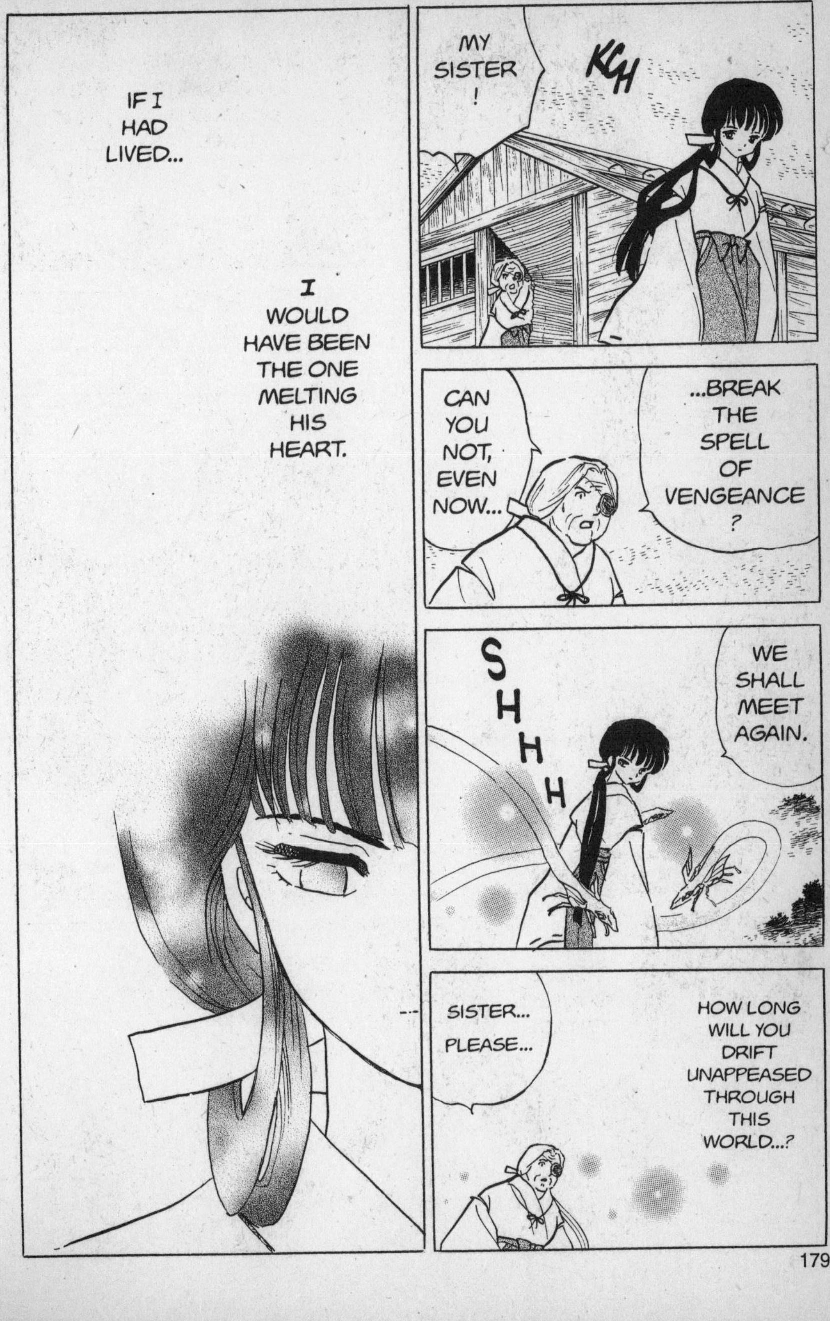
IF I HAD LIVED...
I WOULD HAVE BEEN THE ONE MELTING HIS HEART.
MY SISTER!
KCH
CAN YOU NOT, EVEN NOW...
...BREAK THE SPELL OF VENGEANCE?
SHHH
WE SHALL MEET AGAIN.
SISTER... PLEASE...
HOW LONG WILL YOU DRIFT UNAPPEASED THROUGH THIS WORLD...?

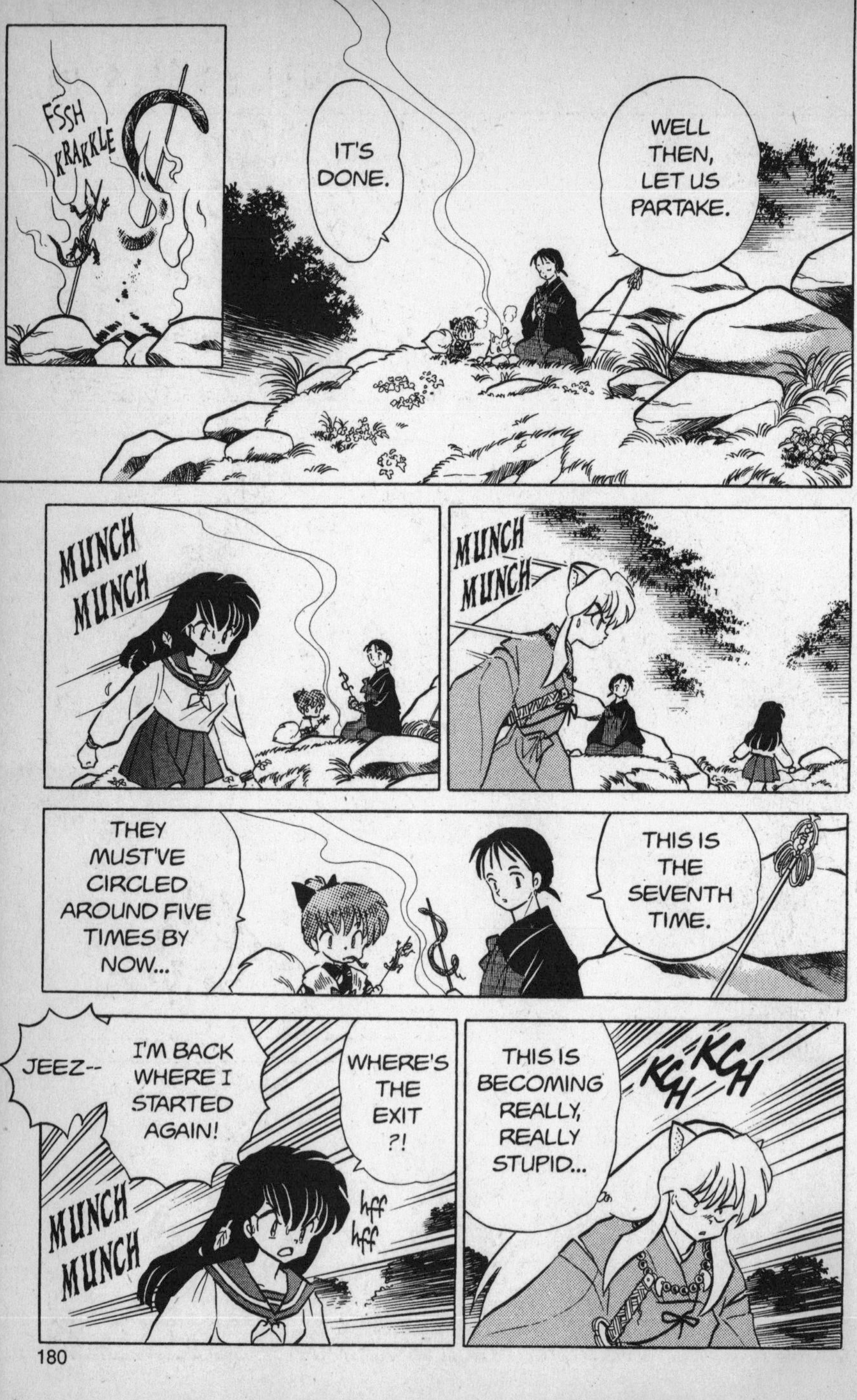
FSSH KRAKKLE
IT'S DONE.
WELL THEN, LET US PARTAKE.
MUNCH MUNCH
MUNCH MUNCH
THEY MUST'VE CIRCLED AROUND FIVE TIMES BY NOW...
THIS IS THE SEVENTH TIME.
JEEZ--
I'M BACK WHERE I STARTED AGAIN!
WHERE'S THE EXIT ?!
hff hff
MUNCH MUNCH
THIS IS BECOMING REALLY, REALLY STUPID...
KCH KCH

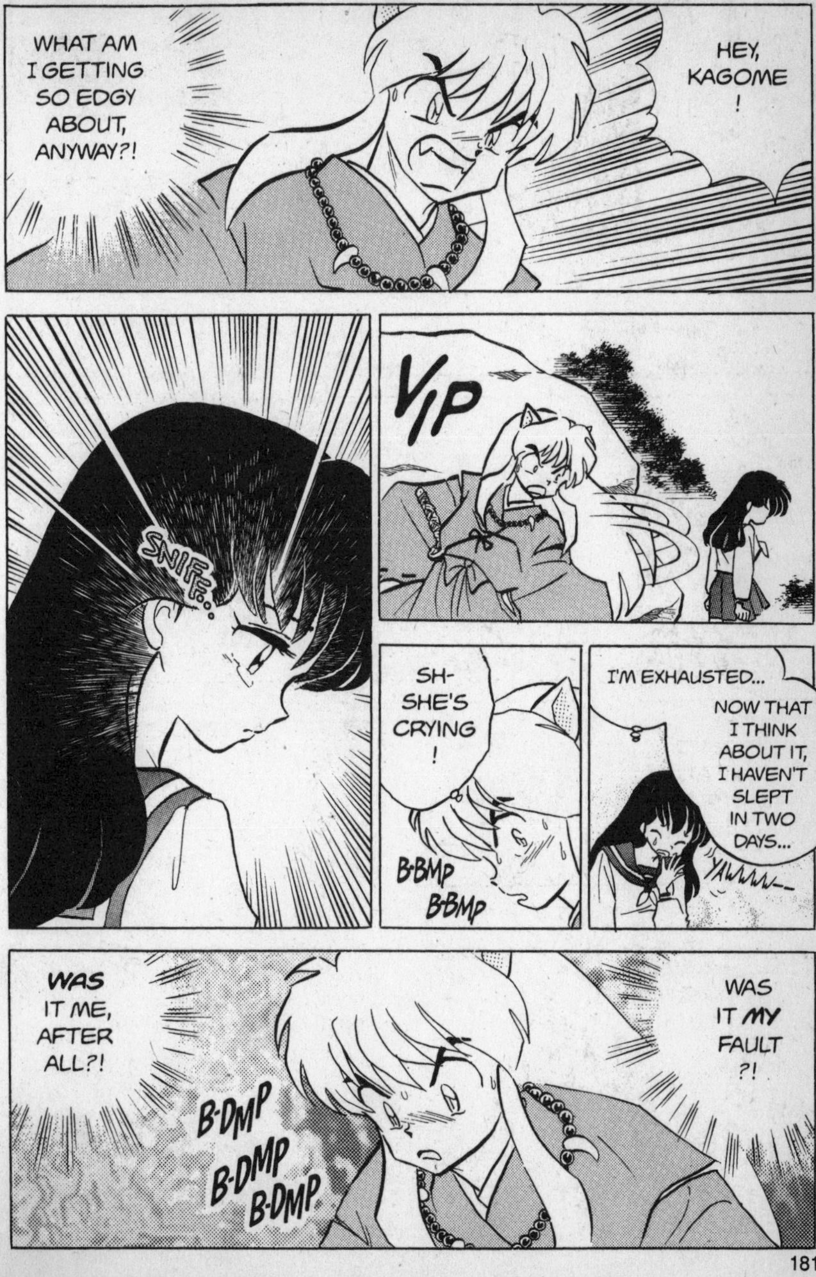
WHAT AM I GETTING SO EDGY ABOUT, ANYWAY?!
HEY, KAGOME!
SNIFFF...
VIP
SH-SHE'S CRYING!
B-BMP
B-BMP
I'M EXHAUSTED...
NOW THAT I THINK ABOUT IT, I HAVEN'T SLEPT IN TWO DAYS...
YAWWWN—
WAS IT ME, AFTER ALL?!
B-DMP
B-DMP
B-DMP
WAS IT MY FAULT?!

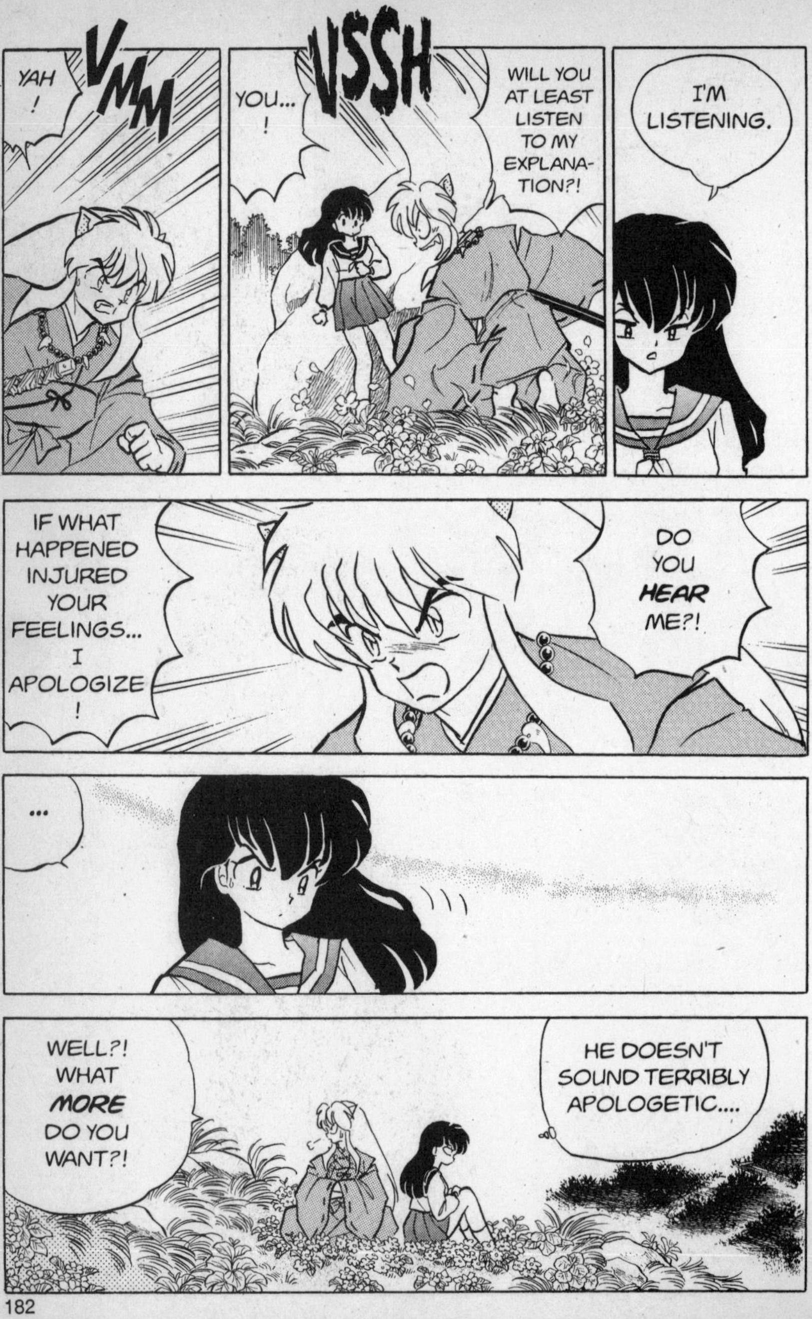
YAH!
VMM
YOU...!
VSSH
WILL YOU AT LEAST LISTEN TO MY EXPLANATION?!
I'M LISTENING.
IF WHAT HAPPENED INJURED YOUR FEELINGS... I APOLOGIZE!
DO YOU HEAR ME?!
...
WELL?! WHAT MORE DO YOU WANT?!
HE DOESN'T SOUND TERRIBLY APOLOGETIC....

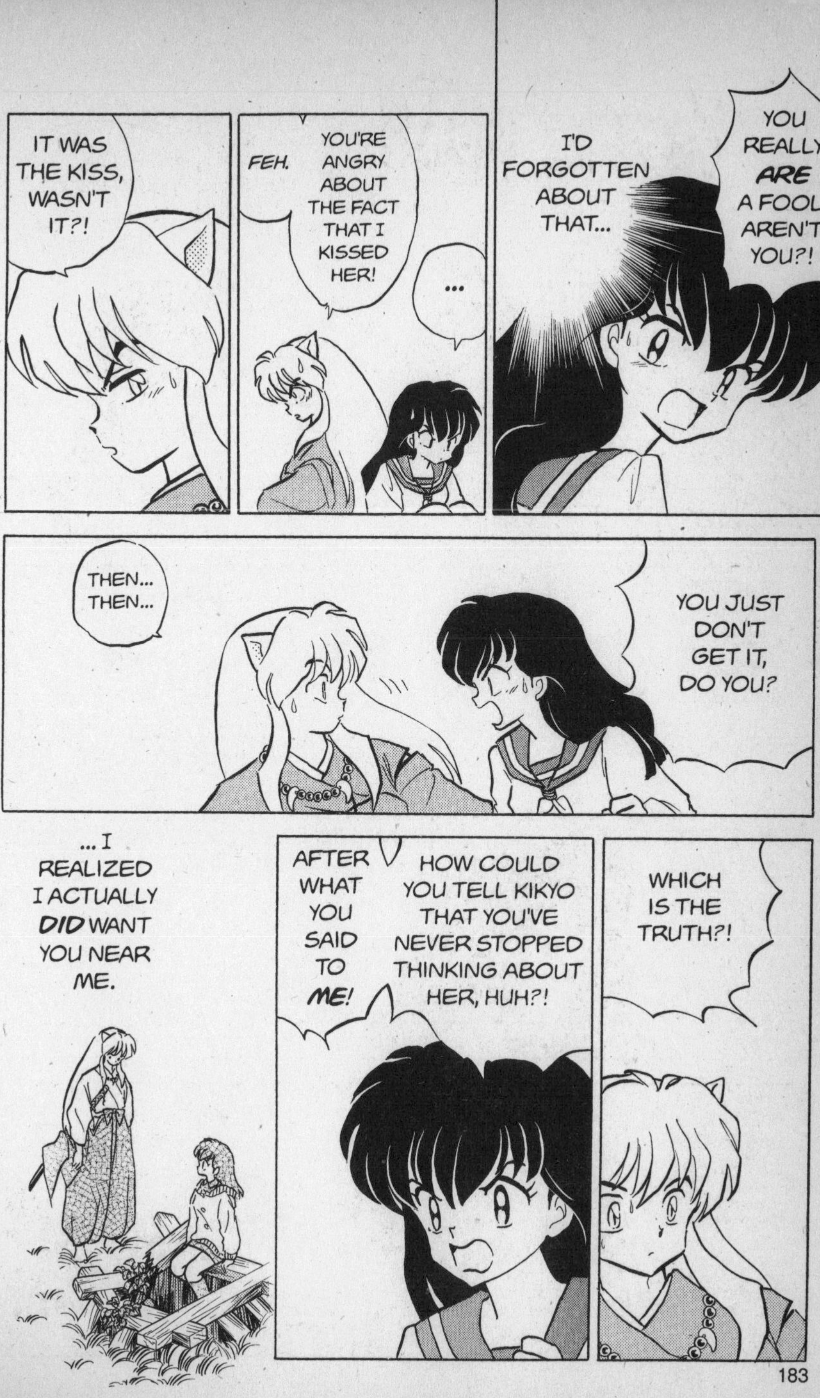
IT WAS THE KISS, WASN'T IT?!
FEH.
YOU'RE ANGRY ABOUT THE FACT THAT I KISSED HER!
...
I'D FORGOTTEN ABOUT THAT...
YOU REALLY **ARE** A FOOL, AREN'T YOU?!
THEN... THEN...
YOU JUST DON'T GET IT, DO YOU?
...I REALIZED I ACTUALLY **DID** WANT YOU NEAR ME.
AFTER WHAT YOU SAID TO **ME**!
HOW COULD YOU TELL KIKYO THAT YOU'VE NEVER STOPPED THINKING ABOUT HER, HUH?!
WHICH IS THE TRUTH?!

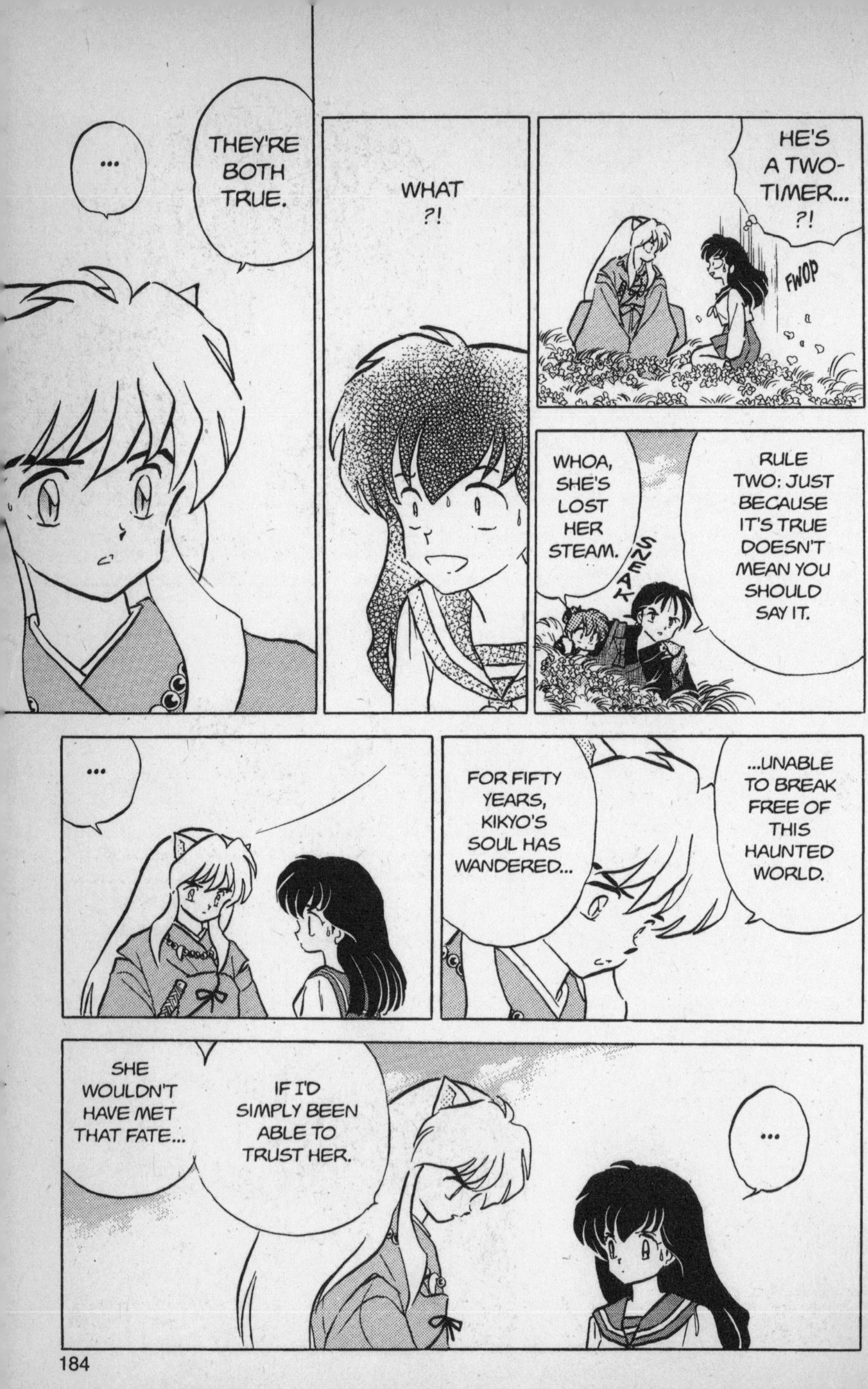
...
THEY'RE BOTH TRUE.
WHAT ?!
HE'S A TWO-TIMER... ?!
FWOP
WHOA, SHE'S LOST HER STEAM.
SNEAK
RULE TWO: JUST BECAUSE IT'S TRUE DOESN'T MEAN YOU SHOULD SAY IT.
...
FOR FIFTY YEARS, KIKYO'S SOUL HAS WANDERED...
...UNABLE TO BREAK FREE OF THIS HAUNTED WORLD.
SHE WOULDN'T HAVE MET THAT FATE...
IF I'D SIMPLY BEEN ABLE TO TRUST HER.
...

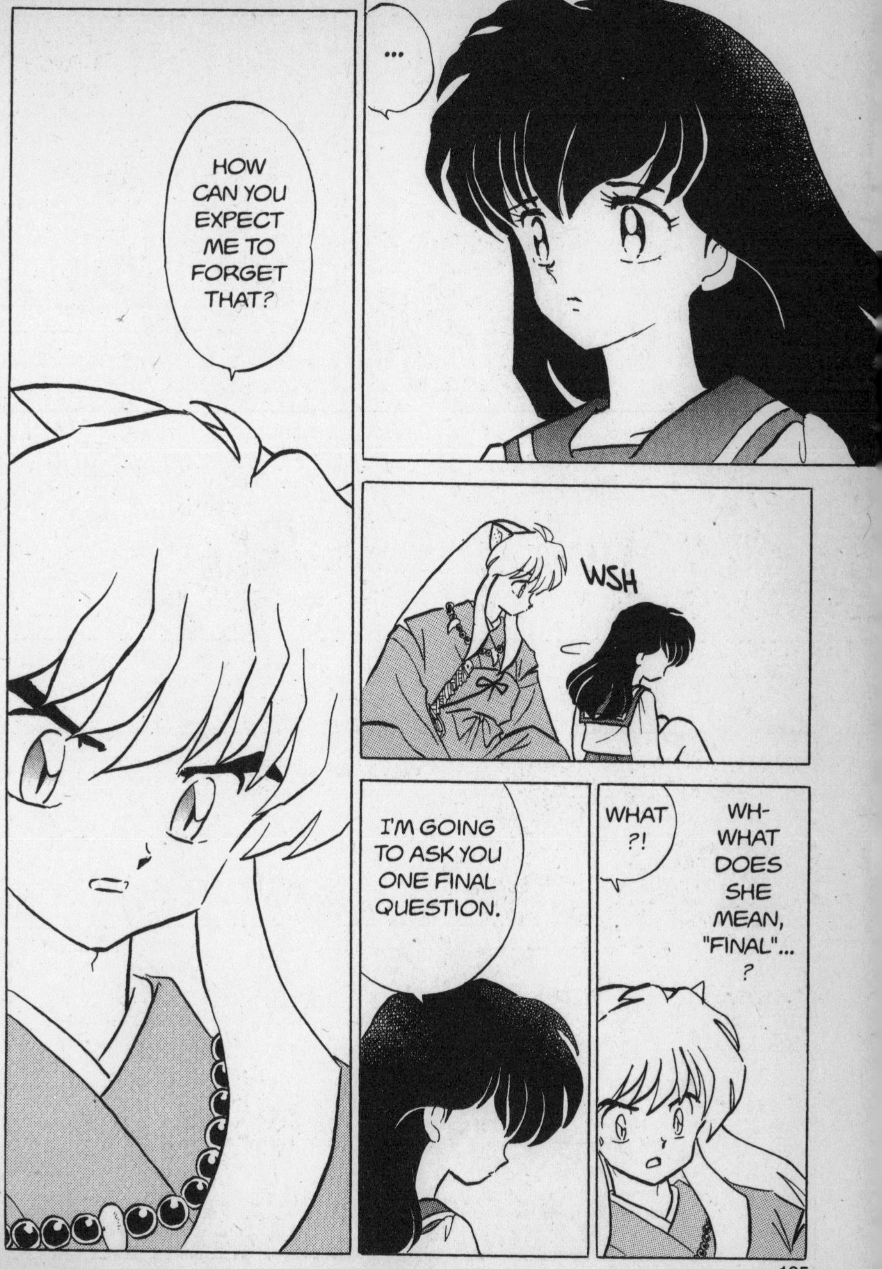
HOW CAN YOU EXPECT ME TO FORGET THAT?
...
WSH
I'M GOING TO ASK YOU ONE FINAL QUESTION.
WHAT?!
WH-WHAT DOES SHE MEAN, "FINAL"...?

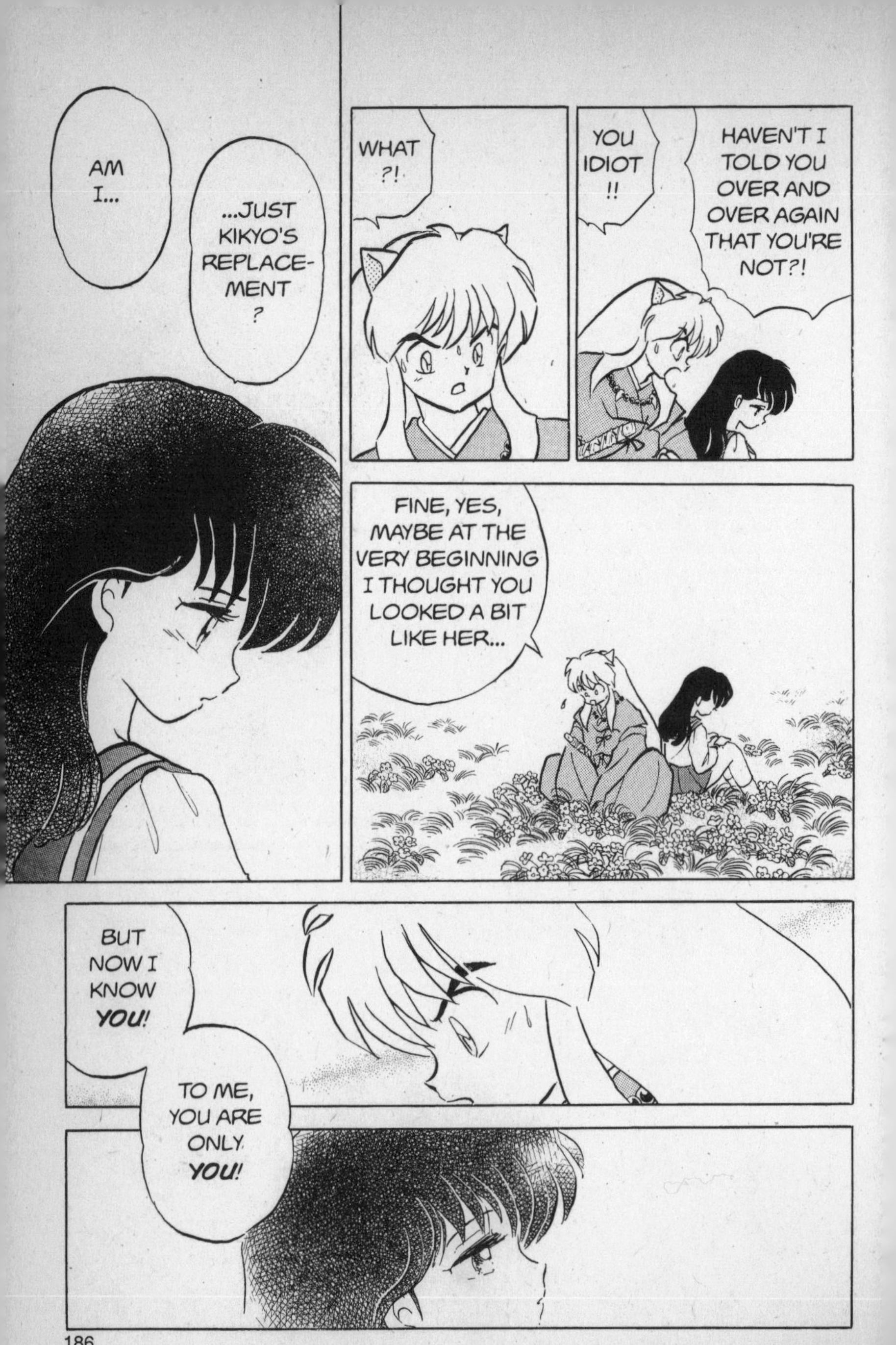
AM I...
...JUST KIKYO'S REPLACEMENT?
WHAT?!
YOU IDIOT!!
HAVEN'T I TOLD YOU OVER AND OVER AGAIN THAT YOU'RE NOT?!
FINE, YES, MAYBE AT THE VERY BEGINNING I THOUGHT YOU LOOKED A BIT LIKE HER...
BUT NOW I KNOW **YOU!**
TO ME, YOU ARE ONLY **YOU!**

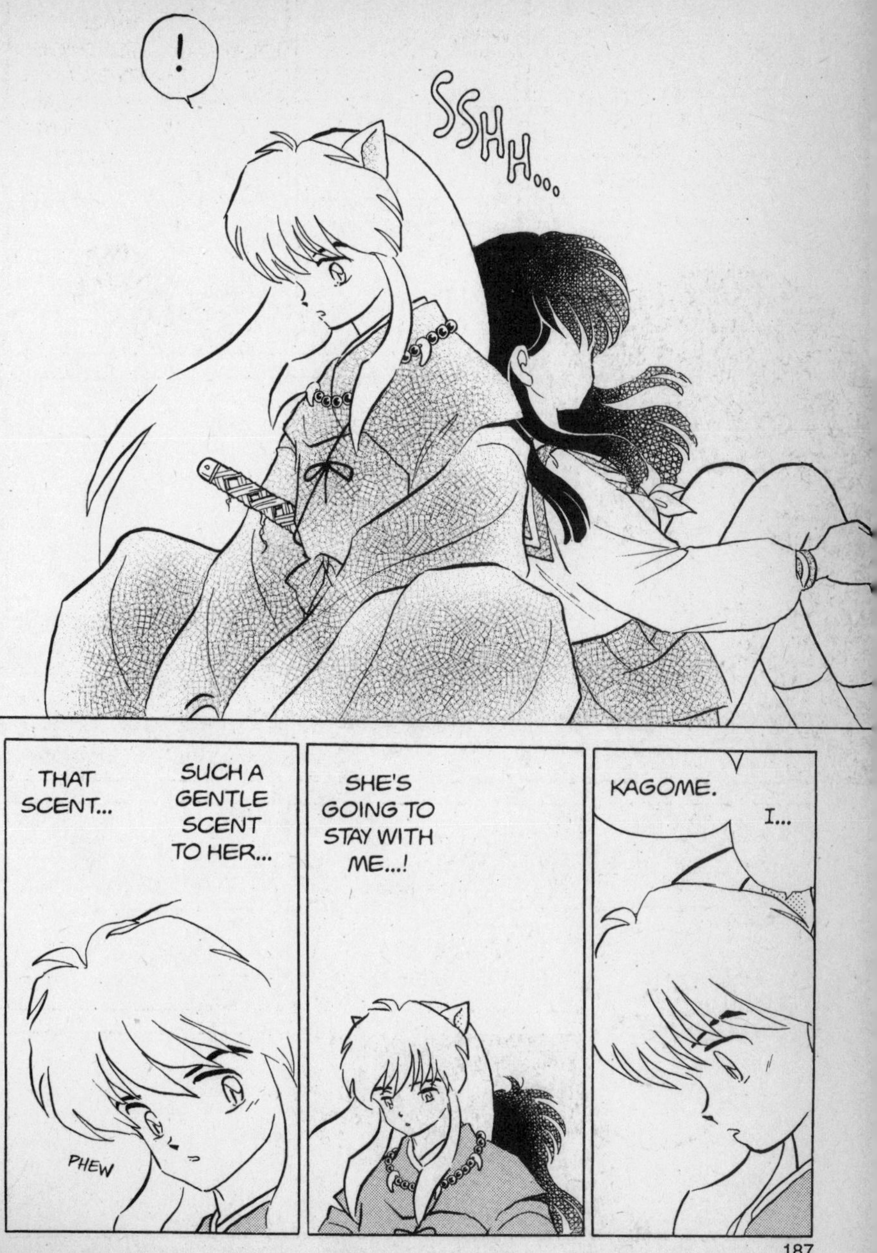
!
SSHH...
THAT SCENT...
SUCH A GENTLE SCENT TO HER...
PHEW
SHE'S GOING TO STAY WITH ME...!
KAGOME.
I...

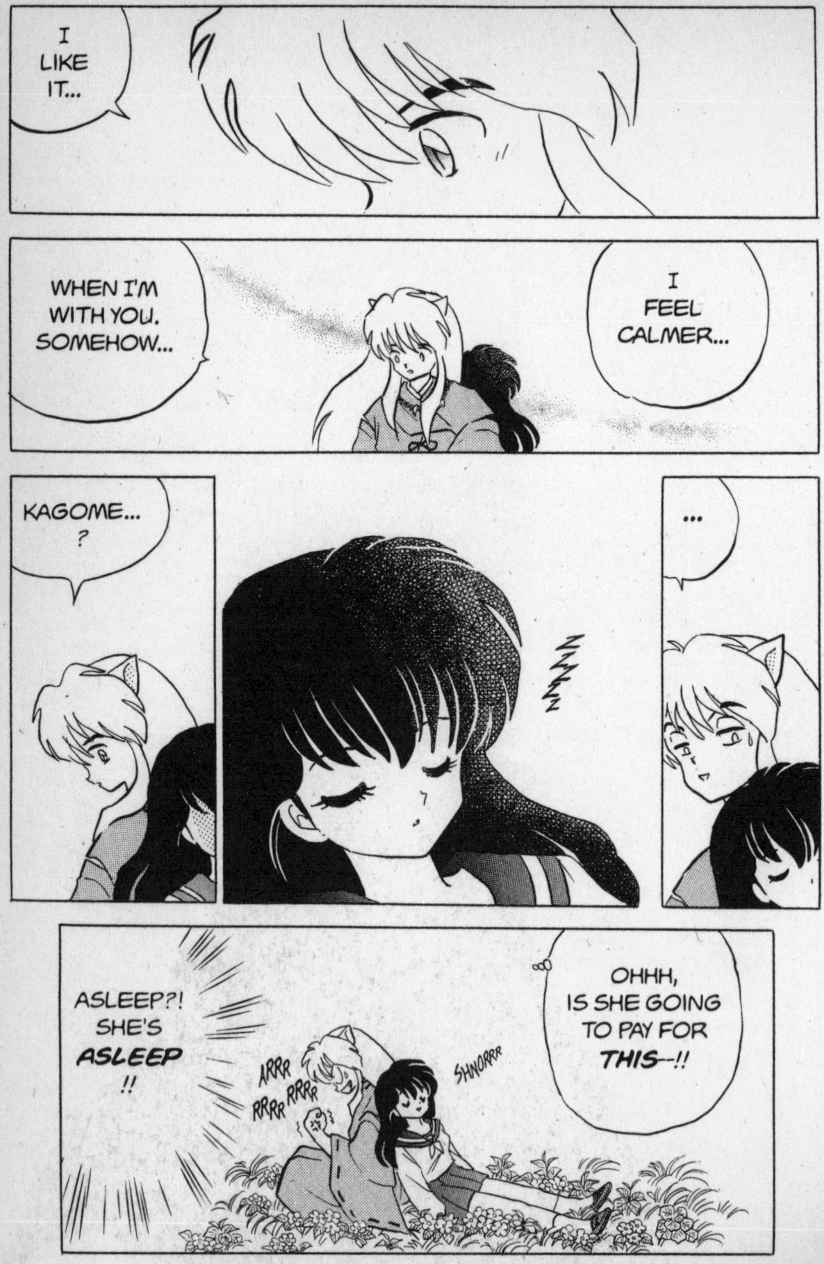
I LIKE IT...
WHEN I'M WITH YOU. SOMEHOW...
I FEEL CALMER...
KAGOME... ?
ZZZZZ
...
ASLEEP?! SHE'S **ASLEEP**!!
ARRR RRRR RRRR
SHNORRR
OHHH, IS SHE GOING TO PAY FOR **THIS**--!!

TO BE CONTINUED...!

Rumiko Takahashi

Rumiko Takahashi was born in 1957 in Niigata, Japan. She attended women's college in Tokyo, where she began studying comics with Kazuo Koike, author of *Crying Freeman*. In 1978, she won a prize in Shogakukan's annual "New Comic Artist Contest," and in that same year her boy-meets-alien comedy series *Lum*Urusei Yatsura* began appearing in the weekly manga magazine *Shônen Sunday*. This phenomenally successful series ran for nine years and sold over 22 million copies. Takahashi's later *Ranma 1/2* series enjoyed even greater popularity.

Takahashi is considered by many to be one of the world's most popular manga artists. With the publication of Volume 34 of her *Ranma 1/2* series in Japan, Takahashi's total sales passed one hundred million copies of her compiled works.

Takahashi's serial titles include *Lum*Urusei Yatsura*, *Ranma 1/2*, *One-Pound Gospel*, *Maison Ikkoku* and *Inu-Yasha*. Additionally, Takahashi has drawn many short stories which have been published in America under the title "Rumic Theater," and several installments of a saga known as her "Mermaid" series. Most of Takahashi's major stories have also been animated, and are widely available in translation worldwide. *Inu-Yasha* is her most recent serial story, first published in *Shônen Sunday* in 1996.

LOVE MANGA? LET US KNOW!

☐ Please do NOT send me information about VIZ Media products, news and events, special offers, or other information.

☐ Please do NOT send me information from VIZ Media's trusted business partners.

Name: _____

Address: _____

City: _____ **State:** _____ **Zip:** _____

E-mail: _____

☐ **Male** ☐ **Female** **Date of Birth** (mm/dd/yyyy): ___ / ___ / ___ (Under 13? Parental consent required)

What race/ethnicity do you consider yourself? (check all that apply)

☐ White/Caucasian ☐ Black/African American ☐ Hispanic/Latino

☐ Asian/Pacific Islander ☐ Native American/Alaskan Native ☐ Other: _____

What VIZ Media title(s) did you purchase? (indicate title(s) purchased) _____

_____

What other VIZ Media titles do you own? _____

_____

Reason for purchase: (check all that apply)

☐ Special offer ☐ Favorite title / author / artist / genre

☐ Gift ☐ Recommendation ☐ Collection

☐ Read excerpt in VIZ Media manga sampler ☐ Other _____

Where did you make your purchase? (please check one)

☐ Comic store ☐ Bookstore ☐ Grocery Store

☐ Convention ☐ Newsstand ☐ Video Game Store

☐ Online (site: _____) ☐ Other _____

How many manga titles have you purchased in the last year? How many were VIZ Media titles?
(please check one from each column)

MANGA
- [ ] None
- [ ] 1 – 4
- [ ] 5 – 10
- [ ] 11+

VIZ Media
- [ ] None
- [ ] 1 – 4
- [ ] 5 – 10
- [ ] 11+

How much influence do special promotions and gifts-with-purchase have on the titles you buy?
(please circle, with 5 being great influence and 1 being none)

1   2   3   4   5

Do you purchase every volume of your favorite series?
- [ ] Yes! Gotta have 'em as my own
- [ ] No. Please explain: _____

What kind of manga storylines do you most enjoy? (check all that apply)

- [ ] Action / Adventure
- [ ] Comedy
- [ ] Fighting
- [ ] Artistic / Alternative

- [ ] Science Fiction
- [ ] Romance (shojo)
- [ ] Sports
- [ ] Other _____

- [ ] Horror
- [ ] Fantasy (shojo)
- [ ] Historical

If you watch the anime or play a video or TCG game from a series, how likely are you to buy the manga? (please circle, with 5 being very likely and 1 being unlikely)

1   2   3   4   5

If unlikely, please explain: _____

Who are your favorite authors / artists? _____

_____

What titles would like you translated and sold in English? _____

_____

THANK YOU! Please send the completed form to:

VIZ MEDIA

NJW Research
42 Catharine Street
Poughkeepsie, NY 12601